The Cambridge Companion to Music and Romanticism

This Companion presents a new understanding of the relationship between music and culture in and around the nineteenth century, and encourages readers to explore what Romanticism in music might mean today. Challenging the view that musical 'romanticism' is confined to a particular style or period, it reveals instead the multiple intersections between the phenomenon of Romanticism and music. Drawing on a variety of disciplinary approaches, and reflecting current scholarly debates across the humanities, it places music at the heart of a nexus of Romantic themes and concerns. Written by a dynamic team of leading younger scholars and established authorities, it gives a state-of-the-art yet accessible overview of current thinking on this popular topic.

BENEDICT TAYLOR is Reader in Music at the University of Edinburgh. He is author of *Mendelssohn, Time and Memory* (Cambridge, 2011), *The Melody of Time* (2015), and *Towards a Harmonic Grammar of Grieg's Late Piano Music* (2016). He is co-editor of the journal *Music & Letters* and the recipient of the Jerome Roche Prize of the Royal Musical Association.

T0381647

Cambridge Companions to Music

Topics

The Cambridge Companion to Ballet
Edited by Marion Kant

The Cambridge Companion to Blues and Gospel Music
Edited by Allan Moore

The Cambridge Companion to Choral Music
Edited by André de Quadros

The Cambridge Companion to the Concerto
Edited by Simon P. Keefe

The Cambridge Companion to Conducting
Edited by José Antonio Bowen

The Cambridge Companion to the Drum Kit
Edited by Matt Brennan, Joseph Michael Pignato and Daniel Akira Stadnicki

The Cambridge Companion to Eighteenth-Century Opera
Edited by Anthony R. DelDonna and Pierpaolo Polzonetti

The Cambridge Companion to Electronic Music
Edited by Nick Collins and Julio D'Escriván

The Cambridge Companion to the 'Eroica' Symphony
Edited by Nancy November

The Cambridge Companion to Film Music
Edited by Mervyn Cooke and Fiona Ford

The Cambridge Companion to French Music
Edited by Simon Trezise

The Cambridge Companion to Grand Opera
Edited by David Charlton

The Cambridge Companion to Hip-Hop
Edited by Justin A. Williams

The Cambridge Companion to Jazz
Edited by Mervyn Cooke and David Horn

The Cambridge Companion to Jewish Music
Edited by Joshua S. Walden

The Cambridge Companion to the Lied
Edited by James Parsons

The Cambridge Companion to Medieval Music
Edited by Mark Everist

The Cambridge Companion to Music and Romanticism
Edited by Benedict Taylor

The Cambridge Companion to Music in Digital Culture
Edited by Nicholas Cook, Monique Ingalls and David Trippett

Composers

Instruments

Musical Examples

Contributors

FRANCESCA BRITTAN is Associate Professor of Music at Case Western Reserve University. Her work focuses on intersections amongst music, magic, and histories of science. She has published widely on these topics, including in her first book, *Music and Fantasy in the Age of Berlioz* (Cambridge, 2017) and in a collection of articles in the *Journal of the American Musicological Society*, *19th-Century Music*, *Nineteenth-Century Music Review*, the *Journal of the American Liszt Society*, and elsewhere. Her current book-in-progress is *The Conductor's Wand: Histories, Technologies and Legacies of Orchestral Power*.

KEITH CHAPIN is Senior Lecturer in Music and Director of Performance at Cardiff University School of Music. Previously, he held positions at Fordham University and the New Zealand School of Music. He researches on issues of aesthetics and analysis in eighteenth- to twentieth-century France and Germany, focusing on changing conceptions of sublimity and their different musical manifestations, the relationship between music and literature, and the aesthetics of counterpoint. He has served as co-editor of *Eighteenth-Century Music* and associate editor of *19th-Century Music*. He is a violist and performs as a chamber musician.

LISA FEURZEIG is Professor of Music at Grand Valley State University in Michigan. Her research is centred on text–music relations in vocal music. In *Schubert's Lieder and the Philosophy of Early German Romanticism*, she argues that Schubert created musical equivalents for complex abstract ideas in settings of Schlegel and Novalis. In addition to lieder, her other research areas include musical quotation and reference, Viennese theatrical traditions, and German-American music. She has been an editor of two critical editions and is co-editor, with Marjorie Hirsch, of the *Cambridge Companion to Schubert's* Winterreise. In 2017–18, Lisa was a Fulbright-IFK Senior Fellow in Cultural Studies in Austria, researching current styles of operetta performance. As a singer, she has emphasised early music, lieder, and music since 1900.

JAMES GARRATT is Professor of Music History and Aesthetics at the University of Manchester, where he also holds the position of University Organist. His research and teaching centre on German music, thought and culture in the long nineteenth century; aesthetic theory and the history of music aesthetics; and music, politics, and political theory. James's publications include three single-author books: *Palestrina and the German Romantic Imagination: Interpreting Historicism in Nineteenth-Century Music* (Cambridge, 2002); *Music, Culture and Social Reform in the Age of Wagner* (Cambridge, 2010); and *Music and Politics: A Critical Introduction* (Cambridge, 2018). Other recent research includes a multimedia project on 'Organ Music from the Great War' (www .youtube.com/c/OrganMusicfromtheGreatWar). He is currently completing a book for Cambridge University Press on *Music, Aesthetics and Values*, and is working on a series of comparative studies of the aesthetics of music and painting in the nineteenth century.

MATTHEW GELBART is Associate Professor in the Department of Art History and Music at Fordham University. His primary scholarship deals with musical categories and identities. His first book, *The Invention of 'Folk Music' and 'Art Music': Emerging Categories from Ossian to Wagner*, was published by Cambridge University Press in 2008. It considers these lastingly influential categories as historically contingent and reliant upon each other. His second book, on *Musical Genre and Romantic Ideology*, is forthcoming from Oxford University Press. It explores the way social belonging buttressed the importance of musical genre in the Romantic period and how Romanticism left a strong imprint on the idea of genre amongst today's scholars, artists, marketers, and listeners in the West. He also writes and teaches on rock and pop music.

DANA GOOLEY is Professor of Music at Brown University. He is the author of *The Virtuoso Liszt* (Cambridge, 2004), a study of Liszt's reputation and reception during his concert career, and *Fantasies of Improvisation: Free Playing in Nineteenth-Century Music* (Oxford, 2018), the first general study of improvisational practices and values in European music in this period. He has co-edited the essay collections *Franz Liszt and His World* (Princeton, 2006) and *Franz Liszt, Musicien Européen: Art, Culture, Politique* (Editions Vrin, 2012). His articles on music criticism, virtuosity, musical mediation, improvisation, cosmopolitanism, and jazz have appeared in *Performance Research, 19th-Century Music, Musical Quarterly, Keyboard Perspectives, Musiktheorie, Journal of Musicology,* and *Journal of the American Musicological Society*, as well as in the edited collections *Taking it to the Bridge: Music as Performance* (2013) and *Music and the Sonorous Sublime in European Culture, 1680–1880* (2020).

NICOLE GRIMES is Associate Professor of Music at the University of California, Irvine. Her books include *Brahms's Elegies: The Poetics of Loss in Nineteenth-Century German Culture* (Cambridge, 2019), *Rethinking Hanslick: Music, Formalism, and Expression* (co-edited with Siobhán Donovan and Wolfgang Marx, Boydell & Brewer, 2012), and *Mendelssohn Perspectives* (co-edited with Angela Mace, Ashgate, 2011), and numerous articles and chapters on the music of Brahms, Clara Schumann, Robert Schumann, Schoenberg, Liszt, Wolfgang Rihm, and Donnacha Dennehy. Her research has been funded by a Marie Curie International Fellowship from the European Commission, the Deutscher Akademischer Austauschdienst, and the Irish Research Council for the Humanities and Social Sciences.

KATHERINE HAMBRIDGE is Assistant Professor in Musicology at Durham University. Her research concerns French and German musical life in the first half of the nineteenth century, in particular music and politics, music theatre, and issues of voice, genre and performance. She has published articles and book chapters on a range of topics, taking in melodrama, royal birthday concerts, canonical discourses, and the German voice, and her article for the *Journal of the American Musicological Society*, 'Staging Singing in the Theater of War (Berlin, 1805)', won the Royal Musical Association's Jerome Roche Prize 2016. The volume *The Melodramatic Moment: Music and Theatrical Culture 1790–1820*, co-edited with Jonathan Hicks, appeared in 2018 with the University of Chicago Press. She is currently completing a monograph which offers new ways to think about musical modernity through the case study of Berlin; her new research concerns the transfer and circulation of 'popular' music theatre repertoire (such as melodrama and vaudeville) and personnel between Paris, London, Vienna, and Berlin, 1789–1848.

SARAH HIBBERD is Stanley Hugh Badock Chair of Music at the University of Bristol. Her research focuses on opera and other forms of music theatre in Paris and London during the first half of the nineteenth century. Her work has appeared in journals such as the *Cambridge Opera Journal*, *19th-Century Music*, *Music & Letters*, *Laboratoire Italien*, and in edited volumes including *London Voices 1820–1840: Vocal Performers, Practices, Histories*, ed. Roger Parker and Susan Rutherford (Chicago, 2020); *The Melodramatic Moment: Music and Theatrical Culture, 1790–1820*, ed. Katherine

Hambridge and Jonathan Hicks (Chicago: University of Chicago Press 2018); and *Sound Knowledge: Music and Science in London, 1789–1851*, ed. James Q. Davies and Ellen Lockhart (Chicago, 2016). Other publications include *French Grand Opera and the Historical Imagination* (Cambridge, 2009); a guest-edited special issue of *19th-Century Music*, 39/2 (2015); and *Music and the Sonorous Sublime in European Culture, 1680–1880* (Cambridge, 2020), co-edited with Miranda Stanyon. She is currently co-editor of the *Cambridge Opera Journal.*

JULIAN HORTON is Professor of Music Theory and Analysis at Durham University. He is author of *Bruckner's Symphonies: Analysis, Reception and Cultural Politics* (Cambridge, 2004) and *Brahms' Piano Concerto No. 2, Op. 83: Analytical and Contextual Studies* (Peeters, 2017); editor of *The Cambridge Companion to the Symphony* (2013); and co-editor with Gareth Cox of *Irish Musical Studies* XI: *Irish Musical Analysis* (Four Courts Press, 2013), with Lorraine Byrne Bodley of *Schubert's Late Style* (Cambridge, 2016) and *Rethinking Schubert* (Oxford, 2016), and with Jeremy Dibble of *British Musical Criticism and Intellectual Thought 1850–1950* (Boydell, 2017). In 2012, he was awarded the Westrup Prize of the *Music & Letters* Trust for the article 'John Field and the Alternative History of Concerto First-Movement Form'. In 2016, he was appointed Music Theorist in Residence to the Netherlands and Flanders. He is currently writing *The Symphony: A History* for Cambridge University Press.

KAREN LEISTRA-JONES is Associate Professor of Music at Franklin & Marshall College. Her research interests include the history and aesthetics of musical performance, the Schumann–Brahms circle, and musical representations of landscape, motion, and travel. Recent publications have appeared in the *Journal of Musicology, Music & Letters, 19th-Century Music*, and the *Journal of the American Musicological Society*. Her current project explores Beethoven performance in the long nineteenth century as a cultural, political, and art-religious phenomenon.

TOMÁS MCAULEY is Assistant Professor and Ad Astra Fellow in the School of Music at University College Dublin. Previously, he held postdoctoral positions at Indiana University and the University of Cambridge. He is author of *The Music of Philosophy: German Idealism and Musical Thought, from Kant to Schelling*, forthcoming with Oxford University Press, and co-editor, with Nanette Nielsen, Jerrold Levinson, and (associate editor) Ariana Phillips-Hutton, of the recently published *Oxford Handbook of*

Western Music and Philosophy. He is currently working on his second monograph, *Hearing the Enlightenment: Music, Philosophy, and the Emergence of Modernity*, under contract with Yale University Press. From 2010 to 2018 he served as founding chair of the Royal Musical Association Music and Philosophy Study Group.

THOMAS PEATTIE is an associate professor of Music at the University of Mississippi. He holds degrees in composition (BMus) and musicology (MA) from the University of Calgary, and a PhD in historical musicology from Harvard University. His research focuses on nineteenth- and twentieth-century music, with a particular interest in the relationship between Romanticism and modernism. He is the recipient of fellowships from the Social Sciences and Humanities Research Council of Canada, the Paul Sacher Foundation, and the Italian Academy for Advanced Studies in America at Columbia University. In addition to his contributions to several edited volumes, including *Mahler and His World* (Princeton), *Music, Modern Culture, and the Critical Ear: A Festschrift for Peter Franklin* (Routledge), *Giacinto Scelsi: Music across the Borders* (Brepols), and *Mahler in Context* (Cambridge), his articles and reviews have appeared in a number of leading journals, including *Acta musicologica, Contemporary Music Review, Journal of the Royal Musical Association, Music & Letters, Nineteenth-Century Music Review*, and *PAJ: A Journal of Performance and Art*. He is the author of *Gustav Mahler's Symphonic Landscapes* (Cambridge, 2015) and is currently preparing a monograph on the transcribing practice of Luciano Berio.

MIRANDA STANYON is Lecturer in Comparative Literature at King's College London, and the recipient of an Australian Research Council Australian Discovery Early Career Award (project number DE200101675) funded by the Australian Government. Her research focuses on British and German literary cultures, especially as they interact with music and sound. Her publications include *Resounding the Sublime* (University of Pennsylvania Press, 2021) and, with Sarah Hibberd, the edited collection *Music and the Sonorous Sublime in European Culture* (Cambridge, 2020).

BENEDICT TAYLOR is Reader in Music at the University of Edinburgh and co-editor of *Music & Letters*. He specialises in the music of the late eighteenth to early twentieth centuries, analysis, and philosophy. His publications include *Mendelssohn, Time and Memory: The Romantic Conception of Cyclic Form* (Cambridge, 2011); *The Melody of Time:*

Music and Temporality in the Romantic Era (Oxford, 2016); *Towards A Harmonic Grammar of Grieg's Late Piano Music* (RMA Monographs, 2017); the edited volume *Rethinking Mendelssohn* (Oxford, 2020); and, as co-editor, a special issue of *19th-Century Music* on subjectivity and song (Spring 2017). He is the 2011 recipient of the Jerome Roche Prize of the Royal Musical Association and has held fellowships at the Institute of Advanced Studies Berlin and from the Alexander von Humboldt-Stiftung.

JOHN TRESCH is Professor and Mellon Chair in History of Art, Science, and Folk Practice at the Warburg Institute, University of London. He is author of *The Romantic Machine: Utopian Science and Technology after Napoleon*, winner of the 2013 Pfizer Prize for outstanding book in history of science. He is also author of a study of Romanticism, technology, and science in the USA in the 1830s and '40s, *The Reason for the Darkness of the Night: Edgar Allan Poe and the Forging of American Science*. He is the editor of the *History of Anthropology Review* and is working on a book called *Cosmograms: How to Do Things with Worlds*.

STEVEN VANDE MOORTELE is Associate Professor of Music Theory at the University of Toronto, where he is also Associate Dean, Research for the Faculty of Music and Director of the Centre for the Study of Nineteenth-Century Music (CSNCM). His principal research interests are theories of musical form, the analysis of large-scale instrumental forms from the late eighteenth to the early twentieth century, and the music of Wagner and Schoenberg. Publications include *Two-Dimensional Sonata Form* (Leuven, 2009); *Formal Functions in Perspective* (Rochester, 2015); *The Romantic Overture and Musical Form from Rossini to Wagner* (Cambridge 2017); and *Robert Schumann: Szenen aus Goethes Faust* (Leuven, 2020). He is the winner of the 2018 Wallace Berry Award from the Society for Music Theory, the 2019 Roland Jackson Award from the American Musicological Society, and the 2020 Westrup Prize from the *Music & Letters* Trust.

HOLLY WATKINS is Professor of Musicology at the University of Rochester's Eastman School of Music, where she has taught since receiving her PhD from the University of California, Berkeley in 2004. Watkins is the author of *Musical Vitalities: Ventures in a Biotic Aesthetics of Music* (Chicago, 2018) and *Metaphors of Depth in German Musical Thought: From E. T. A. Hoffmann to Arnold Schoenberg* (Cambridge, 2011). Her articles on Romanticism, modernism, ecological aesthetics, and intersections between music and philosophy have appeared in such venues as the

Journal of the American Musicological Society, 19th-Century Music, New Literary History, Women and Music, Opera Quarterly, Contemporary Music Review, Current Musicology, and *The New Centennial Review.* In 2014–15, Watkins was the recipient of a fellowship from the American Council of Learned Societies, and in 2010–11 she held a Harrington Faculty Fellowship at The University of Texas at Austin.

SEBASTIAN WEDLER is Departmental Lecturer in the Faculty of Music at the University of Oxford, where he also acts as Director of Studies for Music at Merton College and Lecturer in Music at University College. Previously, he was Junior Research Fellow at St Hilda's College and Lecturer at The Queen's College. He received his DPhil from the University of Oxford in 2017. His research and teaching interests include music history post-1750, musical analysis and criticism, and issues in the philosophy and aesthetics of music. He is currently completing his first monograph on Anton Webern's tonal works (1899–1908). He was elected 'Prize Scholar' at Merton College and is the recipient of the 'Link 2 Future' Award from the Psychoanalytic Seminar Zurich. In recognition of his teaching, he was shortlisted for Outstanding Tutor in the Humanities by the Oxford University Student Union in 2017.

ALEXANDER WILFING works at the Department of Musicology in the Austrian Academy of Sciences. He attained his doctorate in musicology in 2016 with a study on Eduard Hanslick's reception in English-language discourse. A reworked version of this book has appeared recently as *Re-Reading Hanslick's Aesthetics: Die Rezeption Eduard Hanslicks im englischen Sprachraum und ihre diskursiven Grundlagen.* Since 2014 he has undertaken research projects on the historical contexts of Hanslick's aesthetics at the Austrian Academy of Sciences, Vienna. He is editor of *Hanslick in Context: Perspectives on the Aesthetics, Musical Criticism, and Historical Setting of Eduard Hanslick* (Vienna: Hollitzer, 2020); co-editor of *The Aesthetic Legacy of Eduard Hanslick: Close Readings and Critical Perspectives* (New York: Routledge, forthcoming); and is currently preparing further projects on Hanslick's criticism, the historical evolution of musicological methodology, and the political contexts of nineteenth-century Vienna that led to the simultaneous establishment of musicology and art history in Austria. Since 2018, Wilfing has been editor-in-chief of *Musicologica Austriaca: Journal for Austrian Music Studies.*

Preface

'We are accustomed to judge a thing by the title it bears' wrote Robert Schumann concerning the music of his colleague, Hector Berlioz. Titles can indeed be important. This volume is intended as a 'Companion to Music and Romanticism' – not, it should be noted, to 'Romantic Music', or 'Music in the Romantic Era'. Unlike many earlier books on the topic, Romanticism is not taken here primarily to refer to a distinct period in music history, though there is nevertheless a clear historical focus on the long nineteenth century, resulting from the overlapping between the Romantic period as generally understood in literature and art (*c.* 1797–1848) and as commonly received as a musical epoch (from *c.* 1815 to *c.* 1914). Nor, on the other hand, is Romanticism understood simply as a musical style, even one characteristic of a group of figures we might choose to term 'Romantics' (including, no doubt, Schumann and Berlioz). Rather, it is conceived as a constellation of themes, ideas, and responses rooted in the cultural milieu of post-Enlightenment, post-revolutionary Europe, which intersect with music in diverse and challenging ways.

Reflecting both the nature of the topic and the current diversity of disciplinary responses to these questions, the present volume is designed as a series of conceptual approaches that interrogate the relation between Romanticism and music from a range of different viewpoints: *Horizons*, *Worlds*, *Aesthetics*, *Practices*, and *Histories*. Written by a dynamic team of leading younger scholars and established authorities, it seeks to offer a state-of-the-art yet accessible overview of current thinking on this popular topic.

Romanticism is not the easiest topic to elucidate. But it does come with several ostensible advantages for an editor. A Companion clearly aims at a degree of comprehensiveness in coverage; just as evidently, it will never completely fulfil this demand. The advantage of treating a topic like Romanticism, however, is that such failure is not only expected, but singularly apt. I have tried to avoid obvious lacunae in topics covered; still, an unscrupulous editor has a convenient excuse to hand for any omissions by appealing to the aesthetics of incompletion and the Romantic fragment. Moreover, as Isaiah Berlin once argued,

Romanticism marked an epochal change in the history of ideas in that two incompatible views could both be considered right in their own way. A range of viewpoints and approaches to the problem of framing Romanticism and music are given by the different contributors to this volume, not all of which may necessarily harmonise completely with one another (although there is in fact little significant disagreement between them). While some initial framework for the contributors was provided by the opening chapter, as I argue there, the tension between different understandings of Romanticism and its relationship with music – as a movement, historical period, style, or aesthetic – is one that authors will invariably negotiate for themselves. All the Companion's contributors are experts in their field, and I have tried to allow their different voices to come across as clearly as possible, reflecting the topic under discussion and the perspective of the individual author.

Finally, some much-needed acknowledgements. I would like to offer a short but heartfelt thanks here to all those who helped and contributed to the making of this volume. In particular I must mention Kate Brett for initially commissioning this companion and seeing it through to publication, Elaine Kelly for valuable advice when putting it together, Damian Taylor for helpful comments on the sections I wrote, and last but by no means least, all nineteen contributors for their enormous expertise and enthusiasm for the subject.

Chronology

Romanticism is difficult to define in terms of a distinct historical period in music. The following chronology covers a large stretch of time broadly equivalent to the 'long nineteenth century' lasting from the French Revolution to the First World War, in which nearly all discussion of music and Romanticism is located. It concentrates on the period between the late 1790s and 1850, which covers both the eras usually associated with literary and artistic manifestations of Romanticism and music's subsequent 'Romantic generation' of composers. After mid-century the examples given are generally more confined to music, reflecting the oft-noted sense that music's purported 'Romantic' quality in this period was at variance with its surrounding culture.

1781   Mozart moves to Vienna. Kant, *Critique of Pure Reason*.
1782   Rousseau's *Confessions* posthumously published.
1789   Outbreak of French Revolution. William Blake, *Songs of Innocence*.
1790   Death of Joseph II of Austria. Kant, *Critique of Judgement*. Goethe, *Faust: A Fragment*.
1791   Death of Mozart. Haydn travels to London. Thomas Paine, *The Rights of Man*.
1792   Beethoven, aged 21, arrives in Vienna. Mary Wollstonecraft, *A Vindication of the Rights of Woman*.
1793   Execution of Louis XVI; French Revolutionary Terror.
1794   Fichte begins lecturing on the *Wissenschaftslehre* in Jena.
1795   Schiller, *Aesthetic Education of Man*, Goethe, *Wilhelm Meister's Apprenticeship*.
1796   Jean Paul, *Siebenkäs*.
1797   Emergence of early Romantic circle in Jena and Berlin. Wackenroder, *Outpourings of an Art-Loving Friar*. Coleridge writes *Kubla Khan, or a Vision in a Dream. A Fragment*. Birth of Schubert.
1798   Haydn, *The Creation*. First issue of the *Athenäum* published by the Schlegel brothers (six issues, until 1800). Wordsworth and Coleridge, *Lyrical Ballads*.

1799 Hölderlin, *Hyperion*. Wackenroder/Tieck, *Fantasies on Art*, Schleiermacher, *On Religion*, F. Schlegel, *Lucinde*. Goya, *Caprichos*.

1800 Novalis, *Hymns to the Night*. Schelling, *System of Transcendental Idealism*. Volta invents early form of electrical battery.

1801 Birth of Bellini. Act of Union between Great Britain and Ireland.

1802 Beethoven, Piano Sonatas, Op. 31. Chateaubriand, *René*. Schelling, *Philosophy of Art*.

1803 Birth of Berlioz. Jean Paul, *Titan*.

1804 Napoleon crowned Emperor of France by Pope in Rome. Beethoven, *Eroica* Symphony. Senancour, *Obermann*. Declaration of Independence in Haiti.

1805 British Navy defeats French fleet at Trafalgar. Wordsworth completes *The Prelude*. First volume of *Des Knaben Wunderhorn* published by Arnim and Brentano in Heidelberg. Birth of Fanny Mendelssohn, later Hensel.

1806 France defeats Prussia at the Battle of Jena; dissolution of Holy Roman Empire.

1807 Hegel, *Phenomenology of Spirit*. Abolition of slave trade across British Empire.

1808 Premiere of Beethoven, Symphonies Nos. 5 & 6. Goethe, *Faust*, Part 1, Moore, first book of *Irish Melodies*.

1809 Death of Haydn. Birth of Mendelssohn. A. W. Schlegel, *Lectures on Dramatic Art and Literature*.

1810 E. T. A. Hoffmann's review of Beethoven's Fifth Symphony. Birth of Chopin and Schumann. De Staël, *On Germany*. Caspar David Friedrich, *The Monk by the Sea*.

1811 Birth of Liszt. Luddite riots against industrialisation in English Midlands. Austen, *Sense and Sensibility*.

1812 Napoleon's failed invasion of Russia. Byron, *Childe Harold's Pilgrimage*, cantos 1 & 2. J. M. W. Turner, *Snow Storm: Hannibal and his Army Crossing the Alps*.

1813 Napoleon defeated in Peninsula War (cf. Beethoven's *Wellington's Victory*) and at Leipzig at the 'Battle of Nations'. Birth of Wagner and Verdi.

1814 Field publishes first three *Nocturnes*; Schubert, 'Gretchen am Spinnrade'. Scott, *Waverley*.

1815 Final defeat of Napoleon at Waterloo. Congress of Vienna. Schubert, 'Der Erlkönig', 'Heidenröslein'.

1816 Beethoven, *An die ferne Geliebte*, Rossini, *Il barbiere di Siviglia*, Spohr, *Faust*.

1817 Byron, *Manfred*, Coleridge, *Biographia Literaria*.

1818 Schopenhauer, *The World as Will and Representation*, vol. 1. Friedrich, *The Wanderer over the Sea of Clouds*. Mary Shelley, *Frankenstein*.

1819 Birth of Clara Schumann, née Wieck. Gericault, *Raft of the Medusa*. Peterloo Massacre in Manchester. Anti-Semitic Hep-Hep riots and repressive Carlsbad Decrees in German territories.

1820 Hoffmann, *Life and Opinions of Tomcat Murr*, Lamartine, *Poetic Meditations*, Shelley, *Prometheus Unbound*. Ørsted discovers connection between electricity and magnetism.

1821 Weber, *Der Freischütz*. Shelley, *A Defence of Poetry*. Constable, *The Hay Wain*. Death of Napoleon and Keats. Start of Greek War of Independence.

1822 Birth of Franck. Death of Hoffmann and Shelley.

1823 Schubert, *Die schöne Müllerin*.

1824 Premiere of Beethoven, Symphony No. 9. Birth of Smetana and Bruckner. Death of Byron.

1825 Mendelssohn, Octet. Opening of Stockton and Darlington Railway.

1826 Death of Weber. Mendelssohn, Overture to *A Midsummer Night's Dream*.

1827 Death of Beethoven. Schubert, *Winterreise*. Heine, *Book of Songs*, Hugo, Preface to *Cromwell*, Delacroix, *The Death of Sardanapalus*.

1828 Death of Schubert. Auber, *La Muette de Portici*, Marschner, *Der Vampyr*. Paganini starts major European concert tour.

1829 Mendelssohn's pioneering revival of Bach's *St Matthew Passion* in Berlin, and journey to Scotland (inspiration for *Hebrides* Overture and 'Scottish' Symphony). Rossini, *Guillaume Tell*.

1830 July Revolution in Paris. Berlioz, *Symphonie fantastique*. Stendhal, *The Red and the Black*. Tennyson, first collection of *Poems*.

1831 Meyerbeer, *Robert le diable*, Bellini, *La sonnambula* and *Norma*. Faraday discovers principle of electromagnetic induction.

1832 Chopin, *Nocturnes*, Op. 9. Mickiewicz completes *Dziady*. Death of Goethe and Scott. Great Reform Act in Britain.

1833 Mendelssohn, 'Italian' Symphony. Birth of Brahms and Borodin.

1834 Berlioz, *Harold in Italy*. Schumann co-founds *Neue Zeitschrift für Musik*. Death of Coleridge.

1835 Chopin, Ballade No. 1, Donizetti, *Lucia di Lammermoor*, Schumann, *Carnaval*. Death of Bellini. Heine, *The Romantic School*, Leopardi, *Canti*.

1836 Meyerbeer, *Les Huguenots*. Cole, *The Course of Empire*. Dickens, *The Pickwick Papers*.

1837 Eichendorff, *Poems*. Accession of Queen Victoria to British throne. Cooke and Wheatstone patent the electric telegraph.

1839 Berlioz, *Roméo et Juliette*. Schubert's 'Great' C major Symphony, rediscovered by Schumann, premiered under Mendelssohn's direction. Introduction of photographic processes by Daguerre and Talbot.

1840 Gade, *Echoes of Ossian* Overture, Schumann, *Liederkreis* Op. 39, *Dichterliebe*. Birth of Tchaikovsky. Friedrich Wilhelm IV ('the Romantic on the Throne') becomes King of Prussia.

1841 Schumann, Symphonies Nos 1 & 4, Wagner, *The Flying Dutchman*. Birth of Dvořák.

1842 Mendelssohn, *A Midsummer Night's Dream*, incidental music.

1843 Birth of Grieg. Kierkegaard, *Either/Or*.

1844 Elizabeth Barrett Browning, *Poems*. Turner, *Rain, Steam and Speed – The Great Western Railway*.

1845 Franz Brendel takes over *Neue Zeitschrift für Musik*, which becomes mouthpiece for the 'New German School'. Merimée, *Carmen*.

1846 Berlioz, *La Damnation de Faust*. Hensel publishes first works.

1847 Death of Hensel and Mendelssohn. Charlotte Brontë, *Jane Eyre*, Emily Brontë, *Wuthering Heights*.

1848 Revolutionary uprisings across Europe. Death of Donizetti. Liszt stops career as touring virtuoso and settles in Weimar as Kapellmeister. Founding of Pre-Raphaelite Brotherhood. Marx and Engels, *The Communist Manifesto*.

1849 Death of Chopin. Meyerbeer, *Le Prophète*. Wagner flees to Switzerland, pens *Art and Revolution* and subsequent tracts. Courbet, *The Stone Breakers*.

1850 Death of Wordsworth.

1851 Great Exhibition held in London's Crystal Palace. Melville, *Moby-Dick*.

1853 Liszt, B minor Sonata, Verdi, *Il trovatore* and *La traviata*, Wagner begins composition of *Das Rheingold*. Schumann writes 'Neue Bahnen', promoting Brahms.

1854 Liszt introduces the term 'symphonic poem' to describe *Les préludes*. Schumann has psychological breakdown and is institutionalised. Hanslick, *Vom musikalisch-Schönen*.

1855 Whitman, *Leaves of Grass* (first version).

1856 Death of Schumann. Flaubert, *Madame Bovary*.

1857   Birth of Elgar. Liszt, *A Faust Symphony*. Baudelaire, *Les Fleurs du mal*.

1858   Birth of Puccini.

1859   Gounod, *Faust*, Wagner, *Tristan und Isolde*. Darwin, *On the Origin of Species*.

1860   Brahms and Joachim amongst four signees to a declaration objecting to Brendel and New German School. Birth of Mahler and Wolf.

1861   Unification of Italy. Start of the American Civil War.

1862   Birth of Delius and Debussy. Hugo, *Les misérables*.

1863   Premiere of Berlioz, *Les Troyens* (cut version). Helmholtz, *On the Sensations of Tone*.

1864   Death of Meyerbeer. Birth of Richard Strauss. Maxwell proves light is an electromagnetic wave.

1865   Birth of Nielsen, Glazunov, and Sibelius. American Civil War ends.

1866   Bruch, Violin Concerto No. 1. Dostoevsky, *Crime and Punishment*.

1867   Opening of the Suez Canal.

1868   Grieg, Piano Concerto. Death of Rossini.

1869   Death of Berlioz. Brahms, *A German Requiem*. Tolstoy, *War and Peace*.

1870   Tchaikovsky, *Romeo and Juliet* fantasy-overture. Wagner, *Beethoven* essay. Start of Franco-Prussian War.

1871   Verdi, *Aida*. Eliot, *Middlemarch*. Unification of Germany.

1872   Mussorgsky, *Boris Godunov*. Nietzsche, *The Birth of Tragedy*.

1873   Birth of Rachmaninov.

1874   Bruckner, Symphony No. 4 ('Romantic'), first version; Johann Strauss (son), *Die Fledermaus*; Verdi, *Requiem*. Birth of Schoenberg. Term 'Impressionism' coined to criticise Monet's 1872 painting *Impression: soleil levant*.

1875   Bizet, *Carmen*, and death. Grieg, *Peer Gynt*.

1876   Premieres of Wagner's *Der Ring des Nibelungen* at Bayreuth, and Brahms's Symphony No. 1. Alexander Graham Bell patents the telephone.

1877   Thomas Edison demonstrates his new phonograph. Tolstoy, *Anna Karenina*.

1878   Dvořák, *Slavonic Dances*, Op. 46, Sullivan, *H.M.S. Pinafore*, Tchaikovsky, Symphony No. 4.

1879   Smetana, *Má vlast*.

1880   Offenbach, *The Tales of Hoffmann*, and death. Dostoevsky, *The Brothers Karamazov*.

1881   Borodin, String Quartet No. 2.

1882   Wagner, *Parsifal*.

1883   Death of Wagner. Bruckner Symphony No. 7.

1885   Brahms, Symphony No. 4, Dvořák, Symphony No. 7.

1886   Franck, Violin Sonata. Death of Liszt.

1888   Franck, Symphony in D minor, Rimsky-Korsakov, *Scheherazade*. Nietzsche, *The Case of Wagner*. Strindberg, *Miss Julie*.

1889   Premieres of Mahler, Symphony No. 1, and Strauss, *Don Juan*. Tolstoy, *The Kreutzer Sonata*.

1890   Mascagni, *Cavalleria rusticana*. Death of Franck.

1891   Brahms, Clarinet Quintet. Hardy, *Tess of the d'Urbervilles*, Ibsen, *Hedda Gabler*.

1892   Leoncavallo, *Pagliacci*, Sibelius, *En saga*.

1893   Dvořák, Symphony No. 9 ('From the New World'); Tchaikovsky, Symphony No. 6 (*Pathétique*), and death; Verdi, *Falstaff*.

1894   Beach, *Gaelic* Symphony, Debussy, *Prélude à L'après-midi d'un faune*, Dvořák, Cello Concerto. Beginning of Dreyfus affair in France.

1895   Rachmaninov, Symphony No. 1. Lumière brothers patent their *cinématographe* and screen first public films. Röntgen discovers X-rays. Trial of Oscar Wilde.

1896   Mahler, Symphony No. 3, Puccini, *La bohème*. Death of Bruckner and Clara Schumann. Marconi patents radio transmitter.

1897   Death of Brahms. Vienna Secession co-founded by Klimt. Tolstoy, *What Is Art?*

1898   Coleridge-Taylor, *Hiawatha's Wedding Feast*. Rodin's *Monument to Balzac* rejected. Zola publishes *J'accuse*.

1899   Elgar, *Enigma Variations*, Joplin, *Maple Leaf Rag*, Schoenberg, *Verklärte Nacht*. Yeats, *The Wind Among the Reeds*. Freud, *Interpretation of Dreams*.

1900   Elgar, *The Dream of Gerontius*, Puccini, *Tosca*.

1901   Rachmaninov, Piano Concerto No. 2. Death of Verdi. Thomas Mann, *Buddenbrooks*. Death of Queen Victoria.

1902   Debussy, *Pelléas et Mélisande*, Mahler, Symphony No. 5, Sibelius, Symphony No. 2. Klimt, *Beethoven Frieze*.

1903   Wright Brothers achieve first manned powered flight.

1904   Delius, *Sea Drift*, Puccini, *Madama Butterfly*. Death of Dvořák.

1905   Debussy, *La Mer*, Lehár, *The Merry Widow*, Strauss, *Salome*. Einstein, *Special Theory of Relativity*. Russo-Japanese War ends in victory for Japan.

1906   Ives, *Central Park in the Dark*, Smyth, *The Wreckers*.

1907 Rachmaninov, Symphony No. 2. Death of Grieg. Picasso, *Les Demoiselles d'Avignon*.

1908 Elgar, Symphony No. 1, Mahler, *Das Lied von der Erde*, Rachmaninov, *The Isle of the Dead*, Scriabin, *Poem of Ecstasy*, Schoenberg, String Quartet No. 2.

1909 Albéniz, *Iberia*, Mahler, Symphony No. 9, Schoenberg, *Erwartung*.

1910 Strauss, *Der Rosenkavalier*, Stravinsky, *The Firebird*, Vaughan Williams, *Fantasia on a Theme by Thomas Tallis*.

1911 Elgar Symphony No. 2, Nielsen Symphony No. 3, Sibelius Symphony No. 4. Death of Mahler. Amundsen beats Scott to South Pole.

1912 Bartók, *Bluebeard's Castle*, Ravel, *Daphnis et Chloé*.

1913 Riots at premieres of Stravinsky's *The Rite of Spring* in Paris, and at Berg's *Altenberg Lieder* in Vienna. Proust, *Swann's Way*.

1914 Outbreak of First World War.

PART I

Horizons

1 | Defining the Indefinable: Romanticism and Music

BENEDICT TAYLOR

Whatever else it may be, Romanticism is hardly unknown: its characteristic features are in fact familiar to many of us. Take the 1832 painting by Carl Gustav Carus, *Goethe-Denkmal* (Goethe Memorial), reproduced as the cover to this Companion. A wild, lonely landscape of mountains and ravines calls forth the sublimity of nature, the lofty peaks standing out as islands within the mysterious sea of mist. It is already late: the sun has apparently set and evening is drawing on; a full moon, peeping out for a moment from behind the clouds above, provides nocturnal illumination through its refulgent, reflected light. Art and religion are near at hand (even the stylised framing of the picture suggests an altar panel). Two sculpted angels perch on the tomb in the foreground, imparting an aura of sanctity to the scene's already otherworldly quality: alongside the presence of death there is a promise of something beyond. In barely legible, almost hieroglyphic script the name 'Göthe' can be made out on the medieval-looking sarcophagus. The Romantic vision is built on the remains of the classical past, while sequestered within the protecting mountains high above the rest of humanity, the poetic genius has been returned to nature, from whence he arose. (This, lest the national provenance be overlooked, is a distinctly Germanic backdrop too – albeit the Romantic 'Saxon Switzerland' rather than mercantile Frankfurt am Main.) Not the least of these Romantic features is the harp, a favourite symbol for music in Carus's paintings. While the angels pray for the soul of the poet, the harp already suggests the potential for transcendence (note the gleaming star, a flash of gold amidst the surrounding sheen of crepuscular silver and blue, the illuminating lamp of poetic imagination, a second sun), as if the now liberated spirit might rise from the tomb to communicate directly with nature, attaining eternal life through his art. Calling to mind the Romantic cult of the aeolian harp on which the wind would play its natural melodies, the instrument suggests the organic interconnection of self and nature through sound, the living breath of a pantheistic world infused by spirit.

Carus's picture serves as a virtual compendium of Romantic images and themes; indeed, for many observers its Romanticism might have passed well beyond exaggeration into cliché. Yet its creator embodies many of the apparent contradictions of Romanticism. No ill-adjusted artist at odds with the world around him, Carus – a former friend of Goethe – was himself a medical doctor and *Naturwissenschaftler*, a respected professional within civil society and leading man of science. An expert in melancholia and pioneer in studying the unconscious, he was consulted by no less a figure than the ailing Robert Schumann (Carus's recommendation of energetic morning walks appears to have had little effect, however; with paintings like this how could he have hoped to cure any Romantic artist?). For all the Romantic excess, the quotidian worlds of science and society lie not far away. And while few would have difficulties in identifying Carus's painting as 'Romantic', Romanticism itself has long proved strangely recalcitrant to definition.

Romanticism: In Search of a Definition

> Weary of analysing and pondering, finding always empty phrases and incomprehensible professions of faith, we came to believe that this word *romanticism* was no more than a word; we thought it beautiful, and it seemed a pity that it meant nothing.[1]

Romanticism is easy to recognise, but notoriously hard to define. When even undoubted Romantics like Alfred de Musset (quoted above) treat the attempt with ironic condescension, we might well despair of adequately formulating a definition, let alone ever extending our understanding to its relation with music – an art form that has similarly often been found to be beautiful, and yet to mean nothing. No doubt a similar problem haunts attempts to theorise other comparable wide-ranging movements, such as the Enlightenment, modernism, or postmodernism. But the irony for Romanticism is that this endeavour seems to coalesce into one of the critical objectives of the Romantic movement itself: how to define the indefinable; and the inevitable failure of this attempt is perhaps the most Romantic feature of it. This is a movement, after all, which not only resists easy encapsulation (most such general terms do), but in which the search for completion, for a unified whole, truth, or ultimate meaning, is as commonly present as the insistence that this goal is for ever unreachable. To rework a famous fragment by Friedrich Schlegel, the foremost spokesman of German Romanticism, a definition is both impossible – and necessary.[2]

Nevertheless, the difficulties should not be exaggerated: such scruples, while satisfying scholarly consciences, are little use to the student wanting some direction within this topic. In broad terms, of course, some basic outlines can easily be sketched. Romanticism is usually taken to refer to a range of movements arising in Western Europe at the end of the eighteenth century and start of the nineteenth, concentrated originally in Germany and Britain but also finding expression in France soon after.[3] More generally, it can refer to an ethos, aesthetic, or worldview often associated with these movements, though this is where the problems of definition soon become apparent. It might typically include an emphasis on feeling and emotion, with increased value placed on subjectivity and self-expression, on nature and organic growth, the power of the creative imagination and the unconscious; the prizing of art and the aesthetic, the spiritual and fantastic, self-consciousness and freedom, pantheism and the universal power of love; yet also a sense of alienation or even spiritual homelessness that is the flip side of the longing to be part of a larger whole. Recurring themes and images include night, darkness, or twilight, death, loss, memory, and distance, and above all, yearning or longing for something (often undefined) beyond our finite world of experience. The longer the list continues, however, the further we seem to be from ever reaching any end, and the more contradictions emerge. Thus, fragmentation exists alongside a longing for the whole, the systematic alongside the unsystematic; the nostalgic looking back on the past is found alongside a purposeful resolve towards creating a new future, deep pessimism found against high optimism. Romanticism can appear to be politically progressive and yet conservative; the idea of Romantic art as a form of escapism sits strangely alongside Shelley's famous claim of poets being 'the unacknowledged legislators of the world'. Some of these dichotomies are of course only surface contradictions, and it could be just as persuasive in several cases to see Romanticism as arising from the desire to reconcile antithetical positions bequeathed by modernity and the Enlightenment. Still, the difficulty in trying to define the movement through its associated qualities becomes readily apparent.[4]

The multiplicity of features viewed as belonging to Romanticism, and the seemingly impossible task of finding a single unifying theme or essence behind the different manifestations, is indeed the overriding problem for scholars. In an oft-cited article from 1924, the literary historian Arthur Lovejoy famously dismissed attempts to find a unitary definition for Romanticism; short of discarding the term altogether (which he conceded would never take off) he suggested 'that any study of the subject should begin with a recognition of a prima facie plurality of Romanticisms', each of which could be more or less circumscribed by date, representatives, and constituent elements.[5] Still, this has not stopped scholars ever since persisting in trying to find common features underlying Romanticism's multifarious forms. It may be sought in the common norms of 'imagination for the view of poetry, nature for the view of the world, and symbol and myth for poetic style'; in 'the revolution in the European mind against thinking in terms of static mechanism and the redirection of the mind to thinking in terms of dynamic organicism'; in the movement from the model of the creative imagination as a mirror to that of a lamp.[6] In philosophical terms, Romanticism might be grounded in a scepticism towards the idea that reason can explain everything, an anti-foundationalism that questions whether incontrovertible first principles can be found that might ground reason itself, a critique of the rationalism of the Enlightenment. Thus Romanticism marks a turning point in history when two sets of values may be equally right – and yet incompatible; a world where reason cannot be reconciled with reality, and we are thrown back on sincerity and personal integrity as the only arbiters of truth.[7] Some go further in arguing that in its unremitting perspectivism, fragmentation and anti-rationalist thrust, Romanticism is essentially pre-empting postmodernity; others disagree, holding that it carries further the project of the Enlightenment, seeking to reconcile reason with ethics and aesthetic sensibility, not abandoning the belief in an ultimate truth but admitting that we may only ever approach it without ever actually reaching it.[8] The Romantic spirit – the tension between the urge for a meaningful whole and the insistence on the fragmentary and incomplete – lives on, sometimes unwittingly, sometimes self-consciously, in the attempt to define Romanticism itself.

Romanticism and Music

Even greater problems arise, however, when musicological use is introduced. While music is unquestionably an important part of many Romantic formulations, Romanticism as a concept applied to music often bears at best an oblique relationship with Romanticism as more generally understood. The most commonly encountered use of the term is to describe a certain type of music – namely as 'Romantic music', as an adjective on the cusp of forming a compound noun. Thus, as many standard textbooks over the last century will tell us, 'Romantic' refers to European music from Beethoven's late works and Schubert to the rise of Schoenberg and Stravinsky – in other words, almost a century of musical composition, roughly correlate to the nineteenth century, pushed back by a decade or so. But it is often unclear in these accounts whether 'Romantic' is being used to refer to a historical period or as a style – if not an uneasy mixture of the two – and in neither case is the relation with other cultural manifestations of Romanticism straightforward.[9] The entry in the *Harvard Concise Dictionary of Music* from 1978 is a case in point, defining 'Romantic / romanticism' both in chronological terms (music from roughly the 1820s to 1910) and as a distinct 'movement' with a geographical centre (Germany), while also offering some of its typical stylistic traits (an emphasis on subjective expression, formal freedom) and characteristic genres (character piece, song, symphonic poem).[10] More rewarding, perhaps, is to take Romanticism as an aesthetic – as a mode of perceiving music and category of reception. Romanticism becomes less a constitutive element 'in' a musical work, and more a way of understanding music. In this situation, though, the term's chronological and geographical bounds become inevitably loosened; almost any music can potentially be seen as 'Romantic' as a result (which is indeed how music is usually treated in Romantic writings).

Romanticism as a Historical Period

Let us start with the historical question. One of the problems with musical Romanticism as a historical-stylistic category is that it is largely non-coetaneous with the literary and philosophical movements going under that name. Those looking for a starting date for the latter often consider the outbreak of the French Revolution in 1789 as a convenient initial boundary; more precisely, the gathering of an influential group of thinkers in Jena and Berlin around 1797 (including the Schlegels, Novalis, Wackenroder, Tieck, Schleiermacher, and Schelling) is often taken to mark the onset of the *Frühromantik* in Germany, with their journal the *Athenaeum* its mouthpiece, and the publication in 1798 of the *Lyrical Ballads* by Wordsworth and Coleridge the beginning of a specific ('Lakeland') Romantic movement in England. The situation in France is less straightforward, though some time in the first decades of the nineteenth century is often proposed as a starting point. But these Romantic movements were relatively short-lasting. German Romanticism is conventionally divided into 'early' (1797–1802), 'high' (1802–15), and 'late' (1815–30) forms; by 1830, then, it is largely over, while the early 1830s also mark a standard cut-off point in the narrative of English literary Romanticism (Keats, Shelley, and Byron had all died the previous decade, Coleridge would soon follow, and Wordsworth had written all the work for which he is celebrated). French Romanticism is normally considered passé by the later 1840s.

In music-historical terms, of course, 'Romanticism' is supposed to have hardly started by the time its most influential manifestations have finished in other arts. The one period which almost all music histories agree on terming 'Romantic' – the years from around 1830 to 1850, marked by the emergence of the figures sometimes designated 'the Romantic Generation' – is the period after the primary Romantic impulses in England and Germany had already faded.[11] What is more, Romanticism appears to persist much longer in music than in most other art forms. As Carl Dahlhaus notes, the second half of the nineteenth century in Europe is an age of scientific positivism and realism in most other arts; while a good case could be made for considering some of the music in this period under the aegis of Romanticism (or 'neo-Romanticism'), the disparity is none-theless striking.[12]

Geographically, too, the tendency to use 'Romantic' as a blanket label for all nineteenth-century music runs the risk of imposing a centre/periphery model on national styles across Europe: music from countries strongly influenced by Romanticism and Romantic aesthetics (most evidently, the German-speaking lands) becomes thereby privileged, along with particular associated genres and aesthetics (instrumental music or 'national' opera; the idea of 'absolute' or 'pure' music), while the music of cultures less marked by Romanticism is either marginalised or misrepresented through misprision within a purported Romantic aesthetic. Romanticism thus easily becomes a normative category: the music of other cultures must either be accommodated within it, or run the risk of being seen as periph-eral to a nineteenth-century mainstream. The relationship, for instance, between various national movements in the second half of the nineteenth century and certain Romantic ideas is not in dispute; but whether all nineteenth-century national movements should simply be reduced to a larger monolithic 'Romanticism' – and whether all music from outside the Austro-German sphere should be understood as 'nationalistic' – is much more questionable.

Romanticism as a Style

In the absence of any clear chronological and cultural intersection it would at least help if Romanticism in musical terms were a robust stylistic category that would enable the connection to other 'Romanticisms' to be justified, but even here the link can often be tenuous. 'Romantic music' is typically viewed as denoted by an emphasis on emotion and subjective expression, by a freedom from formal constraints and the introduction of 'extra-musical' or programmatic elements, by increased harmonic complexity and richness, the use of song-like melodic material, and the development and expansion of instrumental resources including an emphasis on the colouristic use of sound. Certain genres are seen as Romantic innovations – the lied, song-cycle, characteristic piano miniature, concert overture and symphonic poem, and the notion of opera as a fusion of all the arts or *Gesamtkunstwerk*.

Some of these features undeniably do relate to Romanticism as more generally understood: in some cases the Romantic quality arises from the subject matter (the lied and Romantic lyric poetry; the themes of Romantic national opera); the ideal of the *Gesamtkunstwerk* famously sought by Wagner in his later music dramas relates to earlier discussions by Romantic writers such as Friedrich Schlegel and E. T. A. Hoffmann (although it must be remembered that opera, from its beginnings, has held up a comparable ideal). Specific stylistic and aesthetic features of the earlier Romantic movements – organic, evolving forms, the aesthetics of the fragment, the mixing and fusion of genres – can also be connected to certain aspects of nineteenth-century musical style, which may thus be justified under the stylistic label of Romantic.[13] In such cases, though, the proportion of music from the nineteenth century that can be considered specifically 'Romantic' decreases – often drastically – as the application of the term becomes more refined. Many of the traits commonly associated with Romantic music (such as harmonic richness, lyricism, looser syntax, the colouristic use of sound) could, however, simply be considered stylistic characteristics of nineteenth-century music more generally; they have little intrinsic connection with other cultural manifestations of Romanticism. In certain cases, indeed, the supposed link is rather more deceptive than initially appears. This applies to what are probably the two most popular preconceptions of Romantic music: its emotional expressivity and freedom from classical form.

First, while subjective expression is indisputably an important aspect of Romanticism more widely, the idea of music as 'the language of the emotions' is actually a pre-Romantic aesthetic characteristic of the eighteenth century (Romantic aesthetics are generally distinct in emphasising music's formalist aspects, or when based on emotional qualities, imbuing them with significantly greater metaphysical aspirations than the primarily physiological and ethical basis of earlier eighteenth-century viewpoints). Thus the popular view of music as primarily the expression of emotion has no more connection with Romanticism than with the aesthetics of sensibility or *Empfindsamkeit*, and would apply to C. P. E. Bach at least as well as to Chopin over half a century later. Moreover, one would be entering hazardous territory if venturing to suggest that other music is generally less expressive than that popularly termed 'Romantic'. The gestures and rhetoric of nineteenth-century music have become established in modern Western culture as the pre-eminent language of the emotions, but there is no reason to believe that earlier music was not heard as expressive to a comparable extent. Most problematic of all, though, is the idea – widespread since the late nineteenth century – that Romanticism is inherently opposed to 'purely musical' qualities, emphasising (often 'extra-musical') content over form. This has been partially responsible for introducing a new concept into music historiography, the 'Classical', as an imagined antipode to the 'Romantic'.

It is undeniable that Romantic aesthetics following Schlegel see the Romantic as being manifested in a literary art that is to some extent incomplete, fragmentary, open, evolving, stylistically heterogeneous, in contrast to the perceived formal unity of the works of classical antiquity. To this extent, the dichotomy here constructed between 'Classical' and 'Romantic' could plausibly be extended to musical works embodying such opposed formal qualities. Yet the very idea that music – textless instrumental music specifically – can be considered a work of art in its own right, as an object of aesthetic contemplation, is the most significant contribution of Romantic thought to the history of music aesthetics. In a word, the 'purely musical' is a Romantic invention; listening to instrumental music as a meaningful language, one embodying its own type of logic and form, is the lasting legacy of Romanticism. The 'extra-musical' – the idea that music needs the support of verbal language or conjunction with other arts for its meaning – is an earlier viewpoint, against which Romantic aesthetics form the strongest opposition. It is this that separates the Romantic view of music from that of the eighteenth-century Enlightenment. If we hear the symphonies, quartets, and sonatas of Haydn, Mozart, and Beethoven as embodying purely musical values, we are hearing them Romantically. To put it in pointed form, to see music as 'Classical' is essentially to view it from the perspective of Romanticism.[14]

To be sure, one might propose that, as a stylistic category, 'Romantic' music can still be opposed to 'Classical' music, even if the latter is inherently a Romantic aesthetic. Romanticism – an idea with a tendency towards infinity – may be broad enough to contain both types within its copious contradictions. This is the point, however, when the use of 'Romantic' as a stylistic category is in serious danger of obscuring more than it illuminates. By allowing two contradictory stylistic designations into a single broader aesthetic that shares one of their names, the whole matter becomes irredeemably confusing. This is responsible for one of the most futile debates in music history: whether, and to what extent, 'Classical' music is different to Romantic music; when 'Classicism' ends, when Romanticism starts, whether Beethoven (who always seems the pivotal figure) was 'Classical' or Romantic, et cetera. Both terms are fictitious concepts, heuristic labels that outlive their use when taken too literally as implying a coherent and antithetical historical, stylistic, or aesthetic position.

It is clear that 'Romantic' is typically used in a mixed and rather loose sense, as a broad historical-stylistic label to designate an epoch in Western art music in terms of some of the prominent stylistic characteristics of this music and its associated aesthetics. There is nothing inherently wrong with such broad labels: it should just be remembered that the use of this word to designate all nineteenth-century music may well contradict other, more specific uses of the term. Problems may arise when the various meanings are conflated and it is assumed that Romanticism, in the stricter meaning of the term, is an essential quality of all music from this period – that certain genres, formal principles, and styles constitute a norm against which the music of this era should be evaluated.

Romanticism as an Aesthetic

It may be more productive to approach Romanticism as an aesthetic, a mode of understanding music rather than a style or historical era. After all, Romanticism is often associated with the otherworldly and transcendent: there is an unintended irony in seeking too exact a location in time and space for its musical manifestation. This means, for instance, taking seriously the claim E. T. A. Hoffmann made in 1810 when he described the music of Haydn and Mozart as 'Romantic'. But it also means that the music of other composers not even remotely overlapping with the European movements that go under the name can equally be heard Romantically, as when Hoffmann elsewhere praises the choral music of Leo and Palestrina, or when Kleist treats the Gloria from the Mass of an unknown (and no doubt imaginary) early Italian master as the instantiation of the power of music.

Underlying this is the belief that speaking of 'Romantic music' is less valuable than seeking to understand what Romantic writers heard in music, what they meant when they spoke of music, the role music played in Romantic philosophy and aesthetics. For while Romanticism is on the one hand just as diffuse, contradictory, and confusing in its musical as in any of its other manifestations, two things appear certain: that music is central to many forms of Romanticism, indeed provides what is in many ways the exemplary Romantic art; and that Romanticism in turn is central to music, being responsible for its drastic change in aesthetic status since the eighteenth century, one whose effects have remained with us to this day.

Music is so often accorded a vital function in Romantic thought, whether this relates to an actual piece of music, the practice of music making, the vague idea or literary figure of 'music', or the philosophical properties attributed to this art form. For Novalis, Wackenroder, and many Romantic poets, music serves the function of 'Romanticising the world', of poeticising and re-enchanting, of restoring lost unity and meaning. For other thinkers, music is a model for other forms of intellectual and artistic activity, capable of expressing the ineffable, even of revealing noumenal truths inaccessible to other modes of inquiry. Romanticism has played the biggest part in emancipating music, in promoting the claims of music as not just equal to any of the other arts, but indeed as the most profound of all. Friedrich Schlegel describes it as the highest of the arts, Hoffmann as the most Romantic of the arts, indeed the only truly Romantic art, while it occupies a position above all the other arts in the metaphysical system of Schopenhauer. Under Romantic aesthetics, music was put forward for the first time in millennia – even perhaps in history – as an art and activity that brings us closest to fundamental philosophical truths, the nature of ultimate reality, God, or what have you. Indeed, in some ways music effectively becomes the 'new mythology' sought by the early Romantics, especially by the end of the nineteenth century, when the metaphysical status afforded to it by earlier Romantic writers filters down into a popular truism.

The valorising of music is one of Romanticism's most momentous and yet most troubling legacies. And when more recent writers or artists – many of whom no one would consider 'Romantic' as such – call up music as expressing some otherwise ineffable quality, as linking to another, privileged realm of meaning, they are wittingly or not perpetuating a view of music for which Romanticism is responsible. This Romantic mode of understanding music has proved hard to shake off, partly because it is from this perspective that music can first be seen as uniquely meaningful at all.

From this perspective, Romanticism emerges as a complex and fascinating phenomenon that intersects with music in numerous ways. It is primarily this viewpoint that forms the guiding idea behind this present Companion – less an account of musical style in the nineteenth century than a study of the views, functions, perceptions, and polemical uses of music, as idea and practice, as it intersects with the multifarious forms taken by Romanticism. Still, it is hard to avoid completely the historical and stylistic definitions raised earlier: even if the notion of Romanticism is treated as an aesthetic that is transhistorical in application, it is nonetheless an aesthetic that arose at a particular time in European history and took particular artistic forms of expression. We cannot fully understand Romanticism outside its specific historical and cultural manifestations, which unavoidably brings us back, however warily now, to the previous categories outlined above.

The tension between these three perspectives – Romanticism as a historical period or movement, as a style, and as an aesthetic or mode of perception – is one that needs to be negotiated in any account of Romanticism and its relation to music. It is a challenge to which each of the following chapters will, in their different ways, respond.

Notes

1. Alfred de Musset, *Lettres de Dupuis et Cotonet* (1836), cited in Lilian R. Furst (ed.), *European Romanticism: Self-Definition. An Anthology* (London: Methuen, 1980), 47.
2. Friedrich Schlegel, *Athenaeum* Fragment No. 53: 'It is equally fatal for the mind [*Geist*] to have a system and to have none'; also see Fragment No. 82 on the problems of philosophical definition.
3. Looking to etymology and early use is liable to confuse rather than elucidate matters. 'Romantic' first arises to describe the medieval language of France and the associated literary form of the Romance, marked by fabulous or fantastic qualities. Though the term is prominently used in an adjectival sense by writers (such as the Schlegels) whom we would now consider 'early Romantics', its application to designate this movement itself seems to have occurred retrospectively in the early decades of the nineteenth century.
4. An extensive list of Romantic traits can be found in a classic study by Henry H. H. Remak, 'West European Romanticism: Definition and Scope', in Newton P. Stallknecht and Horst Frenz (eds.), *Comparative Literature: Method and Perspective* (Carbondale, IL: Southern Illinois University Press, 1961), 223–59.
5. Arthur Lovejoy, 'On the Discrimination of Romanticisms', *Proceedings of the Modern Language Association*, 39 (1924), 235–6, 237.
6. See respectively René Wellek, 'The Concept of "Romanticism" in Literary History II: The Unity of European Romanticism', *Comparative Literature*, 1 (1949), 147; Morse Peckham, 'Toward a Theory of Romanticism', *Proceedings of the Modern Language Association*, 66 (1951), 14; M. H. Abrams, *The Mirror and the Lamp: Romantic Theory and the Critical Tradition* (Oxford: Oxford University Press, 1953).

7. See Isaiah Berlin, *The Roots of Romanticism*, ed. Henry Hardy (London: Chatto & Windus, 1999); the lectures that comprise this book were originally given in 1965.

8. See, for instance, Paul de Man, *The Rhetoric of Romanticism* (New York: Columbia University Press, 1984), Philippe Lacoue-Labarthe and Jean-Luc Nancy, *The Literary Absolute: The Theory of Literature in German Romanticism*, trans. Philip Barnard and Cheryl Lester (Albany: SUNY Press, 1988), Manfred Frank, *The Philosophical Foundations of Early German Romanticism*, trans. Elizabeth Millan-Zaibert (Albany: SUNY Press, 2003), and Frederick C. Beiser, *The Romantic Imperative: The Concept of Early German Romanticism* (Cambridge, MA: Harvard University Press, 2003).

9. Thus, surveying some standard English-language surveys of the last century, several use the term 'Romantic' simply as a synonym for 'nineteenth century': e.g., Wilfrid Mellers, *Romanticism and the Twentieth Century (from 1800)* (London: Barrie and Rockliff, 1957); Leon Plantinga, *Romantic Music: A History of Musical Style in Nineteenth-Century Europe* (New York: W. W. Norton, 1984); Gerald Abraham (ed.), *Romanticism (1830–1890), The New Oxford History of Music*, vol. 9 (Oxford: Oxford University Press, 1990); Alexander Ringer (ed.), *The Early Romantic Era. Between Revolutions: 1789 and 1848* (London: Macmillan, 1990); and Jim Samson (ed.), *The Late Romantic Era. From the mid-19th century to World War I* (London: Macmillan, 1991). Others concentrate more on the idea of Romanticism as a style and aesthetic, though often attempt to cover as much of the nineteenth century as possible through this term: see, for instance, Alfred Einstein, *Music in the Romantic Era: A History of Musical Thought in the 19th Century* (New York: W. W. Norton & Co., 1947), who explicitly qualifies that his book is 'not a "History of Music in the 19th Century"' (xi); Rey M. Longyear, *Nineteenth-Century Romanticism in Music* (Englewood Cliffs, NJ: Prentice Hall, 1969); Arnold Whittall, *Romantic Music: A Concise History from Schubert to Sibelius* (London: Thames and Hudson, 1987).

10. 'An important movement of the 19th century, continuing until c. 1910 . . . In music, romanticism was largely a Germanic phenomenon . . . characterized by emphasis on subjective, emotional qualities and greater freedom of form.' *Harvard Concise Dictionary of Music*, ed. Don Michael Randel (Cambridge, MA: Harvard University Press, 1978), 431–2. More recent editions are slightly more circumspect.

11. See for instance Charles Rosen, *The Romantic Generation* (Cambridge, MA: Harvard University Press, 1995). The figures in question were all born around the first decade of the nineteenth century: Schubert (who died in 1828!), Bellini, Berlioz, Mendelssohn, Chopin, and Schumann; with the marginally younger Liszt, Wagner, and Verdi achieving the greater part of their compositional reputation only after mid-century.

12. See Carl Dahlhaus, 'Neo-Romanticism', in *Between Romanticism and Modernism: Four Studies in the Music of the Later Nineteenth Century*, trans. Mary Whittall (Berkeley and Los Angeles: University of California Press, 1980), 1–18; also *Nineteenth-Century Music*, trans. J. Bradford Robinson (Berkeley and Los Angeles: University of California Press, 1989), 192–5. As Dahlhaus argues, it could be persuasive to think of music in the later nineteenth century as providing (in some cases) a form of escapism from the overriding anti-Romantic, materialist ethos of the age; this is the time that the Romantic metaphysics of music, originally propounded in the early nineteenth century, attains widespread cultural acceptance.
13. See, for instance, John Daverio, *Nineteenth-Century Music and the German Romantic Ideology* (New York: Schirmer, 1993), Rosen, *The Romantic Generation*.
14. The concept of the 'Classical' in music seems to have grown up from the second quarter of the nineteenth century onwards to describe earlier music that remained exemplary and canonical; the fact that many pieces of 'Romantic' music are treated as a no less central part of the repertoire nowadays implies that such a distinction is effectively annulled (it is all 'Classical' – as indeed the umbrella term for Western art music suggests). On this matter and the difficulties of applying these terms historically see especially Hans Lenneberg, 'Classic and Romantic: The First Usage of the Terms', *Musical Quarterly*, 78 (1994), 610–25. See further Nicole Grimes's chapter in this volume (Chapter 19).

Further Reading

Beiser, Frederick C. *The Romantic Imperative: The Concept of Early German Romanticism* (Cambridge, MA: Harvard University Press, 2003).

Berlin, Isaiah. *The Roots of Romanticism*, ed. Henry Hardy (London: Chatto & Windus, 1999).

Charlton, D. G. 'The French Romantic Movement', in D. G. Charlton (ed.), *The French Romantics*, 2 vols. (Cambridge: Cambridge University Press, 1984), vol. 1, 1–32.

Cooper, John Michael (ed.). *Historical Dictionary of Romantic Music* (Lanham, MD: Scarecrow Press, 2013).

Dahlhaus, Carl. *Nineteenth-Century Music*, trans. J. B. Robinson (Berkeley and Los Angeles: University of California Press, 1989).

Ferber, Michael. *Romanticism: A Very Short Introduction* (Oxford: Oxford University Press, 2010).

Ferguson, Frances. 'On the Numbers of Romanticisms', *ELH*, 58/2 (1991), 471–98.

Frisch, Walter. *Music in the Nineteenth Century* (New York: W. W. Norton, 2013).

Furst, Lilian R. (ed.). *European Romanticism: Self-Definition. An Anthology* (London: Methuen, 1980).

Lovejoy, Arthur. 'On the Discrimination of Romanticisms', *Proceedings of the Modern Language Association*, 39 (1924), 229–53.

Reibel, Emmanuel. *Comment la musique est devenue 'romantique': De Rousseau à Berlioz* (Paris: Fayard, 2013).

Rummenhöller, Peter. *Romantik in der Musik: Analysen, Portraits, Reflexionen* (Munich: Deutsche Taschenbuch Verlag, 1989).

Samson, Jim. 'Romanticism', *The New Grove Dictionary of Music and Musicians*, ed. Stanley Sadie, 29 vols. (London: Macmillan, 2001), vol. 21, 596–603.

Samson, Jim (ed.). *The Cambridge History of Nineteenth-Century Music* (Cambridge: Cambridge University Press, 2001).

Wellek, René. 'The Concept of "Romanticism" in Literary History II: The Unity of European Romanticism', *Comparative Literature*, 1/2 (1949), 147–72.

2 | The Emergence of Musical Romanticism

KEITH CHAPIN

For all its proponents' protestations of difference, Romanticism emerged from the Enlightenment. The intellectuals and artists who debated the arts and their significance at the end of the eighteenth century belonged to the same well-educated and relatively well-to-do European social circles. They shared tastes for music that ranged from the emotionally intense to the lyrically simple, and from expansive grandeur to intimate delicacy. They had strong interests in antiquity and in the lessons that could be learned for the present. They were aware of the power of music, in particular, to trouble rational discourse.

These common foundations provided the productive framework for competition and discussion. Telling differences could often arise as artists competed with their forebears and with each other, and as people of letters discussed the news and issues of the day. Thus, even as eighteenth- and nineteenth-century musicians cultivated the main genres of vocal and instrumental music – opera, Mass, oratorio, symphony, string quartet, sonata, song – the register of their musical expression shifted from grace to fervency and from wit to exuberant striving. Even as entertainment, religious devotion, and the representation of status remained primary functions of music, those who felt that music should do more shifted their attention away from moral needs towards metaphysical or existential ones. Even as artists looked to the past for inspiration, they began to shift their attention away from classical Greek and Roman civilisation towards the alternate antiquities of 'primitive' folk cultures or medieval religious cults. And even as critics recognised that music did not convey ideas clearly and distinctly, this turned from its failing to its insuperable advantage.

Musicians and Writers

When discussing the origins of musical Romanticism, it is useful to distinguish between its emergence amongst musicians and amongst the writers who often led discussions of taste. Although these groups interacted, they did not always belong to the same social circles and they had different goals.

To track these differences and others, this chapter focuses on composers, not to distract from their position in a complex economy involving performers, teachers, printers and publishers, and a web of amateur listeners and music makers, but rather because shifts in musical style and taste can best be seen today in their works.

Successful musicians in the eighteenth and early-nineteenth centuries often came of age in family craft traditions. J. S. and C. P. E. Bach, Beethoven, Bellini, Cherubini, Couperin, Field, Grétry, Liszt, Mozart, Rameau, Reichardt, Rossini, Salieri, and Weber were all born of professional musicians, and some of them could point to successive generations of musicians behind them. The social level of this group is indicated by the exceptions. Major composers who were not born of families of professional musicians tended to come from artisan or the modest middle levels of society. Handel's father was a barber-surgeon. Clementi's was a silversmith; Gluck's, a forester. Haydn's father and grandfather were wheelwrights and Schubert's and Chopin's fathers were teachers. Donizetti's father's highest attainment was the position of custodian and usher at a pawn shop.

As professionals working in craft traditions, musicians were strongly linked to the institutions that employed them, in particular the court, church and city, but also to the aristocratic classes that dominated society. Their position was often an ambiguous one. They were members of the court or church establishment, but also practitioners of one of the fine arts. The practical result of this ambiguous position was that most musicians were not fully integrated in the discussions that led to the formation of Romantic ideals. Those that were, such as Jean-Philippe Rameau in Paris or Johann Philipp Kirnberger in Berlin, often found that writers and intellectuals failed to understand the basic principles of their craft. In 1756, the philosopher Moses Mendelssohn wanted to supplement his private study of the mathematical side of music theory and took some practical keyboard lessons from Kirnberger. However, he could not understand why the time signatures of 6/8 and 3/4 were not equivalent: they appeared to be fractions, after all. In his report after Mendelssohn's death, the publisher Friedrich Nicolai attributed the misunderstanding to Kirnberger's lack of philosophical clarity of expression. For his part, Rameau eventually fell out with Jean le Rond d'Alembert over the latter's simplification of his harmonic system in the *Eléments de musique* (1752).[1]

The writers and intellectuals who defined the aesthetics of Romanticism or adapted them to the musical sphere tended to come of age in families without such close ties to the world of professional music making. Many came from fathers or even families with equally strong professional links to positions involving the written or spoken word, whether as jurists or lawyers (Beyle, better known under his pen name Stendhal, Wackenroder, E. T. A. Hoffmann, and Wordsworth) or as preachers or ministers (Coleridge, Schelling, the Schlegel brothers, Schleiermacher). Writers whose families were not involved in words directly often came from ones that had earned high positions in society through success in banking and commerce (Hölderlin, Goethe, and de Staël) or in the army or civil service (Hegel, Schiller, and Hugo). Others were of aristocratic lineage (Byron, Chateaubriand, La Motte Fouqué, Leopardi, Mickiewicz, and von Hardenberg, who used the pen name Novalis). These familial backgrounds based in good writing or good breeding often offered educational paths into the art of discussion and debate, whether through specialised secondary schools or universities (such as the Friedrich-Werdersche Gymnasium in Berlin where Tieck and Wackenroder wrote their first poetry, or the Tübinger Stift, the university residence in Tübingen where Hegel, Hölderlin, and Schelling first dreamed of a universal poetry), or through artistic and intellectual salons (such as those of Henriette Herz in Berlin or Suzanne Curchod (Necker) in Paris).

Thus, writers and musicians at the cusp of Romanticism often developed their skills in different arenas, the former in one of intellectual debate and affluence, the latter in one of skilled service. As always, there are exceptions, but often ones that prove the rule. As scions of a well-to-do banking family of assimilated Jews in Berlin, Felix Mendelssohn and his sister Fanny Hensel (née Mendelssohn) may owe their dedication to the craft traditions of music – a dedication exceptional amongst Romantic musicians – in part to the fact that they did *not* stem from the same professional and religious backgrounds as other musicians. That said, while musicians often did follow literary developments, they did not necessarily aim at similar goals. In many of the short stories, novels, and philosophical tracts of the period, music serves as a figure by which writers could explore philosophical issues such as the origins of languages and cultures, the limits of signification in communication, or the nature of interiority.[2] Musicians certainly appreciated the high standing that had been assigned to them by the world of letters. On 23 March 1820 Beethoven included some flattering words in a letter recommending a travelling acquaintance to E. T. A. Hoffmann in Berlin.[3] However, as Carl Dahlhaus noted, the vague terms of the letter do not allow one to assume that Beethoven fully agreed with Hoffmann's seminal review (1810) of the Fifth Symphony.[4]

Musicians worked in a world in which listeners often interpreted music in narrative terms. The music of the highest prestige – opera and oratorio – had its tales written into it, of course, but even ascendant genres of instrumental music such as symphonies, string quartets, and sonatas were often assigned stories or sequences of images to explicate their meanings. Music theorists Jérôme-Joseph de Momigny and Adolf Bernhard Marx, for example, respectively associated the first movement of Mozart's String Quartet in D minor, K. 421 (1783), with Dido's lament from Virgil's *Aeneid*, and Beethoven's Symphony No. 3 ('Eroica', 1804) with the development of a military man. In this context, Berlioz's *Symphonie fantastique* (1830) – with its accompanying programme that functions 'like the spoken text of an opera' to explain the motivation for the music and depict an 'episode from the life of an artist'[5] – exemplifies a general practice of linking instrumental music and narrative. This practice could range from examples of explicit programme music, as with Berlioz's work, to indicative titles to individual movements, as in Beethoven's Symphony No. 6 ('Pastoral', 1808), to entire works, as with Clementi's Piano Sonata Op. 50 No. 3 (*Didone abbandonata*, 1821).[6]

Thus, even as writers began to explore the ways that the arts might 'aspire to the condition of music', as the critic Walter Pater wrote later in the nineteenth century,[7] musicians themselves seem to have aspired to the communicative powers, communal relevance and social status of poets, playwrights, painters, and other artists who could tell a story. Recent work in music theory has shown that theories of narrative and metaphor can be productively applied to 'abstract' instrumental music. Such work does not try to nail down precise meaning, but rather shows how, for example, Chopin's Ballade in G minor, Op. 23 (1835), can evoke the feeling of nostalgia, instil a hope and desire for resolution, and trace the tragedy of the collapse of such hopes. This musical narrative resonated with similar feelings of nostalgia, high hopes for the future, and subsequent deception amongst contemporaries; say, amongst Chopin's fellow Poles exiled in Paris after the failure of the revolutions of 1830.[8] Musicians placed moods into sequences that mirrored the ups and downs of comedy and tragedy, used styles or 'topics' to evoke associations, and in general explored the ways that the forms of music map onto the forms of human experience.

While musicians and writers would always have slightly different interests, musicians gradually joined elite artistic discussions more fully towards the beginning of the nineteenth century. Despite restrictive social attitudes, women played an essential role in this convergence, in particular through their roles as hosts of artistic salons. These informal gatherings where artists and writers mixed with aristocratic patrons gained popularity in

Paris in the seventeenth century, but multiplied there and spread to many other European centres in the eighteenth. The salons of Mesdames Geoffrin, Dupin, d'Epinay, and others were the centre of the intellectual ferment of the French Enlightenment, attracting Voltaire, Rousseau, d'Alembert, Diderot, Grimm, and many other men of letters. As the condescending thinking went, women had a special role in the conversations that took place, softening and smoothing the disputational tendencies of men, allowing them to avoid dry, academic discussions.[9] Parisian salons set both the tone and the vogue for salons throughout Europe well into the nineteenth century, and *salonnières* like Suzanne Curchod and Germaine de Staël (Paris), Henriette Herz and Rahel Varnhagen (Berlin), and Friederike Brun (Copenhagen), amongst others, provided opportunities for artists to try out their ideas and their products before an intimate, sympathetic audience. As assimilated Jews, Herz and Varnhagen encouraged free thinking in their salons in a way that made them essential to the birth of German Romanticism.

Although these high-profile salons had a strong bias towards words, they prepared the ground for a more general flowering of intellectual and artistic debate amongst artists in various media, often in semi-formal friendship circles that occasionally owed some of their intensity to their function as an escape from the political controls on public life. Schubert's circle included the poets Mayrhofer and Schober, the composer Hüttenbrenner, and the painter Schwind, amongst other lovers and practitioners of the arts. The painter Delacroix's journals record his frequent discussions with Chopin and the writer George Sand on artistic matters. E. T. A. Hoffmann drew inspiration from his own friendship with fellow writers Chamisso and La Motte Fouquet to give a framing tale to a collection of his previously published tales (*Die Serapionsbrüder*, 1819–21). In it the eponymous brothers of Serapion discuss 'their' stories and give some sense of the discussions that might have taken place when Hoffmann, Chamisso, and La Motte Fouquet met each other. At times friendship circles were exclusively male, often misogynistically so. At others, women participated as equal members, as artistic creators in their own right or, in a twist on their original role as cultured arbiters of enlightened debate, as romantic muses.

As one looks for the emergence of Romanticism, it is easy to call attention to the university town of Jena – where Fichte, Hölderlin, Novalis, Schiller, Schelling, the Schlegel brothers, Tieck, and others gathered to discuss ideals and idealism – or to the books, journals, philosophical poems, introductions to plays, and other publications that circulated in and between France, Germany, Italy, Britain, and other countries. Ideas mattered, and those that wrote about them are justly recognised for capturing the issues that moved the multitude (or rather that part of it that was literate and at least moderately well-to-do). But the emergence, dissemination, and practical adaptation of Romanticism owed as much if not more to the freewheeling discussions of both men and women who loved and made love, drank and tried drugs, and roamed over moors, along lakes, and through fields and forests, not to mention reading, sketching, painting, telling tales, writing poetry, making music, and so much more. Gathering together at the Stägemann salon in Berlin, a bunch of young friends acted out a story of love and death revolving around a miller maid, improvising poetry to capture the emotions and erotic tensions of the event. The play was serious, as Jennifer Ronyak has noted: the participants in the play and in the salon were themselves enmeshed in a complex web of attachments and infatuations, and the event allowed them to play through issues of identity and attachment in a way both pleasant and rich in philosophical resonances.[10]

Events such as these demonstrate how salons and friendship circles could stimulate imaginations, cross social divides, and draw music, writing, and other artistic media closer together. Many of the participants or onlookers at this song-play were later active in the arts, including Luise Hensel (a poet), Wilhelm Hensel (a painter who later married Fanny Mendelssohn), Clemens Brentano (a poet), and Wilhelm Müller (a poet). In 1818, musical settings of poems from the event were published by the musician Ludwig Berger, another salon attendee, and most memorably, in 1824 by Franz Schubert as *Die schöne Müllerin* (*The Beautiful Maid of the Mill*).

Styles of Emotion: Romanticism and Its Eighteenth-Century Precedents

In both the eighteenth and nineteenth centuries, musicians and writers alike were well aware of the strong link between music and the emotions. As the musician and lexicographer Heinrich Christoph Koch confidently defined music in 1782, 'amongst the fine arts, it is the one that expresses feelings by means of the combination of tones'.[11] By the early nineteenth century, writers – including Koch himself – were beginning to question whether the emotional power of music was the root of its aesthetic value, but no one questioned the empirical power of music over the emotions.

It makes little sense to portray 'classical' music as rational and Romantic as emotional, as if music followed the shift from Enlightenment to Romanticism in lockstep. Still, there were differences in how musicians and critics channelled music's emotional power and how they interpreted it.

In the broadest terms, the pendulum of taste began to swing from grace to expressive intensity towards the end of the eighteenth century, reversing the swing from 'baroque' elaborateness towards the more delicate stirrings of the heart that had occurred towards its beginning. While at work on the *Singspiel, Entführung aus dem Serail* (*Abduction from the Seraglio*, 1782), Mozart noted in a letter to his father that he wished to express Osmin's rage with an adventuresome modulation. Yet he explained that there was a limit to both emotional excess and the modulation plan, as music 'must never cease to be *music*'.[12] The spirit of restraint stood well with an approach to form that emphasised the careful articulation of phrases, and an aesthetic that stressed comprehensibility and the communicative bond between composers, performers, and listeners. Early Romantic composers hardly gave up on negotiations between excess and the demands of taste, but they proclaimed an affinity with excess in a manner that would have been foreign to Mozart.

This shift in emotional register was matched in performance practice. In his performance manual for keyboard players, François Couperin noted that keyboard players should not sit facing the keys straight on, but rather sit slightly turned away from the keyboard and towards listeners. This would allow the performer to look at the listeners with the proper 'air of ease at his harpsichord, without fixating his gaze on any object or looking too vague', thus ensuring that listeners knew that the performer played for them alone.[13] By contrast, those who listened to Beethoven and Chopin noted their sense of distraction from the world as they played, while virtuosos like Liszt were lauded for the intensity of their concentration. Rather than enjoying a connection of conversational ease with performers, Romantics appreciated the intensity of introvert self-absorption or extro-vert showmanship.[14]

Such pendulum swings of taste underpin such convenient historical monikers as the baroque, classical, and Romantic periods, but musicians of the eighteenth and nineteenth century worked within a common stylistic framework, one that complicates any easy distinction between classical and Romantic music. Towards the beginning of the eighteenth century, the basso continuo disappeared (except in religious music), tonal emerged from modal harmony, and the chains of short motivic or metric units typical of baroque *Fortspinnung* ('spinning forth') gradually gave way to more regular phrase lengths. German musicians referred to the resulting style as the *galant* style, borrowing a French term associated with delicacy, agreeableness, and cultured cosmopolitanism. As the eighteenth century progressed, musicians elaborated this into a sophisticated and elegant style flexible enough to be varied across genres, national borders, and ultimately generations, such that early-nineteenth-century composers found it adaptable to their own purposes. The style used cadences to articulate phrases and order them hierarchically into comprehensible large-scale form. It featured a simple homophonic texture that could be enriched to varying degrees by the sharing of motives between melody and accompaniment. It balanced main and subordinate themes judiciously so as to offer both unity and variety, often enriched by the borrowing of stylistic materials from a variety of genres. And it led themes along a harmonic path that treated closely related keys as structural poles, and that used dramatic and surprising modulations to dramatise the movement between these poles.

Romantic musicians learned these procedures, treating the composers who excelled at them (especially Haydn, Mozart, and Beethoven, but also Clementi and Cherubini) as classics and thereby doing much to create the notion of a classical style in music in the first place. They also learned a principle of balance that this panoply of technical means made possible, a principle that, for example, they saw embodied in the visual arts in the statuary of classical Greece and Rome. They thus projected back onto the eighteenth century a notion of the classic and classicism that no musicians of that time would have used with respect to themselves.[15]

Yet this is not all that Romantic musicians learned. Eighteenth-century musicians also worked below or above what might be called a middle style of elegance and grace, in both cases creating a special type of 'sublime' intensity and directness of effect. As they did so, they would often simplify, complicate, or undermine these compositional strategies, along lines dictated by the requirements of particular musical genres. At one point, music historians liked to find various pre-Romanticisms in the eighteenth century, treating the cultivation of extreme emotion as harbingers of things to come. It is wiser to see these genre and style traditions as sites where eighteenth-century musicians explored the lower and upper extremes of style for their own ends, albeit in ways that would resonate for later Romantic composers.

The most obvious site of the cultivation of the extreme in the eighteenth century was the opera house. From its earliest days, opera had allowed characters to show the depth of their love or the height of their rage with a musical language modulated to moments of extreme psychological pressure. Vigorous passagework, audacious harmonies, and rapid breaks in continuity might show storms of the soul. They might also set the storms that raged around characters, linking lightning to licks of the violin or flute and thunder to the dull roar of low tremolo or drum rolls (not to mention to special lighting and sound effects of the theatre). Second, opera offered a stage for gods, goddesses, and other supernatural events to show themselves, surrounded by an aural shadow of slowly unfolding uncanny harmonies and sepulchral timbres, often with generous use of trombones or low strings.

For a long time, such effects were labelled *Sturm und Drang* (storm and stress) in an attempt to connect them to the North German literary movement of that name that flourished during the 1770s. However, the musical use of these techniques was more geographically widespread and lacked the political edge of that proto-nationalist, anti-French, and socially progressive literary movement. Clive McClelland has usefully suggested the terms *tempesta* and *ombra* to describe these speedy and slow theatrical styles respectively.[16] From the theatre they migrated easily to instrumental genres that demanded grandeur and audacity, especially the symphony. In some cases, instrumental works that stormed with stress actually originated as overtures to plays, as in the case of Haydn's symphonies of the 1770s.[17]

A second site for the cultivation of extreme emotion was Northern Germany, where musicians such as Carl Philipp Emanuel Bach channelled the North German tradition of elaborate music making (represented above all by his father, Johann Sebastian Bach). Scholars once referred to this musical tradition as one of *Empfindsamkeit*, a term based on the German translation of the English word 'sentimental' from Laurence Sterne's late novel *A Sentimental Journey through France and Italy* (1768). As the origin of the term indicates, the German literary tradition imitated English literary antecedents. Musicians like C. P. E. Bach may have achieved a style in which the arc of expression is interrupted and undercut by surprising turns of phrase, sudden shifts in style, and an approach to musical form that privileges disruption over formal integration. However, the musical traditions had other roots, especially the keyboard fantasy. Always an opportunity for musicians to show their skill and ingenuity (e.g., J. S. Bach's Chromatic Fantasy and Fugue in D minor, BWV 903), the fantasy became a way for composers to fascinate listeners with picturesque surprises and show inspired genius. When the English music historian Charles Burney visited C. P. E. Bach in Hamburg, he commented not only on the composer-performer's inspired improvising, but also on the fervency that was caught in the sweat of his brow.[18]

It was not just the turbulent end of the scale of passions that caught eighteenth- and, later, nineteenth-century fancy. There was also a halo around styles of seeming innocence and simplicity. In the case of folk song, men of letters such as James Macpherson in Scotland or Johann Gottfried Herder in Germany largely took the lead in identifying folk poetry and songs as a token of immediacy.[19] Although nationalist pride and a jaundiced eye towards the generally celebrated achievements of the Enlightenment gave folk song and poetry special significance, the humble simplicity of traditional melodies offered them an attractive alternative to the elegance and grace that informed musical taste generally.

Professional musicians during the eighteenth century were certainly aware of this fashion for folk music, but many did not musically realise the sound of innocence. Haydn and Beethoven respected the simplicity of Scotch, Irish, English, and Welsh folk songs in settings commissioned by the Scottish publishing entrepreneur George Thomson, but they used accompanimental figuration in the piano that invokes the domesticity of easy piano works. Carl Friedrich Zelter found the Haydn's folk-song collections 'Haydensch' (Haydnesque) rather than 'heidnisch' (heathen).[20]

It was again in Northern Germany that one could find composers willing to adopt a humble style in a way that answered the ideal of unassuming virtue, untouched by the corrupting influences of civilisation. Although composers centred in Berlin, including Zelter and Johann Friedrich Reichardt (both correspondents of the poet Johann Wolfgang von Goethe), may not have thought of themselves as a 'Berlin Song School', as they are sometimes described, they were attuned enough to literary debates to eschew sophistication.

As musicians elsewhere became more aware of literary ideals of innocence and humility, they sometimes followed suit. In the poem 'Heidenröslein' (1771, pub. 1789), Goethe described in simple strophes a conversation between a young boy and a rose on the heath. When Schubert set it in 1815, he maintained simplicity through the regularity of a two-bar rhythmic-melodic pattern (in most cases, a bar of quavers leads to a semiquaver turn; largely stepwise melodic motion is capped by valedictory leaps) and a demure piano accompaniment (chords broken into an easy back-and-forth between bass and upper voices, with good-natured tags at the close of the vocal phrases). Although contemporary reviewers noted that he tended towards the sophistication of art song, Schubert knew well how to apply this sophistication with the light touch appropriate to the ideal of folk song.

Another site of simplicity was church music. When writing religious music, composers had always mediated between the tried-and-trusted styles favoured by churchmen and the catchy styles that pulled in publics in the theatre. The conservatism of church music bespoke the age and stability of the church itself. In addition, the respect for tradition allowed certain works and styles to emerge somewhat contradictorily both as hallmarks of bygone, simpler times and as tokens of an eternal order. In the first part of the eighteenth century, Italian and Italianate composers had simplified ornate, 'baroque' textures along leaner lines, touching the heart with candid melodies of understated drama, invoking counterpoint with the affecting suspension rather than learned motivic working, and pointing meandering modal harmony towards the focussed directionality of functional tonality. Giovanni Battista Pergolesi's *Stabat mater* (1736) and Carl Heinrich Graun's *Der Tod Jesu* (*The Death of Jesus*, 1755) were widely performed and critically celebrated well into the nineteenth century.

Finally, styles inherited from the seventeenth century, often protected from the tides of fashion through their association with the church, persisted through the eighteenth century to find new favour as composers sought to invigorate *galant* vim with dramatic intensity or monumental grandeur. One of these styles was that of learned counterpoint, strict voice leading, and motivic elaboration. The tradition was an old one, defended against the *galant* tendencies of his time by Johann Sebastian Bach. A second, related one was that rooted in commemorative and celebratory choral music, as found for example in the English anthem, the French grand motet, or sections of the Catholic Mass. Particularly when adapted to public occasions, as when Handel's *Messiah* was performed with large forces in 1784 in London, such works achieved a striking monumentality.

As Romantic musicians looked back, they could learn many styles of emotion, both light and intense, and they could learn them from many places. Although they eventually expanded on them, turning a military march or a celebratory Te Deum into a revolutionary hymn, they always listened with cocked ears to their predecessors' sensitivity to balance and the means by which they had complicated, enriched, or undermined this balance. Without an awareness of this diversity of styles, musicians of both centuries would not been able to knock it akilter with such panache.

Ethics and Metaphysics

As the eighteenth century turned to the nineteenth, musicians explored styles of emotion that were either less cultivated or more fervent than the cultured sophistication that best suited Enlightenment ideals of taste, decorum, and common sense. Yet this exploration of the extremes happened within specific aesthetic and ideological contexts. Emotion meant new things in the nineteenth century, and both humble and high registers of music often fuelled new thoughts on the nature and significance of music.

One hallmark of thought about music in the eighteenth century was a focus on the empirical experience of music. Music theorists and critics may have bent enlightened, critical rationality to the development of a music-theoretical vocabulary suited to music, to an aesthetics of expression that took account of the ways that music did *not* imitate nature, and more generally to the ways that music did *not* lend itself to Enlightenment,[21] but they largely refrained from the speculation on music and world harmony that had excited musicians and critics even up through the early eighteenth century. Once divorced from speculative theory, music appeared at times to be little more than entertainment, 'an innocent luxury', as the English music historian Charles Burney wrote.[22] The pleasure may not seem so innocent today; as the term 'luxury' shows, music could also serve as a signifier of social class and education. Yet this relative nonchalance about the powers of music suited an instrumental repertoire of sonatas, concertos, and sinfonias that aimed at *galant* effects, as well as an operatic repertoire that retold stories of heroism and happy ends from ancient history and classical mythology.

Where musicians and writers ascribed more significance to music, they tended to link the emotional power of music, and of the arts generally, to ethics. The emotional power of the arts might make the moral or religious lessons in many eighteenth-century tales and poems more palatable, or they could even elicit the height of feeling that made empathy possible in the first place. As the German encyclopaedist Johann Georg Sulzer (a contemporary of C. P. E. Bach) wrote in the *General Theory of the Fine Arts* (1771–4), 'Expression is the soul of music. Without it, music is but an entertaining diversion. But with it, music becomes the most expressive speech overpowering the heart. It compels us to be tender, then to be resolute and steadfast. It can quickly bring forth our pity, and just as quickly, admiration.'[23]

One also sees this attention to emotion and ethics in the sentimental turn to plays and operas that occurred in the last third of the eighteenth century. As specified by Aristotelian theory of drama, comedy had always focussed on contemporary characters from the middle and lower classes, often subjecting them to the humiliations and comeuppances of slapstick and farce. Dramatists like Goldoni in Italy, Diderot in France, and Lessing in Germany sought to give theatre more respectability with characters that could inspire virtue and empathy. Opera librettos, including those penned by Goldoni himself, showed a similar turn, especially in vernacular operatic genres such as *opera buffa*, *opéra comique*, and *Singspiel*.

As the eighteenth gave way to the nineteenth century, the swing towards the special intensity of innocent naiveté and high drama went hand in hand with a shift away from ethics and towards metaphysics. In his oft-cited review (1810) of Beethoven's Fifth Symphony, E. T. A. Hoffmann wrote that 'Music reveals to man an unknown realm, a world quite separate from the outer sensual world surrounding him, a world in which he leaves behind all feelings circumscribed by intellect in order to embrace the inexpressible.'[24] The turn towards metaphysics could lead in different directions, from the depths of the soul to the heights of religious devotion, or even both.[25]

Between heights and depths, Romantics also developed a form of metaphysics that focussed on rare capacities and rarefied experiences. These could highlight the sheer magic of human presence in the world, often in a way that would continue to chime in less metaphysical, more existentialist strands of twentieth-century criticism and philosophy. Reporting on a performance of an unidentified Haydn quartet, Mozart quintet, and Beethoven's 'Archduke' Trio, Op. 97, the French Romantic painter Eugène Delacroix noted a remark by Chopin on the differences between Haydn and Mozart. Haydn had achieved his perfection through experience, but Mozart 'had no need of experience; knowledge was always found with him at the level of inspiration'.[26] Chopin avoids explanation of Mozart's ability, though he must have known that Mozart had had a famous pedagogue as a father and had travelled the major musical centres of Europe as a child. Rather, Chopin uses words of wonder to capture his experience of numinous presence in the hearing of Mozart's music and to nod towards what he perceived as the miracle of its production. When treated with attitudes of wonder, even the prosaic matter of Mozart's acquisition of skill can bespeak the truth of the world and the human place in it.

The turn towards metaphysics found its way into practices of reception, as when Hoffmann heard Beethoven or Chopin and Delacroix heard Mozart. In particular, it offered a framework by which instrumental music could be heard as an echo of the absolute. It also affected operatic subjects. While comedy did not vanish from nineteenth-century stages, artistic attention turned back towards stories of heroism and the supernatural. Already at the end of the eighteenth century, there was a fascination with magic, as seen in such works as Grétry's *Zémire et Azor* (1771, based on the story of Beauty and the Beast) or Mozart's *Die Zauberflöte* (*The Magic Flute*, 1791). As appropriate to their respective genric roots in *opéra comique* and *Singspiel*, they did not focus on the high-status gods and goddess of classical Greek or Roman mythology. Instead, their plots originated in tales told by Enlightenment men of letters seeking to teach ethics or enlightenment in an exciting way, often by borrowing the humble forms of the folk or morality tale. By the early nineteenth century, composers were turning tales of magic towards more heroic ends, often against a backdrop that emphasised the close relationship between nature and the supernatural.[27]

Carl Maria von Weber's *Der Freischütz* (*The Free Shot*, 1821) shows how styles of humility and excess could take on special significance when refracted through metaphysical prisms. Led astray by fellow forester Kaspar, Max has magic bullets made at midnight by invoking the demonic spirit Samiel. Six will strike true, but one belongs to Samiel. With these bullets, Max hopes to reverse his bad fortune and win the hand of his beloved Agathe in a shooting competition. The battle between good and evil is made musically manifest by a back-and-forth between songs of innocent goodness and evil experience. Innocence is expressed by the folk-song-like choruses of bridesmaids and hunters, who represent the people and their 'natural' relationship to the forest, to tradition, and to God. The evil of the supernatural resonates through the turbulent textures, exotic harmonies, and disruptive gestures that accompany the midnight casting of bullets in the Wolf's Glen. The humble religiosity of hymn also leaves a trace, in particular in the closing communal song of thanksgiving. Agathe might represent a position of ethical goodness, but the opera focusses less on issues of practical morality than it does on religion, the supernatural, and the redemptive power of love. Agathe's innocence and religion saves her from 'Samiel's' bullet, and thereby saves Max as well, despite the error of his ways. More than just an emotion, love carries with it the divine power of salvation.

The role of the forest and the folk in *Der Freischütz* also highlight a turn towards a different type of relationship with the past. Artists of all ages learn from their predecessors, whether it be the techniques associated with particular styles, genres or media, or the works that make them ripe for intertextual quotation and adaptation. Artists also learn standards of excellence, generally ones linked with particular norms of style or genre. Yet the language of this relationship to the past, as well as the models imitated, can vary considerably over history. By the turn of the nineteenth century, artists and intellectuals had lost confidence in perpetual progress. They sought alternatives to the cultivation of the classical past, looking for immediacy rather than reflection, seeking a life within nature rather than a manipulation of it, and idealising the simplicity of rural life over the complexity of urban existence. Yet this glorification of an alternate antiquity – of immediacy over reflected study – did not change the many connections that existed between artists of the eighteenth and nineteenth centuries.

Although brought up in a family of music and theatre professionals and a composition pupil of Michael Haydn (younger brother of Joseph, best known for his old-fashioned church music), Weber (1786–1826) had imbibed the language and ideals of Romanticism, developed his own literary aspirations, and even drafted a Hoffmannesque novel, *Tonkünstlers Leben* (*Tone-Poet's Life*). He was thus well placed to set its dreams to music, giving *Der Freischütz* the telling genre designation of 'Romantic Opera in Three Acts'. Like many of his contemporaries, Weber could reach back to and extend eighteenth-century musical traditions at the same time that he created a new, Romantic musical world.

Notes

1. Laurenz Lütteken, 'Zwischen Ohr und Verstand: Moses Mendelssohn, Johann Philipp Kirnberger und die Begründung des "reinen Satzes" in der Musik', in Anselm Gerhard (ed.), *Musik und Ästhetik im Berlin Moses Mendelssohns* (Tübingen: Niemeyer, 1999), 136–7; Thomas Christensen, *Rameau and Musical Thought in the Enlightenment* (Cambridge: Cambridge University Press, 2004), ch. 9.
2. See the chapters by Gelbart (Chapter 5), Stanyon (Chapter 3), and Watkins (Chapter 12) in this volume.
3. E. T. A. Hoffmann, *Briefwechsel*, ed. Hans von Müller and Friedrich Schnapp, 3 vols. (Darmstadt: Wissenschaftliche Buchgesellschaft, 1967–9), vol. 2, 245.
4. Carl Dahlhaus, *Klassische und romantische Musikästhetik* (Laaber: Laaber, 1988), 108.
5. Hector Berlioz, [Printed Concert Programme] *Episode de la vie d'un artiste Symphonie fantastique, en cinq partie* (Paris: n.p., 1830), n.p. [1].
6. See further Alexander Wilfing's chapter in this volume (Chapter 11).
7. Walter Pater, 'The School of Giorgione' (1873), in A. Phillips (ed.), *The Renaissance: Studies in Art and Poetry* (Oxford: Oxford University Press, 1986), 86.

8. See for instance Karol Berger, 'Chopin's Ballade Op. 23 and the Revolution of the Intellectuals', in John Rink and Jim Samson (eds.), *Chopin Studies II* (Cambridge: Cambridge University Press, 1994), 72–83, and on the Second Ballade, Op. 38, Jonathan Bellman, *Chopin's Polish Ballade: Op. 38 as Narrative of National Martyrdom* (New York: Oxford University Press, 2009).

9. Dena Goodman, *The Republic of Letters: A Cultural History of the French Enlightenment* (Ithaca, NY: Cornell University Pres, 1994), 99–111.

10. Jennifer Ronyak, '"Serious Play", Performance, and the Lied: The Stägemann *Schöne Müllerin* Revisited', *19th-Century Music*, 34/2 (2010), 141–67.

11. Heinrich Christoph Koch, *Versuch einer Anleitung zur Composition*, 3 vols. (Rudolstadt and Leipzig: A. F. Böhme,1782–93), vol. 1, 4.

12. Emily Anderson, *The Letters of Mozart and His Family*, 3rd ed., rev. and ed. Stanley Sadie and Fiona Smart (London: Macmillan, 1985), 769.

13. François Couperin, *L'Art de toucher le clavecin* (Paris: Author, 1716), 4–6.

14. See further Dana Gooley's chapter in this volume (Chapter 18).

15. See my 'Classicism/Neoclassicism', in Stephen Downes (ed.), *Aesthetics of Music: Musicological Perspectives* (Abingdon and New York: Routledge, 2014), 144–69.

16. Clive McClelland, *Ombra: Supernatural Music in the Eighteenth Century* (Lanham, MD: Lexington Books, 2012), and *Tempesta: Stormy Music in the Eighteenth Century* (Lanham, MD: Lexington Books, 2017).

17. Elaine Sisman, 'Haydn's Theater Symphonies', *Journal of the American Musicological Society*, 43/2 (1990), 292–352.

18. Charles Burney, *The Present State of Music in Germany, the Netherlands, and the United Provinces*, 2 vols., 2nd ed. (London: Becket et al., 1775), vol. 2, 270. Annette Richards, *The Free Fantasia and the Musical Picturesque* (Cambridge: Cambridge University Press, 2001).

19. See the chapter in this volume by Matthew Gelbart (Chapter 5).

20. Letter from Zelter to Mendelssohn, 9 June 1829, quoted in Thomas Christian Schmidt, *Die ästhetischen Grundlagen der Instrumentalmusik Felix Mendelssohn Bartholdys* (Stuttgart: M & P, 1996), 95.

21. Laurenz Lütteken, 'Musik in der Aufklärung–Musikalische Aufklärung?', *Musiktheorie*, 14/3 (1999), 213–29.

22. Charles Burney, *A General History of Music*, 4 vols. (London: Author, 1776–1785), vol. 1, xiii.

23. Nancy Kovaleff Baker and Thomas Christensen (eds.), *Aesthetics and the Art of Musical Composition in the German Enlightenment: Selected Writings of Johann Georg Sulzer and Heinrich Christoph Koch* (Cambridge: Cambridge University Press, 1995), 51.

24. E. T. A. Hoffmann, *E. T. A. Hoffmann's Musical Writings: Kreisleriana, The Poet and the Composer, Music Criticism* (Cambridge: Cambridge University Press, 1989), 236.

25. See the chapters by James Garratt (Chapter 9) and Holly Watkins (Chapter 12) in this volume.
26. Eugène Delacroix, *Journal: 1822–1863* (Paris: Plon, 1996), 134 (21 February 1847).
27. See further Francesca Brittan's chapter in this volume (Chapter 8).

Further Reading

Chapin, Keith. 'Classicism/Neoclassicism', in Stephen Downes (ed.), *Aesthetics of Music: Musicological Perspectives* (Abingdon: Routledge, 2014), 144–69.

Dirst, Matthew. *Engaging Bach: The Keyboard Legacy from Marpurg to Mendelssohn* (Cambridge: Cambridge University Press, 2012).

Eigeldinger, Jean-Jacques. *Chopin: Âme des salons parisiens (1830–1848)* (Paris: Fayard, 2013).

Gelbart, Matthew. *The Invention of 'Folk Music' and 'Art Music': Emerging Categories from Ossian to Wagner* (Cambridge: Cambridge University Press, 2007).

Head, Matthew. 'Fantasia and Sensibility', in Danuta Mirka (ed.), *The Oxford Handbook of Topic Theory* (Oxford: Oxford University Press, 2014), 259–78.

Kramer, Lawrence. 'The Schubert Lied: Romantic Form and Romantic Consciousness', in Walter Frisch (ed.), *Schubert: Critical and Analytical Studies* (Lincoln, NE: University of Nebraska Press, 1988), 200–37.

McClelland, Clive. 'Ombra and Tempesta', in Danuta Mirka (ed.), *The Oxford Handbook of Topic Theory* (New York: Oxford University Press, 2014), 279–300.

Richards, Annette. *The Free Fantasia and the Musical Picturesque* (Cambridge: Cambridge University Press, 2001).

Ronyak, Jennifer. *Intimacy, Performance and the Lied in the Early Nineteenth Century* (Bloomington: Indiana University Press, 2018).

Rosen, Charles. *The Romantic Generation* (Cambridge, MA: Harvard University Press, 1995).

Safranski, Rüdiger. *Romanticism: A German Affair*, trans. Robert E. Goodwin (Evanston: Northwestern University Press, 2014).

Spitzer, Michael. *Metaphor and Musical Thought* (Chicago: Chicago University Press, 2004).

PART II

Worlds

3 | Music and Romantic Literature

MIRANDA STANYON

Introduction

> *Heard melodies are sweet, but those unheard*
> *Are sweeter; therefore, ye soft pipes, play on*
> — Keats, 'Ode on a Grecian Urn' (1819)

Music is ubiquitous in Romantic literature. To wander through its poetry and prose is to encounter a landscape crowded with obscure village minstrels, prophetic bards, carefree improvisors, cruelly disfigured and rejected castrati, and enthusiastic kapellmeisters ready to cruise the job market.[1] Genius composers draw us into infinite nocturnal kingdoms (Beethoven), die listening to their own sublime creations (Haydn), and return to life to haunt pubs and opera houses (Gluck).[2] Here, Sappho's song echoes as she leaps from a cliff; there, a 'Hindoo' girl sings a prediction of her love match; Albanian soldiers 'half-scream' war-ballads in the mountains; medievalising lutes sound mysteriously through the darkness to heroines imprisoned in castles; caged birds sing in praise of *Waldeinsamkeit*, while nightingales vie for airtime with the silent pipers on an antique urn.[3]

And this din largely covers just one dimension of the relationship between literature and music: the representation of music in literary texts. Just as significant for Romanticism was the new twilight zone between literature and music theory or criticism, epitomised by E. T. A. Hoffmann's publications of the same material in music journals and collections of 'literary' *Fantasiestücke*. Finally, there is the enormous territory of Romantic literature *in* music, most strikingly poetry settings in lieder, and adaptations of prose for operas, melodramas, and instrumental works (Mérimée's novella for Bizet's *Carmen*; De Quincey's autobiography via Musset for Berlioz's *Symphonie fantastique*; Dumas *fils*'s play for Verdi's *La traviata*; Hugo's novel for Claude-Michel Schönberg's *Les Misérables*).

The task of this chapter is not to survey this vast field, but to ask what work music does for literature in Romanticism. The question is difficult enough, not least given the problems of periodisation endemic to studies of Romanticism. Romanticism is not contemporaneous across European traditions, and nor is literary Romanticism easily synchronised with musical Romanticism. Thus 'Romantic' debates over sublimity, virtuosity and naturalness, spontaneous creativity, and fidelity to the musical work are fought over 'baroque' and 'classical' compositions by Handel, Arne, Mozart, or Gluck.[4] Related to periodisation are broader definitional problems, not infrequently scorned by Romantic writers themselves ('one feels the Romantic, one does not define it', wrote one).[5] Should we talk of Romantic movements (centred on social groupings and affiliations, and often on canonical artists), Romantic eras and generations (at the risk of implying that a spirit of the age permeates all cultural productions), or of Romantic aesthetics, more or less temporally limited (since, for instance, Friedrich Schlegel famously believed 'all poetry is or should be Romantic', a statement difficult to fathom outside the particular moment and milieu of Jena Romanticism (1798–1804))?[6]

As a cluster of values, tendencies, and theories, Romantic aesthetics include engagement with philosophical Idealism, absolutes, and ideals – both 'normative', in the sense that art represented ideals, and 'categorial', in the sense that making and reflecting on art might enact ideals such as freedom, spontaneity, infinite play, indeterminacy, or autonomy.[7] As autonomous, art was imagined to be non-utilitarian (not difficult in a world where personal patronage was increasingly unreliable), although it could be deeply politically and socially engaged. Romanticism was not, of course, concerned with 'emotion' above 'reason' or 'enlightenment', nor with individual subjectivity against community or society. It was, however, bound up with new understandings of such categories: the dominant paradigm of 'emotions' was crystallising in our period (alongside claims that aesthetic responses are *not* passionate); and eighteenth-century ideas about the shaping power of the subject's imagination and perception took on new dimensions and urgency, leading some texts to despair of accessing reality through the 'green spectacles' of our own perceptual apparatus (Kleist's letters), others to revere imagination as a 'power' revealing an 'invisible world' superior to empirical experience (Wordsworth's *Prelude*), and still more to create dialectics between experience as given and self-created.[8] Although metaphors surrounding imagination were often visual, the (for Romantic authors) emotionally charged and time-saturated medium of music was increasingly both a model for literary production, and a source of metaphors for subjectivity – as when Coleridge calls 'Joy' a 'strong music in the soul', given to us by 'Nature', but becoming 'the life and element' 'Of all sweet sounds' available to perception, 'All melodies the echoes of that voice' (lines 64, 68, 58, 74). These words, from 'Dejection: An Ode' (1802), suggest a final Romantic concern: the idea of a malady – melancholy, madness, solipsism, incurable longing – sometimes seen as a universal human asset, but often identified with specific problems of modernity, be they despotic revolutions, repressive old orders, urban and utilitarian pressures, idleness and loss of old meanings, or alienation – a *mal du siècle*.

Other chapters in this book help explain music's distinctive and exalted place in this aesthetic, in particular its connection with origins, of languages and peoples, and with ends, the *telos* of humans' connection with the infinite and undetermined. For our purposes, it suffices to recall the musicological argument that the failures of music within (narrowly) representational artistic paradigms became a strength when representation was seen as limited and determined, making music, in Hoffmann's words, 'the most Romantic of all the arts . . . for only the infinite is its object'.[9] This leaves verbal arts in an uncomfortable position. They not only habitually represent and refer (although texts like Novalis's *Monolog* (1798) will dispute this), but do so using arbitrary signs which differ between places and times, suggesting language's 'determination' by society, and moreover subjectivity's determination by language, so long as we cannot fully prise apart thought and word. Thus while Romantic theory makes expansive claims for literature – the best known being Schlegel's that 'Romantic poetry', aka literature, is 'a progressive universal poetry' which is 'alone infinite, as she alone is free' – literature also faces problems which, I suggest, music helps to navigate.[10]

The following is shaped by two methodological approaches to the question of the work of music for literature: word and music studies, and the somewhat newer field of sound studies. The former often concentrates on representations of music and on word–music relations in text settings. It is shaped by modernist understandings of the specificity and separateness of the arts, and the poignant gaps between them (for instance, literature is silent and textual; literature aspires to but never achieves polyphony).[11] Sound studies, meanwhile, following postmodern media and cultural studies, tend to assume the constructed and so changeable nature of divides between media and senses, while striking an anti-elitist stance which can sideline the 'elite' sources and close musical and textual analysis often found in word and music studies. Both approaches resonate with Romantic-era and pre-Romantic aesthetics – think, on one hand, of the gulf between visual and verbal arts in Lessing, on the other of Romantic ideals of synaesthesia or the reunification of the faculties (split by modern divisions of labour) in Wagner's *Gesamtkunstwerk*. But it is sound studies' stronger questioning of the division between the arts which particularly informs this chapter's two broad answers to the question of the work of music.

First, 'music' has a strong role in forming 'literature', as an art, discipline, and institution whose contemporary form emerges in the latter part of the eighteenth century. A well-known marker in this process is a new division between imaginative and non-imaginative literature: in Johnson's 1755 dictionary, 'literature' means 'Learning, skill in letters', but the term has roughly its modern scope around 1800 (for instance, in the English translation of Madame du Staël's *De la littérature considérée dans ses rapports avec les institutions sociales* (*The Influence of Literature on Society*, 1812)). Other markers include the establishment in Edinburgh of the first chair in rhetoric and *belles lettres*, in 1762, held by Hugh Blair, the principal champion of the supposed primitive bard Ossian; and the establishment in the 1780s of 'philology' in German universities (roughly equivalent to Anglo-Saxon language and literature departments). There are also new pedagogical practices, including a stress on learning reading through motherly *oral* instruction; changing emotional and imaginative investments in reading; and marked rises in literacy and print.[12] These coincide with longings for a lost oral immediacy that supposedly existed before modern print culture, with ballad crazes, stylings of poetry as songs, lyrical ballads, or odes, and fashions for improvisation – alongside justifications of *written* literature as the most comprehensive art after all, reuniting sight, gesture, and sound under the aegis of imagination.[13]

Second, the remainder of this chapter suggests, music helps Romantic literature to fail. Perhaps paradoxically, failure is a key way of responding to and evoking ideals. What is sometimes called the 'literary absolute' flourished in literary theory – a genre, if not separate from, then athwart literary 'works'. Poetry and imaginative prose meanwhile employ music to *suggest* ideals without needing fully to instantiate or capture them, a hubristic task and a self-defeating one insofar as these ideals are infinite and indeterminate. Failure, like music, has varied meanings and uses for Romantic literature, and one of the chief conclusions of this chapter is that, while music often evokes the universal and/or indistinct, there is also a strong alignment between music and particularity. Within the limits of any particular set of aesthetic characteristics or functions, failure thus proves a useful and wide-ranging thread running through the work of music for Romantic literature.

Loss of Sound and Certainty: Blake, Hoffmann, Kleist

The 'Introduction' to William Blake's 1789 *Songs of Innocence* (later, following the French Revolutionary Terror, expanded as *Songs of Innocence and Experience*) is not a prose preface but an energetic poem. Voiced by a rural 'Piper' (line 7), it suggests simple oral origins through compact lines, straightforward and repetitive syntax, an elementary and rough rhyme scheme (abab) and frequently recurring sounds (especially *chear, hear, clear* (6, 8, 10, 12, 18, 20)). But the song – if such it is – does not insist on oral purity. It is an apparently cheerful parable about the emergence of writing from absolute music, and simultaneously about the genesis and fate of the *Songs* as a text.[14] The piper first 'Pip[es] songs of pleasant glee', then, upon the request of a genius- or Christ-like child, gives these songs a programme: 'Pipe a song about a Lamb' (2, 5). He is next told to 'Drop [his] pipe' and 'Sing', and finally to 'sit ... and write / In a book that all may read' (9, 13–14). Making a 'rural pen' from a 'reed', the piper 'wrote [his] happy songs, / Every child may joy to hear' (16–17, 19–20), creating a text that has print's ease of dissemination (*all* may read) and writing's function as record and script for performance (children may *hear*).

We might wonder, however, what tune the words will take, if any, and whether *something* has been lost in the piper's descent from wandering to sitting, from 'valleys wild' to tamer stream (1), from pipe to pen, and from an immediate audience with a seraphic child to a merely potential audience of distant children. The poem does not strongly invite a suspicious reading, yet many experienced readers stumble over such questions, and particularly the ambiguity of the piper 'stain[ing] the water clear' (18), apparently with his pen: does writing stain the water dirty, or 'clear' and repristinate it? Moreover, what stains the flowing water, so suggestive of pure origins, and what is the stream's place in writing? Is the water itself an ink, or a writing surface for the dabbling reed? In the absence of Blake or the piper to answer such questions – so the ideal of immediate presence goes – readers are free to disagree, freer and less certain than in an oral and musical 'beforehand'. The poem thus constructs not just one 'oral-literate conjunction', in Maureen McLane's words, but several.[15] It allows us to imagine literature's all-encompassing nature – its paths out of and back into orality and song – but also to question the idyll presented on the page.

A loss of innocence is deepened in German Romantic texts which complicate their oral-literate conjunctions by acknowledging that music, as well as words, can be written, creating complex matrices of music, word, sound, and text. Kleist's 'Die heilige Cäcilie oder die Gewalt der Musik (eine Legende)' (St Cecilia or the Power/Violence of Music (a Legend), 1810) and Hoffmann's 'Ritter Gluck' (Sir Gluck, 1814), like Grillparzer's Biedermeier novella *Der arme Spielmann* (*The Poor Player*, 1847), all turn on unreadable scores. In Kleist's case, a maternal detective-figure approaches the manuscript of a mass by an 'old master', hoping to unlock the secret to the musical experience which miraculously converted her iconoclast sons to Catholicism. But she is musically illiterate, or at least cannot decipher this old notation. Seeing the score's 'unknown magical signs, with which a fearsome spirit seemed mysteriously to define its circle', she 'thought she would sink into the earth'.[16] She, too, soon converts. What the mother, a truth-seeking Protestant, fails to read *is* legible by others – namely, the nuns of the apparently wealthy and well-connected convent of St Cecilia – and the reader is left wondering about the roles of divine intervention as against worldly power plays and obfuscation in the Protestants' return to the old faith. In Hoffmann's case, an apparition of the dead composer Gluck plays from a richly bound and printed score, yet its notes are invisible to the dilettante narrator – either a sign of his musical-philosophical tone-deafness (for he misunderstands the genius), or the sheer impossibility of translating the infinite, teeming, polymorphous 'forms' (*Gestalten*) of ideal creativity into quotidian life on the page, the letter that kills while the spirit gives life. With Grillparzer, we meet a musical text as botched and cramped as the aspirations of its atrocious 'beggar-musician' to unstained personal and musical harmony in a fallen world.[17]

In each story, music represents for some characters an ideal experience which, to others, looks or sounds incomprehensible. The fact that music is not immediately present within these literary prose texts – as sound or as writing – allows them to stage a gap between the ideal and the prosaic (the latter aligned with the writer-narrator), and furthermore to pass on this gap to the reader as a failure of certainty, the impossibility of contact with a musical 'source' which might prove whether the ideal was an illusion all along or not. This kind of useful failure, created by writers who were themselves composers, players, or commentators on music, contrasts sharply with the desirable failure of musical ideals with a Romantic such as Coleridge.

Avoiding the Ideal: Coleridge

One of Coleridge's best-known treatments of music is 'The Eolian Harp' (1796). This rural and domestic idyll sees the poet sitting with his future wife, musing on the philosophical implications of sounds emanating from an aeolian harp. This instrument fascinated Romantic listeners because it was played by the wind, seeming to activate and manifest the creativity and harmony of nature (even 'the mute still air / Is Music slumbering on her instrument' (lines 33–34)). For Coleridge, the harp suggests first eroticism ('caress'd, / Like some coy maid' (15–16)); then the supernatural ('a soft floating witchery of sound' (20)); then more elevated philosophical material-ism, influenced by Enlightenment nerve theory – Coleridge engaged espe-cially with Hartley's idea that solid nerves, vibrating like instrument strings, grounded all sense perception, movement, and thought – theory tainted by association with scepticism and pantheism.[18] The speaker distances his phil-osophising from scepticism, and recalls the Neoplatonic Christian imagery of a world soul (long associated with music) as well as Romantic scientific work on the underlying unity of sensation and life: there is

> one Life within us and abroad,
> Which meets all motion and becomes its soul,
> A light in sound, a sound-like power in light,
> Rhythm in all thought, and joyance every where. (27–30)

Yet still he imagines his 'passive brain' being *given* thoughts, as the harp is given melodies by 'random gales', and wonders 'what if all of animated nature / Be but organic Harps diversely fram'd, / That tremble into thought, as' they are swept by 'one intellectual breeze', 'the Soul of each, and God of all?' (42–3, 45–9). All this looks ideal: a vision of organic and spiritual unity, and one not only formulated intellectually, but suggested by, even on a continuum with, an empirical musical experience. Moved by music, as harp strings are moved by the wind, the poem seems to enact that flow between individual and universal, mechanical 'motion' and 'soul', which it describes (28). Similar musical visions appear in Schlegel's *Abendröte* (*Sunset*, 1802; 1.1.15–18) – where 'Everything seems to speak to the poet / For he has found the meaning, / And the universe [seems] a single choir, / Many songs from One mouth' – or Eichendorff's miniature 'Wünschelrute' (Divining Rod, 1838):

> A song sleeps in all things
> Which lie dreaming, on and on,

And the world begins to sing
If only you hit upon the magic word.

With Coleridge, however, the ideal and the aural idyll are not the final word. In the last stanza, the speaker accepts the 'mild reproof' of his beloved's 'more serious eye', and abandons his 'unhallow'd' speculations (or, perhaps better, 'auscultations', since this is philosophy as listening) (50, 52).[19] Joy and contentment – the poet's 'Peace, and this Cot, and thee, heart-honour'd Maid!' (65) – arise not from musical nature revealing itself naturally to poet-philosophers, but from the intervention of the biblical God, 'saving' broken natures and revealed, partially, in scripture (62). Likewise, proper poetry emerges not as enthusiastic invention, flowing from 'vain Philosophy's aye-babbling spring', but humble 'praise' of God, 'The Incomprehensible!' (58, 60–61). Readers may regard the final stanza as marring the poem's shape and sentiments. But, for the speaker, claims to ideal plenitude are dangerous, and failure to embody it a saving grace. Poetry responds to the pressures of the given: not a world spirit but actual community (the female companion), revealed religion (and its limits), and, more mutedly, an inherited *poetic* tradition of rural contentment, taken from Virgil's Georgics. In this long tradition, philosophical speculation on nature is situated within *quiet* rural landscapes, like the one with which Coleridge begins (where 'The stilly murmur of the distant Sea / Tells us of silence' (11–12)); and, while Virgil's poet-speaker asks the muses for philosophical enlightenment and elevation, he then falls back into the more humble request for a quiet life and unspectacular contentment (*Georgics* 2.475–89). An internal tension between sound, music, and quiet thus runs through the poem, and prepares the well-tuned reader for the fact that 'wild', 'delicious', exuberant music will *help* poetry to reach its necessary domestication and falling-short (25, 20).

Music plays a no less pivotal role in perhaps the best-known Romantic failure in poetry, Coleridge's 'Kubla Khan' (1797/1816). In a preface which by its nature underscores the poem's lack of self-sufficiency (as will the marginal notes in 'The Rime of the Ancient Mariner'), Coleridge reports that he published this 'fragment' at the request of Byron, 'rather as a psychological curiosity, than on the ground of any supposed *poetic* merits'.[20] Romantic tropes of the exotic or 'other', spontaneous, and ideal are on full display. During a vivid opium dream, inspired by reading an antique travelogue which narrated the still older history of the Mongol khan Kublai, the author experienced a spell of spontaneous 'composition'. This original poem was composed in an ideal psycho-physiological state, 'without any sensation or consciousness of effort', and an ideal quasi-Adamic language, whose 'expressions' 'correspond[ed]' perfectly with the '*things*' they represented. Seeming 'to have a distinct recollection of the whole' upon awakening, Coleridge 'instantly and eagerly wrote down the lines' we know as 'Kubla Khan' before being interrupted by a visitor from the quotidian world.[21] Fled was the vision, and the remaining 150–250-odd lines of poetry Coleridge imagined himself to have composed in his altered state. 'Kubla Khan' is thus presented as a monument to a lost ideal poetic experience – a witness to a 'whole' that is all the more evocative of perfection for being itself broken. The imaginative stakes are high, but the pressures on the words on the page relatively low. Internally, the poem also describes imperilled, utopian perfection. First, there is the 'miracle of rare device' that is Kubla Khan's heterotopic 'pleasure-dome', arising as if by magic through his creative 'decree' and seemingly channelling the violent forces of nature (35, 2). Yet its pleasures and musical 'mingled measure' cannot drown out the labours of kingship, the sound of 'Ancestral voices prophesying war!' (33, 30).

Third-person description now breaks off, replaced by a first-person reflection on a past 'vision' of an 'Abyssinian' 'damsel with a dulcimer' (37–9). She sings of another artificial paradise, Abyssinia's 'Mount Abora' (41). The speaker's now-indistinct 'vision' was apparently sonic – although the visual term builds in extra distance between reader and music – since its (non)sounds become a stimulus for his own potential construction of an artificial paradise:

> Could I revive within me
> Her symphony and song,
>   To such a deep delight 'twould win me,
> That with music loud and long,
> I would build that dome in air,
> That sunny dome! those caves of ice! (42–7)

This conditional act of creation with its lost possible ground – music – is bracketed one further step by the hypothetical reaction of 'all who heard' the music: 'all should cry, Beware! Beware!' at the enthusiastic (and implicitly opiated) creator, should enclose him in a quasi-magical, protective triple 'circle' and close their eyes to him (48–9, 51). The underlying structure here is significant: an exotic woman, singing about a legendary mountain in her native land – one long associated with the hidden source of the sacred river Nile – represents poetic creation's lost source of plenitude (a 'loud and long' 'symphony', or *sounding-together* (45, 43)).

Moreover, *as* lost, the singer represents the stimulus for the existing poetic fragment, in its mode of imperfect recollection, wish, or lament, strategically distanced from an encircled ideal.

Coleridge's very different treatments of strange stringed instruments in these poems use music to figure an ideal which it is actually in the poem's interests to avoid. 'Kubla Khan' arguably has a pragmatic rationale for avoidance: the perfection of altered states cannot be communicated directly, and gesturing towards their loss becomes a good bet in persuading readers something was really there. But in both poems there is a dimension of moral danger and delusion in the ideal that makes failure to reach it valuable. What explains this danger and its alignment with music? It should be acknowledged that the scenario does not fully capture the range of music's work for Coleridge, let alone for other English Romantics, and figures including Fanny Burney, Leigh Hunt, William Hazlitt, the Shelleys, and Thomas De Quincey engaged more closely and positively with musical culture. Nonetheless, the lurking suspicion of music in the two poems perhaps holds some trace of broader English Protestant suspicions of music as sensual distraction and self-display.[22] If not typical, the poems find many echoes elsewhere. The moral questions raised in 'The Eolian Harp' are shared by Wordsworth's ambivalent depiction of excessive musical absorption in 'The Power of Music'. Meanwhile, the less clearly denounced artificial paradise of Coleridge's opium vision is echoed by De Quincey's depiction of the 'Pleasures of Opium' in his *Confessions of an English Opium-Eater* (1821) – recalled from the other side of this 'Paradise', when he has suffered and apparently overcome the 'Pains of Opium'. Opium's pleasures are epitomised by visits to the opera, where he heard alongside opera singers the passionate 'music' of Italian women speaking in the audience, a musicality enhanced by its separation from utilitarian signification – since De Quincey understood no Italian – and which he compared with the musicality of 'Indian' women's speech, as recounted by a contemporary traveller to Canada.[23]

The connection of music with exotic women's language deserves further exploration. It suggests associations of music with the non-semantic, a- or irrational, undetermined and vague; with passion, sensuality, wildness; and with racial, national, epistemological, and gendered otherness. These are alterities that modern male European authors might claim to harness and mediate to readers without embodying them, making music a useful 'constitutive other' for literature. But the exotic woman can also suggest music's associations with things more particular, determinate, and grounded, leading us to a final and complex case of literary failure.

Exoticism and Philological Failure: Mérimée

Prosper Mérimée's novella *Carmen* (1845/47) is not always counted amongst the Romantic works of this archaeologist, historical conservationist, and master of short fiction. Yet it reflects and interrogates key developments stemming from Romantic-era literature and literary-critical method, still important to the discipline today – namely historicism and hermeneutical philology. Nor is *Carmen* obviously concerned with music: despite her name, and unlike Bizet's gypsy, Mérimée's does not seduce through song. Music is incidental, scattered through the novella, integrated into larger soundscapes and broader depictions of character, custom, and place.

This is as it should be in a novella shaped by historicism, a term coined by Friedrich Schlegel but with roots in Enlightenment-era philosophy and its reception by Herder and others.[24] Historicism assumed that character and action vary across nations and their specific stages of historical development; influenced by history, national languages are great repositories and transmitters of cultural specificity, revealing a people's nature and pointing to its origins. For Herder, the origins of language and song were conjoined. The first language indeed was song, and present-day orally preserved folk songs offered a better insight into the spirit of a people than more alienated modern languages. Within the historicist paradigm, consciously or not (self-consciously in Mérimée's case), literary authors will show the organic connection between language, social milieu, and individual plots. Literary historians and critics will give close attention to the specificities of language (philology) in order to interpret or divine a text's original meaning (the hermeneutic task). While German Romantics are usually held to have concentrated on the specificities of distant lands or times, especially the Middle Ages, Mérimée's friend Stendhal is credited with applying historicism to the here and now, showing in his realist novels how both unremarkable everyday mores and apparently idiosyncratic individual fates are shaped by larger socio-historical forces.[25] Tellingly, Stendhal connected music with national origins and specificities in his *Memoirs of Rossini* (1824), recounting how the changeable timbres of Giuditta Pasta's voice inspired in an exiled Neapolitan a vivid moonlit vision of his 'unhappy homeland'.

Set in near-modern-day Spain, Mérimée's *Carmen* combines realism with a romanticising, exotic location. Philology and historical interpretation are built into its premise: the narrator is a travelling French dilettante-scholar who comes across Carmen's lover and murderer, Don José, during an archaeological 'excursion' which he hopes will prove the exact site of the classical Battle of Munda, a 'fascinating question' supposedly 'holding all learned Europe in suspense'.[26] The narrator recounts the 'little story' of *Carmen* to fill in time before his dissertation on Munda's origin takes the scholarly world by storm. We soon find he is also a keen linguist and ethnographer, recording in footnotes details of language use (Carmen switches between Spanish, Basque, and 'chipe calli'), pronunciation, and telling idioms, and using his observations in faltering attempts to discern the geographical and 'national' origins of Don José and Carmen herself (mistaken for an Andalusian, a Moor, or a Jew).

Music and sound are crucial here. The undercover bandit José is initially taciturn (a stance affirmed in the novella's last sentence, which quotes a 'gypsy' proverb, 'A closed mouth, no fly can enter' (339)). The pronunciation of José's 'first words' marks him as a stranger in Andalusia (3). But only his singing to a mandolin, with incomprehensible words and a 'melody plaintive and exotic', suggests to the narrator that he is specifically Basque (7). The song – a characteristic 'zortziko' – affects José in a way that on one hand reveals his ethnic traits and origins, and on the other hints at his individual character and fate. José grows 'sombre', 'profound[ly] melancholy', and resembles 'Milton's Satan'. 'Perhaps, like' that Romantic antihero, he is brooding on 'the abode he had left behind [Heaven/ Navarre], and of the exile he had earned by some transgression' (7). (The same is true of Carmen's only conventional musical performance, a *romalis* dance for a high-society party. Glimpsing this dance accompanied by 'tambourine' and 'guitar', José 'fell in love with her in earnest' – yet he introduces this pivotal personal moment in quasi-historicist, sociological terms, as generally characteristic of gypsies and their place in Spanish society: 'They always have an old woman ... and an old man with a guitar .... As you know, Gypsies are often invited to social gatherings to entertain guests' (27–8).[27])

José's melancholy seems not simply associative, but directly prompted by sound's affective and aesthetic qualities. For, much later, he tells the narrator: 'Our language is so beautiful, señor, that when we hear it spoken far from home our hearts leap at the sound of it' (23). Rousseau had linked sound with nostalgia – originally a longing for a specific place, one's homeland – citing Swiss soldiers' propensity to fall fatally ill if they heard their native (verbally incomprehensible) cow-herding songs in distant lands. This trope has a decisive narrative function in *Carmen*: when José, then a soldier, arrests Carmen for attacking her fellow worker, it is Carmen's recognition of José's Basque accent, her ability as a polyglot gypsy to speak Basque, and her false claim to be José's compatriot which persuade him to let her escape. This plunges him into a series of punishments and transgressions ending in the lovers' isolation and deaths. The sonic effect is double-pronged, specific and general; since not only Basque, but Carmen's vocalising in any language (along with her laughter) always overpowers José's reason, he claims, making him a 'fool', 'drunken', 'mad', bending him irresistibly to her will (24).

José's response to Carmen's voice suggests a kind of sympathetic magic: sound makes him resemble her wild and exotic character. The cluster of associations – madness, drunkenness, magic, transgression, passion, exoticism – belongs to cultural clichés about music as 'other' to modern rationality and rule-bound civilisation. Music represents an alluring ideal of sorts – freedoms, extremes, and rebellions in an age of staid moderation, inertia, and inward-looking pedantry (recall the 'fascinating' question of Munda) – but not an ideal realist literature can straightforwardly embrace. Mérimée deploys these associations in Carmen's incidental uses of music. The lovers' first orgiastic one-night stand begins with Carmen 'danc[ing] and laugh[ing] like a madwoman, singing, "You are my *rom* [husband], I am your *romi* [wife]"', before violently smashing an old woman's 'only plate' to fashion makeshift castanets (30). Like her other words, Carmen's song lies: she is already married. But on another level the music is incantatory and interpellative, helping to effect José's deracination and transformation from an honour-bound Basque-speaker into something like a Roma. After the resurfacing of Carmen's real *rom*, she will idly sing and 'rattl[e] her castanets' as a cover for kissing José at their shared campsite (prompting his accusation, 'You are the Devil incarnate', to which she replies, 'Yes' (39)). She 'clack[s] her castanets' like protective talismans or noisy carnival instruments to 'banish' any 'disturbing idea' (46), and just before her death, 'engrossed' in a weird mental state as she undertakes rituals that predict her murder, she 'sing[s]' 'magic songs invoking' the original 'great Queen of the Gypsies' (51).

This is a world where sounds are identifiers and signatures, typifying characters and groups like the timbre of an instrument. José has his Basque accent; the narrator a repeating watch (a novelty in Spain, leading Carmen to misidentify him as an upper-crust Englishman); even King Pedro I, a footnote claims, was easily recognised in a dark alley by an old woman through his 'extraordinary disability' of 'loudly' 'crack[ing]' 'knee-joints' (29). Carmen has her castanets, but gypsy sounds are also an anomaly and problem for the narrator's methods. Polyglot, code-switching, wild, magical – these sounds of course delocalise and exoticise gypsies, failing to specify their origins or locality. The novella's belated fourth instalment, a free-standing ethnographic sketch of the gypsies, hammers home the anomaly. Their pre-European origins are unknown; their reasons for migrating unknown; 'strangest of all, no one knows how . . . their numbers soon increased so prodigiously in several countries so far apart' (337) – in other words, even the assumption that peoples emanate from *single* origins is undermined. Finally, the origin of gypsy language is unsettled, and, flouting the logic of hermeneutic philology and the tie between nation and speech, '[e]verywhere they speak the language of their adopted country in preference to their own' (337).

These anomalies help the novella to stage its failures and instal its central character as, not merely an enigmatic femme fatale in the tradition of French literature, but an inscrutable force of resistance and autonomy who tells her lover, 'you have the right to kill your *romi*. But Carmen will always be free' (52). José's failure to control Carmen, and the narrator's scholarly failure fully to place the gypsies in general and Carmen in particular, join a series of imperfections: the lovers' deaths and failed relationship; half-accidental murders; incomplete linguistic crossings (Basque and 'chipe calli' are essentially closed to the narrator, and even Carmen speaks the former 'atrociously' (24)); the forever-suspended proof that the narrator has located Munda; incomplete plot arcs (characteristic of modern short fiction) concerning José's death and the narrator's promise to return a medallion to José's mother at home – narrative promises of closure or return to origins left hanging by the focus on Carmen's end. As in 'Kubla Khan', music helps to evoke lost origins, wholeness, and creative freedoms not possessed by the literary work itself judged as a set of words on the page. It creates something like a 'transcendence' or 'ideality effect', a sense of something further that literature can strive to become and represent.

Conclusion

However unappealing the stereotypes of music in a text like *Carmen*, the work of music within this novella and the other examples discussed aligns it with the aspirations of Romantic literature as defined by Schlegel:

Other kinds of poetry are complete and can now be fully analysed. The romantic kind of poetry is still becoming; indeed, that is its actual essence, that it can only eternally become, never be complete. . . . Only she is infinite, because only she is free and acknowledges, as her first law, that the caprice of the poet suffers no law above itself.[28]

Schlegel's definition is both infinitely demanding and absolves literary works of embodying any perfections – classically associated with completeness – or living up to any particular ideal, since standards would make poetry determined and unfree. The 'ideal' of Romantic poetry can only be provided by 'a divinatory criticism' like Schlegel's, not by analysing a canon of extant exemplary works.[29] Romantic poetry is great in theory; in practice, in order to 'never be complete' it frequently cultivates smallness, showy incompleteness, and failure. Although Schlegel claims that Romantic literature has no real boundaries – 'encompass[ing]' multiple arts, non-arts like philosophy, and the 'artless song' breathed out by a 'child' – nevertheless one of the most effective 'caprices' of Romantic writers is precisely to construct limits and acknowledge laws above and outside literature – perhaps above all the law of music.

Methodologically, this observation brings home a foundational argument of media studies, now also important for sound studies and musicology, that different media have porous and changing boundaries, and, in Georgina Born's words, exist 'relationally'.[30] This insight encourages us to see relationships between literature and music within the broader framework of sound, and to attend to matters as seemingly external to music as hermeneutic philology. This reinforces the fact that the 'work' of music for literature extends beyond any trope or structure such as failure, to forming the institution and discipline of literature itself. Nonetheless, the uses and timbres of failure are manifold and revealing. It might spur melancholy, frustration, madness, longing, humility, suspicion, or an awareness of interdependence. Its flipside is promise and possibility – the sense taken from Romanticism into the commonplaces of later culture: that life and art are epitomised by 'Effort, and expectation, and desire, / And something ever more about to be' (Wordsworth);[31] the drive 'To strive, to seek, to find, and not to yield' (Tennyson);[32] that the failure of pleasure drives the formation of civilisation and individual psyches (Freud); or that, in words claimed by postmodernist ironists and popular self-help books alike, we are condemned and free to 'Try Again. Fail Again. Fail Better' (Beckett).[33] Even E. M. Forster has a little of it when he declares in 'Not Listening to Music' – a celebration of his failure to concentrate on or write about music – that while his 'own performances upon the piano' (usually Beethoven) 'grow worse yearly', 'never will [he] give them up': 'Even when people play as badly as I do, they should continue: it will help them to listen.'[34]

Notes

1. John Clare, *The Village Minstrel* (1821); James Beattie, *The Minstrel* (1774); James Macpherson, *Fragments of Ancient Poetry* (1760); Letitia Elizabeth Landon, 'The Improvisatrice' (1824); Hans Christian Andersen, *The Improvisatore* (1835); Joseph von Eichendorff, *Aus dem Leben eines Taugenichts* (1826); Leigh Hunt, 'Velluti to his Revilers' (1825); E. T. A. Hoffmann, *Fantasiestücke in Callot's Manier* (1814–19).
2. Hoffmann, 'Beethovens Instrumental-Musik' (1810) and 'Ritter Gluck' (1809/14); Heinrich von Kleist, 'Über Haydns Tod' (1811).
3. Landon, 'Sappho' (1822) and 'The Hindoo Girl's Song' (1835); Lord Byron, *Childe Harold* (1812), 2.72; Ann Radcliffe, *Mysteries of Udolpho* (1794); Ludwig Tieck, *Der blonde Eckbert* (1797); John Keats, 'Ode to a Nightingale' and 'Ode on a Grecian Urn' (1819).
4. See Sarah Hibberd and Miranda Stanyon (eds.), *Music and the Sonorous Sublime in European Culture, 1680–1880* (Cambridge: Cambridge University Press, 2020); Gillen D'Arcy Wood, 'The Castrato's Tale: *Artaxerxes* and the Feminization of Virtuosity', *The Wordsworth Circle*, 39/3 (2008), 74–9; Günter Schnitzler, '"Ritter Gluck": Produktive Musikkritik', in Günter Saße (ed.), *E. T. A. Hoffmann: Romane und Erzählungen* (Stuttgart: Reclam, 2004), 13–30; Rachel Cowgill, 'Mozart Productions and the Emergence of *Werktreue* at London's Italian Opera House, 1780–1830', in Roberta Montemorra Marvin and Downing Thomas (eds.), *Operatic Migrations* (Aldershot: Ashgate, 2006), 145–86.
5. Louis-Sébastien Mercier, *Néologie*, vol. 2 (Paris: Moussard, 1801), 230. Unless noted, all translations are my own.
6. Friedrich Schlegel, '*Athenäum* fragment 116' (1798), in Wolfdietrich Rasch (ed.), *Kritische Schriften* (Munich: Carl Hanser Verlag, 1958), 38.
7. Stefan Matuschek, 'Romanticism as Literary Idealism', in *The Impact of Idealism*, vol. 3, *Aesthetics and Literature*, ed. Christoph Jamme and Ian Cooper (Cambridge: Cambridge University Press, 2013), 72.
8. Kleist, *Sämtliche Werke und Briefe*, ed. Helmut Sembdner, rev. ed., vol. 2 (Munich: Deutscher Taschenbuch Verlag, 2001), 634; William Wordsworth, *Prelude* (1805), book 6, lines 530, 539.
9. Hoffmann, 'Beethovens Instrumental-Musik', in *Fantasiestücke in Callot's Manier*, vol. 1 (Bamberg: Kunz, 1814), 108–9.
10. On Schlegel's 'romantic poetry' as 'modern literature', see Matuschek, 'Romanticism as Literary Idealism', 88–90.
11. Louise Hornby, *Still Modernism: Photography, Literature, Film* (New York: Oxford University Press, 2017), discusses modernism and 'medium specificity'.

12. Friedrich Kittler, *Aufschreibesysteme 1800/1900* (Munich: Fink, 1985); Deidre Lynch, *Loving Literature: A Cultural History* (Chicago: University of Chicago Press, 2015); Andrew Piper, *Dreaming in Books: The Making of the Bibliographic Imagination in the Romantic Age* (Chicago: Chicago University Press, 2009).

13. Angela Esterhammer, *Romanticism and Improvisation, 1750–1850* (Cambridge: Cambridge University Press, 2008); Maureen McLane, 'Ballads and Bards: British Romantic Orality', *Modern Philology*, 98 (2001), 423–43; Günter Oesterle, 'Arabeske, Schrift und Poesie in E. T. A. Hoffmanns Kunstmärchen "Der goldne Topf"', *Athenäum: Jahrbuch für Romantik*, 1 (1991), 60–96.

14. Compare McLane, 'Ballads and Bards', 427–8.

15. McLane, 'Ballads and Bards'.

16. Kleist, 'Die heilige Cäcilie oder die Gewalt der Musik (eine Legende)' (1810), *Sämtliche Werke*, 226.

17. Franz Grillparzer, *Der arme Spielmann. Anmerkungen und Nachwort von Helmut Bachmaier* (Stuttgart: Reclam, 2002), 7.

18. See further Shelley Trower, *Senses of Vibration: A History of the Pleasure and Pain of Sound* (New York: Continuum, 2012), 13–26.

19. For an influential discussion of auscultation, see Jonathan Sterne, *The Audible Past: Cultural Origins of Sound Reproduction* (Durham, NC: Duke University Press, 2003), 100–37.

20. Samuel Taylor Coleridge, 'Of the Fragment of Kubla Khan', in Ernest Hartley Coleridge (ed.), *The Complete Poetical Works of Samuel Taylor Coleridge*, vol. 1 (Oxford: Oxford University Press, 1912), 295–7, at 295.

21. Ibid., 296.

22. On English Romantic wariness of virtuosity and praise of 'natural' performance, see Gillen D'Arcy Wood, *Romanticism and Music Culture in Britain* (Cambridge: Cambridge University Press, 2010).

23. *The Works of Thomas De Quincey*, ed. Grevel Lindop et al. (London: Pickering & Chatto, 2000–3), vol. 2, 334.

24. See Edward Said, 'Introduction', in Erich Auerbach, *Mimesis: The Representation of Reality in Western Literature*, trans. Willard R. Trask (Princeton: Princeton University Press, 2013), ix–xxxii, at xii–xvi. Further James Chandler, *England in 1819: The Politics of Literary Culture and the Case of Romantic Historicism* (Chicago: University of Chicago Press, 1998).

25. Auerbach, *Mimesis*, ch. 18.

26. For English translations, see Prosper Mérimée, *Carmen and Other Stories*, trans. Nicholas Jotcham (Oxford: Oxford University Press, 1989), here 1 (subsequent page numbers are provided in the text in parentheses).

27. Compare Mérimée's aim in his Romantic historical novel *Chronique de règne de Charles IX* (1829) of creating '[u]ne peinture vraie des mœurs et des caractères à une époque donnée' (a true picture of the customs and characters

of a given epoque), and his combination there of what Charlton identifies as a passion for 'significant details and revealing anecdotes' with flattened character 'types'. Donald Charlton, 'Prose Fiction', in *The French Romantics*, 2 vols. (Cambridge: Cambridge University Press, 1984), vol. 1, 189, 195.

28. Schlegel, *Athenäum* fragment 116, 37–8.

29. Ibid.

30. Georgina Born, 'For a Relational Musicology: Music and Interdisciplinarity, Beyond the Practice Turn', *Journal of the Royal Musical Association*, 135 (2010), 205–43.

31. William Wordsworth, *Prelude* (1805), book 6, lines 541–2.

32. Alfred, Lord Tennyson, 'Ulysses' (1833), line 70.

33. Samuel Beckett, 'Worstward Ho' (1983).

34. E. M. Forster, 'Not Listening to Music' (1939), in *Two Cheers for Democracy* (San Diego: Harcourt Brace & Co., 1951), 127–30, at 130.

Further Reading

Barry, Kevin. *Language, Music and the Sign* (Cambridge: Cambridge University Press, 1987).

Chapin, Keith Moore, and Clark, Andrew Herrick (eds.). *Speaking of Music: Addressing the Sonorous* (New York: Fordham University Press, 2013).

Esterhammer, Angela. *Romanticism and Improvisation, 1750–1850* (Cambridge: Cambridge University Press, 2008).

Gess, Nicola, and Honold, Alexander (eds.). *Handbuch Literatur & Musik* (Berlin: De Gruyter, 2017).

Hoeveler, Diane. *Long: Gothic Riffs: Secularizing the Uncanny in the European Imaginary, 1780–1820* (Columbus: Ohio State University Press, 2010).

Jamme, Christoph, and Cooper, Ian (eds.). *The Impact of Idealism: The Legacy of Post-Kantian German Thought*, vol. 3: *Aesthetics and Literature*, ed. Nicholas Boyle and Liz Disley (4 vols.) (Cambridge: Cambridge University Press, 2013).

Kittler, Friedrich, Macho, Thomas, and Weigel, Sigrid (eds.). *Zwischen Rauschen und Offenbarung: zur Kultur- und Mediengeschichte der Stimme* (Berlin: Akademie Verlag, 2002).

Lacoue-Labarthe, Philippe. *Musica ficta: Figures of Wagner*, trans. Felicia McCarren (Stanford: Stanford University Press, 1994).

Lubkoll, Christina. *Mythos Musik: Poetische Entwürfe des Musikalischen in der Literatur um 1800* (Freiburg: Rombach, 1995).

McClary, Susan (ed.). *Georges Bizet: Carmen* (Cambridge: Cambridge University Press, 1992).

McLane, Maureen. *Balladeering, Minstrelsy, and the Making of British Romantic Poetry* (Cambridge: Cambridge University Press, 2011).

Stanyon, Miranda. *Resounding the Sublime: Music in English and German Literature and Aesthetic Theory, 1670–1850* (Philadelphia: University of Pennsylvania Press, 2021).

Thym, Jürgen (ed.). *Of Poetry and Song: Approaches to the Nineteenth-Century Lied* (Rochester: University of Rochester Press, 2010).

Weliver, Phyllis, and Ellis, Katharine (eds.). *Words and Notes in the Long Nineteenth Century* (Woodbridge: Boydell Press, 2013).

Wood, Gillen D'Arcy. *Romanticism and Music Culture in Britain, 1770–1840: Virtue and Virtuosity* (Cambridge: Cambridge University Press, 2010).

4 | Music, Romantic Landscape, and the Visual

THOMAS PEATTIE

Long regarded as the paradigmatic example of Romantic musical land-scape, Felix Mendelssohn's overture *The Hebrides (Fingal's Cave)*, Op. 26, remains unique insofar as the surviving evidence related to its composition allows us to trace the inspiration for the work's distinctive opening con-tours to a specific time and place. The broad outlines of this story are well known.[1] During the summer of 1829 Mendelssohn travelled to Scotland with the diplomat and writer Karl Klingemann, a trip that included a walking tour of the Highlands and the Hebridean archipelago. On the afternoon of 7 August near the small town of Oban on the Scottish mainland, Mendelssohn attempted to document his impressions of the surrounding landscape in a pencil drawing that offers a tantalising glimpse of the archipelago for which the composer was about set sail (see Fig. 4.1). Arriving later that evening on the Isle of Mull, Mendelssohn continued to record his impressions, this time in the form of a twenty-one-bar sketch whose musical substance closely resembles the opening of the completed overture. Of particular interest here is Mendelssohn's prefatory note in which he claims a direct connection between his own reaction to the landscape of the Hebrides and the music that he immediately felt com-pelled to jot down. Indeed, it is precisely the directness of this claim that demonstrates why the overture in its final form has continued to serve as an important point of reference for anyone wrestling with the fraught ques-tion of how a musical work can be said to evoke a particular landscape or, indeed, the idea of landscape more generally.[2]

In the case of *The Hebrides*, discussions concerning its presumed con-nection to the place by which it was inspired have naturally been informed by other factors including, most prominently, the suggestive power of the work's title.[3] This serves to remind us that while in recent years our understanding of Mendelssohn's overture as a 'landscape' has been shaped by the musical sketch and accompanying commentary described above, as is the case for many Romantic works, the perceived presence of visual and scenic elements has for most listeners been determined largely by the overture's more immediately accessible 'programmatic' layer. With respect to Romantic instrumental music more generally, such programmatic layers

Figure 4.1 Felix Mendelssohn (1809–47), *Ein Blick auf die Hebriden und Morven* (A View of the Hebrides and Morven), graphite, pen, and ink on paper, Tobermory, 7 August 1829 (Bodleian Library, University of Oxford, MS. M. Deneke Mendelssohn D.2, Fol. 28)

have traditionally included work and movement titles, as well as printed programmes and other kinds of programmatic descriptions. In vocal and choral music, it is the poetry itself that has tended to play the most important role in establishing a sense of place, while in opera a similar role has been played by libretti, staging manuals, and the like. Of course, there are other kinds of texts that have been used to make interpretive claims about the relationship between music and landscape in the nineteenth century, including (1) a composer's letters, diaries, and other writings; (2) paratexts, including autograph annotations in a composer's sketches, manuscripts, and printed scores; and (3) contemporary performance reviews and other forms of written commentary and analysis. Whereas our understanding of the relationship between music and landscape continues to be shaped by such texts, the question of how this relationship is manifested in specifically musical terms continues to pose considerable interpretive challenges. With this in mind, I will focus my attention in what follows on two larger issues raised by Mendelssohn's overture, both of which are relevant to the perceived presence of the visual and scenic in Romantic music in all its manifestations. I will begin by considering the claim that a musical work has the ability to *evoke* landscape in the first place, whether in general or specific terms. Following a brief exploration of the depiction of music and music making in Romantic art, I will turn my attention to the notion of landscape as an object of *contemplation*, considering it both as an activity from which composers frequently drew creative inspiration, and as a metaphor that has often been used to make sense of individual works whose musical identity is in some way bound up with the idea of landscape broadly construed.

Evoking Landscape

When Mendelssohn jotted down his musical impressions of the Hebrides in 1829, the notion that instrumental music had the potential to illustrate already had a long and distinguished history. Amongst the most important precedents are the *pièces de caractère* of François Couperin (1668–1733), works whose evocative titles often seem to align closely with their musical character. Of more immediate relevance is the characteristic symphony, the illustrative genre par excellence that emerged during the second half of the eighteenth century. Often remembered for their vivid depictions of storms, battles, hunts, and pastoral idylls, these works also frequently gave musical expression to a range of national and regional characters.[4] While not programmatic in the Listzian sense, such works anticipate the Romantic conception of programme music insofar as their descriptive titles are often supplemented by elaborate prose descriptions. But to the extent that the characteristic symphony draws on an established tradition involving the musical representation of things or events, it is important to remember that the genre also placed a strong emphasis on human emotions and expressive content. Indeed, it is precisely this duality that allows us to make sense of Beethoven's own contribution to the genre in his Sixth Symphony (1808), a work whose title he gave in a letter to his publisher as *Pastoral Symphony or Recollections of Country Life: More the Expression of Feeling than Tone-Painting*.[5] Yet, as it turns out, Beethoven's apparent rejection of *Tonmalerei* as suggested by this subtitle is not borne out by the completed symphony. For in addition to the numerous examples of musical illustration that can be found throughout the work, the very form of the second movement ('Scene by the brook') appears to have been determined by the kind of landscape it purports to evoke. In his discussion of an early sketch containing material for this movement, Lewis Lockwood has observed that underneath a preliminary version of the 12/8 figure, which in its final form has been widely understood to represent the motion of the brook, Beethoven wrote: 'je grosser der Bach je tiefer der Ton' (the greater the brook the deeper the tone). For Lockwood the significance of this annotation as it relates to the movement as a whole is that Beethoven ultimately went on to establish a 'correlation between the image of the widening and deepening brook and the orchestral forces that develop the form of the movement'.[6] We might even go so far as to say that it is precisely the movement's sense of motion that ultimately informs Beethoven's attempt to evoke this particular landscape. Indeed, as Benedict Taylor has recently proposed, 'music can successfully model a landscape to the extent that it implicates its moving, dynamic aspects, its temporal processes'.[7]

Whereas the early reception of Beethoven's *Pastoral Symphony* reflects the competing aesthetic claims embedded in the work's subtitle, the first half of the nineteenth century witnessed the emergence of a critical vocabulary that revealed another kind of tension in the reception of Romantic music: namely, between musical works that were understood to illustrate and those that were thought to possess narrative qualities. In his discussion of the role of metaphor in nineteenth-century music criticism, Thomas Grey identifies a '"pictorial" mode (appealing to a range of "natural", rather than abstract, imagery), and a "narrative" mode, which ascribes to a composition the teleological character of an interrelated series of events leading to a certain goal, or perhaps a number of intermittent goals that together make up a more or less coherent story'.[8] But as Grey goes on to argue, these modes are by no means mutually exclusive:

[t]he 'story' conveyed by an instrumental work might, for some critics, have more in common with the kind of story conveyed by a series of images: a story expressed in mimetic rather than diegetic terms, in which levels of 'discourse' cannot be distinguished from the medium itself, and in which the events 'depicted' resist verbal summary. Furthermore, the categories of 'pictorial' or 'descriptive' music – *malende Musik* – most often embraced concepts of musical narration as well, at least in the critical vocabulary of the earlier nineteenth century.[9]

The extent to which these metaphorical modes often overlapped is made plain in a rarely discussed passage that Grey cites from the second part of Franz Liszt's essay on Berlioz's *Harold in Italy* first published in the *Neue Zeitschrift für Musik* in 1855. This overlap is particularly evident in the context of Liszt's discussion of the emerging interpretive tradition around the symphonies, sonatas, and quartets of Beethoven, in which critics had endeavoured, in Liszt's words, 'to fix in the form of picturesque, poetic, or philosophical commentaries the images aroused in the listener's mind' by these works.[10]

At first glance Franz Brendel's often-cited tribute to Robert Schumann's early piano works appears to offer a straightforward example of the 'pictorial mode'. Upon closer examination, however, it becomes apparent that the way in which Brendel uses the metaphor of landscape to illuminate specific musical features in Schumann's music does not, strictly speaking, draw on 'natural imagery', but rather on the representation of such images.

Schumann's compositions can often be compared to landscape paintings in which the foreground gains prominence in sharply delineated, clear contours while the background becomes blurred and vanishes in a limitless perspective. They may be compared to fog-covered landscapes from which only now and then an object emerges glowing in the sunlight. Thus the compositions contain certain, clear primary sections and others that do not protrude clearly at all but rather serve merely as backgrounds. Some passages are like points made prominent by the rays of the sun, whereas others vanish in blurry contours. These internal characteristics find their correlate in a technical device: Schumann likes to play with open pedal to let the harmonies appear in blurred contours.[11]

If, for Brendel, this description pertained most directly to the *Fantasiestücke*, Op. 12, Berthold Hoeckner has shown that it applies equally well to Schumann's celebrated evocation of distant sound in his *Davidsbündlertänze*, Op. 6 (1837), specifically at the beginning of the cycle's penultimate number, 'Wie aus der Ferne', where the use of the damper pedal gives rise to a distinctive texture that 'easily compares to Brendel's image of a landscape with a blurred harmonic background against which melodic shapes stand out like sunlit objects'.[12] Given that the relationship between music and landscape being proposed here is more precisely a relationship between music and the visual *representation* of landscape, it is worth considering whether the desire to draw technical and formal parallels between musical composition and painting risks over-interpreting the presumed visual dimension of the works under discussion, especially given that Schumann was not attempting to *compose* landscape in the way that would become increasingly common in the decades that followed.

During the second half of the nineteenth century conscious attempts to compose landscape often drew on a compositional device referred to as a *Klangfläche* (sound sheet), a device that as Carl Dahlhaus has noted gave rise to the most 'outstanding musical renditions of nature' in Romantic music.[13] Dahlhaus provides three examples (the 'Forest Murmurs' from

Act II of Richard Wagner's *Siegfried*, the 'Nile Scene' from Act III of Giuseppe Verdi's *Aida*, and the 'Riverbank Scene' from Act III of Charles Gounod's *Mirielle*), each of which functions as a self-contained musical tableau. Characterised by outward stasis and inward motion, these passages are suggestive of landscape in part because the *Klangfläche* is 'exempted both from the principle of teleological progression and from the rule of musical texture which nineteenth-century musical theorists referred to, by no means simply metaphorically, as "thematic-motivic manipulation", taking Beethoven's development sections as their *locus classicus*'.[14] Indeed, Dahlhaus goes on to observe that 'musical landscapes arise less from direct tone-painting than from "definite negation" of the character of musical form as a process', something that is particularly evident in the later nineteenth-century use of the *Klangfläche* where the status of the resulting tableaux is determined partly in relation to the larger symphonic narratives in which they are embedded.[15]

Perhaps even more common during the latter half of the nineteenth century are those works whose relationship to landscape is bound up with the claim that their creation has been inspired by an *actual* geographical locale. Amongst the most ambitious attempts to compose a large-scale instrumental work in these terms is Franz Liszt's *Années de pèlerinage* (composed between 1837 and 1877), a sort of musical travelogue inspired by the composer's 'pilgrimages' to Switzerland and Italy. As Liszt writes in the preface to the work's first volume, 'Suisse', his aim was to give 'musical utterance' both to the 'sensations' (*sensations*) and 'impressions' (*perceptions*) that he encountered during his travels. How precisely this is conveyed to the listener in terms of specificity of place is, of course, more complicated. Whereas in the earliest published editions of the work each individual piece is preceded by a full-page engraving that was presumably meant to put the performer in mind of the specific locales being evoked, for most contemporary listeners the work of musical illustration would have been carried out by the individual movement titles, as well as through the use of well-established musical topics.

This desire to draw connections between musical works and the places in which they were composed has long played an important role in accounts of one composer in particular: Gustav Mahler. The history of this interpretive tradition can be traced, in part, to the testimony of the conductor Bruno Walter. In the summer of 1896 Walter visited Mahler at his lakeside retreat in the Austrian village of Steinbach am Attersee where the composer was at work on his Third Symphony. Walter later reported that as he stepped off the boat and glanced up towards the surrounding mountains Mahler offered a most unconventional greeting: 'You don't need to look – I have composed this all already' ('Sie brauchen gar nicht mehr hinzusehen, das habe ich alles schon wegkomponiert').[16] Earlier that year Mahler provided a more detailed account of his belief in the mimetic power of his own music. Commenting on the Third Symphony's minuet, which at the time still bore the title 'What the flowers in the meadow tell me' (Was mir die Blumen auf der Wiese erzählen), Mahler reportedly said:

You can't imagine how it will sound! It is the most carefree thing that I have ever written – as carefree as only flowers are. It all sways and waves in the air, as light and graceful as can be, like the flowers bending on their stems in the wind. . . . As you might imagine, the mood doesn't remain one of innocent, flower-like serenity, but suddenly becomes serious and oppressive. A stormy wind blows across the meadow and shakes the leaves and blossoms, which groan and whimper on their stems, as if imploring release into a higher realm.[17]

In addition to his belief that this landscape served as the primary source of inspiration for the movement as a whole, Mahler also went one step further by suggesting that the listener would be able to envision Steinbach and its surroundings in the music's very fabric: 'Anybody who doesn't actually know the place . . . will practically be able to visualise it from the music, so unique is its charm, as if made just to provide the inspiration for a piece such as this.'[18] While connections of this sort have remained an important thread in the reception of Mahler's music, such interpretive moves have also been treated with scepticism. Theodor W. Adorno was amongst the first to resist the idea that these works might reflect specific features of the landscapes in which they were composed. And while it is true that his discussion of *Das Lied von der Erde* makes reference to its place of composition amongst the 'artificially red cliffs of the Dolomites', Adorno is careful not to propose any direct link between this singular landscape and the musical fabric of this remarkable work.[19] It is nevertheless worth remembering that Mahler's symphonies have long been thought to aspire to the visual, an aspiration that is particularly evident in those passages that invoke the rich tradition of the operatic landscape tableau.

Of course, the presence of landscape imagery in Romantic music was not always bound up with these illustrative modes. Daniel Grimley has been particularly attentive to this issue as it relates to questions of landscape and nationhood in the music of Edvard Grieg, Carl Nielsen, Jean Sibelius, and Frederick Delius. And while for Grimley the idea of landscape in this music is closely tied to broader cultural formations of national identity, he also substantially broadens our understanding of this topic by drawing on perspectives from historical-cultural geography and environmental studies, including a range of ecocritical discourses. In the context of Grieg's music, for example, he has argued persuasively that landscape is not 'merely concerned with pictorial evocation, but is a more broadly environmental discourse, a representation of the sense of being within a particular time and space'.[20] Grimley also encourages us to think of the function of landscape here both as a spatial phenomenon (through associations with pictorial images connected to the Norwegian landscape and the folk traditions of its inhabitants) and as a temporal one (involving historical memory and attempts to recover or reconstruct past events). In his close readings of individual works, he also interrogates their formal properties in a way that forces us to think about landscape not only in terms of the evocation of a particular place, but also in terms of a 'more abstract mode of musical discourse, one grounded in Grieg's music with a particular grammar and syntax'.[21]

Excursus: Making Music in Romantic Art

Nowhere are the connections between nineteenth-century musical culture and the visual and scenic manifested more clearly than in the depiction of music making in Romantic art. Prominent examples include Moritz von Schwind's *Eine Symphonie* (1852) and Gustav Klimt's *Schubert at the Piano* (1899), the former depicting a performance of Beethoven's Choral Fantasy, Op. 80, and the latter offering an idealised portrait of Franz Schubert. In contrast to these composer-centric canvases, the works of the German painter Adolph Menzel are particularly notable for their emphasis on the social dimension of music making. In *The Interruption* (1846), Menzel captures the moment in which a group of unannounced house guests interrupt two young women who have been making music in a lavish drawing room, while in *Clara Schumann and Joseph Joachim in Concert* (1854, Fig. 4.2) the focus is entirely on the two musicians whose studied concentration reflects the intensity of an unfolding performance.[22] More explicit in its diagnosis of music as a social phenomenon is Menzel's *Bilse Concert* (1871, Fig. 4.3). Although the orchestra here occupies a prominent position in the middle of the canvas, Menzel devotes equal space to the audience (at the bottom of the frame) and the candlelit busts of composers who keep silent watch over the performers and their audience (at the top).[23] Finally, in *Flute Concert of Frederick the Great at Sanssouci* (1852,

Figure 4.2 Adolph Menzel (1815–1905), *Clara Schumann and Joseph Joachim in Concert* (1854), coloured chalks, 27 × 33 cm, Private Collection (Wikimedia Commons)

Fig. 4.4), Menzel draws our attention both to the elaborate setting in which the performance takes place and to the absorption of the musicians and auditors in attendance. So popular was this painting that on the occasion of Menzel's seventieth and eightieth birthdays it was transformed into a *tableau vivant*, demonstrating the continued vitality of a tradition that flourished during the nineteenth century as entertainment for the educated middle class.

Contemplating Landscape

Amongst the most important functions of Romantic landscape painting was to provide the viewer with an opportunity to (re)experience the sublimity of the natural world through an act of private contemplation. So central was this impulse to the painterly imagination in the nineteenth century that the act of contemplation would itself become the focus of numerous canvases. This is particularly evident in the tradition of the *Rückenfigur*, in which the

Figure 4.3 Adolph Menzel, *Bilse Concert* (1871), gouache, 17.8 × 12 cm, Kupferstichkabinett, Berlin (bpk Bildagentur / Kupferstichkabinett, Staatliche Museen, Berlin / Jörg P. Anders / Art Resource, NY)

depicted figure is seen from behind. Caspar David Friedrich's *Wanderer above the Sea of Fog* (1818) remains the most representative example of this tradition, while Carl Gustav Carus's *Pilgrim in a Rocky Valley* (c. 1820) offers a useful point of comparison in that it makes explicit the religious dimension often associated with this mode of solitary contemplation. Composers were often depicted in similarly contemplative poses, including in the *Rückenfigur* of Beethoven by Joseph Weidner and Arnold Schoenberg's *Self-Portrait from Behind* (1911).

Figure 4.4 Adolph Menzel, *Flute Concert of Frederick the Great at Sanssouci* (1850–2), oil on canvas, 142 × 205 cm, Alte Nationalgalerie, Berlin (Wikimedia Commons)

In the context of nineteenth-century compositional traditions this mode of private contemplation occupies a particular place of prominence in the genre of the lied. Beethoven's *An die ferne Geliebte* (1816) offers a particularly compelling manifestation of this tendency. In the first song the speaker contemplates the landscape that separates him from his beloved, a present-tense reflection shot through with a sense of melancholy that is carefully matched by Beethoven's setting of the poem's first stanza: 'Upon the hill I sit / Gazing into the blue land of mist / Looking towards the far pastures / Where I found thee, beloved.' But as the speaker begins to dwell on his own isolation, the music takes on an increasing urgency; not in the vocal line, which remains largely the same from stanza to stanza, but rather in the accompaniment, which undergoes a further intensification midway through the final stanza.

This isolation is further highlighted in the cycle's second song, above all in the unusual treatment of the vocal line in the middle stanza. Here the melody is transferred to the piano while the singer declaims the text on a single pitch: 'There in the peaceful valley / Grief and suffering are silenced: / Where in the mass of rocks / The primrose dreams quietly there / The wind blows so lightly / Would I be.' To the extent that this hushed meditation reflects the experience of someone lost in thought, this moment represents a deepening of the cycle's contemplative mode. Yet as we bear witness to the speaker's innermost thoughts, we are also provided with an opportunity to experience the stillness of the landscape by which he is surrounded.

Although the contemplation of nature is often understood to be an act of communion that requires the subject to be quiet, reverent, and immobile, many composers had an active relationship to the landscapes they inhabited. While these composers rarely 'worked' outside in the manner of the *plein-air* painters, they often sketched as they walked. Beethoven's pocket sketchbooks, for example, reveal the extent to which the composer's surroundings inspired creative activity. Mahler, too, is reported to have composed in this manner, sketching out *Das Lied von der Erde* (1908) during the course of his daily walks through the mountain landscapes of the eastern Dolomites.[24] Of course, the idea of traversing a given landscape was thematised in many nineteenth-century works, from Schubert's *Winterreise* (1827) to Schoenberg's *Verklärte Nacht* (1899). In the case of *Verklärte Nacht* our understanding of the sextet's narrative power is shaped in part by the eponymous poem by Richard Dehmel that was included in the first published edition of the score. Indeed, the music ultimately seems to convey the spirit and the sweep of Dehmel's goal-oriented narrative, which begins with an unnamed woman confessing to her partner that the child she is carrying is not his. And while at the outset the night is cold and the landscape bare, through an act of forgiveness and acceptance the night is transfigured and transformed into something that is at once lofty and bright. That the narrative is presented as a nocturnal walk, recounted alternately by the narrator and the unnamed couple, is relevant insofar as the piece not only appears to reflect Dehmel's imagery, but also possesses a musical trajectory that conveys the shifting moods of the poem. Schoenberg would later provide a detailed programme note that offers a literal mapping of poetic image and musical gesture, demonstrating the extent to which he understood this work to operate both at the level of the pictorial and the narrative.[25]

Whereas the musical personae devoted to the contemplation of landscape in Romantic music commonly occupied an elevated perspective (a tradition that runs from Beethoven's *An die ferne Geliebte* to Richard Strauss's *Eine Alpensinfonie* a century later), there is also a parallel tradition running from Schubert to Schoenberg in which the wanderers and walkers are more properly earthbound creatures, far removed from the lofty perspectives of hill and mountaintop. In the early twentieth century this tradition found an unlikely continuation in the music of Charles Ives, a composer whose embrace of the quotidian often seems to suggest a ground-level view of the world as filtered through the eyes and ears of the modern urban subject. Ives's interest in the evocation of place is particularly evident in his orchestral works, where the use of programmatic titles making reference to specific geographical locales is often supplemented by detailed prose descriptions. In *Central Park in the Dark* (1906), Ives's self-described 'picture-in-sounds', the composer aims to capture what might have been heard by an attentive listener 'some thirty or so years ago (before the combustion engine and radio monopolized the earth and air), when sitting on a bench in Central Park on a hot summer night'.[26] In spite of the obvious emphasis here on listening, Ives also provides a succession of richly detailed images that allow the listener to envision the source of the sounds that are being attended to so carefully by the work's unnamed subject.

In 'The "St. Gaudens" in Boston Common (Col. Shaw and his Colored Regiment)', from Ives's *Orchestral Set No. 1: Three Places in New England* (*c.* 1911–14), the act of contemplation once again plays out in the context of an urban landscape. Here the object of contemplation is Augustus Saint-Gaudens's Memorial to Robert Gould Shaw and the Massachusetts Fifty-Fourth Regiment, a high-relief bronze that pays tribute to Shaw and his soldiers, who comprised one of the first African-American regiments to fight for the Union Army during the American Civil War. Perhaps the greatest interpretive challenge posed by Ives's work concerns the question of what exactly this music is attempting to depict. While it is possible to identify a narrative dimension (one that reflects the ill-fated battle at Fort Wagner that culminated in the deaths of Shaw and more than half of his soldiers), when taken together with Ives's accompanying poem this piece might also be heard as a musical response to the memorial itself, one that reflects the 'auditory image of men moving together'.[27]

Finally, in 'From Hanover Square North, at the End of a Tragic Day, the Voice of the People Again Arose' from *Orchestral Set No. 2*, we are presented with a composition that purports to describe an event witnessed by Ives in New York City on the morning of 7 May 1915: namely, the spontaneous reaction of a large crowd of New Yorkers to the reported loss of 1,198 lives in the tragic sinking of the British passenger ship RMS *Lusitania*. The illustrative power of Ives's accompanying note makes it worth quoting at length.

I remember, going downtown to business, the people on the streets and on the elevated train had something in their faces that was not the usual something. Everybody who came into the office, whether they spoke about the disaster or not, showed a realization of seriously experiencing something. (That it meant war is what the faces said, if the tongues didn't.) Leaving the office and going uptown about six o'clock, I took the Third Avenue 'L' at Hanover Square Station. As I came on the platform, there was quite a crowd waiting for the trains, which had been blocked lower down, and while waiting there, a hand-organ or hurdy-gurdy was playing in the street below. Some workmen sitting on the side of the tracks began to whistle the tune, and others began to sing or hum the refrain. A workman with a shovel over his shoulder came on the platform and joined in the chorus, and the next man, a Wall Street banker with white spats and a cane, joined in it, and finally it seemed to me that everybody was singing this tune, and they didn't seem to be singing in fun, but as a natural outlet for what their feelings had been going through all day long. There was a feeling of dignity all through this. The hand-organ man seemed to sense this and wheeled the organ nearer the platform and kept it up fortissimo (and the chorus sounded out as though every man in New York must be joining in it). Then the first train came in and everybody crowded in, and the song gradually died out, but the effect on the crowd still showed. Almost nobody talked – the people acted as though they might be coming out of a church service. In going uptown, occasionally little groups would start singing or humming the tune.[28]

As was the case with *Central Park in the Dark*, there is a clear relationship here between the note's descriptive detail and the work's chaotic surface. But whereas *Central Park in the Dark* looks to an imagined past, *From Hanover Square North* attempts to capture Ives's own lived experience as an eye- and ear-witness to the remarkable event he so eloquently describes in his note. Indeed, Ives creates a musical analogue to the 'multiple, competing aspects of the city' in part by dividing the orchestra into a distant choir and a main orchestra, two distinct ensembles whose relative autonomy creates a 'visual perspective' that allows us to 'hear behind the foreground sounds'.[29] Equally remarkable is the presence of narrative elements that foreground what Ives went on to describe as a desire to convey the 'ever changing multitudinous feeling of life that one senses in the city'.

The Persistence of Romantic Landscape

Whereas Ives's unique approach to the evocation of place may have found few immediate followers, the same cannot be said about the music of his British contemporaries, including Edward Elgar, Ralph Vaughan Williams, and Frederick Delius, who together engaged with this tradition in a particularly influential way during the first half of the twentieth century. Indeed, it is hardly coincidental that more recent generations of British composers have continued to breathe new life into that tradition, including Peter Maxwell Davies (*An Orkney Wedding, with Sunrise* and *Antarctic Symphony*), and Thea Musgrave, whose *Turbulent Landscapes* offers an extension of the Lisztian programmatic ideal. Less obviously illustrative is Jonathan Harvey's . . . *towards a pure land*, a work that nevertheless takes the listener on a journey towards an imagined place that Harvey has described as

a state of mind beyond suffering where there is no grasping. It has also been described in Buddhist literature as landscape – a model of the world to which we can aspire. Those who live there do not experience ageing, sickness or any other suffering . . . The environment is completely pure, clean, and very beautiful, with mountains, lakes, trees and delightful birds.[30]

Despite the staggering plurality of compositional and aesthetic priorities represented by the works of this eclectic group of composers, what binds them together is the extent to which they are part of an ongoing dialogue with musical Romanticism writ large. Indeed, their renewed exploration of the visual and scenic, as well as their engagement with questions surrounding the narrative and expressive qualities of individual works that once dominated discussions of musical representation in the late-eighteenth and early-nineteenth centuries, make clear the continued relevance of these traditions amongst twentieth- and twenty-first-century composers, audiences, and critics.

Notes

1. See in particular Roger Fiske, *Scotland in Music: A European Enthusiasm* (Cambridge: Cambridge University Press, 1983), 116–49; and Thomas S. Grey, 'Fingal's Cave and Ossian's Dream: Music, Image, and Phantasmagoric Audition', in M. L. Morton and P. L. Schmunk (eds.), *The Arts Entwined: Music and Painting in the Nineteenth Century* (New York: Garland, 2000), 63–99.
2. For a particularly sensitive account of these challenges, see Benedict Taylor, 'Seascape in the Mist: Lost in Mendelssohn's *Hebrides*', *19th-Century Music*, 39 (2016), 187–222.
3. The work's title underwent numerous changes, including *Die Hebriden* (The Hebrides), *Ouvertüre zur einsamen Insel* (Overture to the Solitary Island), *The Isles of Fingal*, and *Fingalshöhle* (Fingal's Cave).
4. Richard Will, *The Characteristic Symphony in the Age of Beethoven* (Cambridge: Cambridge University Press, 2002), 1.

5. Lewis Lockwood, *Beethoven's Symphonies: An Artistic Vision* (New York: W. W. Norton & Co., 2015), 128.

6. Ibid.

7. Taylor, 'Seascape in the Mist', 193.

8. Thomas Grey, 'Metaphorical Modes in Nineteenth-Century Music Criticism: Image, Narrative, and Idea', in Steven P. Scher (ed.), *Music and Text: Critical Inquiries* (Cambridge: Cambridge University Press, 1992), 96.

9. Ibid., 96–7.

10. Ibid., 97.

11. Franz Brendel, 'Robert Schumann with Reference to Mendelssohn-Bartholdy and the Development of Modern Music in General', trans. Jürgen Thym, in R. Larry Todd (ed.), *Schumann and His World* (Princeton: Princeton University Press, 1994), 322–3.

12. Berthold Hoeckner, 'Schumann and Romantic Distance', *Journal of the American Musicological Society*, 50 (1997), 96.

13. Carl Dahlhaus, *Nineteenth-Century Music*, trans. J. B. Robinson (Berkeley and Los Angeles: University of California Press, 1989), 307. The term, which can be traced to Ernst Kurth's *Musikpsychologie* (1931; 1947) was developed by Monika Lichtenfeld in connection with the music of Wagner and Mahler. See Lichtenfeld, 'Zur technik der Klangflächenkomposition bei Wagner', in Carl Dahlhaus (ed.), *Das Drama Richard Wagners als musikalisches Kunstwerk* (Regensburg: G. Bosse, 1970), 161–7, and 'Zur Klangflächentechnik bei Mahler', in P. Ruzicka (ed.), *Mahler – eine Herausforderung: Ein Symposion* (Wiesbaden: Breitkopf & Härtel, 1977), 21–34.

14. Dahlhaus, *Nineteenth-Century Music*, 307.

15. Ibid.

16. Bruno Walter, *Gustav Mahler*, trans. L. Walter Lindt (New York: Schocken Books, 1974), 28.

17. Natalie Bauer-Lechner, *Recollections of Gustav Mahler*, trans. Dika Newlin, ed. Peter Franklin (Cambridge: Cambridge University Press, 1980), 52.

18. Ibid., 52–3.

19. Theodor W. Adorno, *Mahler: A Musical Physiognomy*, trans. E. Jephcott (Chicago: Chicago University Press, 1992), 149.

20. Daniel M. Grimley, *Grieg: Music, Landscape and Norwegian Identity* (Woodbridge: Boydell Press, 2006), 57.

21. Ibid., 108.

22. See Claude Keisch and Marie-Ursula Riemann-Reyher (eds.), *Adolf Menzel, 1815–1905: Between Modernism and Impressionism* (New Haven, CT: Yale University Press, 1996), 270–2.

23. Ibid., 355–6.

24. Alma Mahler, *Gustav Mahler: Memories and Letters*, ed. Donald Mitchell and Knud Martner, trans. Basil Creighton, 4th ed. (London: Cardinal, 1990), 123.

25. The programme is reproduced in Joseph Auner (ed.), *The Schoenberg Reader* (New Haven, CT: Yale University Press, 2003), 38–40.

26. Charles Ives, *Central Park in the Dark* (Hillsdale, NY: Mobart Music Publications, 1978), 31.

27. Stuart Feder, *Charles Ives, 'My Father's Song': A Psychoanalytic Biography* (New Haven, CT: Yale University Press, 1992), 232.

28. Charles E. Ives, *Memos*, ed. J. Kirkpatrick (New York: W. W. Norton, 1972), 92–3.

29. Denise von Glahn, 'From Country to City in the Music of Charles Ives', in *The Sounds of Place: Music and the American Cultural Landscape* (Boston, MA: Northeastern University Press, 2003), 94.

30. Quoted in Michael Downes, *Jonathan Harvey: Song Offerings and White as Jasmine* (Farnham: Ashgate, 2009), 121.

Further Reading

Bohlman, Philip V. 'Landscape – Region – Nation – Reich: German Folk Song in the Nexus of National Identity', in Celia Applegate and Pamela Potter (eds.), *Music and German National Identity* (Chicago: Chicago University Press, 2002), 105–27.

Bullock, Philip Ross. 'Lyric and Landscape in Rimsky Korsakov's Songs', *19th-Century Music*, 40 (2017), 223–38.

Burnham, Scott. 'Landscape as Music, Landscape as Truth: Schubert and the Burden of Repetition', *19th-Century Music*, 29 (2005), 31–41.

Dolp, Laura. 'Between Pastoral and Nature: Beethoven's *Missa Solemnis* and the Landscapes of Caspar David Friedrich', *Journal of Musicological Research*, 27 (2008), 205–25.

Grey, Thomas. '*Tableaux-Vivants*: Landscape, History Painting, and the Visual Imagination in Mendelssohn's Orchestral Music', *19th-Century Music*, 21 (1997), 38–76.

Grimley, Daniel M. *Delius and the Sound of Place* (Cambridge: Cambridge University Press, 2018).

 Grieg: Music, Landscape and Norwegian Identity (Woodbridge: Boydell Press, 2006).

 '"In the Mood": *Peer Gynt* and the Affective Landscapes of Grieg's *Stemninger*, op. 73', *19th-Century Music*, 40 (2016), 106–30.

Johnson, Julian. 'Mahler and the Idea of Nature', in Jeremy Barham (ed.), *Perspectives on Gustav Mahler* (Aldershot: Ashgate, 2005), 23–36.

Morton, Marsha L. and Schmunk, Peter L. (eds.). *The Arts Entwined: Music and Painting in the Nineteenth Century* (New York: Garland, 2000).

Peattie, Thomas. *Gustav Maher's Symphonic Landscapes* (Cambridge: Cambridge University Press, 2015).

Rosen, Charles. 'Mountains and Song Cycles', in *The Romantic Generation* (Cambridge, MA: Harvard University Press, 1995), 116–236.

Taylor, Benedict. 'Seascape in the Mist: Lost in Mendelssohn's Hebrides', *19th-Century Music*, 39 (2016), 187–222.

Volioti, Georgia. 'Landscaping the Gaze in Norwegian Visual Art and Grieg's Op. 66 Folksong Piano Arrangements', *Music & Letters*, 98 (2017), 573–600.

von Glahn, Denise. *The Sounds of Place: Music and the American Cultural Landscape* (Boston, MA: Northeastern University Press, 2003).

5 | Romanticism, the Folk, and Musical Nationalisms

MATTHEW GELBART

Less ink has been spilled over musical nationalism than blood over political nationalism – but a great deal of ink nonetheless. And arguably some blood, for the two phenomena are closely linked. Musical nationalism has supported and been supported by political nationalism: in the nineteenth century an opera performance could be the catalyst for a revolution, or a tone poem could rally the pride of a politically prostrate nation. Musical nationalism is clearly a Romantic concept – not just because modern nationalism and musical Romanticism are systems of thought that emerged contemporaneously, but because of a common idea at their nexus: 'the folk'. It is a concept that depends on both Romanticism and nationalism to make sense, and which in return has undergirded musical nationalism. Indeed, in English, German, Russian, and other languages, 'national music' and 'folk music' began as synonyms. Over the long nineteenth century 'national' and 'nationalist' music were terms that frequently came to apply to types of art music. Yet they never separated fully from 'folk music'. Evaluations of the 'national' characteristics of art composers such as Grieg or Glinka have frequently fastened on the perceived connection to folk music in their work. At other times, the connection is less direct. The iconic national status of Beethoven or Verdi, for example, has nominally been built on carrying forward traditions rather removed from folk music. And yet 'the folk' still lurk underneath, an indelible legacy of Romanticism.

The Nation

To unravel this knot, we should begin by tracing the history of the ideas themselves. Most historians agree that, in the form in which it has been disseminated around the world, nationalism was a phenomenon born in the eighteenth century.[1] Earlier ideas of 'nation', 'liberty', and 'self-government' were tied to feudal fealty and competition. It was only when the idea of divine right was rejected that those who would govern had to find new answers to the question of what united 'a people' under their government. If, as Jean-Jacques Rousseau argued, government was a social contract, then who should be bound together by or excluded from such an arrangement? The answer came in appeals to (and sometimes dogged invention of) a shared culture that could become central to 'national' identities: languages, laws, religious customs, literature – and artistic products. 'Cultural' and 'political' nationalism have thus always been two sides of the same coin, the latter reliant on identities built up by the former. Since these identities included music, the first real assertions of ethno-national ownership of musical styles, techniques, and traditions date to the early eighteenth century.[2]

Such appeals to shared culture became many times stronger, however, when they could evoke ancient, mythical origins. By the second half of the eighteenth century, Europeans were increasingly encountering cultures very different from their own. More importantly, they had begun conceiving such cultures not simply as heathen outsiders of a divine order they themselves represented, but as frozen earlier stages of humanity on its fixed path away from 'nature' and towards modernity – stages they believed their own cultures to have passed through as well. These European ethnocentric understandings of human development were shared by so-called pro- and anti-Enlightenment thinkers, despite the fact that the former saw 'progress' towards the European present as positive and the latter saw it as an intangible loss. In terms of nationalism, however, it was the latter 'Romantic' viewpoint that most frequently shaped the discourse, because when proto-Romantic thinkers such as Rousseau began to envision modern civilisation as representing a breach with a purer, more natural human past – for which they yearned nostalgically – the idea of 'authenticity' emerged.[3] Tracing cultural traditions backwards towards hoary natural ethnic roots could add a great essentialist force to any national claims.

The Folk and Their Music

The idea of 'the folk' originates from just this urge. Europeans found 'the folk' the moment they conceived of the natural, 'primitive' Other not abroad but within their own midst: as pure peasants untouched by the corrupting forces of industrialisation, urbanisation, and modernity in general. These people, seen as living preservations of any nation's past, were first 'discovered in plain sight' on the geographic edge of Europe, in the Scottish Highlands. The apparent unearthing by James Macpherson of pre-Christian epics by the Celtic bard Ossian still living in oral tradition catalysed a discussion across Europe about the potential of isolated groups to create and to preserve delicate literature and music without writing. From a modern point of view, Macpherson was a fraud. He had assembled into a coherent whole his English 'translations' from diverse oral fragments of Gaelic poetry he had picked up, modifying them and adding the connective tissue to make them narrative epics. But these facts did not diminish the cultural earthquake caused by the Ossian publications in the 1760s. The debates they immediately spurred about non-literate creativity, collective creation versus modern reproduction, and the reliability and power of oral tradition spread across the continent, playing a prominent role in establishing modern standards of authorship and authenticity in the first place.

Since rural oral poetry, including Ossianic poetry, was generally sung, it is no surprise that the term 'national music' – tied to these authentic 'natural' roots of a culture – entered the English language in the disputes around Ossian. It meant something close to our term 'folk music', which is actually a later retranslation of 'national music' back into English. Johann Gottfried Herder, the early Romantic Prussian thinker who coined the word *Volkslied*, first introduced it in a 1773 essay on Ossian, as a translation of 'national song'.[4] *Volk* in German captured the mystical collective properties of nationalism perfectly – like the Slavic *narod*, it can be rendered in English as 'people', 'folk', or 'nation' in different contexts. After Herder, discourse on *narodnaya* song and music seeped into Slavic languages (and decades later, 'folk song' and 'folk music' seeped slowly into English). The expanding vocabulary indicated the international potential of the ideas: Herder's foray into the Ossian debate had been motivated by his ardent belief that pure, authentic rural groups similar to the Scottish Highlanders could be found all over Europe ('we Germans too' had them, he gushed). He had encouraged literate Europeans to collect folk poetry and song from every nation, and a year later (1774) published the first edition of his own international collection, soon retitled *Volkslieder*.[5] As if in answer to Herder's call, other collections – such as Achim von Arnim and Clemens Brentano's famous *Des Knaben Wunderhorn* – rapidly followed, in Germany and beyond.

The understandings of the relationships between words and music in these Ur-Romantic collections also exposed typical Romantic thought patterns. Mid-eighteenth-century thinkers – such as Condillac, Monboddo, Rousseau, and Herder – had begun to argue that 'music' in some form was a primal medium of communication prior to language.[6] Versions of this theory became extremely influential (resurfacing in Darwin's work and even modern evolutionary theory), and led to the famous Romantic cliché that music was a 'universal' or 'natural' language, which helps explain why many published collections of national song across Europe, such as those just mentioned, contained words but no music. For many editors, the lack of printed music in no way indicated its lack of import. Just the opposite: there was more effort expended on pinning down on paper specific, sanctioned versions of the words of songs because collectors assumed that the music needed less help to spread intact orally across time and space. Music could perpetuate itself naturally and primally – as a more direct and untutored expression of the soul. The same assumption guided the famous national song collectors of the period who *did* print both words and music (e.g., Vasily Fyodorovich Trutovsky and then Nikolay Lvov and Ivan Prach in Russia; Robert Burns and his partners in Scotland; and Johann Friedrich Reichardt and others in Germany; or later Théodore Hersart de la Villemarqué in France).[7] In their editorial decisions and in their prefatory material they made it clear that they too considered words subject to 'decay' in oral transmission amongst the national populace (often because they came upon bawdy texts where they had hoped for idealised 'national' poetry). They assumed that the different versions of texts they found could be traced back to a single high-quality original representing the nation's natural values. With music, however, the same collectors were prepared to accept different variants and even allow that continued changes in oral tradition could lead to equally 'authentic' versions. By the middle of the nineteenth century, folklorists acquiesced to a similar idea of valid variants in living tradition in other media (poetry, stories, myths, etc.);[8] but early on, 'national music' had a particular cachet, worthy of the generally high status of (ineffable) music amongst the arts in Romantic ideologies.

National Art Music: Old Cultivated Traditions versus New National Schools

Despite these common assumptions, the national implications of music varied heavily from place to place. In the roughest terms, claims over music as national cultural capital split into two types based on the strength of local traditions of educated, cultivated music. In France as well as (the future) Italy and Germany, there were centuries-old religious and operatic training systems that had created musical styles far removed from those of the rural 'folk'. The funding, organisation, and achievements of such well-established educational and professional traditions could themselves be staked out as national property. Indeed, German nationalists had even more: the recent explosion of prestigious instrumental music from Vienna and the North could be newly leveraged as a cultivated heritage allowing Germany to bid for musical dominance against its neighbours in specifically 'Romantic' terms. Champions of modern German composition increasingly framed 'pure' instrumental music as the most direct window into the human psyche (a twist on the idea of music's primacy discussed in the previous paragraph).[9] As several of the other chapters in this volume touch upon, promoters could frame this music – full of modern artistic ambition but devoid of words that might tie it directly to a particular time and place, even to a particular language – as 'universal'. And yet, as the same writers pointed out happily, it was the Germans who had led the way.

Meanwhile, unlike the musical 'centres' above, most nations in the rest of Europe, and many others around the world, could not claim well-funded professional musical traditions as their cultural property. Whether through proximity to the dominant musical nations or through political subjugation, these musically 'peripheral' nations, to the extent that they supported elite music making, had historically sent their 'best and brightest' to the metropoles to be educated or had imported educators from those centres. Their trained musicians thereby found themselves in a weak position to argue that they represented autochthonous culture. Instead – as we might expect given the centrality of 'the folk' in nationalist discourse – bourgeois nationalists in such places directly promoted 'national music' in its original 'folk' sense. They collected and published 'their' rural traditional music with particular purpose and speed.

In the longer term, however, this focus proved unsatisfactory to professionally ambitious nationalist musicians. Romanticism might almost be defined through an obsession with organic metaphors, and so it was with the folk. Despite their importance, the folk were consistently framed as relics. Pure and authentic, they could stand as the organic *roots* of nations, but not as the blossoms and sprouts of a nation's modern achievement on the international stage. For this reason, as Romantic nationalism spread, each musically 'peripheral' nation soon sought to build upon its distinctive folk-musical roots a modern, individualist, elite compositional tradition, what came to be called a national 'school' of music.

National schools were both figurative (educational traditions) and often literal (conservatory buildings in the urban centres of the aspirant nations). They aimed to show young musicians how to integrate their nations' unique and 'authentic' folk roots with international professional standards – or vice versa depending on the emphasis. The schools were responsible for a long list of composers that come to mind when people speak of 'nationalism in music'. Amongst the earliest areas to adopt the school approach were Eastern Europe and Scandinavia (giving us Mikhail Glinka, Niels Gade, Frédéric Chopin, Franz Liszt, Bedřich Smetana, Edvard Grieg, the Russian 'Mighty Handful', Jean Sibelius, etc.). By the later nineteenth century the same approach had spread through the British Isles (Edward Elgar, Ralph Vaughan Williams, etc.), the Iberian peninsula (Enrique Granados, Manuel de Falla, etc.) and to the United States (including, famously, Jeanette Thurber's invitation to Dvořák to run her National Conservatory in New York – to some it seemed necessary initially to import a European 'nationalist' to teach Americans how to mine their own 'folk' material for national 'art' music).[10] The trend reached most countries in the Americas (Antônio Carlos Gomes, Heitor Villa-Lobos, Carlos Chávez, Alberto Ginastera) and continued through the twentieth century and even beyond, carrying on the legacy of Romanticism in many modern postcolonial African and Asian nations, especially if they were multiethnic constructions without their own long-established 'classical' musical traditions from precolonial days to unify them (Fela Sowande, Lucrecia Kasilag).[11]

Musicians from national schools seemed liberated to create fusion styles that could join a national past and present, collective folk 'authenticity' and individual, original artistic 'genius' – thus fulfilling a Romantic ideal nearly perfectly. As Carl Dahlhaus noted, art music 'prompted to harmonic [or other stylistic] experiment by procedures or material originating in folk music was on the one hand technically progressive', while on the other hand potentially immediate in its popular appeal; it thus 'seemed to suspend or resolve the conflict between the avant-garde and popular taste'.[12] Composers from the national schools engrained themselves successfully in local histories, becoming heroes in many cases. The main airports in the capitals Warsaw and Budapest are still named after Chopin and Liszt respectively.

Centre and Periphery as a Covert Value System

At the same time, the power structure (cultural and political) that rendered these nations musically peripheral in the first place also worked against the international reputations of their star composers in ways both obvious and more insidious. By the mid-nineteenth century the musical hegemony of

Germany was complete in terms of prestige. Influential German writers and critics had relentlessly extended their claims for the 'universal' qualities of German *instrumental* music to assert that German music in general was the most universal – an argument buoyed by claims that German culture overall took the best of all others and synthesised it. Through this process, German art music took the role of the 'unmarked norm': even as the shared standards themselves were framed as German achievements, they provided the rules and set the aspirational goalposts and criteria against which all other music would come to be measured. Richard Taruskin has outlined a 'double bind' that musicians born outside these traditions accordingly faced. If they observed the dominant rules fully and wrote music that sounded German (and hence, 'neutral' or 'universal'), they would be denigrated as non-German imitators of German music, unable to create their own sounds. But if they worked *only* with local traditions, they would be ignored on the international stage, seen merely as representatives of 'primitive' foreign music. The 'school' approach was thus their logical recourse; it played up exotic 'folk' elements from their respective nations that set them apart – using those features, as Dahlhaus outlined, to create a 'modern' hybrid with the international standard. Yet however successful this strategy was locally within the nations that used it, it nevertheless allowed the German critics who made the rules to stop short of awarding such composers the highest, 'universal' status given to Bach, Mozart, or Beethoven.[13]

Even the vocabulary quietly indicated the hierarchy: 'National(ist) music' in common parlance came to mean peripheral music. Towering figures of German musical prose as different as Robert Schumann, Eduard Hanslick, and Richard Wagner all argued in different ways that musical 'nationalism' itself was provincial, because music should be universal. As Wagner put it, other countries' music (both folk and art music) was 'national' (i.e., local), while Germany's was 'purely human'.[14] The irony of manifesting German nationalism by decrying musical 'nationalism', akin to those in privileged positions in our times decrying 'identity politics' on the assumption that their dominant position is not itself an identity, perpetuated itself as Germans went on to found the modern discipline of musicology and determine its foundations internationally. Until quite recently, Wagner, and to a lesser extent Verdi, because they represented central traditions, were included in 'mainstream' chapters of textbooks, somehow separate from the sections on 'nationalists'. It has taken the development of new approaches for nationalism to be considered in a more balanced light.[15]

Complicated Realities

Wagner's own music makes clear another issue: despite the general trend for 'peripheral' composers to rely more on 'folk music' to build their national claims and 'central' composers to rely more on adherence to educated national traditions, there was actually a great deal of variation in this respect from composer to composer and even within the output of single artists. The extent to which a given composer used pre-existing melodies or even folk-like melodies to evoke nationalism, and the extent to which a given composer allowed such 'folk' styles to alter or create a personal style, was not entirely predictably correlated to the centre–periphery opposition outlined above.

First of all, because of its centrality to broader nationalist claims, the 'folk' retained a kind of talismanic importance even in nations with strong traditions of cultivated music. This is certainly true of Germany. The very idea of organically integrating folk roots into individual modern art (indeed the entire Romantic obsession with organicism and organic metaphors, joining biology and the arts) was of German Romantic origin. Herder's greatest influence in forming the modern international idea of 'folk song' was not creating the term (*Volkslied* was a translation from English after all), but rather his suggestion that *Volkslied* was valuable not (or not only) in its own right, but as 'raw material' for individual Romantic artists. As I have argued elsewhere, the Romantic idea of 'art music' is thus itself built on a contrast with 'folk music' – a binarism that was not an equal opposition but involved the organic integration of one into the other.[16]

Thus, depending on which Romantic strands a German nationalist picked up, different approaches to the folk presented themselves. Whereas Hanslick's nationalism drew upon idealist philosophy to argue for cultivated traditions of instrumental music as the German achievement of universality (he had little time for 'national melodies' as 'art'), Wagner internalised a notion of art music as dependent organically on the folk. He accordingly sought to emphasise any connection to the folk that he could find in Beethoven's music, as a stepping stone to his own. The anchor of his argument was the 'Ode to Joy' in the Ninth Symphony, which he framed as an assimilation of the spirit of German folk song – a folk song by Beethoven himself. By thus defining 'the folk' as including any composers who organically absorbed the spirit of their people (and united words and music, as 'the folk' did when composing), he could make similar claims about the folk roots of his own music dramas, however far-fetched those claims usually were in terms of sonic resemblance to any German music in oral tradition.[17]

On the other side of the coin, there were composers born on the 'periphery' who were not particularly interested in 'folk music'. Chopin, for example, was generally most concerned with furthering the cosmopolitan elite piano traditions he found in his adoptive homeland of France. He wrote some character pieces that were 'national' dances (the Polonaises and Mazurkas), but long-standing attempts to find direct connection between their sounds and Polish peasant music have been shown up as rather strained.[18] And Grieg himself was compelled to rebut the constant search for folk music in his work, denying, in later life, that he had had in-depth knowledge of peasant music when he wrote his earlier compositions that people often claimed were folk-inspired, and instead opting for a different typical nationalist argument: that his music already sounded Norwegian simply because he was organically Norwegian.[19]

Another factor complicating relationships between 'the folk' and 'national music' is the presence of racial minorities within ethnically conceived nations. Notably, for example, in both Hungary and Spain, the Roma and Calé/Gitano ethnic minorities (the so-called 'Gypsies') over centuries contributed strongly to the styles that were picked up as essentially 'national' by the Romantics.[20] The cognitive dissonance this caused amongst nationalists was resolved in one of two ways. They could recognise Romani contributions but relegate them to the role of wild, untrained 'natural music' – again organic 'roots' that magically created something beautiful but needed the majority population to blossom into a modern national symbol. (This is how Liszt framed the 'Gypsy' style as Hungarian national music, and it points to how both peasants and minorities could be viewed as 'noble savages'.) Alternatively, nationalists could use notions of (racial) purity to lead a backlash, searching to find national music roots not 'corrupted' by the 'foreign' Romani influence. These might be a different body of 'authentic' peasant folk music (in Hungary, this approach culminated with Bartók's fieldwork, prose, and composition) or might be educated 'national' art music of the past (such as in Spain, when nationalists sought to oust Andalusian flamenco as the national musical symbol). One historiographical model, then, allowed Romani musicians to play the role of the fertile but unthinking, naïve folk inventors; the other excluded them completely. In neither is the minority population read as possessing agency and intellectual development of its own as part of the modern nation.

Questions about the music of ethnic minorities can be reframed as part of a larger thorny issue: national claims to music may be based on the (supposed) first origins of melodic material amongst an authentic folk, but they may also be based on later 'domestic' developments in imported, internationally shared, or minority-sourced material. Generally, nationalists have seized on whichever answer allowed the majority ethnic group to get credit. Certainly, this was true in the above cases involving Romani music. This trend was exacerbated when multi-ethnic and settler colonial nations developed their own musical nationalisms. For example, White American nationalists have historically barred the musical contributions of Black Americans from representing 'national' culture by calling them 'foreign' (African), or mere 'developments' of White styles (thus placing the 'national' at the point of supposed origins). *Or* just the opposite: Black music was allowed as valid American folk 'roots' but in need of 'development' into art by the White population or traditions (thus placing the 'national' as evolution).[21]

Reception Methods for Reading Music as National since the Romantic Era

Both the ability of influential arbiters sometimes to embrace origins and other times to embrace subsequent development as national, and the ability of audiences and scholars to posit folk music connections regardless of their tenuousness, highlight the mediated aspect of folk and national claims. Ultimately, as recent scholarship has noted, the national has always been in the eye (and ear) of the beholder.[22] Aspects read as national in a piece of music vary in degree and kind at different geographical and chronological points in its existence, and for different audiences. It thus seems helpful to consider five common reception methods (often also internalised by composers) through which music has since the Romantic era been perceived or claimed as national. All may be used by insiders or by outsiders of a national culture, but that distinction may lead to very different reactions to the claims.

1) The **creator(s)** of a piece can be framed as a source of national pride, as representations of their countries, by simple virtue of being from there. Such creators can be 'the folk' as a group (Irish peasants as the original creators of Irish national music), or individuals (Beethoven the German; Verdi the Italian). This approach also allowed Romantic nationalists to claim local figures who lived before the era of nationalism too (Bach the German, Palestrina the Italian, O'Carolan the

Irishman). It also encompasses debates about when minority groups, expatriates, and so forth count as 'national'.

2) The linguistic or musical **materials** of a piece can be seen as national heritage. This may involve the words set to music, but it may also be a question of collective claims to musical **style** (e.g., the pervasive use of motivic development seen as 'German') or musical **idioms** (such as the harmonies or rhythms typical of a national folk song or dance repertoire) including when these idioms are perceived in 'art music' that builds on folk origins (as with claims about Chopin's mazurkas). Musical **genres** may also be framed as nationally representative (e.g., *opéra comique* as the French 'national genre').

3) The **values** of a piece can be framed as representative of a nation, drawing on homologies between national cultures and their musical products (e.g., German music seen by German critics as 'serious', 'masculine', and 'rational' like the German people; Italian music seen by Italians as full of a gift for melody like the Italian people; French music seen by the French as showing clarity and wit like the French people; both French and Italian music seen by the Germans as 'feminine' and 'bodily').[23] Particular composers and performers may be seen as embodying those values (Beethoven as 'manly' for so many critics).

4) The **subject matter** of music, such as opera plots or open or secret programmes in instrumental music, can relate to a national event, hero, myth, or landscape (e.g., Sibelius's *Finlandia*; Grieg's *Peer Gynt*; Wagner's *Meistersinger* as German history). But note that even something as supposedly simple as topical plots were filtered through radically different perceptions. Thus many of Verdi's early and middle operas were read retrospectively as thinly veiled Italian nationalist parables.[24] Chopin's Ballade Op. 38 could be read as encoding a story of the crushing of Poland – but to radically different degrees by Polish audiences in Poland, Polish audiences in Paris, and French artists sympathetic to Poland's plight.[25] That the duet 'Sacred Love for the Fatherland' from (the French) Auber's opera *La Muette de Portici* (about Spanish rule over Naples) sparked brawls that spilled out of the opera house during a (Brussels) performance two years after the premiere, and led to the Belgian Revolution of 1830, is entirely due to the ability of audiences to filter pieces to apply topically or allegorically to themselves.

5) The **uses** of melodies or pieces (on their initial appearance or even much later), especially by governments and institutions, can make them into important national symbols. These uses create meanings that stick

to music indefinitely in many cases. Examples here include twentieth-century applications of Romantic music, such as Nazi use of *Die Meistersinger* in film and rallies, or the use of Elgar's 'Nimrod' on Remembrance Sunday in Britain. More immediately, they include the general case of national anthems, themselves a phenomenon dating from the Romantic era, due to their appeals to a people or folk.[26]

These reception methods can support each other or be combined, of course, but they can also be pitted against each other rhetorically at different times, depending on the needs of different interlocutors.

A Case Study: *The Moldau*

We might instructively end with a brief case study that looks at the different variables in flux. Bedřich Smetana was, according to legend, inspired to father the 'Czech school' of composition by a slight from an Austrian who stated that the Czechs were good musicians but had no creative identity separate from Germanic music; Smetana cemented this role through his operas on national themes, such as *Libuše* (which opened the Czech national theatre in 1881), and also by his cycle of tone poems *Má vlast* (*My Fatherland*), the second of which, *Vltava* (*The Moldau*), was written at a feverish pace in late 1874.

At the most obvious level, this programmatic piece focuses on reception method 4 above (subject matter) as the key to nationalism. In this case, landscape weaves together and binds various other symbols of the nation: the Vltava is the Czech national river, beginning from springs in the south of the country and eventually flowing grandly through Prague before emptying into the Labe (Elbe). This aspect (which ties the piece to the historical and geographical subjects of the other works in *Má vlast*) was immediately recognised as 'national'. Smetana's programme is labelled into the score; it traces the river from its sources, which are illustrated by trickling watery adumbrations of the main theme (Ex. 5.1) before that famous melody bursts forth (Ex. 5.2). The piece then follows a rondo form, the main 'flowing Moldau' theme alternating with depictions of what the river snakes past: a woodland hunt, a rustic wedding, the water nymphs of Czech mythology playing in the moonlight, and St John's rapids. The final section, in which the river 'flows grandly' into Prague past the Vyšehrad, the old fortress above the banks, converts the main theme to major for its apotheosis and briefly quotes the motive of *Vyšehrad*, the previous tone poem in the collection.

Example 5.1 Smetana, *Vltava* (1874), from *Má vlast*, opening, bb. 1–6

Example 5.2 Smetana, *Vltava*, main theme, bb. 39–47

But the programme's subject matter is tied to other 'national' connotations. Notably, nationalist music journalists immediately claimed a close connection to Czech folk song for the piece (reception method 2). One early reviewer called the broad main melody itself 'a naively simple motive of Czech folk song'. Another, arguing that '*Czech* folk song' was an 'endlessly minable source' that must be the basis for any Czech national [art] music, claimed that it was, admirably, the basis for the entire piece here.[27] In fact, it is unclear whether Smetana's main melody was drawn directly from any existent Czech folk song (unlikely), whether it in fact *became* taken up as a children's song (changed to major as 'The Cat Crawls through the Hole', Ex. 5.3), or whether it (like the cat song) simply mimics a whole family of very similar tunes in use in both 'folk' and art music across Europe – not least in Sweden where Smetana had recently been living and was probably familiar with a very similar minor version of the melody.[28] Nevertheless, it was clearly important to early nationalist audiences (and to many since) that the melodic materials be seen as fundamentally Czech and of folk origin – specifically or abstractly. An interesting aspect of the piece is that the riverside wedding episode, which presents a peasant dance melody, a polka (which, despite its name, is a Czech national dance, see Ex. 5.4), in fact uses stylised 'folk music' *as* landscape: it becomes part of the sounds and sights along the river – like shepherds in a rural landscape painting.

Example 5.3 'The Cat Crawls through the Hole', Czech children's song

Example 5.4 Smetana, *Vltava*, polka, bb. 122–30

At the same time, the piece needed to stand for Czech modernity, and here genre and artistic values came to the fore. Tone poems were specifically associated with the 'New German' School – and it took some contortion from Czech nationalists to reclaim the genre as appropriate for Czech art music. Smetana's champions did so by arguing that the Czechs were uniquely capable of *developing* the genre, thereby demonstrating Czech presence amongst the most 'modern' nations (reception method 3) and Czech 'readiness' for increasing political independence within the Hapsburg empire.[29] In this context, it was particularly important to affirm Smetana's own 'Czechness' (reception method 1), despite the fact that he was mainly a German speaker (hence the insistence on the Czechness of the folk-musical materials, and on Smetana's intimate familiarity with Czech folksong). The movements of *Má vlast* could thus be presented and read as organically integrating 'natural' elements of the Czech lands – landscape and folksong – with internationally competitive modern composition techniques perfected on

Czech soil, by a Czech. Such instrumental music was ideally poised (even more than Smetana's Czech operas, which, tied to the Czech language, had their greatest impact domestically) for exhibition on the international stage.

Finally, Czech institutions have continued to use Smetana's work as national symbolism (reception method 5). Indeed, *Má vlast* has served almost as a shibboleth. Public announcements in Prague's train station are cued by the short motive of *Vyšehrad*, and on Czech Airlines flights *The Moldau* has been piped briefly over the speakers to announce arrival in Prague. In this layered history we can see how Romantic claims of an organic relationship between nineteenth-century composition techniques and a national 'folk' can be parlayed though the creation and reception of one composition.

Notes

1. See, e.g., Ernest Gellner, *Nations and Nationalism* (Ithaca, NY: Cornell University Press, 1983); Eric Hobsbawm, *Nations and Nationalism since 1780: Programme, Myth, Reality* (Cambridge: Cambridge University Press, 1990); Benedict Anderson, *Imagined Communities: Reflections on the Origin and Spread of Nationalism*, 3rd ed. (London and New York: Verso, 2006).

2. See Matthew Gelbart, 'Allan Ramsay, the Idea of "Scottish Music" and the Beginnings of "National Music" in Europe', *Eighteenth-Century Music*, 9/1 (2012), 81–108.

3. See esp. Regina Bendix, *In Search of Authenticity: The Formation of Folklore Studies* (Madison: University of Wisconsin Press, 1997).

4. See Matthew Gelbart, *The Invention of 'Folk Music' and 'Art Music': Emerging Categories from Ossian to Wagner* (Cambridge: Cambridge University Press, 2007), esp. chapters 2–3; also Philip V. Bohlman, *Song Loves the Masses: Herder on Music and Nationalism* (Berkeley and Los Angeles: University of California Press, 2017).

5. Johann Gottfried Herder, *Sämmtliche Werke*, ed. Bernhard Suphan, 33 vols. (Berlin: Weidmann, 1877–1913), vol. 5, 174, 189.

6. See Downing Thomas, *Music and the Origins of Language: Theories from the French Enlightenment* (Cambridge: Cambridge University Press, 1995).

7. See Matthew Gelbart, '"The Language of Nature": Music as Historical Crucible for the Methodology of Folkloristics', *Ethnomusicology*, 53/3 (2009), 363–95.

8. Music collection thus presented the archetype of the methodology that later came to underlie all folkloristics (ibid.).

9. See, e.g., Mary Sue Morrow, *German Music Criticism in the Late Eighteenth Century: Aesthetic Issues in Instrumental Music* (Cambridge: Cambridge University Press, 1997), esp. chapter 3.

10. See also Douglas Shadle, *Orchestrating the Nation: The Nineteenth-Century American Symphonic Enterprise* (New York: Oxford University Press, 2015).

11. As an example of the dilemmas involved in this process in a postcolonial context, see Christi-Anne Castro, *Musical Renderings of the Philippine Nation* (New York: Oxford University Press, 2011).

12. Carl Dahlhaus, 'Nationalism in Music', in *Between Romanticism and Modernism: Four Studies in the Music of the Later Nineteenth Century*, trans. Mary Whittall (Berkeley and Los Angeles: University of California Press, 1980), 99.

13. Richard Taruskin, *Defining Russia Musically: Historical and Hermeneutical Essays* (Princeton: Princeton University Press, 1997), 48; see also Taruskin, 'Nationalism', in *The New Grove Dictionary of Music and Musicians*, esp. sections 4, 10–11.

14. Richard Wagner, *Richard Wagner's Prose Works*, trans. William Ashton Ellis (London: Kegan Paul, 1892–9), vol. 2, 48–54.

15. A good summary and list of further references is in Matthew Riley and Anthony D. Smith, *Nation and Classical Music: From Handel to Copland* (Woodbridge: Boydell, 2016), 1–2.

16. See Gelbart, *'Folk Music' and 'Art Music'*, 102–10, 191–203. Also Benjamin W. Curtis, *Music Makes the Nation: Nationalist Composers and Nation Building in Nineteenth-Century Europe* (Amherst: Cambria, 2008), esp. chapter 3.

17. *Richard Wagner's Prose Works*, 107; Gelbart, *'Folk Music' and 'Art Music'*, chapter 6.

18. See Barbara Milewski, 'Chopin's Mazurkas and the Myth of the Folk', *19th-Century Music*, 23/2 (1999), 113–35.

19. See Piero Weiss and Richard Taruskin (eds.), *Music in the Western World: A History in Documents*, 2nd ed. (New York: Schirmer, 2007), 350–1.

20. For a short overview, see Anna Piotrowska, *Gypsy Music in European Culture: From the Late Eighteenth to the Early Twentieth Centuries* (Boston, MA: Northeastern University Press, 2013), 15–85.

21. See, e.g., Henry Finck, 'Creative Americans', in *The Outlook*, 22 December 1906, 983–9. Similar issues have gone on to underlie writing about jazz (as a kind of art music as well), rock, and other Black styles as American 'national' culture.

22. See, e.g., Michael Beckerman, 'In Search of Czechness in Music', *19th-Century Music*, 10 (1986), 61–73.

23. Claims of masculinity could also be presented in other nationalist discourse, see, e.g., Annegret Fauser, 'Gendering the Nations: The Ideologies of French Discourse on Music (1870–1914)', in Harry White and Michael Murphy (eds.), *Musical Constructions of Nationalism: Essays on the History and Ideology of European Musical Culture 1800–1945* (Cork: Cork University Press, 2001), 72–103.

24. See John Rosselli, 'Music and Nationalism in Italy', in White and Murphy (eds.), *Musical Constructions of Nationalism*, 181–96; Mary Ann Smart, 'Verdi, Italian Romanticism, and the Risorgimento', in Scott L. Balthazar (ed.), *The Cambridge Companion to Verdi* (Cambridge: Cambridge University Press, 2004), 29–45.

25. See Jonathan Bellman, *Chopin's Polish Ballade: Op. 38 as Narrative of National Martyrdom* (New York: Oxford University Press, 2010).

26. The only anthems that date earlier (those of the United Kingdom and the Netherlands) are pledges of allegiance to a monarch, whereas, starting with the *Marseillaise*, anthems from the Romantic period onwards are attempts to establish a shared culture by appeal to reception methods 1–4 on the list.

27. *Dalibor*, 10 April 1875, 117. *Hudební Listy*, 8 April 1875, 55. Translated by the author.

28. Jan Racek, *Motiv Vltavy* (Olomouc: Velhrad, 1944); Brian Large, *Smetana* (London: Duckworth, 1970), 275–6.

29. See Kelly St. Pierre, *Bedřich Smetana: Myth, Music, and Propaganda* (New York: University of Rochester Press, 2017), esp. chapter 2.

Further Reading

Beckerman, Michael. 'In Search of Czechness in Music', *19th-Century Music*, 10 (1986), 61–73.

Bendix, Regina. *In Search of Authenticity: The Formation of Folklore Studies* (Madison: University of Wisconsin Press, 1997).

Bohlman, Philip V. *Song Loves the Masses: Herder on Music and Nationalism* (Berkeley and Los Angeles: University of California Press, 2017).

Castro, Christi-Anne. *Musical Renderings of the Philippine Nation* (New York: Oxford University Press, 2011).

Curtis, Benjamin W. *Music Makes the Nation: Nationalist Composers and Nation Building in Nineteenth-Century Europe* (Amherst: Cambria, 2008).

Frolova-Walker, Marina. *Russian Music and Nationalism: From Glinka to Stalin* (New Haven and London: Yale University Press, 2008).

Gelbart, Matthew. *The Invention of 'Folk Music' and 'Art Music': Emerging Categories from Ossian to Wagner* (Cambridge: Cambridge University Press, 2007).

'"The Language of Nature": Music as Historical Crucible for the Methodology of Folkloristics', *Ethnomusicology*, 53/3 (2009), 363–95.

Riley, Matthew, and Smith, Anthony D. *Nation and Classical Music: From Handel to Copland* (Woodbridge: Boydell, 2016).

Shadle, Douglas. *Orchestrating the Nation: The Nineteenth-Century American Symphonic Enterprise* (New York: Oxford University Press, 2015).

St. Pierre, Kelly. *Bedřich Smetana: Myth, Music, and Propaganda* (Rochester, New York: University of Rochester Press, 2017).

Taruskin, Richard. 'Nationalism', in Stanley Sadie (ed.), *The New Grove Dictionary of Music and Musicians*, 29 vols. (London: Macmillan, 2001), vol. xvii, 689–706.

Trumpener, Katie. *Bardic Nationalism: The Romantic Novel and the British Empire* (Princeton: Princeton University Press, 1997).

White, Harry, and Murphy, Michael (eds.). *Musical Constructions of Nationalism: Essays on the History and Ideology of European Musical Culture 1800–1945* (Cork: Cork University Press, 2001).

6 | Music, Romanticism, and Politics

KATHERINE HAMBRIDGE

Call to mind the most familiar tendencies of Romantic aesthetics – the breaking of aesthetic conventions, nostalgia for the past, the highlighting of individual subjectivity, idolisation of wild nature – and you would be hard-pressed to extrapolate from them a characteristically Romantic political position. The pursuit of the ineffable, or the prizing of the unconscious, meanwhile, seems to shortcut this possibility altogether by suggesting a deliberate disavowal of the political world – and that is before you add music into the equation. Drawing parallels between aesthetics and politics is always a risky business, and with music *and* Romanticism particularly tricky. The themes of this chapter are thus best teased out by questioning their possible intersections. How did the political beliefs of Romantic musicians affect their creative endeavours? Can we speak of styles having political tendencies – and if so, what is/was the politics of 'Romantic' music? Which political tendencies contributed to Romanticism in music? Which Romantic political positions influenced musical life? Which Romantic elements of musical life influenced political life? What are the political implications of Romantic theories about music?

The first two questions raise thorny issues of musicological method. Composers' politics have received significant treatment in scholarship, not least because of the influence of the Romantic hero on musicological historiographic models: the centrality of the individual as a structure for studying music (as well as other arts) has been long-lasting, if not unchallenged. The sizeable academic literature on Beethoven's politics, for instance, not to mention the stories circulating about him in musical culture more broadly, attest to the difficulties of pinning down the political beliefs of historical figures who were not prone to straightforward or consistent political statements. This is, in fact, one of the best places to observe both the pitfalls and the critiques of reading political positions onto musical choices, or – as is implied by my second question – political positions *from* musical choices: often Beethoven's music has been seen as a site of resistance.[1] But such approaches are now well problematised: connections that we might see between musical choices and contemporary politics were not necessarily intended by the composer nor legible to audiences at the time, and such connections have to be established as more or less plausible, based on the conventions and discourses of the time. Thus the second of my six questions should rather ask which political tendencies (if any) have been attributed *by whom* (whether composer, critics, or audiences) to musical Romanticism or Romantic musical style.

For all these reasons, and for the purposes of showing the breadth of possible approaches to this topic, it is the remaining four questions that I'll explore in this chapter, outlining some of the ways that connections between music, politics, and Romanticism can be drawn. This includes discussion of Romantic theories of state governance or political organisation, and how they influenced Romantic conceptions of art, as well as exploring how Romantic aesthetics could be given different political spins in different political contexts; my focus on German lands and France is particularly instructive on this latter point, where the intersections of revolutions and Romanticism vary considerably. In the second section, I look at the political mobilisation of Romantic symbols in musical life, before ending with a brief consideration of politicised anti-Romanticism amongst music critics in 1848.

Romanticism and Revolution

While it is possible to trace proto-Romantic tendencies across the second half of the eighteenth century, in the cult of individual sensibility, for example, or in Rousseauvian reactions against the reification of rationality, few would deny the impact of the French Revolution of 1789 in forming Romantic aesthetics. The failure of the Revolution – its descent into the Terror and disorder, its subsequent usurping by Napoleon – was seen by many to demonstrate the failure of reason itself, and of attempts to order the world logically and systematically, which fed the Romantic emphasis on individual perception and interpretation over objective truths. The sense of rupture brought about by Revolutionary attempts to erase the *ancien régime* – not least the execution of Louis XVI and Marie Antoinette – and the turmoil of the Revolutionary and Napoleonic wars (1792–1815) contributed to a longing to return to a simpler past, or to wild, unspoilt nature. Moreover, that sense of turmoil, of unstoppable social forces and violence, increased the salience of the category of the sublime in art (as opposed to the beautiful).

Romanticism can be seen as a response to the Revolution, then, but that does not mean that all Romantics were reactionary or anti-revolutionary.

To be sure, many of the early Romantics in France, the German lands, and England, after initial support, recoiled in horror at the violence unleashed in France. But their impulse was not to preserve a pre-Revolutionary status quo; if any single tendency amongst the early Romantics can be generalised, it is a critique of the 'mechanistic administration of society' (to use Novalis's term for Enlightenment rationality) that they saw as culminating in the Revolution.[2] For Friedrich Schlegel, the aesthetic provided a space to reverse this process: in his 'Gespräch über die Poesie' (1800), he presents the purpose of poetry (understood as a quality of all arts) as being to 'annul the progression and laws of rationally thinking reason and to take us back to the beautiful confusion of imagination, into the original chaos of nature'.[3] Such a statement might suggest the tension between the Romantic emphasis on individual imagination, not to mention chaos, and *any* system of political organisation. Elsewhere, though, Schlegel and others did contemplate alternative models of society in more concrete terms, emphasising the interdependence of the individual and the collective. Indeed, the Romantics sought to combat the perceived atomisation of a rationalised society through various sources of community, including religion, love, and art.

Novalis's *Die Christenheit oder Europa* (*Christendom or Europe*, 1799), for example, extols the unity of medieval Europe, when 'one Christendom inhabited this humanly fashioned part of the world; one grand common interest bound the most distant provinces of the wide spiritual realm'.[4] Love, meanwhile, was 'the completion of community' for Schlegel,[5] and the subject of Novalis's treatise *Glaube und Liebe* (*Faith and Love*, 1798), which advocated for the emotional bonds within family and marriage as the basis of society. Schleiermacher too argued that without love 'no individual life or development is possible ... everything must degenerate into a crude, homogeneous mass',[6] and in his *Versuch einer Theorie des geselligen Betragens* (*Essay on a Theory for Social Conduct*, 1799) proposed intimate sociability and conversation as a way of developing meaningful bonds that served both the individual and the wider society. For Schlegel, art could serve such a purpose, in a Romantic outgrowth of the Herderian idea of shared culture creating communities.[7] Romantic conceptualisations of the state emphasised *organic* bonds, in other words, rather than systemised relations or social contracts: Adam Müller, in *Die Elemente der Staatkunst* (*The Elements of Statecraft*, 1809), argued that 'the state is not a mere factory, a farm, an insurance, institution or mercantile society; above all, it is the inward association of all physical and spiritual needs, of all physical and spiritual riches, of all the inner and outer life of a nation into one great, energetic, infinitely moving and living whole'.[8] The prizing of organicism was of course apparent in Romantic approaches to artworks too: as Ethel Matala de Mazza has pointed out, 'The social models of the Romantics were aesthetic constructs in the most precise sense: they grounded their postulate of togetherness on the imaginative "evidence" of aesthetic experience.'[9] This should not lead us to read any trace of organicism in music as a political statement, however, but rather to see the power of the organic model in both spheres, the political and artistic, and the importance of such interconnection for the Romantics.

The German Romantics' political programme was not, therefore, a mere reversion to pre-Revolutionary times, and indeed contained elements of radical anti-capitalism. It was nonetheless strongly hierarchical. With the idealisation of the medieval period came its feudal structures (explicitly advocated by Müller in his later work), and the elitist tendencies of Romantic political thought are latent in Schlegel's statement that 'A perfect republic would have to be not just democratic but aristocratic and monarchic at the same time: to legislate justly and freely, the educated would have to outweigh and guide the uneducated, and everything would have to be organized into an absolute whole.'[10] Moreover, many of the Romantics would ally themselves with restoration causes or employers: both Schlegel and Müller worked for the conservative Austrian politician Klemens von Metternich. But in their advocacy of medieval structures, the Romantics were in fact far more extreme than their reactionary overlords, and increasingly, the vintage of their political and social models (and their view of art's purpose) reflected an impulse to retreat from rather than transform contemporary society.

If the trajectory of many German Romantics is one of increasing conservatism and withdrawal, elsewhere the political tendencies of Romantic movements are more ambivalent. In England Wordsworth and Coleridge similarly recoiled inward in reaction to the Revolution, but the younger Shelley and Byron would continue to support republicanism. In France, Chateaubriand quickly turned against the Revolution and joined a royalist emigré army based in Germany; beguiled by the individuality of British literature, he published a number of articles from 1800 onwards on figures such as Ossian and Shakespeare, followed by his paean to Christianity (*Génie du christianisme*) in 1802. Other French advocates of Romanticism in those early years – such as Madame de Staël, whose *On Germany* in 1813 was central in defining Romanticism for Europe as a whole – were politically liberal: de Staël, a moderate Revolutionary in the 1790s, opposed Napoleon's authoritarianism, and advocated instead a constitutional monarchy along a

British model.[11] Common to both de Staël and Chateaubriand was a rejection of the rigid control and ordering of society (whether by utilitarian rationality or an authoritarian leader), which finds a parallel in their aesthetic stances.

Such a parallel should not be assumed. The Romantic principle of resistance to ordering or convention has often been divorced from its specific historical and individual contexts in ways that have cast all Romantic art works and artists as politically progressive simply by virtue of the aesthetic experimentation and freedom they pursued. Certainly, the Romantics proposed the breaking of artistic conventions: Schlegel, advocate of the 'confusion of the imagination', also complained that 'All the classical genres are now ridiculous in their rigorous purity', and that the celebration of individual subjectivity and genius was antithetical to abstract rules.[12] The political corollary of this aesthetic stance can vary, however. One of the reasons that the association between Beethoven and the Revolutionary has been so enduring, for example, is because of an (over-) easy equivalence drawn between aesthetic and political 'liberation', between the (artistically) revolutionary and the Revolutionary. This takes some unravelling. In the first place, French Revolutionary politicians in fact tended to be somewhat conservative in their aesthetic pronouncements as a result of their concern for the wide legibility of art: official Revolutionary music was often far from artistically revolutionary.[13] But there are ways in which the ruptures of the Revolution did prompt musical experimentation that would become associated both with the Revolutionary and the Romantic: Sarah Hibberd has argued that attempts by composers such as Cherubini to reflect the power and sublimity of Revolutionary violence prompted harmonic and formal experimentation that was associated at the time with political radicalism, regardless of the political viewpoints of the composers generating it. François-Joseph Gossec, for example, heard clear (and to him, worrying) political connotations in the 'noisiness' of the music of Cherubini and others: '[M]elody, melody! That is the refrain of sensible men and the sane part of the public. Harmonic detours, barbaric transitions, exaggerated chromaticism, that is the truck of fools and fanatics.'[14]

Harmonic detours, barbaric transitions, exaggerated chromaticism: these sounds might be *of* the Revolution – but does that make them always an incitement to revolution, intended or perceived, whether in a French or other national context? Many of the features that appeared so dramatically new in Beethoven's music can be traced to Cherubini, whose influence the German composer was happy to admit. Indeed, Kaiser Franz was reported to dislike Beethoven's music because 'There is something revolutionary in the music.'[15] Some of the vocabularies and innovations now associated with musical Romanticism can be traced to French Revolutionary music, in other words – and their appeal to the Romantic sensibility traced to the disorder, sublimity or 'liberation' they conveyed: while Kaiser Franz may have perceived it as a threat, E. T. A. Hoffmann admiringly described Beethoven's music as a setting 'in motion the machinery of awe, of fear, of terror, of pain'.[16] But, again, we should be careful about drawing too easy a parallel between an aesthetic experience of, or references to, Revolution at one remove, and any desire to dismantle the political status quo; all the more so between those aesthetic innovations that are merely aesthetically revolutionary (which have no connection to the sounds of the Revolution) and political radicalism. After all, the aesthetic experimentation that Beethoven pursued later in his life has more often been traced to a withdrawal from the world (because its esotericism rules out unambiguous political communication of any nature) or to conservative politics (aligned with the medievalism and mysticism of German Romantics such as Schlegel and Müller).[17]

The parallel – between Romantic aesthetic experimentation and political liberation – has more obvious contemporary salience in a nineteenth-century French context, and this is partly because those rigid artistic rules that Romantics were so keen to transcend – classicism – were more deeply embedded in the 'establishment' in France, and more associated with the official culture of the Bourbon monarchy; there was, in other words, a direct link between political control and aesthetic restrictions. Napoleon's regime (1799–1815) reinforced this association, propagating neo-classicism both as a way of legitimating his rule by referencing the aesthetic of the pre-revolutionary *ancien régime*, and as a way of distancing Napoleonic society and art from Revolutionary chaos and experimenta-tion. Thus de Staël's *De L'Allemagne* was censored for its suggestion that the Germans could rejuvenate the French, and for its promotion of Romanticism at the expenses of the national tradition of classicism. From a figure who also opposed Napoleon politically (de Staël was banished from Paris in 1803), such a suggestion in the aesthetic sphere was considered both unpatriotic and anti-Napoleonic, and in 1814, the Bonapartist journal *Le Nain Jaune* drew up a mock treaty of a 'Romantic Confederation' calling for the utter defeat of French literature and language, 'signed' by de Staël and others.[18]

That *Le Nain Jaune* was a liberal Bonapartist journal should again serve as a check to any easy equation between progressive politics and Romantic aesthetics: its own anti-Romantic stance reflected a concurrent association between royalism and Romanticism (de Staël, after all, advocated a constitutional monarchy). But let us pursue a little longer the growing tendency for that first equation in France, which takes some unexpected musical directions. While politicised disputes about Romanticism in literature were already underway in the 1810s, it was a little later that music got drawn in, by which point certain binary oppositions had become established in criticism with varying degrees of pejorative intent: liberal vs royalist; Romantic vs classical; freedom or anarchy vs order; foreign vs French. Although German music was not automatically classed as Romantic, German libretti with supernatural tendencies were: when Carl Maria von Weber's *Der Freischütz* was performed in Paris as *Robin des bois* (1824), it was criticised for its 'Romantic devils'[19] by opponents, just as it was celebrated by Victor Hugo's Romantic circle.[20] The transferral of those binaries to musical characteristics came into focus more in the discourse around Italian opera in the second half of the 1820s, prompted, at least in part, by the publication of Romantic manifestos by literary figures in 1823–5 (Victor Hugo's *Nouvelles odes* and Stendhal's *Racine et Shakespeare*), Rossini's increasing dominance of the Parisian operatic scene, and a growing association of Romanticism with modernity and the present (this despite its affinity for the past!).[21] In 1825, Charles de Salvo's account of *Lord Byron en Italie et en Grèce* contained an anecdote in which Rossini himself (apparently) acknowledged his music's categorisation as Romantic, and linked this to its deliberate contemporaneity. Noting that he had been criticised for bringing together large forces, trumpets and drums and the like (and labelled Romantic in doing so), Rossini suggested that 'if the war continued in Europe, I would have put the cannon in every finale, and I would have made music with guns'.[22]

Rossini's innovative noisiness – paradoxically – takes us back to the 1790s, and this aesthetic-political association is made explicit in the critic Louis Vitet's articles on Romanticism in the liberal paper *Le Globe* in 1825. Recognising the complicated history of the term, Vitet sought to consolidate the movement and its political resonances, declaring that 'Taste in France awaits its 14 July . . . Practical Romanticism is a coalition animated by diverse interests, but which has a common goal, the war against the rules, the rules of conventions.' The political language is not merely metaphorical: the restrictiveness of aesthetic institutions such as the royal opera house and the sterility of classical conventions are directly linked to absolute monarchy and its regulation of the artistic sphere. Rossini, moreover, is heralded as a genius, and Vitet also identifies musical features associated with Romanticism, namely, harmonic and orchestral innovation.[23] The politicisation of Rossini's musical style is as apparent from the arguments of its detractors. As Emmanuel Reibel has shown, the opera composer Henri-Montan Berton, declared by Stendhal the 'champion' of the 'counter-revolution in music',[24] associated musical rules with political stability, classicism with the *ancien régime*, and declared himself at war with those who praised Rossini for 'shaking the rules of the old musical regime'.[25] While Berton had come to prominence as a composer during the Revolutionary decade, he was by this point a solid establishment figure, having worked at the Opéra, taught at the conservatoire since its foundation, and been honoured as a member of the Institut de France (the prestigious national learned society). Back in 1821, seemingly in response to Rossini's success in Paris with *Otello*, he had published a serious of articles identifying the new decadence he detected:

Ambitious modulations, extraordinary transitions, multiplicity of parts, incoherence of rhythms, pretentious searches for harmony, mannered turns of melody, and above all an immeasurable profusion of semiquavers . . . supported in their lead fire by that of the heavy artillery of the trumpets, trombones, timpani and tom-toms . . .[26]

As already suggested, though, these two opposing positions were not the only ones in this debate. It was perfectly possible to find liberals who were anti-Romantic, who saw the aesthetic as conservative in its mysticism or decadence, and maintained a commitment to clarity and rationality: thus *Le Corsaire* attacked Rossini as the 'sublime leader' of a school propagating 'hustle and bustle' and 'double gibberish'.[27] Similarly, it was possible to find conservative monarchists who remained attached to the mystical, nostalgic elements of Romanticism, in the vein established by Chateaubriand at the start of the 1800s. In fact, one of the reasons that Rossini's *Guillaume Tell* (1829) was such a powerful symbol of Romanticism in 1820s France was its combination of 'modern' music by one of the figureheads of Romanticism, on a theme of Revolution, with an older, nostalgic Romanticism that revelled in the authenticity of folk culture and mountains.[28] Published that same year, Toreinx's *Histoire du romantisme*, which singled out Rossini for his own chapter (Beethoven and Weber only had a chapter between them), described the composer as a 'true Romantic author', commending, along with his bold modulations and rich and varied orchestration, his capacity to paint 'local and historical colours'.[29] In this same history, Toreinx himself wondered at the changing political fortunes of Romanticism – 'at first . . . the defender of liberty. Then it was the accomplice of despots' – and described the recent (re-alliance) of Romanticism with progressive politics as itself a 'revolution'.[30]

Romantic Isms

If the above section was structured around the relation between Romanticism and r/Revolution, it was also about the contrasting tendencies of Romantic liberalism and conservatism in the nineteenth century (or indeed liberal Romanticism and conservative Romanticism). This section develops those themes in relation to some other 'isms', particularly nationalism and dynasticism (or dynastic patriotism), within a Prussian and German context.[31] In the first half of the nineteenth century, 'Germany' did not exist as a political entity, but rather as an idea defined by shared language and culture, which the national movement sought to realise politically. The importance of Romantic aesthetics and symbols to both nationalist and dynasticist discourses lies in the way they contributed to narratives of political identity: appeals to the rightness of any particular grouping on account of a shared past or culture. As Matthew Gelbart has pointed out elsewhere in this volume, any claim to a shared culture is strengthened by the evocation of its ancientness. Looking at these two political movements allows us to see the Romanticisation of the past as politically ambivalent (as with Chateaubriand and de Staël): the nationalist movement in nineteenth-century German lands tended to be populated by those of liberal politics, who saw unification as a way to increase individual liberties; the cause of dynastic patriotism tended to be more conservative, preserving the status quo in terms of leadership and social organisation. To both, a Romanticisation of the past was useful to unite populations around a heritage, however mythologised, elaborated, and invented.

The rehabilitation of J. S. Bach provides one telling example of how Romantic aesthetics enabled a new appreciation of older artworks – and how such heritage could be a politically unifying force. The complexity of Bach's music, neglected in the second half of the eighteenth century in favour of Italianate 'noble simplicity', became once more appealing as qualities of profundity and complexity emerged as positives.[32] Carl Maria von Weber's celebration of Bach's 'most unexpected progressions' in part-writing and 'long successions of unusual rhythms in the most ingenious contrapuntal combinations' gives some indication of the points of connection with an aesthetic of 'beautiful confusion', and his comparison of 'this sublime artist' with 'a Gothic cathedral' indicates the way that the aura of age fed the sense of profundity: Bach's 'individuality' was, according to Weber, both 'Romantic' and 'truly German'.[33] Indeed, the Romantic rehabilitation of Bach had a distinctly nationalist flavour, of which Johann Nikolaus Forkel's 1802 biography presents the most (in)famous example: 'this man – the great musical poet and the greatest musical orator that there has ever been and probably ever will be – was a German. Be proud of him, fatherland, be proud of him, but also be worthy of him!'[34]

Weber's own musical endeavours included a sustained attempt to create distinctively German artworks, particularly in the field of opera. His *Der Freischütz*, premiered in Berlin 1821, was only the most successful of early nineteenth-century efforts to define German music theatre through subject matter or self-conscious stylistic markers. Kotzebue's libretto *Hermann und Thusnelde* (1813), for example, had drawn on the myth of the warrior Arminius/Hermann, who united disparate tribes to defeat the Romans in 9 CE, as recorded by Tacitus. Intended as a grand opera with spoken dialogue, and containing a supernatural appearance from Germania herself and the transfiguration of Thusnelde in Valhalla, the work was set by three composers, without either critical or popular success.[35] E. T. A. Hoffmann's opera *Undine* (1816), which sets Friedrich de la Motte Fouqué's 1811 story, is set near the Danube in medieval times, but features a water nymph, combining the appeal of the national chivalric past with elements of fairy tale. The stage design thus presented both Gothic architecture and the German (super)natural environment, while the costumes imitated the paintings of German masters from the fifteenth and early sixteenth centuries.[36] Weber reviewed the Berlin production for the *Allgemeine musikalische Zeitung*, measuring Hoffmann's opera against the 'German ideal' of organic unity, though it has to be said that his vested interests led him to a more favourable opinion of its merits than many other critics.[37]

Der Freischütz is clearly in the *Undine* rather than *Hermann* mould. Set in the seventeenth century and featuring the forests, hunting, and hunting horns of German folklore and Romantic sensibility, this opera too combined the appeal of the natural and supernatural. Richard Wagner would later testify to the significance of the forest to the German nation when he sought to explain it to the French: the French word 'bois' could not capture it.[38] While, as several scholars have now argued, there is much that is musically Italian and French in this depiction of German country life, Weber did attempt to mark it sonically as German through the use of folkish melodies, horns, and male-voice choir writing. These musical elements were not exclusive to German musical traditions, but were increasingly defined as German musical symbols: in the case of the male-voice choirs, the association was both with traditional hunting culture and masculinity and with the contemporary student singing societies that acted as a cover for liberal political organisations. Certainly, *Der Freischütz* served not only as a focus for pan-German efforts to create a German opera tradition, but also, in the context of Berlin, as something of a covert rallying cry for those who opposed the monarch's traditionalism but were censored from overt statements of opposition.[39]

Although liberals saw in *Der Freischütz* a symbol of a pan-German community united by a Romanticised shared culture and past, dynastic monarchies opposing that vision could use similar tactics. The same year that he was writing *Undine*, for example, Hoffmann was commissioned to write a theatrical prologue celebrating the Prussian hereditary dynasty, the Hohenzollerns, on the anniversary of the beginning of their reign as Margraves of Brandenburg in 1415. *Thassilo* was performed in October 1815 with music also by Hoffmann. Set in the time of Charlemagne, with Thassilo, the first of the Hohenzollerns, credited with saving the Fatherland by uniting all Germans, the prologue thus trod the delicate tightrope of acknowledging the German cultural nation while amplifying the historic importance of the dynasty. In the years following the Napoleonic Wars, the need to shore up the dynastic identities of the German states that made up the German Federation (the loose association created at the Congress of Vienna in 1815 to replace the Holy Roman Empire, which had been dissolved in 1806) only increased as the movement for political unification, and thus the dissolution of the individual states, grew in strength: this movement would lead to the revolutions of 1848, where the demands for a German nation of shared culture and history were allied with calls of individual liberty, in opposition to hereditary and autocratic rulers. Thus Friedrich Wilhelm VI of Prussia (reigned 1840–61), like his Hohenzollern forebears, faced the challenge of uniting his diverse and discontinuous territories, not all of them German speaking, not all of them Protestant. Known as the 'Romantic on the Throne', he sought to locate his authority – and the integrity of the Prussian state – in the past: both in the lineage of the Hohenzollerns, which gave him a divine right to rule, and whose hereditary lands had historically been diverse and discontinuous; and in a pre-Reformation Christian (Catholic) unity, which overcame the contemporary confessional and linguistic divides in Prussia. This strategy, in which we can see the influence of the German Romantics at the start of the century, was at least in part derived from his personal mysticism, aesthetic preferences, and convictions, but was also a strategic, anti-Revolutionary 'monarchical project' which sought to preserve the political status quo.[40]

Friedrich Wilhelm's support for the reconstruction of the medieval, Catholic cathedral in Cologne (part of the Kingdom of Prussia since 1815) can be seen as part of this project, combining a specifically confessional statement of inclusivity with a monument to German medieval architecture: the completed building, begun in the thirteenth century, was inaugurated in 1842. The king's preference for historical repertoires such as Palestrina (the *Missa Papae Marcelli* was apparently one of his favourites)[41] and his cultivation of historicist church music also reflect his conception of Prussia. To be sure, church music has historically contained references to earlier styles to a much greater extent than secular repertoires have, and as James Garratt has shown, German Romantics of both Protestant and Catholic persuasions were drawn to Palestrina: E. T. A Hoffmann's 'Old and New Church Music' is a good example of the former.[42] But the self-conscious historicism of court-appointed composers writing for the Prussian Union Church (a Protestant body combining Lutheran and Calvinist churches, created in 1817), and their references to specifically Catholic repertoires of church music, suggests that this wider tendency could be politicised. Thus Laura Stokes has argued that choral settings of the *Deutsche Liturgie* for the Prussian Union Church in the 1840s use gestures to earlier church music to evoke either a harmonious 'pre-sectarian past', or the shared history of religious change: in the case of the settings of Eduard Grell (organist at the Berliner Dom from 1829 and later director of the Singakademie), and Wilhelm Taubert (Kapellmeister from 1841), a more or less strict evocation of a Palestrinian style; in the case of Mendelssohn (Kapellmeister from 1843 to 1844), a more eclectic set of historical references, including chant, modalism, antiphonal and imitative writing, chorale structures, and strict treatment of dissonance, which combined could be interpreted as an evocation of the multiple historical and denominational elements making up Prussia's religious identity.[43]

The musical Romanticisation of Prussian dynastic identity can be seen in Meyerbeer's opera *Ein Feldlager in Schlesien*, performed in Berlin in 1844. The narrative of this opera revolves around the revered eighteenth-century Hohenzollern monarch Frederick the Great, accompanied by Enlightenment ideas about the assimilation of diverse groups into the state – which suited present-day Prussian needs, as well as Meyerbeer's own status as an assimilated Jew in Berlin. In many ways it is a typical patriotic work – containing pre-existing military music and an unambiguous narrative of loyalty and sacrifice to the state – but the central character of the gypsy woman Vielka, who can read the future, adds a mystic element to this retelling of Prussian history, and at the end of Act 3 she prophesies a glorious future for Frederick's house and his realm, presented in a series of *tableaux vivants*. The history of the Hohenzollerns is thus presented as a historical epic, including scenes from the life of Frederick the Great (with one of his star opera singers, Madame Mara, singing an Italian aria by Graun), the Napoleonic Wars (volunteer soldiers singing a patriotic song in 1813; Friedrich Wilhelm III's victorious return to Berlin in 1814), and the burning of the royal opera house in 1843. Rather like *Thassilo* and the *Deutsche Liturgie*, the *tableaux* fold non-German (cosmopolitan) and pan-German (volunteer songs) together with the figures of the Prussian monarchs, romanticising the dynastic alongside the national.

Romanticising the Politics out of Music?

Friedrich Wilhelm IV's commitment to dynastic monarchy, and his sense of his position as grounded in an older tradition of political organisation, was one of the reasons that he refused the crown of a unified Germany in 1848. At a stretch, we might say that Friedrich Wilhelm IV's Romanticism was one of the many reasons that the 1848 revolutions, in which liberals sought to unite German states, failed. Certainly, at the time there were voices that directly criticised Romantic aesthetics for inhibiting political change, even when those aesthetics were not allied with conservative politics: while the recourse to the past or to other worlds had the potential for radical critique of contemporary society, too often (so ran the criticism) it served to draw attention and energy away from the present. Music – considered the 'most Romantic of all the arts' precisely because of its capacity to gesture towards other worlds or the ineffable in a relative absence of specific or stable content – was particularly susceptible to this criticism, not least because it was an art form considered to have remained Romantic, while others had begun to embrace new tendencies towards realism.[44] In fact, for some critics of Romanticism, music represented the worst of it, leading to a devaluing of this art form relative to other arts (a recursion to an eighteenth-century hierarchy), which naturally led others to a defence of music's role.[45]

The year 1848 thus sees a debate – largely conducted between two differently orientated music journals, the *Allgemeine musikalische Zeitung* (*AmZ*) and the *Neue Zeitchrift für Musik* (*NZfM*) – precisely about the themes of this chapter: the relationship between music, Romanticism, and politics. Some sought to rescue music from politics (via Romanticism); others, to rescue music *from* Romanticism *for* politics. In an article on

'Relationships between Art and Politics' for the *AmZ*, Eduard Krüger defended music against its apparent political failings by declaring that it did not have anything to do with politics, but rather the 'contemplation of the beautiful'. Carl Kretschmann in the *NZfM*, on the other hand – writing after the Revolution had clearly failed – distinguished music per se from Romanticism in music, which he characterised as an 'over-reliance on the feminine in artistic production' that had led to 'enervation, weakness, and disease': music must become masculine again, by becoming democratic.[46] As Sanna Pederson has pointed out, critics promoting a politically engaged, democratic music generally only contrasted it to the decadence of Romantic music, rather than defining it more explicitly. The one figure who historically had represented this political ideal seems – for several commentators – to have been none other than Beethoven: another *NZfM* journalist would claim that 'Beethoven was a democrat not only in his life but also in his art; he was filled with the spiritual forces [*geistigen Mächte*] of his age and attested to this in his works'.[47] This brings us full circle to some of the powerful legacies of the nineteenth century for our own received understandings of music, those enduring ideas that were presented at the start of the chapter for unpicking: that music is the least political by being the most Romantic of the arts; and that Beethoven is a prime example of political progressivism in music. Neither of these truisms captures the complexity of the interrelations of music, Romanticism, and politics: the political ambivalence of Romanticism as a movement; the adoption of Romantic aesthetics and music by opposing political movements; and the fickle associations of political and aesthetic progress. Both Romanticism and music, and Romantic music, turn out to be rather unstable in their political meanings, but no less politically powerful for all that.

Notes

1. For recent discussion of these tendencies, see David B. Dennis, *Beethoven in German Politics, 1870–1989* (New Haven: Yale University Press, 1996); Leon Plantinga, 'Beethoven, Napoleon and Political Romanticism', in Jane F. Fulcher (ed.), *The Oxford Handbook of the New Cultural History of Music* (New York: Oxford University Press, 2011), 484–500; and Nicholas Mathew, *Political Beethoven* (Cambridge: Cambridge University Press, 2013).

2. Novalis, *Glauben und Liebe* (1798), cited and translated in Stephen Rumph, *Beethoven after Napoleon: Political Romanticism in the Late Works* (Berkeley: University of California Press, 2004), 170.

3. Cited and translated in James Garratt, *Music, Culture and Social Reform in the Age of Wagner* (Cambridge: Cambridge University Press, 2010), 24.

4. Cited and translated in Rumph, *Beethoven after Napoleon*, 18.

5. Friedrich Schlegel, *Philosophical Fragments*, trans. Peter Firchow (Minneapolis: University of Minnesota Press, 1991), 101.

6. *Schleiermacher's Soliloquies: An English Translation of the Monologen*, ed. and trans. Horace Leland Friess (Eugene, OR: Wipf and Stock Publishers, 2002), 39.

7. See F. Schlegel, *Dialogue on Poetry and Literary Aphorisms*, ed. and trans. Ernst Behler and Roman Struc (University Park, PA: Pennsylvania State University Press, 1968), 53.

8. Cited and translated in Rumph, *Beethoven after Napoleon*, 28.

9. Ethel Matala de Mazza, 'Romantic Politics and Society', in Nicholas Saul (ed.), *The Cambridge Companion to German Romanticism* (Cambridge: Cambridge University Press, 2009), 192.

10. *Athenaeum Fragment*, No. 214, cited and translated in G. N. Izenberg, *Impossible Individuality: Romanticisms, Revolution, and the Origins of Modern Selfhood* (Princeton: Princeton University Press, 1992), 136.

11. See Fabienne Moore, 'Early French Romanticism', in Michael Ferber (ed.), *A Companion to European Romanticism* (Oxford: Blackwell, 2005), 172–91; and Biancamaria Fontana, *Germaine de Staël: A Political Portrait* (Princeton: Princeton University Press, 2016), 198.

12. *Lyceum Fragment*, No. 60, Schlegel, *Dialogue on Poetry and Literary Aphorisms*, 127.

13. James H. Johnson, 'Musical Expression and Jacobin Ideology', in *Listening in Paris: A Cultural History* (Berkeley: University of California Press, 1995), 137–54.

14. Sarah Hibberd, 'Cherubini and the Revolutionary Sublime', *Cambridge Opera Journal*, 24/3 (2012), 293.

15. Rhys Jones, 'Beethoven and the Sound of Revolution in Vienna, 1792–1814', *The Historical Journal*, 57/4 (2014), 950, 953.

16. *E. T. A. Hoffmann's Musical Writings*, ed. David Charlton, trans. Martyn Clarke (Cambridge: Cambridge University Press, 1989), 238.

17. See Rumph, *Beethoven after Napoleon*, 92–132.

18. See René Wellek, *A History of Modern Criticism 1750–1950, Volume 2: The Romantic Age* (Cambridge: Cambridge University Press, 1981), 216.

19. Emmanuel Reibel, *Comment la musique est devenue 'romantique': De Rousseau à Berlioz* (Paris: Fayard, 2013), 210.

20. Mark Everist, *Music Drama at the Paris Odéon, 1824–1828* (Berkeley: University of California Press, 2002), 124.

21. In his *Histoire du romantisme* (1829), Toreinx defined Romanticism as 'everything that is new'. See *Histoire du romantisme en France* (Paris: Dureuil, 1829), 164.

22. Charles de Salvo, *Lord Byron en Italie et en Grèce* (1825), cited in Reibel, *Comment la musique est devenue 'romantique'*, 382. For more on Rossini's

reception in Paris – as Romantic or otherwise – see Benjamin Walton, *Rossini in Restoration Paris: The Sound of Modern Life* (Cambridge: Cambridge University Press, 2007).

23. Louis Vitet, 'De la musique moderne', *Le Globe* (15 January 1825), 269–71; and 'De l'indépendance en matière de gout', *Le Globe* (2 April 1825), 442–5 and (23 April 1825), 491–3. Unless otherwise stated, all translations are by the author.

24. Stendhal, *Memoirs of Rossini* (London: Hookham, 1824), 58.

25. Cited in Reibel, *Comment la musique est devenue 'romantique'*, 257.

26. Henri-Montan Berton, 'De la musique mécanique et de la musique philosphique', *L'Abeille*, 3 (1821), 292–8. Reproduced in Reibel, *Comment la musique est devenue 'romantique'*, 377–81, at 378.

27. Reibel, *Comment la musique est devenue 'romantique'*, 262–3.

28. See Walton, 'Looking for the Revolution in *Guillaume Tell*', in *Rossini in Restoration Paris*, 257–92.

29. Toreinx, *Histoire du romantisme*, 405. Other chapters by Toreinx (including one on music) are excerpted and translated in Peter le Huray and James Day (eds.), *Music and Aesthetics in the Eighteenth and Early-Nineteenth Centuries* (Cambridge: Cambridge University Press, 1988), 406–19.

30. Le Huray and Day, *Music and Aesthetics*, 408–9, translation modified.

31. These are not the only 'isms' one might pursue, of course. One recent development has been the study of Romantic Cosmopolitanism: see the special issue 'Romantic Cosmopolitanism', *European Romantic Review*, 16/2 (2005); and Esther Wohlgemut (ed.), *Romantic Cosmopolitanism* (Basingstoke: Palgrave Macmillan, 2009).

32. See Bernd Sponheur, 'Reconstructing Ideal Types of the "German" in Music', in Celia Applegate and Pamela Potter (eds.), *Music and German National Identity* (Chicago: University of Chicago Press, 2002), 48–52.

33. Carl Maria von Weber, 'Johann Sebastian Bach' (1821), in *Carl Maria von Weber: Writings on Music*, ed. John Warrack, trans. Martin Cooper (Cambridge: Cambridge University Press, 1981), 296–9.

34. Johann Nikolaus Forkel, *Ueber Johann Sebastian Bachs Leben, Kunst und Kunstwerke* (Leipzig: Hoffmeister & Kühnel, 1802), 69.

35. Kaspar van Kooten, '"Ein dürftiger Stoff": Hermann and the Failure of German Liberation Opera (1815–1848)', *Nineteenth-Century Music Review*, 16 (2018), 249–72.

36. Francien Markx, *E. T. A. Hoffmann, Cosmopolitanism, and the Struggle for German Opera* (Leiden: Brill, 2016), 238–68.

37. Weber, 'Review of E. T. A. Hoffmann's *Undine*', in *Writings on Music*, 200–5.

38. Richard Wagner, '*Der Freischütz*. To the Paris Public (1841)', in *Pilgrimage to Beethoven and Other Essays*, trans. William Ashton Ellis (Lincoln, NE: University of Nebraska Press, 1994), 169–82, at 176.

39. Stephen C. Meyer, *Carl Maria von Weber and the Search for a German Opera* (Bloomington: Indiana University Press, 2003).

40. David E. Barclay, *Friedrich Wilhelm IV and the Prussian Monarchy* (Oxford: Clarendon Press, 1995), 10.

41. James Garratt, *Palestrina and the German Romantic Imagination: Interpreting Historicism in Nineteenth-Century Music* (Cambridge: Cambridge University Press, 2002), 115.

42. *E. T. A. Hoffmann's Musical Writings*, 351–76. See also James Garratt, 'Mendelssohn's Babel: Romanticism and the Poetics of Translation', *Music & Letters*, 80 (1999), 23–49.

43. Laura K. T. Stokes, 'Mendelssohn's Deutsche Liturgie in the Context of the Prussian Agende of 1829', in Benedict Taylor (ed.), *Rethinking Mendelssohn* (New York: Oxford University Press, 2020), 346–75.

44. See Carl Dahlhaus, *Realism in Nineteenth-Century Music*, trans. Mary Whittall (Cambridge: Cambridge University Press, 1985).

45. See Sanna Pederson, 'Romantic Music Under Siege in 1848', in Ian Bent (ed.), *Music Theory in the Age of Romanticism* (Cambridge: Cambridge University Press, 1996), 57–74.

46. Cited and translated in ibid., 66–9.

47. Cited and translated in ibid., 70.

Further Reading

Garratt, James. *Palestrina and the German Romantic Imagination: Interpreting Historicism in Nineteenth-Century Music* (Cambridge: Cambridge University Press, 2002).

Hindenlang, Karen. 'Eichendorff's "Auf einer Burg" and Schumann's *Liederkreis*, Opus 39', *Journal of Musicology*, 8/4 (1990), 569–87.

Matala de Mazza, Ethel. 'Romantic Politics and Society', in Nicholas Saul (ed.), *The Cambridge Companion to German Romanticism* (Cambridge: Cambridge University Press, 2009), 191–207.

Meyer, Stephen C. *Carl Maria von Weber and the Search for a German Opera* (Bloomington: Indiana University Press, 2003).

Moore, Fabienne. 'Early French Romanticism', in Michael Ferber (ed.), *A Companion to European Romanticism* (Oxford: Blackwell, 2005), 172–91.

Morrow, John. 'Romanticism and Political Thought in the Early Nineteenth Century', in Gareth Stedman Jones and Gregory Claeys (eds.), *The Cambridge History of Nineteenth-Century Political Thought* (Cambridge: Cambridge University Press, 2011), 39–72.

Plantinga, Leon. 'Beethoven, Napoleon and Political Romanticism', in Jane F. Fulcher (ed.), *The Oxford Handbook of the New Cultural History of Music* (New York: Oxford University Press, 2011), 484–500.

Pederson, Sanna. 'Romantic Music Under Siege in 1848', in Ian Bent (ed.), *Music Theory in the Age of Romanticism* (Cambridge: Cambridge University Press, 1996), 57–74.

Reibel, Emmanuel. *Comment la musique est devenue 'romantique': De Rousseau à Berlioz* (Paris: Fayard, 2013).

Rumph, Stephen. *Beethoven after Napoleon: Political Romanticism in the Late Works* (Berkeley and Los Angeles: University of California Press, 2004).

Walton, Benjamin. 'Looking for the Revolution in *Guillaume Tell*', in *Rossini in Restoration Paris* (Cambridge: Cambridge University Press, 2007), 257–92.

7 | Music and Technology

JOHN TRESCH

The French Romantic novelist George Sand, born Aurore Dupin, wrote *The Seven Strings of the Lyre* during the early days of her decade-long affair with Frédéric Chopin. This 'woman's version of the *Faust* legend', published in 1839, featured a magical instrument – not a piano, but a richly ornamented lyre of ivory. The heroine, Hélène, receives it at her birth, though she is forbidden to play it. Mephistopheles, disguised as an antiques dealer, tries to get hold of the harp and through it, the souls of Hélène and her protector, the philosopher Albertus.

When Hélène at last plucks the lyre's strings, she awakens its spirit. Its vibrations immerse her in 'powerful harmonies' and a 'dazzling spectacle' which evoke sorrow and joy, the entire chromatic scale of human emotion and experience. A gloomy 'sea of sand' becomes a glorious cityscape of gleaming towers, fountains, and a river like 'a serpent of gold and azure', while the 'confused clamour' of human activity modulates into an 'imposing concert':

myriads of terrible or sublime harmonies are confused in a single roar, a thousand times more powerful than that of the tempest: this is the voice of industry, the noise of machines, the hissing of steam, and the blow of hammers, the rolling of drums, the fanfare of military phalanxes, the declamation of orators, the melodies of a thousand different instruments, cries of joy, of war and of work, the hymn of triumph and of might.[1]

Sand's enchanted lyre was one of the many magical instruments, tools, and machines that danced through the music of the long nineteenth century: from Mozart's Magic Flute, the charmed bullets in Carl Maria von Weber's *Der Freischütz*, or the 1805 collection of folk songs, *Des Knaben Wunderhorn* (*The Boy's Magic Horn*, set to music by Mendelssohn, Schumann, Brahms, and Mahler), through to the animated machines and toys in Offenbach's *Tales of Hoffmann* and Tchaikovsky's *The Nutcracker*. Yet Sand, the great Romantic author, set her play not in the time of childhood or fairy tales, but her own: the early Industrial Revolution. In the mid-nineteenth century, production of all kinds was being concentrated and amplified with new forms of organisation and new inventions, much of it driven by steam engines and other inventions.

In the Romantic era, critics and theorists sometimes portrayed music as ideal and transcendent, as the sound of feeling, a force striving to realise the purity of immaterial spirit or abstract form. This strand of interpretation, focusing on works' pure musicality, runs from German Idealism and the writings of Romantic authors such as E. T. A. Hoffmann through to Richard Wagner and his followers. Yet the composers, performers, critics, audiences, and promoters of Romantic music – including Hoffmann and Wagner themselves – were also sharply aware of the unavoidable necessity and importance of concrete technology, in new instruments, stage design, architecture, and printed publicity. Inventions and technical adaptions, from new and improved instruments to new lighting and staging techniques, were at the heart of many of the defining characteristics of Romantic music: the sense of wild, dangerous, creative energies in both nature and human arts, the exploration of the most exalted and sombre of human emotions and visionary states, restless formal invention, and appeals to both the intimacy of the individual soul and to vast audiences.

George Sand's vision of the harmonies of labour and industry was partly inspired by the ideas of the social philosopher Pierre Leroux, who envisioned the ongoing spiritual evolution of humanity through symbolism, the arts, and the redistribution of property. Leroux was one of many utopian thinkers of the early nineteenth century, including such early socialists as Charles Fourier, Etienne Cabet, Flora Tristan, and the young Karl Marx, all of whom were imagining a more just and equal society in which industrial machinery would play a central role. This was also an era of intensified European imperial expansion, with organised military technology making possible the violent acquisition of new territories and subjugation of their inhabitants. In the sounds and visions summoned by Hélène's lyre – of steam, banging hammers, and marching armies – Sand conjured up the creative, destructive, world-changing powers of industry, oscillating between dissonance and consonance.

The cultural critic Edward Said wrote that Giuseppe Verdi's 1870 opera *Aida* – whose central plot concerns the doomed love between an Egyptian general and an Ethiopian slave – 'is not so much *about* but *of* imperial domination'; in complicated ways, Said argued, every aspect of the work participated in the logic of the conquest and colonisation of foreign peoples.[2] At the end of this essay, we will return to Said's suggestion about Verdi's opera. More generally, we might adapt his formulation to think about the relationship between Romantic music and technology. Romantic music is *of* technology: entirely dependent on well-established and radically novel arrangements and uses of material implements for its effects. Yet Romantic music is also frequently *about* technology. Its conception, performance, and reception often directly or indirectly reference, portray, and allegorise the promises and dangers of machines and technical domination, participating in wider logics of analysis, production, and control.

Romantic music often presented itself as a consolation against the violent changes, profound uncertainties, and fierce social tensions of industrial modernity – an entertaining or distracting flight into a nostalgic past, the comforts of nature, erotic bliss, spiritual uplift, or dream-like mythologies, including fantasies of national unity. Through its dependence on technology, and its ability to reflect upon its consequences, Romantic music was also an exemplary manifestation of its age.[3]

An Extended Palette

Romantic artists used all available technical means to create strong impressions and remarkable experiences in their audiences. For musicians and composers, this meant an obsessive focus on instrumentation, selecting the instrument which would provide the exact colour or timbre for each moment. At the time of Haydn and Mozart the orchestra typically contained two dozen instruments, with melodies largely carried by the strings, and brass filling in background tone, led by a seated performer – often the composer at the harpsichord or fortepiano. Instruments like the clarinet and trombone were introduced in certain works by Mozart, but by the middle of the nineteenth century the orchestra had expanded greatly. Beethoven introduced the contrabassoon, Mendelssohn the ophicleide (a kind of tuba), while Berlioz brought in the cornet and the harp, and further deepened the low end with the gigantic 'octabass'. The early nineteenth century saw technical developments in wind instruments, introducing new valves and keys as well as pad extensions in woodwinds and brasses, allowing performers to play notes more rapidly and to allow the brass to remain in tune in multiple keys. Using methods of mass production and assembly lines, instrument makers such as inventor Adolphe Sax rolled out new horns, including brasses with reeds, as in the saxophone.

Instrumental innovations often involved collaborations between composers, performers, instrument makers, and scientists. The field of acoustics was on the rise, with studies and treatises from scientists including Ernst Chladni, Felix Savart, Jean-Baptiste Biot, and Ernst and Wilhelm Weber paving the way for Hermann von Helmholtz's monumental work on the physics of sound and music in the 1860s. Similar partnerships were formed to examine the anatomical dimensions of musical performance.[4] Devices were applied to teach and trace ideal hand posture on the piano; the 'laryngoscope' made it possible to inspect those aspects of soprano's throats that allowed them to soar into higher registers, and created science-based norms of good vocal performance. Studies of the ear – including the building of artificial ears – informed the design of instruments as well as the theorisation of the chain of musical transmission, from instrument to vibrating air to the ear's 'tympani' and onwards to the nerves, brain, and soul. The scientific study and optimisation of musicians' bodies implied a treatment of human performers as tools or machines within a wider technical assemblage.[5]

A remarkable development of late eighteenth-century music, with profound implications for the following century, was the consolidation of the orchestra as a relatively standard form, defined by several performers on each of the string, reed, and brass instruments, accompanied by percussion. Haydn's works did much to explore the capacities of the orchestra, effecting an 'orchestral revolution' which carried into the next century. Haydn demonstrated the flexibility of a large ensemble, playing one set of instruments off the other, moving themes across instruments, drawing out the unique meanings and tones of each – their 'personalities' – to assert a harmonious order to nature's diversity and a 'harmony between individuals and the collective whole'.[6]

The orchestra itself came to be seen as a single instrument, a machine composed of specialised parts – skilfully arranged by the composer and governed by the conductor, a role which became increasingly prominent in the early nineteenth century.[7] This conception was reinforced in actual machines built around the turn of the nineteenth century, such as the Orchestrion, which could be programmed to perform multipart symphonies to amused crowds. Beethoven's 'Battle Symphony', *Wellington's Victory*, Op. 91, was originally composed for the Panharmonicon, built by Johann Maelzel, a Bavarian instrument maker who also designed a metronome, a mechanical trumpeter, and a speaking machine. It has been said the two loudest sounds anyone had ever heard in the early nineteenth century came from the battlefields of the Napoleonic wars and the concert halls in which the modern orchestra performed; the 'Eroica' Symphony, which Beethoven originally dedicated to Napoleon himself, linked both forms of technological bombast.

Some of the new instruments used in Romantic music came from other cultures. Musical treatises of the eighteenth century, such as Charles

Burney's *General History of Music*, had inventoried the world's musical offerings. Romantic music was often set in exotic locations – the Middle East, Asia, Africa – and composers added instruments from the musical traditions of these places in order to produce 'local colour', in a kind of auditory tourism – though often with the instruments' uses and meanings altered from their original settings. For example, the tam-tam or gong was traditionally used in South East Asia and China in court ceremonies and processions to mark the rank of different nobles and officials. In Romantic music, its sudden and shocking sound could mark endings and beginnings, as well as signifying magic and a violent entrance from another metaphysical realm.[8]

New and modified instruments were crucial for the high-impact mass performances of symphonies and operas. If the classical music of the eighteenth century most often involved command performances in royal and aristocratic courts, Romantic music was a central part of the nineteenth century's emerging mass entertainment aimed at the rising bourgeoisie. New concert halls were built with acoustic impact in mind; opera houses became sources of civic pride, showcases for architectural beauty and technical prowess, featuring indoor gas lighting which could now be lowered, focusing attention on the stage and away from the crowd. There was furthermore a large marketplace for printed music, along with abundant criticism in specialist and general journals, carried forwards in unprecedented floods of mechanically printed words.

Technological innovations also played an important role in the more intimate settings of parlour and salon music. A steady stream of improvements to the pianoforte made it far more responsive than the harpsichord or clavichord – including the sustaining pedal, dampers to mute the sound of each note after being struck, and the double escapement mechanism, introduced by Sebastian Érard in 1821, which made it possible to sound the same note in very quick succession without waiting for it to return to its starting position. The result was a supple instrument with a wide dynamic range, covering several octaves, which allowed for extremely rapid successions of notes as well as sustained and resonant tones. Paganini dazzled audiences through his virtuosic mastery of the violin; with the improvements to the piano, the space was cleared for Liszt to demonstrate his prowess on the larger instrument, making it an extension of his own individuality. The music of figures such as Chopin and Schumann likewise made use of the piano's effects and dynamics to convey a wide range of emotional states, from melancholy and perplexity to exuberance and devotion.

Music in the era of Romanticism went beyond merely an 'application' of technology to being defined by what the media scholar Jonathan Sterne calls 'technicity': every aspect of music, in its production and its reception, whether sensory, emotional, philosophical, or critical, operated within a logic of mechanical manipulation and enhancement, precision and repeatability.[9]

Pipe Dreams

The exploration of imagination and fantasy, of pathological and altered states of mind, defined the arts of the Romantic era. The 'pipe dreams' of the opium addicts Samuel Taylor Coleridge and Thomas de Quincey, and of the 'Club des Hashischins' which included Charles Baudelaire, Théophile Gaultier, and Eugène Delacroix inspired major works, while Berlioz's *Symphonie fantastique* musically conveyed the effects of opium. Yet in even Romantics' lush internal reveries, industry and technology were not far away. Experiments with drugs were taken as data in the emerging field of psychology, while philosophy inquired into the foundations of consciousness.[10] Nitrous oxide, or laughing gas, was the first hallucinogen discovered in a laboratory, by chemist Joseph Priestley; it was tested by Coleridge's friend, the chemist and poet Humphry Davy, and refined in a process developed by James Watt, the steam-engine inventor.

Explorers of the psyche – whether artists or scientists – also investigated the possibilities of mesmerism or animal magnetism. First popularised in the late eighteenth century by the Viennese doctor Anton Mesmer, in animal magnetism, sensitive individuals claimed to be able to access and control the invisible fluid responsible for life and thought. The magnetiser's rhythmic magnetic 'passes' upon a patient placed him or her into an altered state, bringing about ecstatic pleasures and medical cures. Although a commission at the French Académie des Sciences in 1784 attributed Mesmer's effects to patients' overactive imaginations, a new generation of practitioners appeared in the 1820s and claimed new powers – reading and seeing at a distance, telepathy, communication with spirits – and suggested links between animal magnetism and the new science of character, phrenology.[11] Animal magnetism also resonated with the lightning-quick, elusive qualities of electricity, and both mesmerism and electricity helped inspire a musical aesthetics focused on 'effects'. The electric telegraph's ability to communicate and command at a distance formed a further link: figures 'entranced' or hypnotised appeared on stage in musical opera, likened to automata or androids acting under invisible but mechanical command.[12] In a performance of 1844 Hector Berlioz actually employed an 'electric metronome' to transmit an impulse from a conductor to 'subconductors' of a large orchestra, while electricity was integrated into such musical spectacles as Luigi Manzotti's 1881 ballet *Excelsior*, which featured a 'Dance of the Telegraph Operators'.[13]

Both telegraphy and mesmerism drew upon the invisible forces, fluids, and ethers being actively researched in the mechanical sciences. While in the late eighteenth century, electricity, magnetism, heat, and light – called the 'imponderable fluids' – were seen to be independent of one another, after 1800 a wave of researchers in what has been called *Naturphilosophie* or 'Romantic science' examined the interrelations of these phenomena and the ways they could be converted into each other. A path-breaking discovery was made in 1820 by Hans Christian Ørsted, who showed that electricity and magnetism were modifications of a single underlying principle. Later researchers including Michael Faraday, Charles Wheatstone, and Joseph Henry investigated the relations amongst electromagnetism, light, and heat, while fundamental research on steam engines by Helmholtz, Sadi Carnot, and James Joule laid the foundations of thermodynamics, the laws of conversion of heat into motive force. By the middle of the century, physicists had embraced the notion of a single 'energy' which could be converted into any one of these forms with the proper technical interface. These phenomena were understood to travel as vibrations in an ether which surrounded and penetrated all bodies. This concept informed the understanding of music, and spurred reflections on the nature of the mind, soul, or spirit, and its ability to act upon the world. Ether was the vibratory medium within which all other media, including thought and feeling, made their impact.[14]

In these ways the fantasies of Romantic dreamers were closely tied to technical and scientific developments. Even more widespread 'pipe dreams' captured public attention in the Romantic era, in visions of industrial expansion: the Industrial Revolution was in fact a matter of pipes – tubes, valves, and cylinders, as in the cycle from hot to cold in the steam engine.[15] Industrialisation meant conveying forces, fluids, and other materials from one location to another – from one end of a factory to the other, from sites of extraction to those of production, sale, and consumption. Engineers and scientists worked out calculations to maximise the efficiency of forces, goods, and people as they moved through a reticulated system of intersecting flows.

The general concept of 'communication' underwrote schemes to design large technical systems and networks to join distant places. Saint-Simonian engineers, including the political economist Michel Chevalier, and Prosper Enfantin, who led a mission of engineers to Algeria and Egypt, saw roads, railroads, and waterworks as the blood vessels for a new, peacefully organised civilisation, which would make national and regional boundaries obsolete; they devised plans to open canals in Panama and Egypt, joining East, West, North, and South, in a vast system of efficient circulation. Industrialisation, properly administered, would liberate the productive forces of the earth and society; guided by the emotional works of artists, the slumbering power and idealism of humanity could be awakened, to create a new, harmonious global society. The reflections of composers, instrument makers, architects, and performers to improve, direct, and increase the flow of sound were in keeping with these other forms of industrial speculation.[16]

Romantic Audiovisuality

In the Romantic era, music was deeply embedded in the culture of urban spectacle. Cities were drastically increasing their populations; the growing middle class had money to spend on entertainments: magic shows, comedies, tragedies, and 'vaudeville' stages. Industrial expositions promoted machines to make clothing, books, sculpture, and music, such as Maelzel's mechanical trumpeters and harpsichordists. A wide audience grew for scientific lectures, in Paris's Athenée and Conservatoire des Arts et Métiers, and in London in the Royal Polytechnic Institute, where Davy, Michael Faraday, Charles Wheatstone, and John Tyndall expounded the principles of chemistry and the physical sciences. Their performances featured striking experiments and demonstrations including explosions, demonstrations of electric lighting, magic lantern displays, optical illusions such as 'Pepper's Ghost', and the seemingly self-playing 'magic lyre' display of Wheatstone, with harps suspended in the air which appeared to play themselves.[17] In such spectacles, the sonic and visual were closely entwined.

Other new popular entertainments in London included the Cyclorama, which simulated geological catastrophes, and the Colosseum, which housed concerts, plays, and natural history collections. Many cities hosted the panorama – a large cylindrical building containing an elevated viewing platform from which spectators viewed 360-degree realistic painted landscapes, city views, or battle scenes. The scale and optical principles of the panorama were repeated in painting, as in Géricault's *Raft of the Medusa*, and employed in stage design, where gigantic realistic painted backdrops sought to transport viewers to distant regions in line with the aesthetic ambitions of Romantic music.[18] One prominent Parisian stage painter, with a studio near the vaudeville theatre and panoramas, invented a new entertainment he called 'the diorama', a painting on a semi-transparent screen of a landscape or interior, connected to a lighting system which gradually shifted to bring out different colours and shadings, changing a scene in spring to one in winter, or a daylight view into one of night, often accompanied by music and props – a technology of contrasts, of transformation. The inventor was Louis Daguerre, whose more famous invention, the daguerreotype – the first commercially viable form of photography – was originally intended as a technical aid for painting stage sets, including for operas.

Already in the late eighteenth century popular entertainments were fusing optical devices with music. Deirdre Loughridge has shown how a series of optical inventions, such as the microscope, shadow play, peep show, and phantasmagoria, created new visual experiences – picturing the very small; projecting images; separating spectators from the space of the objects they observed – which affected musical imaginaries: Haydn's *Creation* was the sonic equivalent of a 'magic lantern', while Beethoven created phantasmagoric musical effects heard as the interplay of dark and light. As the nineteenth century began, popular displays took on encompassing views of nature, including orreries and planetariums, machines which showed the moving order of the planets around the sun.[19]

Musical and visual technologies were brought dramatically together in Romantic opera, where it was impossible to separate appreciation for the music from the reception of the plot, acting, dancing, costumes, lighting, backdrops, sets, or special effects. The full suite of techniques of Romantic audiovisuality were brought together in the Paris Opera, notably in the work of Giacomo Meyerbeer. Meyerbeer's brother was the director of the astronomical observatory in Berlin; he was also in correspondence with the great scientist Alexander von Humboldt, who had a hand in most of the scientific and sensory inventions of the time and was an enthusiast of the panorama, daguerreotype, and telegraphy.

In his smash Parisian opera of 1831, *Robert le diable*, Meyerbeer joined audacious orchestration with new sights. A ballet of lascivious nuns cavorted in flesh-coloured tights to the sound of sinister bassoons; a diorama-like backdrop shifted its appearance from light to dark; explosions were made by blowing clouds of seed on to gaslights; the entrance of the chords of a church organ was an unexpected 'sublime invasion'.[20] Critics and audiences commented as much on the visual spectacle as on the music. The libretto offered a compelling character who was the son of a devil; Robert worked witchcraft with a magical branch, which he broke to free his soul. This theme of Meyerbeer's opera cemented the impression, already made prominent in *Faust*, that there was something both magical and diabolical about technology.

The emphasis on technical control was taken yet further by Richard Wagner, who defined opera as a *Gesamtkunstwerk* – a total work of art – where material technologies of all sorts ensured an organic, ideal unity (even though Wagner sneered at the 'materialism' of Meyerbeer's works in a notorious anti-Semitic broadside, 'Jewishness in Music', a source for later attacks against Meyerbeer). To place all elements of the opera under his control, Wagner had a new hall built in Bayreuth where he could be the supreme master of puppets. The audience at his Festspielhaus, pilgrims in a religion of art, adopted a reverent awe towards Wagner's musical dramatisations of Norse mythology.

Technology was indispensable to Wagner's instrumentation and the design of the hall. Wagner also ordered brilliant lighting arrangements, flames, and hidden wires to simulate flight, and made use of billowing clouds of steam for the breath of a dragon and as a 'fade-out' in the transition between scenes. The special stage drapery that came to be associated with Bayreuth, the 'Wagner Curtain', performed a subtle but swift demarcation between dramatic units.[21] The quasi-sacred aura of Wagnerian opera, with its aspiration towards a spiritual experience of pure musicality, was inseparable from an incomparable technological investment in every aspect of the performance. As if to bury the contradiction, unlike in previous concert halls, where the musicians were in the audience's line of sight, in Bayreuth Wagner hid his orchestra in a lowered space before the stage, making the source of the music invisible – a technical invention through which the technological dimension of music was either sublimated or denied.

Music and Technology as Show of Force

Our discussion so far has primarily shown how Romanticism was *of* technology: thoroughly dependent on technical interventions to realise its aims. The extent to which it was *about* technology is a somewhat different matter. Can we say that a Schumann lied or a Chopin nocturne is 'about' technology? Each explores the sonic, emotional, and semiotic affordances of the voice and piano, and might be understood – at least by critics today – as a commentary on them. Likewise, the use of audiovisual technologies to produce enthralling visions, ecstatic transports, and uncanny or magical access to a supernatural realm – all recurrent themes in critical responses to Romantic arts – could be seen to reinforce a new understanding of the relationship between humans and nature: that art is nature continued by other means. Such a view recalls Renaissance theories of art as both a mirror and an improvement of nature. Yet with the vast new scale of the nineteenth century's 'mechanical arts' – and after passing through the Enlightenment's polarisation of art and nature, in which art was often considered a corrupting influence – the deliberate surpassing of nature in Romantic art often took on uncanny, colossal, or monstrous aspects.[22]

Some works of Romantic music explicitly took technology as their theme, as in Berlioz's programme for the National Exposition of the Products of French Industry in 1844, which included his 'Hymn to France', praising his homeland's technological achievements. He repeated the feat in 1855 for the opening of the Palais de l'Industrie, France's answer to the Crystal Palace, with an orchestra of 1,200 instruments performing in a 'gallery of machines'. The Crystal Palace, at the Great Exhibition of the Works of Industry of All Nations in London in 1851, proclaimed a new control over nature: a gigantic transparent structure in which the entirety of the natural and human worlds could be presented as an interior, a mastered environment. In this enormous hothouse, plants from around the world thrived, while well-behaved masses observed, evaluated, and were suitably awed by the technical inventions and commercial goods produced by nations and their colonies. Other international expositions and World's Fairs soon followed. In 1861, Berlioz planned another 'monster-concert' to be performed in the Crystal Palace itself with a chorus of 10,000; his composition, 'The Universal Temple', with lyrics by Viard, proclaimed European unity and freedom for 'all the children of labour and art'.

Such works praised the benefits of technical progress. Yet the fascination in Romantic arts with demonic and diabolical technologies suggested a fundamental ambivalence about the 'magic' of new industrial forces and their staggering ability to accelerate production, shrink distances, and ferry information at lightning speed. Both sinister and optimistic portrayals of nineteenth-century technology highlighted anxieties about agency and personhood. New inventions promised mastery, yet could easily escape those who used them, as in the legend of the sorcerer's apprentice. The recurrent image of mechanised (or mesmerised) subjects highlighted the blurring of boundaries between humans and machines, as well as technology's power to dominate and enslave.[23]

Meyerbeer's opera *Le Prophète* premiered in Paris in 1849, during the period when the Provisional Government was in power in France after the worker's revolution of 1848. Technically, it was a wonder: Berlioz praised its orchestration, it packed delirious special effects onto enormous stage sets, including an ice-skating scene using roller skates; it concluded with a stunningly bright artificial sunrise, produced by an electric arc-lamp invented and operated by the physicist Léon Foucault. Thematically, it was read as a commentary on recent events. In the French Revolution of 1848, echoed worldwide, impromptu armies of republican and socialist workers, inspired by utopian aspirations for a just reorganisation of labour and industry, had overthrown the Orleans Monarchy. The revolution was violently repressed in the bloody 'June Days' of 1848, followed by a tense return to order under the imperially inclined President, Louis Napoleon Bonaparte. Meyerbeer's opera, about a revolutionary messiah manipulated by power-mad conspirators, could be seen to condemn both the uprising and the forces of order it opposed.[24]

The new arrangements of industry had created new fortunes for owners and investors. They also threw thousands of labourers out of work by replacing them with machines or re-employing them at unliveable wages. The promise of improved sanitation, an abundance of consumer goods, an end to hunger, and beautiful new habitations were held out and, to widely varying extents, realised in projects of urban renewal such as that directed by Baron von Haussmann in Paris after Louis Bonaparte's *coup d'état* in 1851. Yet these changes to everyday life came at the cost of the destruction of traditions of guilds and artisanship and local networks of support, and contributed to a sense of dislocation and disorientation with the new pace and intensity of urban life. The progress of national industry also made possible imperial expansion – the growth of the British Empire in Asia and Africa, France's new acquisitions in the South Pacific and North Africa, and Germany and Italy's projects of unification, quickly followed by dreams of colonial acquisitions. The growth of industry was inseparable from the growth of empire.

To return, in conclusion, to the opera *Aida* – a work that is 'not so much *about* but *of* imperial domination' – we might also consider the ways in which Verdi's landmark work is both *of* and *about* technology. And while musicologists' rising interest in the technological and scientific dimensions of music might seem to direct attention away from the politics of colonialism and race, *Aida* suggests how technology and empire often went hand in hand in Romanticism and music.

The original invitation for Verdi to compose a work for Egypt came from the ruling Viceroy, Ismail Pasha, in 1869, who wished to commemorate the opening of the Suez Canal – a technological project long dreamed of by the Saint-Simonians as a step towards increasing peaceful communication and exchange throughout the Mediterranean. Verdi declined, but he later accepted an invitation to debut a work in 1871 to open the new Opera House in Cairo. Arrangements were negotiated by a French archaeologist, Auguste Mariette, who had in 1867 co-ordinated Egypt's exhibits for Paris's International Exposition of 1867, where the Egyptian display had taken the medal for best in show.[25] With his support of Verdi, the Viceroy was exhibiting the modernity of Egypt and participating in the international culture of Romantic music and opera. The opera house was situated in the 'new city' of Cairo, a Haussmann-style enclave of wide avenues, gas lighting, and civic halls.

Verdi's work, too, was a colossal, technologically enhanced spectacle – a show of forces. The imposing sets reconstructed ancient Egyptian buildings to Mariette's specifications. Verdi sought to evoke exoticism and archaeological authenticity, and to create distinctive orchestral effects by writing parts for a newly constructed 'Egyptian trumpet' (with an extra-long stem and bell) and 'hyper-flutes', both of which were louder and stronger than normal, and which were to sound as if by magic when a giant statue in one of the stage-set's temples was struck by sunlight. Following Wagner, Verdi chose to hide the orchestra, burying the 'indecent' view of the 'tops of the harps, the necks of the double basses, and the baton of the conductor all up in the air'.[26] Verdi exerted a dictatorial command over all aspects of the production; its grandiosity was a testament to the largesse, power, and glory of the Viceroy.

In the opera's processionals, ballet, and victory march (following the Egyptian army's victory over Ethiopia), viewers were subjected to a protracted display of a gigantic, disciplined organisation of human labour and technical prowess. Whether this was meant to inspire or repulse the audience was unclear; likewise, just what the story of *Aida* says about imperial domination is notoriously ambiguous. Ralph Locke has identified nine distinct interpretations, including either celebrating *or* protesting Egyptian domination over its southern African neighbours; European domination over North Africa and other non-European regions; Prussian domination over the French; or Austro-Hungarian domination over Italy.[27] However it is read, though, the opera undeniably dramatises technically co-ordinated domination and its effects.

In the final scene – containing some of the most moving music in the operatic canon – Aida is locked in a tomb with her lover, the Egyptian general, Radames, who has refused to give her up and has thus been condemned by the Pharaoh and his jealous daughter. Above them, in the high-ceilinged temple, Egyptian priests conduct a ritual of immortality, singing out in low monotones. In contrast, the lovers duet in soaring, even eerie harmony, announcing the opening of heaven to receive them; above them, the Egyptian princess who loves Radames sorrowfully prays for peace.

Aida's finale enacts power, labour, and control on a stunning scale: in the complexly divided stage design lit differently above and below, in the philologically researched and realised Egyptian sets, painting, and costumes, in the gigantic company of singers who have crossed the stage on their way to war and back – and, of course, in the virtuosity of the singers, musicians, and composer. This power and control reflected and communicated with the power on display in the gaslit streets of the new city of Cairo, the gigantic engineering feat of the Suez Canal, and the international race to develop and deploy the powers of industry and invention to remake the world and gather up its wealth. In just a few years, crippled by debt to European banks for the building of the canal, Egypt would fall under French, then British rule, making *Aida*'s portrayal of Egyptian supremacy – and its colonial domination of the Ethiopians – newly ironic.

When the lights go out on the tragic lovers, the ravished audience explodes in applause. Romantic music and spectacle, made possible through technology, glorify technology's reign. They draw attention to its destructive, suffocating potential and its mesmerising, nearly irresistible appeal.

Notes

* The author thanks Deirdre Loughridge, Benedict Taylor, Emily MacGregor, and Emily Dolan for advice and assistance.
1. George Sand, *A Woman's Version of the Faust Legend: The Seven Strings of the Lyre*, trans. George Kennedy (Chapel Hill: University of North Carolina Press, 2013), 126, 145.

2. Edward Said, 'The Empire at Work: Verdi's *Aida*', in *Culture and Imperialism* (New York: Vintage, 1994), 138.

3. Carl Dahlhaus argued that early Romantic music was well-attuned to the early nineteenth century, but later 'neo-Romanticism', appearing after mid-century, was 'untimely': out of step with the later era's positivism and realism (*Between Romanticism and Modernism: Four Studies in the Music of the Later Nineteenth Century*, trans. Mary Whittall (Berkeley and Los Angeles: University of California Press, 1980), 5). Instead, throughout the century, scientific, realist, 'positivist', and technical interests were closely woven into the aesthetic aims and meanings of Romanticism; on the situation in France before 1848, see John Tresch, *The Romantic Machine: Utopian Science and Technology after Napoleon* (Chicago: University of Chicago Press, 2012).

4. See David Trippett, 'Sound as Hermeneutic, or Helmholtz and the Quest for Objective Perception', *19th-Century Music*, 43/2 (2019), 99–120; Julia Kursell, 'Visualizing Piano Playing, 1890–1930', *Grey Room*, 43 (2011), 66–87; Benjamin Steege, 'Vocal Culture in the Age of Laryngoscopy', in David Trippett and Benjamin Walton (eds.), *Nineteenth-Century Opera and the Scientific Imagination* (Cambridge: Cambridge University Press, 2019), 44–62.

5. Studies of the relations of music, science, and technology (often focused on the nineteenth century) have multiplied in recent years. See collections including Alexandra Hui, Julia Kursell, and Myles W. Jackson (eds.), *Music, Sound, and the Laboratory from 1750–1980*, Osiris, 28/1 (2013); Sarah Hibberd (ed.), 'Music and Science in London and Paris', special issue of *19th-Century Music*, 39/2 (2015); James Q. Davies and Ellen Lockhart (eds.), *Sound Knowledge: Music and Science in London, 1789–1851* (Chicago: University of Chicago Press, 2016); Karen Henson (ed.), *Technology and the Diva: Sopranos, Opera, and Media from Romanticism to the Digital Age* (Cambridge: Cambridge University Press, 2016); Trippett and Walton (eds.), *Nineteenth-Century Opera and the Scientific Imagination*.

6. Emily Dolan, *The Orchestral Revolution: Haydn and the Technologies of Timbre* (Cambridge: Cambridge University Press, 2013), 160.

7. John Spitzer, 'Metaphors of the Orchestra – The Orchestra as a Metaphor', *The Musical Quarterly*, 80/2 (1996), 234–64.

8. Gundula Kreuzer, *Curtain, Gong, Steam: Wagnerian Technologies of Nineteenth-Century Opera* (Berkeley: University of California Press, 2018), 109–20.

9. Jonathan Sterne, 'Afterword: Opera, Media, Technicity', in Karen Henson (ed.), *Technology and the Diva*, 159–64.

10. Francesca Brittan, *Music and Fantasy in the Age of Berlioz* (Cambridge: Cambridge University Press, 2017); Jacques-Joseph Moreau de Tours, *Du hachisch et de l'aliénation mentale: Études psychologiques* (Paris: Fortin, Masson, et cie., 1845); Wolfgang Schivelbusch, *Tastes of Paradise: A Social History of Spices, Stimulants, and Intoxicants* (New York: Pantheon Books, 1992).

11. Céline Frigau Manning, 'Phrenologizing Opera Singers: The Scientific "Proofs of Musical Genius"', *19th-Century Music*, 39/2 (2015), 125–41.

12. Sarah Hibberd, '"Dormez donc, mes chers amours": Hérold's La somnambule (1827) and Dream Phenomena on the Parisian Lyric Stage', *Cambridge Opera Journal*, 16/2 (2004), 107–32; Alison Winter, *Mesmerized: Powers of Mind in Victorian Britain* (Chicago: University of Chicago Press, 2000), 314–20.

13. Ellen Lockhart, 'Circuit Listening', and Gavin Williams, '*Excelsior* as Mass Ornament: The Reproduction of Gesture', in Trippett and Walton (eds.), *Nineteenth-Century Opera and the Scientific Imagination*, 227–48 and 251–68.

14. Carmel Raz, '"The Expressive Organ within Us": Ether, Ethereality, and Early Romantic Ideas about Music and the Nerves', *19th-Century Music*, 38/2 (2014), 115–44.

15. Helmut Müller-Sievers, *The Cylinder: Kinematics of the Nineteenth Century* (Berkeley: University of California Press, 2012).

16. Armand Mattelart, *The Invention of Communication* (Minneapolis: University of Minnesota Press, 1996); Richard Wittman, 'Space, Networks, and the Saint-Simonians', *Grey Room*, 40 (2010), 24–49; Ralph P. Locke, *Music, Musicians, and the Saint-Simonians* (Chicago: University of Chicago Press, 1986).

17. See David Trippett and Benjamin Walton, 'Introduction: The Laboratory and the Stage', in Trippett and Walton (eds.), *Nineteenth-Century Opera and the Scientific Imagination*, 1–18, esp. 10–13.

18. Sarah Hibberd, '*Le Naufrage de la Méduse* and Operatic Spectacle in 1830s Paris', *19th-Century Music*, 36/3 (2013), 248–63.

19. Deirdre Loughridge, *Haydn's Sunrise, Beethoven's Shadow: Audiovisual Culture and the Emergence of Musical Romanticism* (Chicago: University of Chicago Press, 2016), and 'Celestial Mechanisms: Adam Walker's Eidouranion, Celestina, and the Advancement of Knowledge', in Davies and Lockhart (eds.), *Sound Knowledge*, 47–76.

20. See Emily I. Dolan and John Tresch, 'A Sublime Invasion: Meyerbeer, Balzac, and the Opera Machine', *The Opera Quarterly*, 27/1 (2011), 4–31.

21. See further in Kreuzer, *Curtain, Gong, Steam*.

22. See M. H. Abrams, *Natural Supernaturalism: Tradition and Revolution in Romantic Literature* (New York: Norton, 1971); Darcy Grimaldo Grigsby, *Extremities: Painting Empire in Post-Revolutionary France* (New Haven: Yale University Press, 2002), and *Colossal: Engineering the Suez Canal, Statue of Liberty, Eiffel Tower, and Panama Canal: Transcontinental Ambition in France and the United States during the Long Nineteenth Century* (Pittsburgh: Periscope, 2011).

23. On the close connections between slavery and industrialisation and the impact of both on nineteenth-century musical imaginaries, with sound as 'the primary nexus of race and technology', see Louis Chude-Sokei, *The Sound of Culture: Diaspora and Black Technopoetics* (Middletown, CT: Wesleyan University Press, 2015); on uncanny aspects of mechanized singers and performers see Carolyn Abbate, *In Search of Opera* (Princeton: Princeton University Press, 2001).

24. Sarah Hibberd, *French Grand Opera and the Historical Imagination* (Cambridge: Cambridge University Press, 2009), ch. 6; John Tresch, 'The Prophet and the Pendulum: Sensational Science and Audiovisual Phantasmagoria around 1848', *Grey Room*, 43 (2011), 16–41.

25. Katherine Bergeron, 'Verdi's Egyptian Spectacle: On the Colonial Subject of Aida', *Cambridge Opera Journal*, 14/1–2 (2002), 149–59.

26. Giuseppe Verdi, quoted by Gabriela Cruz in 'Aida's Flutes', *Cambridge Opera Journal*, 14/1–2 (2002), 177–200 at 186.

27. Ralph P. Locke, 'Aida and Nine Readings of Empire', *Nineteenth-Century Music Review*, 3/1 (2006), 45–72.

Further Reading

Davies, James Q., and Lockhart, Ellen (eds.). *Sound Knowledge: Music and Science in London, 1789–1851* (Chicago: University of Chicago Press, 2016).

Dolan, Emily. *The Orchestral Revolution: Haydn and the Technologies of Timbre* (Cambridge: Cambridge University Press, 2013).

Dolan, Emily I., and Tresch, John. 'A Sublime Invasion: Meyerbeer, Balzac, and the Opera Machine', *The Opera Quarterly*, 27/1 (2011), 4–31.

Henson, Karen (ed.). *Technology and the Diva: Sopranos, Opera, and Media from Romanticism to the Digital Age* (Cambridge: Cambridge University Press, 2016).

Hibberd, Sarah (ed.). *19th-Century Music*, 39/2 (2015), special issue: 'Music and Science in London and Paris'.

Hibberd, Sarah. 'Le Naufrage de la Méduse and operatic spectacle in 1830s Paris', *19th-Century Music*, 36/3 (2013), 248–63.

Hui, Alexandra, Kursell, Julia, and Jackson, Myles W. (eds.). *Music, Sound, and the Laboratory from 1750–1980, Osiris*, 28/1 (2013).

Kreuzer, Gundula. *Curtain, Gong, Steam: Wagnerian Technologies of Nineteenth-Century Opera* (Berkeley: University of California Press, 2018).

Loughridge, Deirdre. *Haydn's Sunrise, Beethoven's Shadow: Audiovisual Culture and the Emergence of Musical Romanticism* (Chicago: University of Chicago Press, 2016).

Müller-Sievers, Helmut. *The Cylinder: Kinematics of the Nineteenth Century* (Berkeley: University of California Press, 2012).

Tresch, John. *The Romantic Machine: Utopian Science and Technology after Napoleon* (Chicago: University of Chicago Press, 2012).

Trippett, David, and Walton, Benjamin (eds.). *Nineteenth-Century Opera and the Scientific Imagination* (Cambridge: Cambridge University Press, 2019).

8 | Music, Magic, and the Supernatural

FRANCESCA BRITTAN

The Real Supernatural

Amongst the best-known supernatural evocations of the nineteenth century is Franz Schubert's setting of Goethe's 'Der Erlkönig', a piece that catapults us headlong into a wild scene: a father's desperate ride on horseback, a boy terrorised by unseen forces, and the spirit-whisper of the malevolent Erlking (see Fig. 8.1). In and beyond Schubert's own time the song was received as strikingly original, notable for its recasting of Goethe's narrative (such that a storm is raging from the outset) and its tendency towards genre-bending (a conflation of ballad and lied traditions). But most novel of all, according to critics, was the character of the Erlking himself, whom Schubert depicted not as a distant phantasmagorical creature, as in Goethe's poem, but instead as an uncannily human figure crooning a lullaby-like melody.[1] The Erlking's song is first heard *pianissimo*, separated from the musical world of father and son by its higher range, major mode, and rounded lyricism. But slowly, as the lied unfolds, his vocal compass begins to expand, deepening in range, absorbing motives from the two 'real' characters and finally breaking out of the make-believe stasis of the major mode into minor-mode actuality. His final D-minor cadence (b. 123) marks the moment when the supernatural explodes irrevocably into the natural, severing the father's hold on his son and claiming the boy's life (Ex. 8.1).[2] The Erlking proves uncontainable, an ontological blur of human/inhuman, masculine/feminine, real/imagined, a creature hovering on the boundary between phenomena and noumena. It was for this reason that nineteenth-century listeners feared Schubert's song – but it was also why they revered it. Indeed, the German novelist Jean Paul (Johann Paul Friedrich Richter) asked to hear the piece on his deathbed, particularly the passages of the Erlking, which 'drew him, like everyone else, with magic power towards a transfigured, fairer existence'.[3] What attracted Jean Paul was also what made Schubert's supernatural

Example 8.1 Schubert, 'Der Erlkönig', D. 328 (1815): the Erlking's final minor-mode cadence 'And if you are not willing, I shall use force', bb. 119–23.

Figure 8.1 Moritz von Schwind (1804–71), *Der Erlkönig* (*c.* 1830). Oil on canvas, 32 × 44.5 cm, Österreichische Galerie Belvedere, Vienna (Wikimedia Commons)

world quintessentially 'Romantic': its erosion of stable distinctions between this world and the next, its promise of an enchanted real.

To understand more clearly the shift in musico-magical ontology exemplified by 'Der Erlkönig', and by other supernatural evocations of the period, it is helpful to start by widening our lens – considering the backdrops against which Romanticism's newly tangible enchantment emerged. Of course, a comprehensive history of musical magic is not our aim here, but we might begin a concise overview by considering the critical terminology associated with the reception of Schubert's song. It was, as many listeners argued, a piece whose Romanticism was rooted in modern forms of 'fantasy'.[4] This reference was not casual but gestured towards a wide and rich discourse on the fantastic, associated with the literary theory of Friedrich Schlegel, the tales of E. T. A. Hoffmann, Novalis, and Wilhelm Heinrich Wackenroder, and (later) the fiction of Charles Nodier, Théophile Gautier, and Jules Janin. As Gautier put it in 1836, the fantastic was a newly forged mode that jettisoned the make-believe wands, castles, and spells of eighteenth-century fairy tales in favour of a *surnaturel vrai*, a 'true' or 'real' supernatural reconciling imagination with science, dream visions with physical realities, the material with the ethereal.[5]

A generation earlier, Friedrich Schlegel, in his 'Letter About the Novel' (1799), had provided the foundation for such a definition, introducing the fantastic as a revolutionary impulse eliminating all boundaries and classifications, uniting fictional and factual narratives in an arabesque-like mixture of 'storytelling, song, and other forms'. Fantasy dissolved not only generic constraints, but also entrenched epistemological boundaries. The source of its supernaturalism, for Schlegel, was a 'sentimental' or 'spiritual' force, a spirit of divine love permeating the created universe itself. Not otherworldly or elusive, divine magic was immanent, expressed 'in the sphere of nature'.[6] Though palpable, it was not easily captured or described; indeed, only art could apprehend it. And of all the arts, according to Schlegel, *music* was best suited to achieve this:

Painting is no longer as fantastic. … Modern music, on the other hand … has remained true on the whole to its character, so that I would dare to call it without reservation a sentimental art. … [The spiritual] is the sacred breath which, in the tones of music, moves us. It cannot be grasped forcibly and comprehended mechanically, but it can be amiably lured by mortal beauty and veiled in it. The magic words of poetry can be infused with and inspired by its power.[7]

Poetry, for Schlegel, was fantastic only when animated by spiritual sound; the two are united in his theory of Romantic fantasy in an inextricable pairing, together providing an intimation of true magic: 'something higher, the infinite, a hieroglyph of the one eternal love and the sacred fullness of life or creative nature'.[8]

Backdrops for Romantic Fantasy

Schlegel's natural conception of enchantment was not entirely novel but, as he acknowledged, recuperative, 'tending toward antiquity in spirit and in kind'.[9] His fantastic ontology represented a partial return to an earlier magical paradigm: that of the sixteenth and seventeenth centuries, when visible and invisible, physical and metaphysical realms were conceived as parts of a resonant whole. Mingling Platonic ideas with Pythagorean and Christian tenets, Renaissance cosmologists had conceived an all-encompassing enchantment, a network of harmonic concordances flowing downwards from God, linking celestial, intellectual, and mundane planes in sacred musico-mathematical logic. Every facet of the created universe was animated by divine sound, connected to every other via resonant sympathies. The result was an organic unity – a *spiritus mundi* – animated by ubiquitous musical magic. Magician-philosophers harnessed its power by penetrating the secrets of the universal sympathies, the occult relationships between macrocosm and microcosm. In doing so, they achieved Orphic sway, translating divine resonance into composed melody, which could bring bodies into (or out of) tune with the surrounding universe. Spoken poetry, clothed in cosmic music, had similar powers, vibrating within material bodies to transform and illuminate. Magic was real, powerful, and proximate, intimately connected to the pursuit of natural science and philosophy.[10]

For Schlegel and the early German Romantics, the intellectual-magical unity of this world seemed a lost utopia, a golden age that had slowly dissipated through the late seventeenth and eighteenth centuries, eroded by the forces of secularism, scepticism, and materialism. Natural magic, as Friedrich Schiller put it, had been repressed by 'the faith of reason'.[11] Of course, occult beliefs did not disappear suddenly or entirely during the so-called Enlightenment, but were marginalised, no longer associated openly with reliable philosophical and scientific knowledge. Enchantment itself ceased to be regarded as 'real', emerging instead as imaginary, the stuff of entertainment, fraud, or childhood whimsy. The epoch of natural magic gave way to what eighteenth- and nineteenth-century critics alike referred to as the age of the 'marvellous'.[12] Amongst the key literary signals of this shift was an explosion of fairy-tale literature beginning around 1700, ushered in by collections including the Comtesse d'Aulnoy's *Les contes de fées* (1696) and Antoine Galland's free translation of Arabic stories, *Les mille et un nuits* (1704). Emanating largely from France, these fictions relocated enchantment to make-believe and foreign places, demoting spirits and genies (old harbingers of natural magic) to the status of illusions, pedagogical instruments, or vehicles for satire. Such tales were widely translated and imitated, establishing an 'enlightened' form of fictional magic, a rationalist bulwark against antiquated (but still latent) forces of superstition.

A similar trend emerged in the theatrical world: an outpouring of operatic tales of make-believe and exoticism, which shored up the idea of magic as illusory, the province of entertainment rather than serious intellectual enquiry. Music, once a key agent of magic, suffered a parallel loss in status. No longer linked to mystical mathematics or cosmic resonance, it was associated instead with the production of theatrical effects. David J. Buch describes this shift as the moment when 'composers, theorists, and critics could define music in purely rational terms', when sound was no longer inherently divine but simply aesthetic. By the mid-eighteenth century, this transformation had allowed 'a distinct category for magical topics' to emerge, a sounding marvellous.[13] Jean-François Marmontel, in an entry for the famous *Encyclopédie*, identified 'le théâtre du merveilleux' as a broad category of supernatural representation defined in contrast to 'simple nature'. His compatriot, Louis de Cahusac, in an article on 'Féerie', located it as a style of music distinguished by 'an enchanting sound productive of illusions'.[14] These 'illusions' were generated by a collection of musical topics carefully cordoned off from the realm of the actual, designed to evoke imaginary domains: muted registers, modal harmonies, and wind instruments to invoke scenes of dream or sleep; diminished harmonies and low brass scoring to conjure the underworld; static harmony and unison scoring for oracle scenes; and so forth. Such devices defined and constrained magic, which emerged as the 'Other' against which reason and reality were constructed.[15]

As the marvellous paradigm solidified through the last half of the eighteenth century, the authors and composers with whom it was associated began to strain against its boundaries, resisting the idea of magic as superficial or purely illusory. Their reaction was motivated in part by a sense of loss, a nostalgia for direct human access to mystery, enchantment, and spiritual experience, often yoked in modern criticism to burgeoning Romanticism.[16] With it came early signs of a renegotiation of magic's status. Schlegel's real supernatural, as he described it in 1799, was clearly not just recollective, meant to reanimate aspects of Neoplatonic natural magic, but also reactive, a rejection of the constraints associated with eighteenth-century illusions. But how did the new fantastic ontology emerge? How was the domain of reason reconnected with that of enchantment? Answers to these questions are many and complex, but two major catalysts may be noted here.

The Recuperation of Magic

The first involves philosophical innovations proposed by a group of young German Romantics – the *Frühromantiker* – centred in Jena and Berlin in the last decade of the eighteenth century. These included Friedrich Schlegel himself, his brother August Wilhelm Schlegel, Friedrich Hölderlin, Novalis, Friedrich Schelling, and Friedrich Schleiermacher (amongst others). Amongst the primary achievements of this group was a reassessment of the ideas of Immanuel Kant, whose system of critical idealism had aimed, in part, to reconcile old Enlightenment tensions between rationalism and empiricism. Though it had done much to breach this divide, Kant's work had, in so doing, generated a new and equally problematic separation between understanding and sensibility, phenomena and noumena. The new 'Romantic' or 'Absolute' Idealism of the young Romantics sought to eliminate this dualism, generating a philosophical model uniting real and ideal, natural and supernatural in a logical whole.[17] Key to such a project was an embrace of pantheistic impulses inherited from the seventeenth-century thinker Baruch Spinoza, and updated by Gottfried Herder. Drawing on these tenets, the forgers of Romantic Idealism dismantled the idea of divine magic as emanating from a personal, removed God, replacing it with the notion of divinity as an organic force, a metaphysical animator of the natural world. Their work combined Spinoza's monism (the notion of God as the abstract, underlying Substance of all creation) with the tenets of vital materialism (the concept of matter as enlivened, invested with active power) to produce a dynamic deity, 'the infinite, substantial force ... that underlies all finite, organic forces'.[18] The result was an integration of spirituality and materiality, imaginary and actual worlds, which were subsumed into 'an organic whole, where the identity of each part depends on every other ... [as] aspects of a single living force'.[19] Recast in this form, divine enchantment became compatible with – indeed, inextricable from – the material world. Perceiving magic again meant looking at and *listening to* God's physical creation, the voice of nature itself, whose sound was re-endowed with magical efficacy. What emerged, as we have seen in Schlegel, was the notion of God-through-nature: the idea of a real or natural supernatural.

The second catalyst was the series of major political upheavals roiling the last decades of the eighteenth century, emanating from (though not confined to) France. These clashes, which led up to and followed the 1789 revolution, destabilised the intellectual structures that had sustained the

Age of Reason; in particular, as Michel Foucault has influentially argued, they dismantled systems of marginalisation that had confined poor, ill, mad, and criminal populations to the fringes of cities and therefore the outskirts of social discourse. As the impulses of revolution gathered impetus, these populations came flooding back, crowding the streets of Paris, demanding recognition and representation. They brought with them many of the old magical beliefs that had been contained and disciplined by reason: the demons of a repressed past.[20]

The sense of encroaching menace that preceded the events of 1789 was felt not just in France but across Europe; indeed, the return of dark supernaturalism was anticipated in England as early as the 1760s by the rise of Gothic culture. Ushered in by Horace Walpole's *The Castle of Otranto* (1764) and extended through the late eighteenth century by the novels of Ann Radcliffe and Matthew Lewis, Gothic tales feature monsters of all sorts, from vampires to succubi and ghouls, which hover on the peripheries of the known world in medieval castles, underground caverns, and foreign locales. From these (worryingly close) places, they terrorise the domain of reason, morality, and order, suggesting a world under threat. But in the final hour, Gothic supernaturalism is almost always explained away as illusion or misconception, demons are vanquished, and order restored. The pattern is linked, in modern literary criticism, to the idea of a world teetering on the edge of collapse, a last-ditch attempt to shore up the crumbling intellectual and political structures of rationalism.[21]

As the century drew to a close, Gothic containment began to erode and, rather than hovering on the margins, literary monsters began to infiltrate the centre, escaping from distant or underground hiding places into the space of the modern real. It was this ontological conflation that characterised the emerging fantastic culture, which recuperated not just divine forms of enchantment but also demonic impulses.[22] Post-revolutionary tales of fantasy are replete with doppelgängers, emblems of supernatural darkness who are also characters of the 'actual' world: E. T. A. Hoffmann's demonic seductress Giulia in 'A New Year's Eve Adventure' is also the young girl Julietta; Alexandre Dumas's enchanting socialite in 'La femme au collier de velours' is also a dead guillotine victim. No resolution or explanation for these doubles is offered. In fantastic worlds, the dark supernatural is placed alongside the natural as its inescapable, inevitable counterpart, the signal of a newly integrated but also fractured world.

And it was not just the forces of revolution that produced the new 'real' demonism, but also those of burgeoning imperialism. From Napoleon's continental incursions of the early 1800s to the rapid colonisation of India, Africa, and America by the major European powers, the nineteenth century was a time of unstable (expanding, contracting, collapsing) borders. Cultures of reason were threatened not just by ill and mad spectres on the edges of cities, but by the idea of monsters in more remote places which, once distant and separate, now became real and proximate. Foreign – babbling, threatening, illegible – bodies were increasingly wedded to legible 'enlightened' ones, the 'civilised' self to an imperial shadow.[23] Small wonder, then, that theorists of the fantastic often describe the mode in terms of grotesque conflation or paradox. It was a mode of rupture, a recuperation of magic that was rooted not just in Romantic Idealism (including the pantheistic recovery of divine nature) but in political dislocation and violence (the return of repressed demonism). Its *surnaturel vrai* was enticing as well as threatening and had a marked impact on all the arts, especially, as Schlegel suggested, on cultures of musical production and reception.

We have already examined 'Der Erlkönig' as a symptom of the new fantastic ontology, but Schubert's supernaturalism was by no means unique; nor was the idea of 'real' enchantment confined to German-speaking lands, as it extended across Continental Europe, the British Isles, Russia, and America. Magical worlds of all sorts were naturalised, rendered compatible with both reason and science in the late eighteenth and nineteenth centuries, from fairy lands to angelic domains and hellish invocations. Below, we take brief tours of two such spaces, though it is important to note that many others existed, and that the influence of the *surnaturel vrai* was neither total nor unchallenged. Rather than a universal shift, the rise of Romantic fantasy might be understood as a general cultural drift which coexisted with fragments of the older marvellous and Gothic traditions, taking a variety of forms depending on local circumstances and conventions.

Fairies, Science, and Natural Magic

The naturalisation of the supernatural may be seen especially clearly in Romantic fairy evocations, especially those of Felix Mendelssohn, which showcase the new interweaving of magic, reality, and reason.[24] Like Schubert, Mendelssohn forged an early reputation by writing supernatural music, focusing in particular on Shakespearean elfin scenes. The most widely known of these was the Overture to *A Midsummer Night's Dream*,

Op. 21 (1826), although the sound world of this piece had been anticipated less than a year before in the scherzo of the Octet, Op. 20 (1825), and would be invoked again in another scherzo – the opening piece in Mendelssohn's collection of incidental music for Shakespeare's play (1842). In all three works, we encounter *presto*, *pianissimo* wind and string textures, breathless motivic exchange, and an array of virtuosic whirring and fluttering figures. These effects were received by critics as strikingly original; indeed, the Overture seemed so new that it was deemed by one reviewer to have 'no sisters, no family resemblance'.[25] And, as in the case of 'Der Erlkönig', the work's novelty was yoked explicitly to the new aesthetics of fantasy (the term is highlighted in a number of nineteenth-century reviews of the Overture, including those of Ludwig Rellstab and Gottfried Wilhelm Fink).[26]

Of course, Mendelssohn's fairy music was not entirely unmoored from tradition. It owed a debt to earlier operatic and theatrical scores, which often cast fairy music in dance forms featuring quick tempi, quiet dynamic levels, and contrapuntal writing. But his scherzo sound departs from the elfin 'topic' established during the eighteenth-century marvellous epoch in that it is too quick to operate as dance music, and lacks what Buch calls the 'elegant' or ornamental aesthetic of such pieces, tending instead towards microscopic buzzing and humming.[27] It was Fanny Mendelssohn who revealed the template for Felix's new elfin sound in a letter describing the origins of the Octet's scherzo. The piece, she revealed, took its direction not from musical models but from literary description and natural sound: a passage from Part I of Goethe's *Faust* called the Walpurgisnacht Dream, which describes a celebratory masquerade performed in honour of Shakespeare's fairy king and queen, Oberon and Titania.[28] The music for their performance is furnished by a miniature orchestra composed largely of insects: 'Fly-Snout and Gnat-Nose, here we are, / With kith and kin on duty / Frog-in-the-Leaves and Grasshopper – / The instrumental tutti!'[29] To their buzzing and whirring, Puck dances, Ariel sings, and other supernatural creatures flit and hover. This was the imagined entomological soundscape that inspired Mendelssohn's fairy scherzo; indeed, his insect effects were what made Fanny feel, as she put it, 'so near the world of spirits, carried away in the air, half inclined to snatch up a broomstick and follow the aerial procession'.[30] For both her and her brother, the sound of fairies was inextricable from that of bees and grasshoppers, captured and rendered into music by Felix's novel orchestral textures.

The same close attention to nature also shaped Mendelssohn's elfin supernaturalism in the *Midsummer Night's Dream* Overture. According

Example 8.2 Mendelssohn's 'buzzing fly': *A Midsummer Night's Dream* Overture, Op. 21 (1826), bb. 264–70

to Julius Schubring, Felix spent much of the summer of the Overture's composition outside, observing botanical forms and textures and listening to insect song:

> On the sole occasion I rode with him, we went to Pankow, walking thence to the Schönhauser Garden. It was about that time when he was busy with the Overture to *A Midsummer Night's Dream*. The weather was beautiful, and we were engaged in animated conversation as we lay in the shade on the grass when, all of a sudden, he seized me firmly by the arm, and whispered: 'Hush!' He afterwards informed me that a large fly had just then gone buzzing by, and he wanted to hear the sound it produced gradually die away. When the Overture was completed, he showed me the passage in the progression, where the violoncello modulates in the chord of the seventh of a descending scale from B minor to F sharp minor [Ex. 8.2], and said: 'There, that's the fly that buzzed past us at Schönhauser!'[31]

Audiences (as reported in numerous reviews) heard not only flies but other small creatures including gnats in the Overture, whose textures seemed to them to vibrate with insect sound. The piece hovered in a space between natural imitation and poetic expression – in the uncertain domain of the fantastic. Its effects were borrowed and extended in a host of other 'fantastique' scherzi, so labelled by composers from Berlioz to Stravinsky.[32]

An intersection between fairy magic and entomological life was apparent not just in musical works but in literature and popular science. A survey of nineteenth-century fairy stories (including the fantastic tales of E. T. A. Hoffmann, Charles Nodier, and George Sand) reveals that elfin creatures were pervasively figured as insects, their magical miniaturism shading fluidly into microscopic realism as if one world might be housed secretly within the other. And texts on entomology made the same link, interspersing images of butterflies, beetles, and flies with fanciful renderings of fairies, sometimes to appeal to children and in other cases to personify nature's 'magic'.[33] Across disciplines, there was a sense that looking at nature and listening closely its voice could reveal enchanted realities – a hint of the pantheistic magic that Schlegel and other Idealist thinkers associated with the organic world. Modern technology was crucial to this venture. Microscopes, newly affordable and available, promised to reveal hidden botanical and entomological wonders, and virtuosic orchestras functioned similarly, capturing ever-more delicate and inaccessible soundscapes. New instruments, both scientific and musical, breached the gap between science and magic, generating a characteristically fantastic blurring.[34]

But access to enchanted realities was not available to all; only the special few were gifted with senses sufficiently honed to perceive the magical sights and sounds at the heart of the created world. Acute, quasi-divine perception was the province of artistic genius, the basis of a new hierarchy elevating poets, painters, and especially composers to priest-like status. Revered, though often depicted as tortured or mad, the fantastic musician was suspended between the material and ethereal, apprehending both physical surfaces and supernatural (Platonic or vitalist) essences. This model for the inspired listener was, in some regards, a reanimation of the old Renaissance magus, though rather than manipulating the inaudible mathematical resonances of a Pythagorean universe, the Romantic composer harnessed the real sounds of a pantheistic world. Preserving these in composed 'hieroglyphs', he wielded not just aesthetic but metaphysical power, producing works with the capacity to transform, enliven, and elevate.[35]

Imperial Demons

If fairies were rationalised, given new life, by fantasy's *surnaturel vrai*, so too were demons. From Goethe's Mephistopheles (in *Faust* settings by Berlioz, Liszt, Gounod, Boito, and others) to Carl Maria von Weber's Samiel in *Der Freischütz* and the bloodthirsty Lord Ruthven in Heinrich Marschner's *Der Vampyr*, figures of supernatural evil loomed large in Romantic theatrical and instrumental repertories. Their proliferation can be dated, in part, to the rise of Gothic culture (mentioned above) as well as to burgeoning fears of political violence during the years surrounding the French Revolution. However, on the musical stage, demonic evocation also had an older provenance, hearkening back to depictions of monsters, spectres, and the underworld in opera since the seventeenth century. What was new and compelling about Romantic demons – what set them apart from older theatrical horrors – was their partial release from the imaginary world into the realm of the scientific real. Like fairies, sylphs, and angels, they were naturalised, but not by the Idealist longing and pantheistic belief that recalled benevolent magic; instead, the 'nature' with which demons became associated was manufactured by theories of physiological difference emanating from the human and social sciences.[36]

In marvellous opera of the eighteenth century from Niccolò Jommelli to Wolfgang Amadeus Mozart, scenes of dark supernaturalism were associated with the so-called 'terrifying style' (later also called the *ombra* topic), marked by low brass outbursts, the minor mode, diminished harmonies, bare octave or unison sonorities, rhythmic disruption, and sudden dynamic contrasts.[37] This collection of gestures served to depict a range of horrors from witches to flying dragons and hell itself, acting as a carefully cordoned-off magical semiotics separating dark imaginings from 'actual' life. Such effects were not lost in the Romantic period, but they began to coexist with another set of topical markers: those of the exotic. These included noisy percussion (especially the janissary combination of cymbals, triangle, and drum), downbeat thumping, syllabic text-setting, static rhythms, and non-progressive harmonic structures associated with the (alleged) primitivism and ferocity of Turks, Scythians, and other heathen groups.[38] Gradually, the markers of otherworldly demons began to blur into the sounds of these *human* 'savages' in a new convergence of 'real' and mythological malevolence.

This shift took root towards the end of the eighteenth century, when belief in the dark aspects of Christian supernaturalism (including hell and the devil) had been almost completely dismantled, rejected as medieval superstition. There was no room, amongst the educated classes, for the old demons – creatures who had once contained and focused fantasies of sadism, violence, and depravity. Such fantasies persisted, however, floating around in the collective consciousness, attaching to the poor fringes of society and increasingly, to colonial bodies on the edges of expanding Western empires. The new sciences of anthropology and ethnology fuelled this transference, generating theories of racial difference that demoted European peasants along with colonial Others to inferior status. Both populations were categorised as physically and morally inferior, inclined towards violence, gluttony, and lasciviousness. The result was a justification of imperial incursion and domestic oppression as well as the invention of what H. L. Malchow terms the 'racialized Gothic', a class of human fiends.[39]

The sonic markers of the new demonism appear clearly in Meyerbeer's grand opera *Robert le diable* (1831), a work that influenced virtually every infernal evocation of the following three decades. The most famous portion of this opera was (and remains) the Act 3 finale, the dance of the damned nuns, which takes place in a quintessentially Gothic landscape: a graveyard in the courtyard of an ancient moonlit monastery. The evil Bertram has lured the opera's hero, Robert (Duke of Normandy), to the spot, convincing him to commit a sacrilege – to pluck the evergreen branch on the tomb of Saint Rosalie, which will grant him immortality and unlimited power. The traditional signals of the 'terrifying style' (low brass, tremolo, minor mode, and diminished harmonies) accompany Bertram's recitative as he calls the faithless nuns sleeping beneath the monastery stones to awake and aid him in his plan. As they come slowly back to life, however, a different set of effects begins to creep into the orchestra: a ringing triangle and a quiet, staccato motive in the upper strings. To this accompaniment, the nuns rediscover the objects of pleasure to which they had succumbed during their lives, including wine and dice. They urge Robert to complete his task and, when he plucks the fatal branch, the topical convergence already underway is fully realised: the scene shifts from minor mode to a raucous D major marked by noise, percussive clashing, and downbeat thumping. Gone are the sonic effects of Meyerbeer's airy wraiths, replaced by those of savage revellers. The nuns are joined by demons shouting a jerky, syllabic message, and together they form 'a disordered circle', commencing a *fortissimo* bacchanale. Over the course of the scene, ghostly spirits become exotic primitives. The otherworldly collapses into the Other.

Berlioz, in one of several essays on *Robert*, wrote that Meyerbeer's use of percussion signalled a newly savage 'fantastique' aesthetic. And the critic François-Joseph Fétis deemed the whole third act a 'monde fantastique', an infernal vision unlike any that had come before.[40] Especially memorable, for him (as for many reviewers), was the bacchanale, a dance originally associated with Greek pagan ritual but long since appropriated by Western travel writers as a signal of primitive societies. Its telltale circle of revellers appeared in numerous nineteenth-century depictions of native African, American, Australian, and Mexican cultures. Differentiated from one another only superficially, the ring-dances associated with these places became inextricable, for many Western readers, from pagan abandon and debauchery (see Fig. 8.2).[41] Meyerbeer was the first to employ the form in an infernal evocation, but he was by no means the last. In the wake of *Robert le diable*, a host of other composers invoked bacchanalian circles and related exotic effects in demonic scenes, including Adolphe Adam in the ballet *Giselle* (the 'Bacchanale des Wilis'), Berlioz in the Pandemonium scene of *La Damnation de Faust,* and Liszt in the *Mephisto Waltz* No. 1 ('Der Tanz in der Dorfschenke').

In these pieces, as in Meyerbeer, *ombra* markers intermingle vertiginously with the images and sounds of an 'undeveloped' colonial world, and demons themselves hesitate, like Hoffmann's menacing doppelgängers, between mythology and ethnography. The fear they articulate is no longer that of biblical devils or eternal damnation but of vengeful slaves and savage colonies – a threat born of guilt, racial prejudice, and the terrors of modern empire.

Further Threads

The above sketches are points of departure, meant to encourage a wider consideration of music's interface with Romantic forms of natural or scientific magic, several of which are discussed in other chapters of the present volume. We could, for instance, contemplate enchantments produced via composerly interactions with new electrical, optical, and telegraphic technologies;[42] intersections amongst sound, vitalist magic, and physiology forged by instruments including the aeolian harp and glass harmonica;[43] or forms of magical-musical embodiment bound up with nineteenth-century theories of sex and gender.[44] Understanding

Figure 8.2 *La danse du sabbat*, an infernal bacchanale. Metal engraving, in Paul Christian, *Histoire de la magie* (Paris: Furne, 1884) (http://fantastic.library.cornell.edu /imagerecord.php?record=68)

Romantic sound worlds means, in many senses, tracing the history of magic – documenting music's reinstatement as an agent of *puissant* enchantment, a conduit between material and metaphysical domains. The 'end' of the Romantic period (in so far as we can identify such a thing) might be understood as the moment when sound was, once again, divested of such power, slipping back to the status of the aesthetic, rational, or merely marvellous.

Notes

1. See Christopher H. Gibbs, '"Komm, Geh' Mit Mir": Schubert's Uncanny *Erlkönig*', *19th-Century Music*, 19/2 (1995), 115–35.
2. See Deborah Stein, 'Schubert's *Erlkönig*: Motivic Parallelism and Motivic Transformation', *19th-Century Music*, 13/2 (1989), 145–58.
3. Gibbs, 'Komm, Geh' Mit Mir', 132.
4. The term appears repeatedly in Viennese reviews of the 1820s; see Gibbs, 'Komm, Geh' Mit Mir', 122 n. 32; and Christopher H. Gibbs, 'The Presence of Erlkönig: Reception and Reworkings of a Schubert Lied', Ph.D. diss. (Columbia University, 1992).
5. Théophile Gautier, 'Contes d'Hoffmann', *Chronique de Paris* (14 August 1836).
6. Friedrich Schlegel, 'Letter About the Novel', in J. M. Bernstein (ed.), *Classic and Romantic German Aesthetics* (Cambridge: Cambridge University Press, 2003), 287–96 at 291, 293–4.
7. Ibid., 291.
8. Ibid., 291.
9. Ibid., 293.
10. For a broader sense of this magical ontology, see Gary Tomlinson, *Music and Renaissance Magic: Toward a Historiography of Others* (Chicago: University of Chicago Press, 1993).
11. Friedrich Schiller, *The Piccolomini*, trans. Samuel Taylor Coleridge in *The Dramatic Works of Samuel Taylor Coleridge*, ed. Derwent Coleridge (London: Edward Moxon, 1857), 226.
12. On the marginalising (and covert continuation) of musico-magical beliefs, see Penelope Gouk, *Music, Science, and Natural Magic* (New Haven: Yale University Press, 1999). On the emergence of the marvellous paradigm, see David J. Buch, *Magic Flutes and Enchanted Forests: The Supernatural in Eighteenth-Century Musical Theater* (Chicago: University of Chicago Press, 2008).
13. Buch, *Magic Flutes and Enchanted Forests*, 74.
14. Jean-François Marmontel, 'Merveilleux', in *Supplément à l'Encyclopédie, ou Dictionnaire raisonné des sciences, des arts et des métiers* (Amsterdam: M. M. Rey, 1776–7), 906. Louis de Cahusac, 'Féerie', in *Encyclopédie ou Dictionnaire raisonné des sciences, des arts et des métiers*, vol. 6 (Paris: Briasson, 1760), 464.
15. For a summary of magical musical topics, see Buch, *Magic Flutes and Enchanted Forests*, 47–9 and 74–6.
16. For a classic articulation of this shift, see M. H. Abrams, *Natural Supernaturalism: Tradition and Revolution in Romantic Literature* (New York: Norton, 1971).

17. See Frederick C. Beiser, *German Idealism: The Struggle against Subjectivism, 1781–1801* (Cambridge, MA: Harvard University Press, 2002).

18. Julia A. Lamm, 'Romanticism and Pantheism', in David Fergusson (ed.), *The Blackwell Companion to Nineteenth-Century Theology* (Chichester and Malden, MA: Wiley-Blackwell, 2010), 165–86, at 172.

19. Beiser, *German Idealism*, 372.

20. Michel Foucault, *Folie et déraison: Histoire de la folie à l'âge classique* (Paris: Plon, 1961).

21. See David Punter and Glennis Byron, *The Gothic* (Malden, MA: Blackwell, 2004); and Fred Botting, *Gothic*, 2nd ed. (New York: Routledge, 2014).

22. For a seminal study of fantastic literature, see Tzvetan Todorov, *The Fantastic: A Structural Approach to a Literary Genre*, trans. Richard Howard (Ithaca, NY: Cornell University Press, 1973). A helpful historical window onto the genre is provided by José Monleón in *A Specter Is Haunting Europe: A Sociohistorical Approach to the Fantastic* (Princeton, NJ: Princeton University Press, 1990).

23. See H. L. Malchow, *Gothic Images of Race in Nineteenth-Century Britain* (Stanford: Stanford University Press, 1996); and Ruth Anolik and Douglas L. Howard (eds.), *The Gothic Other: Racial and Social Constructions in the Literary Imagination* (Jefferson, NC: McFarland, 2004).

24. See Francesca Brittan, 'On Microscopic Hearing: Fairy Magic, Natural Science, and the *Scherzo fantastique*', *Journal of the American Musicological Society*, 64/3 (2011), 527–600.

25. Roger Nichols, *Mendelssohn Remembered* (London: Faber and Faber, 1997), 106.

26. For Rellstab's description, see *Iris im Gebiete der Tonkunst* (23 November 1832). For Fink's commentary, see the *Allgemeine musikalische Zeitung* of 25 June 1834 and 6 May 1835.

27. Buch describes earlier elfin sound worlds in *Magic Flutes*, 56–7; 63–77.

28. Sebastian Hensel, *The Mendelssohn Family (1729–1847) from Letters and Journals*, 2nd ed., trans. Karl Klingemann (New York: Harper & Brothers, 1882), vol. 1, 131.

29. Johann Wolfgang von Goethe, *Faust*, Part One, trans. David Luke (Oxford: Oxford University Press, 1987), 135.

30. Hensel, *Mendelssohn Family*, 131.

31. Schubring, 'Reminiscences of Felix Mendelssohn-Bartholdy', *Musical World*, 31 (12 and 19 May 1866).

32. See Brittan, 'On Microscopic Hearing', 574–94.

33. See Nicola Bown, *Fairies in Nineteenth-Century Art and Literature* (Cambridge: Cambridge University Press, 2001); and Carol Silver, *Strange and Secret Peoples: Fairies and Victorian Consciousness* (Oxford: Oxford University Press, 1999).

34. On interactions amongst science, magic, and romantic instrumentality see John Tresch, *The Romantic Machine: Utopian Science and Technology after Napoleon* (Chicago: University of Chicago Press, 2012).

35. This new model for the composer is articulated especially clearly by E. T. A. Hoffmann; see *E. T. A. Hoffmann's Musical Writings: Kreisleriana, The Poet and the Composer, Music Criticism*, ed. David Charlton, trans. Martyn Clarke (Cambridge: Cambridge University Press, 1989).

36. For a fuller working-out of this idea, see Brittan, *Music and Fantasy in the Age of Berlioz* (Cambridge: Cambridge University Press, 2017), 191–267.

37. See Buch, *Enchanted Forests*, 48–57; and Clive McClelland, *Ombra: Supernatural Music in the Eighteenth Century* (Plymouth: Lexington Books, 2012).

38. As delineated in Ralph Locke, *Musical Exoticism: Images and Reflections* (Cambridge: Cambridge University Press, 2009).

39. Malchow, *Gothic Images of Race*.

40. For Berlioz's remarks, see the *Gazette musicale* (12 July 1835). Fétis's remarks appear in the same journal (3 December 1831).

41. See Christopher B. Steiner, 'Travel Engravings and the Construction of the Primitive', in Elazar Barkan and Ronald Bush (eds.), *Prehistories of the Future: The Primitivist Project and the Culture of Modernism* (Stanford: Stanford University Press, 1995), 202–25.

42. See Deirdre Loughridge, *Haydn's Sunrise, Beethoven's Shadow: Audiovisual Entertainment and the Emergence of Musical Romanticism* (Chicago: University of Chicago Press, 2016); Inge van Rij, '"A Living, Fleshy Bond": The Electric Telegraph, Musical Thought, and Embodiment', *19th-Century Music*, 39/2 (2015), 142–66; Gabriela Cruz, *Grand Illusion: Phantasmagoria in Nineteenth-Century Opera* (New York: Oxford University Press, 2020).

43. See Heather Hadlock, 'Sonorous Bodies: Women and the Glass Harmonica', *Journal of the American Musicological Society*, 53/3 (2000), 507–42; Carmel Raz, '"The Expressive Organ Within Us": Ether, Ethereality, and Early Romantic Ideas about Music and the Nerves', *19th-Century Music*, 38/2 (2014); and James Kennaway, *Bad Vibrations: The History of the Idea of Music as a Cause of Disease* (Farnham and Burlington, VT: Ashgate, 2012).

44. See Linda Austern and Inna Naroditskaya (eds.), *Music of the Sirens* (Bloomington: Indiana University Press, 2006).

Further Reading

Abrams, M. H. *Natural Supernaturalism: Tradition and Revolution in Romantic Literature* (New York: Norton, 1971).

Austern, Linda Phyllis and Naroditskaya, Inna (eds.). *Music of the Sirens* (Bloomington: Indiana University Press, 2006).

Botting, Fred. *Gothic*, 2nd ed. (New York: Routledge, 2014).

Brittan, Francesca. *Music and Fantasy in the Age of Berlioz* (Cambridge: Cambridge University Press, 2017).

Buch, David J. *Magic Flutes and Enchanted Forests: The Supernatural in Eighteenth-Century Musical Theater* (Chicago: University of Chicago Press, 2008).

Cruz, Gabriela. *Grand Illusion: Phantasmagoria in Nineteenth-Century Opera* (New York: Oxford University Press, 2020).

Gibbs, Christopher H. "'Komm, Geh' Mit Mir": Schubert's Uncanny *Erlkönig*', *19th-Century Music*, 19/2 (1995), 115–35.

Gouk, Penelope. *Music, Science, and Natural Magic in Seventeenth-Century England* (New Haven: Yale University Press, 1999).

Hoffmann, E. T. A. *E. T. A. Hoffmann's Musical Writings: Kreisleriana, The Poet and the Composer, Music Criticism*, ed. David Charlton, trans. Martyn Clarke (Cambridge: Cambridge University Press, 1989).

Loughridge, Deirdre. *Haydn's Sunrise, Beethoven's Shadow: Audiovisual Culture and the Emergence of Musical Romanticism* (Chicago: University of Chicago Press, 2016).

Malchow, H. L. *Gothic Images of Race in Nineteenth-Century Britain* (Stanford: Stanford University Press, 1996).

Monleón, José. *A Specter Is Haunting Europe: A Sociohistorical Approach to the Fantastic* (Princeton: Princeton University Press, 1990).

Richards, Annette. *The Free Fantasia and the Musical Picturesque* (Cambridge: Cambridge University Press, 2006).

Todorov, Tzvetan. *The Fantastic: A Structural Approach to a Literary Genre*, trans. Richard Howard (Ithaca, NY: Cornell University Press, 1973).

Tomlinson, Gary. *Music and Renaissance Magic: Toward a Historiography of Others* (Chicago: University of Chicago Press, 1993).

A Kingdom Not of This World: Music,
Religion, Art-Religion

JAMES GARRATT

The philosopher Peter Sloterdijk recently posed the question 'where are we when we hear music?'[1] Romantic responses are consistent in their religious and often specifically Christian imagery: a 'better world' (Jean Paul), 'paradise' (Tieck), the land of 'faith' and 'holy peace' (Wackenroder), a 'kingdom not of this world' (Hoffmann), and so on.[2] Like Sloterdijk's question, these responses are more complex than they may at first appear, pointing to more than just subjective piety or religiosity (not coincidentally a term introduced into the German language in the years around 1800).[3] Since the time of Heine's *Die romantische Schule* (1835), the Romantic investment in religion has often been disparaged as regressive and equated with 'throne-and-altar nostalgia'.[4] A more sympathetic, though no less one-sided standpoint is to treat such religious rhetoric as an arbitrary 'jargon of ultimacy' servicing purely secular conceptions of transcendence.[5] In different ways, both these approaches reflect how, more broadly, the master narrative of secularisation has shaped conceptions of the relationship between Romanticism and religion.[6] Although scholars have long abandoned clunky notions of an Age of Reason sweeping aside an Age of Faith, the view that religion became a marginal force fighting a doomed rearguard action continues to shape attitudes towards post-Enlightenment religious art. While we may no longer share the confidence with which modernist commentators such as Adorno blasted the false consciousness and 'poisonous' religiosity tainting the products of art-religion, something of this suspicion still clings to works such as Wagner's *Parsifal* and Mahler's Symphony No. 8 (let alone Gounod's *Ave Maria*).[7] The issues yoked together by the secularisation paradigm are far from irrelevant to Romantic religion, art, and art-religion; indeed, the secular-modernist brand of critique epitomised by Adorno feeds on the anxieties of its host, converting Romantic concerns over the continuing possibility of religious art into accusations of mystification and falsity. But to understand the nature of the religion within art-religion, we need to approach it with an alternative model of secularisation in mind: one that emphasises the continuous, dynamic unfolding of religion and the dialogic nature of art's encounters with it.

As Daniel Weidner argues, secularisation and art-religion do not wipe the slate clean; rather, both resemble palimpsests in which the sacred meanings they overwrite remain tangible and active.[8]

Most discussions of the relationships between Romanticism, religious art, and art-religion divide the field into three broad categories, each encompassing a distinct set of attitudes:

  i. art considered as an element within traditional religious practices, such as music for use in the liturgy or private devotions
 ii. art as offering its own points of access to the truths, meanings, and experiences of religion, serving to complement, supplement or interpret them (in Claudia Stockinger's phrase, primary art-religion)[9]
iii. art as co-opting the claims and cultic functions of religion, reconstructing, critiquing, or negating it, or simply taking its place; in Adorno's phrase, 'the self-exaltation of art as the absolute' (secondary art-religion).[10]

Two caveats are needed before exploring these categories further. First, we should avoid pre-emptively treating them as successive stages within the process of secularisation (or music's journey from being 'the most religious among the arts' (Tieck) to what Georg Simmel described as 'the religion of today').[11] Art-religion – particularly in the secondary form outlined above – has often been represented as one of the secular forces filling the void left by the retreat of religion; this model is at work in Max Weber's view that in modernity art 'takes over' religion's functions, laying claim to its own form of redemption.[12] While this perspective fits well with some works from Weber's own period (such as Delius's *Eine Messe des Lebens* or Strauss's *Eine Alpensinfonie*) it exaggerates the secularity of earlier forms of art-religion, which tend to be heterodox or syncretic rather than post-Christian in orientation. Second, we need to resist the polarised view of sacred and secular fostered by the secularisation paradigm. Under Romanticism, the borders between religious art and art-religion were porous, and often the same genres and works were approached from all three of the perspectives outlined above. Consider, for example, the Romantic reception of Raphael's *Sistine Madonna*, elevated by Wackenroder as an emblem of the Christian calling of the artist, by Hoffmann as an intimation of infinity, and by Wagner as a symbol of a 'redemption through love' that transcended religious dogma.[13] Within individual compositions, too, these strands overlap and collide, in spite of energetic attempts by critics and institutions to police the boundaries of the sacred.[14]

Listening Religiously: Art-Religion and Music Aesthetics

Romantic conceptions of art-religion percolated only gradually into the musical sphere, shaping attitudes towards listening and performing music well before they had an impact on composition. Although art-religion emerges in the years around 1800, the term itself is seldom found in discussions of music prior to the 1850s, when it was invoked by critics seeking to burst the bubble of the Wagnerian *Gesamtkunstwerk*. Tellingly, his opponents, such as the literary historian Julian Schmidt, presented Wagner's vision of the 'oneness of religion, art and society' as a stale rehash of the ideas of the theologian Friedrich Schleiermacher and the Romantic school from half a century earlier.[15] While Schmidt's aim was polemical, he is right to identify Schleiermacher and the Romantic school as the key sources for what has been described as the 'convergence' model of art-religion: the view that art and religion – functioning as separate reality compartments in modernity – needed to be drawn into unity.[16] In his *Über die Religion* (1799), Schleiermacher argued that such convergence provided a vital route for reviving religion and reconciling it with the present: 'Religion and art stand alongside one another like two friendly souls whose inner affinity, whether or not they feel it to the same degree, is as yet unknown to them ... To bring them together and to unite them in one bed is the only thing that can bring religion to completion on the path on which we are heading.'[17] Schleiermacher's conception of this convergence assumes that each of these partners has its own autonomous capacity for revelation. In the writings of the Romantic school, however, the boundaries between the two are often blurred, dissolving art and religion into equivalence or identity: for Hölderlin, 'that which is most beautiful is also holiest', while Tieck apostrophises music as 'the completely revealed religion'.[18]

For Carl Dahlhaus, the impulse to draw art and religion together reflects not only the new metaphysical claims being made for art around 1800, but also the primacy given to feeling within contemporary religious thought.[19] One of the most important legacies of art-religion is the heightened awareness it helped to generate of the proximity between aesthetic and religious experience. In terms derived from aesthetics, Schleiermacher describes religion as 'a sense and taste for the infinite', metaphorically linking it to the feelings instilled by art (religious feelings are 'like a piece of sacred music' accompanying human actions, while religious communication aims at transmitting 'heavenly tones' in a manner akin to Orpheus).[20] For Schleiermacher, both art and religion share the capacity to enable individuals to 'lose the finite and find the infinite', generating moments of revelation in which 'the sense of the universe bursts forth as if through immediate inner illumination'.[21] While Schleiermacher is keen to recruit art as a conduit to religion, he is careful not to treat aesthetic and religious feelings as equivalent, arguing that he does not himself grasp 'how the artistic sense [*Kunstsinn*], by itself alone, merges into religion'; indeed, he coins the term art-religion (*Kunstreligion*) in the context of denying the possibility of art being the dominant element in such a partnership.[22] Less caution is displayed in the two other foundational texts of Romantic art-religion, Wackenroder and Tieck's *Herzensergießungen eines kunstlie-benden Klosterbruders* (1797) and *Phantasien über die Kunst* (1799). In these texts, religion and art are folded into one another to the extent that they become interchangeable; artworks become altars, artists priestly medi-ators with the divine, and aesthetic experience a force capable of triggering religious conversion:

The all-powerful music began in slow, full, sustained chords, as if an invisible wind was gusting over our heads; it surged in ever greater waves like an ocean, and the tones drew out my soul entirely from my body. . . . A priest stepped up to the altar, elevated the Host before the people with a gesture of rapture, and all the people fell to their knees as trombones and I know not what other mighty sounds thundered and roared sublime reverence through every limb. . . . Art had wrought a powerful change in me, and now for the first time I truly understood and inwardly compre-hended art.[23]

Wackenroder and Tieck's *Herzensergießungen* and *Phantasien* are best known for their idealisation of medieval and Renaissance religious art, playing a significant role in fostering the Nazarene movement in painting and the Palestrina revival in music. In discussing painting, they focus almost exclusively on old Italian and German art, idealising it as a model of art in the service of the Church, a relic of an authentic, unreflective religious belief lost to modernity. Their picture of music is more nuanced, elevating both early church music and modern instrumental music as sources of religious revelation. In common with most early Romantic writers, Wackenroder and Tieck treat the former as a kind of artless mood music whose naivety, simplicity, and purity exercises an immediate effect on the listener.[24] In contrast, they imbue modern instrumental music with a distinctively modern form of religiosity.[25] In the musical essays and experiences of the fictional composer Joseph Berglinger, such music is presented as a mysterious, otherworldly language, an object of religious devotion on account of its 'deep-seated, immutable holiness'.[26] With

Berglinger, the experience of 'divine, magnificent symphonic movements' becomes a religious exercise, transforming the concert hall into a sacred space in which he 'listened with just the same devotion as if he were in church'.[27]

Given the extent to which such perspectives helped to shape both art-religion and the reception of absolute music, it is worth probing the conception of religion at work in them. Here, we are not dealing with the 'heavenly innocence' or 'purity and sanctity of devotion' that Romantic commentators discerned in premodern art, but with the inscription of new meanings onto a religious background.[28] When Tieck speaks of instrumental music as revealed religion, or when Hoffmann evokes the unknown kingdom unlocked by Beethoven's Fifth Symphony, they employ metaphors and imagery that diverge significantly from those they apply to early church music.[29] As Tom Spencer notes, Wackenroder and Tieck present a 'loose patchwork' of religious references and allusions, stitching together language drawn from the Bible, the Pietist tradition, classical mythology, and the poetics of the sublime in order to create a modern form of aesthetic religiosity, akin to the new mythology invoked by Schelling and Schlegel.[30] These ingredients call attention to the capacity of instrumental music to convey religious truth, while at the same time giving that truth a specifically modern character. If this music, for Wackenroder and Tieck, imparts revelation, it does so through a glass darkly, offering incomprehensibility, infinite longing and a 'frightful, oracularly ambiguous murkiness'.[31]

The kind of primary art-religion epitomised by Wackenroder and Tieck fits well with Rüdiger Safranski's description of Romanticism as 'the continuation of religion by aesthetic means'.[32] In places, however, the Berglinger pieces flirt with the secondary form of art-religion outlined above; not merely through their syncretic language, but through drifting towards an aestheticism in which art and its cult seemingly aspire to replace religion rather than renew it. Thus Berglinger presents music as a seductive alternative reality cut off from the everyday world, a 'beautiful poetic delirium' in which life becomes a musical work.[33] This view of art is simultaneously proposed and critiqued, giving these texts what Marco Rispoli describes as a 'manic-depressive dynamic'; Wackenroder's final piece on Berglinger dwells mercilessly on the delusions of aestheticism, rejecting its presumptuous elevation of the artist as an 'autonomous, human God' and damning its view of art as a 'deceptive, fraudulent superstition'.[34] The presence of such multiple, competing conceptions of art-religion within these and other early Romantic texts enabled a wide range of artists and movements to draw inspiration from them. But it also explains why the concept met with hostility from both those (such as Goethe) who equated it with religious regression and those (such as Eichendorff) who saw it as a Trojan horse for secularising tendencies.

Composing Religiously

Art in the Service of the Church

The idea that premodern religious art was the product of unreflective belief had a fundamental impact on Romantic artistic production. In the paintings of the Nazarenes, the desire to rekindle the Christian mission of art becomes programmatic; works such as Friedrich Overbeck's *Der Triumph der Religion in der Künsten* (1831–40) have a manifesto character, rededicating art to 'the glorification of God' and celebrating artists who 'consecrated their gifts to the service of religion'.[35] The quest to recapture the spiritual fervour of Renaissance painting led Overbeck and the other Nazarenes to imbibe and emulate its styles, symbols, and techniques. Similar goals impelled composers, spurred on by the notion that the composition of authentic Christian music was a near-hopeless venture in modernity; for Hoffmann, in terms echoed by commentators throughout the nineteenth century, 'it is probably completely impossible for a composer today to be able to write in the same way as Palestrina, Leo, and later Handel and others. That age, pre-eminently when Christianity still shone in its glory, appears to have vanished from the earth, and with it the holy dedication of the artist.'[36] This stance had not precluded Hoffmann from composing his own compositional essays on the problem of church music, the *Canzoni per 4 voci alla Capella* (1808): Latin-texted, quasi-liturgical pieces that engage with the idioms of the Italian *stile antico*. For Felix Mendelssohn and other composers of his generation, emulating the styles of old Italian and German compositions was the key to retrieving their spiritual content; the composition of church music becomes a salvage operation with the aim, as Mendelssohn's father put it, of 'combining old ways of thinking with new materials'.[37]

Alongside the emulation of earlier sacred works, Romantic commentators demanded that composers practise what Hoffmann terms 'self-renunciation' (*Selbstverleugnung*) in composing church music.[38] For Hoffmann, this entailed not only suppressing external motives but also those aspects of modern musical practice antithetical to the ideals epitomised by Palestrina; his own *Canzoni* tread a starkly ascetic path, stripping away any musical elements that might be perceived as secular. This approach points to the anti-aesthetic dimension of Romantic religiosity, equating service to the Church with self-effacement and the elimination of art-ness. It parallels the literary work of the Catholic author Clemens Brentano, who aimed to subsume art into religion, regarding his writings as tools of belief rather than artworks. While a similar suppression of artistry pervades Romantic liturgical and quasi-liturgical music, it finds its apogee in Liszt's late church pieces. In music such as *Via crucis* (1878–9) and even more radically in *De profundis* (1883) and *Qui Mariam absolvisti* (1885), Liszt rejects compositional artifice in favour of stark, emotionally charged fragments, translating into practice Wackenroder and Tieck's feeling-oriented view of church music.

Symbols, Frames, and Riddles

If art-religion draws the infinite through the finite, August Wilhelm Schlegel observes, it can do so 'only symbolically, through tropes and signs'.[39] To understand how this symbolic divination of the absolute functions in practice, it makes sense to turn to the artist most associated with Romantic art-religion, Caspar David Friedrich. Rather than cultivating one form of art-religion, Friedrich's paintings circle fluidly through a range of models: some seemingly overdetermined in their Christian symbolism, some employing what Kant described as the 'cipher language' of nature to hint at a pantheist drift, while others present open spaces stripped of anchoring symbols.[40] Paintings such as *Abtei im Eichwald* (1808–10), *Kreuz und Kathedrale im Gebirge* (1812), and *Winterlandschaft mit Kirche* (1811, see Fig. 9.1) draw on multiple familiar religious tropes. In the latter, the wooden wayside crucifix, prayerful penitent, and visionary Gothic church concealed in the mist point to a specifically Christian vision of redemption, an impression confirmed by the discarded crutches in the foreground, which suggest the kind of sudden conversion experience described by Schleiermacher. Even here, where the Christian dimension of the symbols seems transparent, their placing within nature serves to broaden the painting's vision of transcendence. Elsewhere, as in *Der Mönch am Meer* (1808–10), Friedrich empties his canvases of clear religious symbolism, drawing on imagery associated with the secular sublime to imbue his works with an unspoken plenitude of meaning. (For those unsympathetic to Friedrich's work, such as Hegel, the riddle character of his paintings amounted to no more than 'mystery-mongering' [*Geheimniskrämerei*].)[41] But perhaps the most interesting works for our purposes are those in

Figure 9.1 Caspar David Friedrich (1774–1840), *Winterlandschaft mit Kirche* (Dortmund version) (1811). Oil on canvas, 33 × 45 cm, Museum für Kunst und Kulturgeschichte, Dortmund (Wikimedia Commons)

which religious symbols are withheld, but appear present in absence. In *Fichtendickicht im Schnee* (*c.* 1828, see Fig. 9.2) the religious symbolism of *Winterlandschaft mit Kirche* is gone, yet seems to cling imperceptibly to the thicket of spruce trees recalled from the earlier picture. While there, the thicket enclosed a penitent gazing at a crucifix, here the sanctuary-like configuration of trees seems to generate a similarly intense focus, relying on the viewer to imbue it with meaning. The lack of explicit signs of religious transcendence has the result, as Ian Cooper argues, that 'their reference is entirely interiorised in our sense of the scene as revelation, and specifically as revelation occurring through the framing effect of the picture'.[42]

In music, works of art-religion traverse a similar spectrum of symbolisation, and are also inscribed with religious meanings as a result of framing effects. Some works, such as Spohr's Symphony No. 4 *Die Weihe der Töne*, Op. 86 (1832), and Mendelssohn's Symphony No. 2 *Lobgesang*, Op. 52 (1840), proclaim their proximity to religion through multiple ingredients: titles, texts or poetic programmes, musical topics, and the use of pre-existing materials with religious associations (in Spohr's case, the Ambrosian Te Deum and funeral chorale 'Begrabt den Leib in seine Gruft', while in Mendelssohn's, the chorale 'Nun danket alle

Figure 9.2 Caspar David Friedrich, *Fichtendickicht im Schnee* (*c.* 1828). Oil on canvas, 31.3 × 25.4 cm, Neue Pinakothek, Munich (Wikimedia Commons)

Gott' as well as allusions to religious works by Handel and Bach). Not all art-religion, it should be noted, involves a quest for transcendence; in the case of the *Lobgesang*, it is the community effect of religion that is reconstituted, while *Die Weihe der Töne* celebrates the blessings and consolations bestowed by music.[43] While these works present a dense array of verbal and stylistic pointers, other compositions rely purely on musical topics to draw religious resonances into their fields of meaning. Like the monk's habit in *Der Mönch am Meer*, the concluding chorale in Anton Rubinstein's Symphony No. 2 'Océan', Op. 42 (1851) injects religion into the natural sublime, an effect not lost on the critic August Wilhelm Ambros:

The work turns at its end to the loftiest thoughts of which man is capable. Where the ocean is concerned, such declarations are hardly necessary: the roar of the waves is the sound of the organ, the altar candles shine in the eternal stars, plumes of mist ascend as incense, and the gathering clouds serve as altar hangings! All these elements coalesce into a ceremonious chorale like the thrilling one with which Rubinstein concludes his final movement.[44]

As seen earlier, absolute music was prone to being heard through the filter of art-religion, even in the case of works lacking the kind of conspicuous symbols found in Rubinstein's symphony. In a recent essay, Wolfram Steinbeck seeks to refute the long-established tendency to treat Bruckner's symphonies as 'masses without texts' and 'cathedrals in sound'; for Steinbeck, Bruckner's musical materials – including his so-called 'chorales' – lack clear connections to church music, while the composer's fervent Catholicism would have rendered him immune to the claims of art-religion.[45] Much of what Steinbeck has to say is convincing; there is, after all, little intrinsic relationship between, for example, the four root-position chords that mark the climax of the first movement of Bruckner's Ninth and either the Lutheran chorale or Catholic chant harmonisations. Yet his arguments ignore the extent to which, like Friedrich's *Fichtendickicht im Schnee*, works of absolute music were imbued with a religious dimension as a result of framing factors. Sacralised by the consecrated space of the concert hall and the discourses of art-religion, such music could rely on subtle hints – akin to the traces of blue sky in Friedrich's painting – to point listeners towards the transcendent.

Recovering Religion: Heterodox and Syncretic Approaches

Perhaps the most interesting musical products of art-religion are those which juggle multiple forms of the concept, or which aspire to transform both religion and art. Liszt's piano cycle *Harmonies poétiques et religieuses* (1840–53) epitomises the former, juxtaposing arrangements of settings of liturgical texts (his own *Ave Maria* and *Pater noster*, as well as the so-called *Miserere d'après Palestrina*) with movements inspired by verses by the deist poet Alphonse de Lamartine. At least two divergent aesthetics of religious music come together in this cycle: on the one hand, a pantheism-inflected religion of art, and on the other, a liturgically grounded approach that points to Liszt's growing rapprochement with Catholicism.[46] Liszt's largest work, the oratorio *Christus* (1866), offers a similar pluralism, integrating quasi-liturgical pieces and large-scale choruses within the framework of a giant sacralised symphonic poem. The aesthetic and stylistic diversity of *Christus* makes it resemble a kind of spiritual autobiography, ranging from the young Liszt's Christian socialist ideal of a *musique humanitaire* uniting church and theatre, to austere chant harmonisations redolent of his identification with the Ultramontane Catholicism of the 1860s. According to Liszt's 'authorised' biographer, Lina Ramann, the work also combines the primary and secondary forms of art-religion identified above, simultaneously present-ing the Christ of the Church while satisfying pantheist conceptions of the divinity of humanity. For Ramann, *Christus* thematises rather than embodies religious worship, taking as its subject the historical unfolding of the idea of Christ as manifested in the Catholic liturgy.[47] The multiple textural and stylistic layers of the work thus serve as a means to differen-tiate the superseded dogmas of the Church from Christ's living relevance as an icon of purely human values; the choral sections (particularly those that draw on the idioms of early church music) represent the past of Christianity while the symphonic portions – 'hymns to the heartbeat of our age' – grasp hold of its enduring core.[48]

The idea of art-religion as a salvage exercise, a means to preserve the truths at the core of religion, is also crucial for Wagner's *Parsifal*. Often *Parsifal* has been upheld as the supreme exemplar of art usurping religion's place or elevating itself as a 'counter-church', a perspective that is no less mistaken than treating it as a straightforwardly Christian work.[49] The idea that Wagner was aiming to create a substitute for religion takes its cue from the opening lines of his essay 'Religion und Kunst' (1881):

One could say that where religion becomes artificial, it remains for art to salvage the core of religion by grasping the figurative value of its mythic symbols – which religion would have us believe in their literal sense – in order to show forth their profound, hidden truth through an ideal representation. While the sole concern of the priest is that religious allegories be regarded as factual truths, this matters not a jot to the artist since he presents his work freely and openly as his own invention.[50]

In isolation, this passage suggests a secularising agenda in which art seizes the baton from a moribund religion; the impression that Wagner approaches religion solely as an aesthetic resource is seemingly confirmed by the exaggerated contrast he draws between the priest's truths and the artist's invention. But Wagner is not diagnosing a crisis in modernity, but rather what he perceives to be the normal condition of organised religion. Rather than viewing art as a substitute for religion, Wagner casts them in a reciprocal relationship, arguing that art compensates for the dogmatising tendencies of religion by revealing 'its inner essence, ineffably divine truth', a function he sees as embodied by Beethoven's symphonies no less than Raphael's paintings.[51] The nature of the religion evoked in this essay – as in *Parsifal* – is protean and wilfully syncretic, aiming at a synthesis of Christian symbolism, Buddhist ethics, and Schopenhauerian renunciation.

But what is consistent here, as in Wagner's other writings from the period, is his enduring fascination with Christ as redeemer (a concept he understands not in terms of substitutionary sacrifice but rather 'divine compassion').[52] In portraying the flaws of established religion in *Parsifal* while concluding with a message of 'redemption to the redeemer', Wagner thematises the logic of loss and recovery that lies at the core of Romantic art-religion.

Whether *Parsifal* succeeds, even fleetingly, in this mission of religious re-enchantment is a moot point; as with the *Ring*, its critique of the existing order seems more compelling than its vision of a new one. Like most of the other works discussed above, it relies heavily on pre-existing materials and gestures in staging its religious effects, some of which were distinctly shop-worn even at the time of composition (I am thinking in particular of the chromatic-third progressions that strain for the epiphanic at the work's close). And like Friedrich's paintings, *Parsifal* seems to veer between hyper-explication and mystery-mongering, overburdened with messages yet dependent on obscurantism for its allure (the notion that the work transmits a hidden secret, accessible only to initiates, fuelled its popularity with occultists and theosophers well into the twentieth century). Stripping away something of the work's superabundance of religious symbolism has become the norm in recent productions, a process that brings the whole closer to what is surely its most effective part: the orchestral prelude. Even for those resistant to the religious claims of the rest of *Parsifal*, such as Nietzsche, the prelude offers one of the most sublime monuments to the nostalgia and hope invested in art-religion. While Nietzsche focused on the melancholic gaze with which Wagner painted religious feeling, the most impressive aspect of the prelude is surely the chain of seventh chords which bring it to a poised, expectant close; it is hard to imagine a more apt sonic realisation of the 'infinite longing' of Romantic religiosity.[53]

Notes

1. Peter Sloterdijk, 'Where Are We When We Hear Music?', in *The Aesthetic Imperative: Writings on Art*, ed. Peter Weibel, trans. Karen Margolis (Cambridge: Polity Press, 2014), 26–45.
2. Jean Paul, *Hesperus, oder 45 Hundsposttage* (Berlin: Matzdorff, 1795), vol. II, 370; Ludwig Tieck, *Phantasus* (Berlin: G. Reimer, 1828), vol. I, 429; Wilhelm Heinrich Wackenroder and Ludwig Tieck, *Phantasien über die Kunst*, ed.

Wolfgang Nehring (Stuttgart: Reclam, 1973), 65; and E. T. A. Hoffmann, *Kreisleriana*, in *E. T. A. Hoffmann's Musical Writings: 'Kreisleriana', 'The Poet and the Composer', Music Criticism*, ed. David Charlton, trans. Martyn Clarke (Cambridge: Cambridge University Press, 1989), 163.

3. Ernst Müller, 'Religion/Religiosität', in *Ästhetische Grundbegriffe*, ed. Karlheinz Barck et al. (Stuttgart and Weimar: J. B. Metzler, 2003), vol. V, esp. 243–7.

4. Conrad Donakowski, *A Muse for the Masses: Ritual and Music in an Age of Democratic Revolution, 1770–1870* (Chicago: University of Chicago Press, 1977), 155.

5. Thomas Weiskel, *The Romantic Sublime: Studies in the Structure and Psychology of Transcendence* (Baltimore and London: Johns Hopkins University Press, 1976), 36.

6. On this paradigm, see Charles Taylor, *A Secular Age* (Cambridge, MA: Belknap Press, 2007), and Daniel Weidner, 'The Rhetoric of Secularization', *New German Critique*, 41/1 (2014), 1–31.

7. Theodor W. Adorno, *The Jargon of Authenticity*, trans. Knut Tarnowski and Frederic Will (Evanston: Northwestern University Press, 1973), 22.

8. Weidner, 'Rhetoric of Secularization', 30.

9. Claudia Stockinger, 'Poesie und Wissenschaft als Religion: Kunstreligiöse Konzepte im 19. Jahrhundert', in Albert Meier, Alessandro Costazza, and Gérard Laudin (eds.), *Kunstreligion: Ein ästhetisches Konzept der Moderne in seiner historischen Entfaltung* 3 vols. (Berlin: De Gruyter, 2011–14), vol. II, 11–39 at 20.

10. Theodor W. Adorno, *Aesthetic Theory*, ed. Gretel Adorno and Rolf Tiedemann, trans. Robert Hullot-Kentor (London: Continuum, 1997), 197.

11. Tieck, *Phantasus*, 435; Georg Simmel (the attribution is not secure), as quoted in Bernd Sponheuer, 'Popmusik und Kunstreligion. Theoretische Überlegungen', in Siegfried Oechsle and Bernd Sponheuer (eds.), *Kunstreligion und Musik: 1800–1900–2000* (Kassel: Bärenreiter, 2015), 147–60 at 149.

12. Max Weber, 'Religious Rejections of the World and their Directions' (1916), in Hans H. Gerth and C. Wright Mills (eds.), *From Max Weber: Essays on Sociology* (New York: Oxford University Press, 1946), 342.

13. Wilhelm Heinrich Wackenroder and Ludwig Tieck, *Herzensergießungen eines kunstliebenden Klosterbruders*, ed. Martin Bollacher (Stuttgart: Reclam, 2005), 9–11; E. T. A. Hoffmann, 'Die Jesuiterkirche in G', in *Nachtstücke* (Berlin: Realschulbuchhandlung, 1817), vol. I, 236–7; and Richard Wagner, 'Religion und Kunst', *Sämtliche Schriften und Dichtungen*, 16 vols. (Leipzig: Breitkopf & Härtel, 1911), vol. X, 211.

14. See my *Palestrina and the German Romantic Imagination: Interpreting Historicism in Nineteenth-Century Music* (Cambridge: Cambridge University Press, 2002), esp. 37–47, 65–7, 85–6, 144–9, and 173–5.

15. Julian Schmidt, *Geschichte der deutschen National-Literatur im neunzehnten Jahrhundert*, 2 vols. (Leipzig: Friedrich Ludwig Herbig, 1853), vol. I, 421–2.

16. Heinrich Detering, 'Was ist Kunstreligion? Systematische und historische Bemerkungen', in Meier, Costazza, and Laudin (eds.), *Kunstreligion*, vol. I, 11–28 at 14.

17. Friedrich Schleiermacher, *Über die Religion. Reden an die Gebildeten unter ihren Verächtern* (Berlin: Johann Friedrich Unger, 1799), 169–70 (translation based on *On Religion: Speeches to Its Cultured Despisers*, trans. and ed. Richard Crouter (Cambridge: Cambridge University Press, 1996)).

18. Friedrich Hölderlin, *Hyperion oder das Eremit in Griechenland*, in Jochen Schmidt (ed.), *Sämtliche Werke und Briefe* (Frankfurt: Deutscher Klassiker Verlag, 1994), vol. II, 90; Tieck, 'Symphonien', in *Phantasien über die Kunst*, 197.

19. Carl Dahlhaus, *The Idea of Absolute Music*, trans. Roger Lustig (Chicago: University of Chicago Press, 1989), 88.

20. Schleiermacher, *Reden*, 53, 68, 190.

21. Ibid., 167.

22. Ibid., 167, 168.

23. Wackenroder and Tieck, *Herzensergießungen*, 79–80, 81.

24. See in particular Wackenroder and Tieck, *Phantasien*, 74.

25. See Müller, 'Religion/Religiosität', 247.

26. Wackenroder and Tieck, *Phantasien*, 78, 80.

27. Ibid., 85; Wackenroder and Tieck, *Herzensergießungen*, 101.

28. Tieck, *Phantasus*, 426.

29. See Garratt, *Palestrina*, 54–7.

30. Tom Spencer, 'Revelation and *Kunstreligion* in W. H. Wackenroder and Ludwig Tieck', *Monatshefte*, 107/1 (2015), 26–45 at 27–8.

31. Wackenroder and Tieck, *Phantasien*, 86.

32. Rüdiger Safranski, *Romantik: Eine deutsche Affäre* (Munich: Hanser, 2007), 393.

33. Wackenroder and Tieck, *Herzensergießungen*, 100.

34. Marco Rispoli, 'Kunstreligion und künstlerischer Atheismus: Zum Zusammenhang von Glaube und Skepsis am Beispiel Wilhelm Heinrich Wackenroders', in Meier, Costazza, and Laudin (eds.), *Kunstreligion*, vol. I, 115–33 at 119; Wackenroder and Tieck, *Phantasien*, 88.

35. Friedrich Overbeck, 'Eigenkommentar' (1840), in Jutta Assel and Georg Jäger (eds.), *Friedrich Overbeck: Der Triumph der Religion in den Künsten: Kommentar und Kritik* (2005), www.goethezeitportal.de/digitale-bibliothek /forschungsbeitraege/autoren-kuenstler-denker/overbeck-friedrich/jutta- assel-und-georg-jaeger-friedrich-overbeck-der-triumph-der-religion-in-den- kuensten-teil-i.html

36. E. T. A. Hoffmann, 'Alte und neue Kirchenmusik', *Allgemeine musikalische Zeitung*, 16 (1814), 577–84, 593–603, 611–19, at 614.

37. Abraham Mendelssohn, 'Letter of 10 March 1835', in Paul and Carl Mendelssohn Bartholdy (eds.), *Briefe aus den Jahren 1833 bis 1847* (Leipzig: Hermann Mendelssohn, 1863), 86.

38. E. T. A. Hoffmann, *Die Serapionsbrüder: Gesammelte Erzählungen und Mährchen* (Berlin: G. Reimer, 1819), vol. II, 366.

39. August Wilhelm Schlegel, *Vorlesungen über schöne Litteratur und Kunst* (Heilbronn: Henninger, 1884), vol. I, 91.

40. Tanehisa Otabe, 'Die Chriffreschrift der Natur: Ihr Zusammenhang mit der Kunst bei Kant, Schelling und Novalis', in Lothar Knatz and Tanehisa Otabe (eds.), *Ästhetische Subjektivität: Romantik & Moderne* (Würzburg: Königshausen & Neumann, 2005), 233–47.

41. Laure Cahen-Maurel, 'An Art of False Mysteriousness? Hegel's Criticism of the Painting Style of Caspar David Friedrich', *Hegel-Studien*, 51 (2017), 29–58.

42. Ian Cooper, '"Winterabende": A Romantic and Post-Romantic Motif in Friedrich, Büchner and Stifter', *Publications of the English Goethe Society*, 86/1 (2017), 42–54, at 45.

43. On Spohr's Op. 86, see Jonathan Kregor, *Program Music* (Cambridge: Cambridge University Press, 2015), 24–8. On Mendelssohn's Op. 52, see James Garratt, *Music, Culture and Social Reform in the Age of Wagner* (Cambridge: Cambridge University Press, 2010), 110–16; and Benedict Taylor, 'Beyond the Ethical and Aesthetic: Reconciling Religious Art with Secular Art-Religion in Mendelssohn's "Lobgesang"', in Jürgen Thym (ed.), *Mendelssohn, the Organ, and the Music of the Past: Constructing Historical Legacies* (New York: University of Rochester Press, 2014), 287–309.

44. August Wilhelm Ambros, 'Feuilleton. Wiener musikalische Revue' (1872), in Markéta Štědronská (ed.), *Musikaufsätze und -Rezensionen 1872–1876. Historisch-kritische Ausgabe* (Vienna: Hollitzer Verlag, 2017), vol. I, 159–60.

45. Wolfram Steinbeck, '"Messen ohne Text"? Zur Sakralisierung der Symphonik Anton Bruckners', in Oechsle and Sponheuer (eds.), *Kunstreligion*, 61–8.

46. See Serge Gut, 'Des Harmonies poétiques et religieuses de Lamartine à celles de Franz Liszt', *Studia musicologica*, 54/1 (2013), 21–34.

47. Lina Ramann, *Franz Liszt's Oratorium Christus. Eine Studie als Beitrag zur zeit- und musikgeschichtlichen Stellung desselben* (Weimar: T. F. A. Kühn, 1874), 12–14.

48. Ibid., 16.

49. Detering, 'Was ist Kunstreligion?', 15.

50. Wagner, 'Religion und Kunst', 211.

51. Ibid.

52. Richard Wagner, 'Heldentum und Christentum', in *Sämtliche Schriften*, vol. X, 281.

53. Friedrich Nietzsche, *Writings from the Late Notebooks*, ed. Rüdiger Bittner, trans. Kate Sturge (Cambridge: Cambridge University Press, 2003), 111–12.

Further Reading

Bruhn, Siglind (ed.). *Voicing the Ineffable: Musical Representations of Religious Experience* (Hillsdale, NY: Pendragon Press, 2002).

Dahlhaus, Carl. *The Idea of Absolute Music*, trans. Roger Lustig (Chicago: University of Chicago Press, 1989).

Garratt, James. *Palestrina and the German Romantic Imagination: Interpreting Historicism in Nineteenth-Century Music* (Cambridge: Cambridge University Press, 2002).

Gockel, Matthias. 'Redemption and Transformation: Making Sense of Richard Wagner's *Parsifal*', *Religion and the Arts*, 20 (2016), 419–41.

Grewe, Cordula. *Painting the Sacred in the Age of Romanticism* (Abingdon: Ashgate, 2009).

Kinderman, William, and Syer, Katherine R. (eds.). *A Companion to Wagner's Parsifal* (Rochester, NY: Camden House, 2005).

Koerner, Joseph Leo. *Caspar David Friedrich and the Subject of Landscape*, 2nd ed. (London: Reaktion Books, 2009).

Meier, Albert, Costazza, Alessandro, and Laudin, Gérard (eds.). *Kunstreligion: Ein ästhetisches Konzept der Moderne in seiner historischen Entfaltung*, 3 vols. (Berlin: De Gruyter, 2011–14).

Merrick, Paul. *Revolution and Religion in the Music of Liszt* (Cambridge: Cambridge University Press, 1987).

Oechsle, Siegfried, and Sponheuer, Bernd (eds.). *Kunstreligion und Musik: 1800–1900–2000* (Kassel: Bärenreiter, 2015).

Weidner, Daniel. 'The Rhetoric of Secularization', *New German Critique*, 41/1 (2014), 1–31.

PART III

Aesthetics

10 | Music in Early German Romantic Philosophy

TOMÁS MCAULEY

What was the Romantic view of music? And where did it come from? To ask those questions in the singular – as if there were just one, unchanging view of music, shared by all Romantic thinkers – is to betray the variety, multiplicity, and constant change at the heart of the Romantic movements that first arose in late eighteenth-century Europe. Yet it is also to recognise that, amidst this diversity, there was a remarkable unity. For it is indeed possible, if only at the broadest level, to isolate a distinctively Romantic view of music.

According to the dominant view of music throughout the eighteenth century – the conception held by most thinkers of the so-called Enlightenment – the purpose of music is to move the affects (or the emotions) of its listeners, in a somewhat mechanical fashion, for their pleasure, for their moral improvement, for the betterment of their physical or spiritual health, or for some combination of these. In the closing years of the eighteenth century, however, this view was rejected by the leading figures of the movement now known as early German Romanticism. In its place, they developed a wholly new – and characteristically Romantic – conception of music. According to this new conception, the purpose of music is to provide non-linguistic knowledge or insight, most usually into one's inner self or, especially, into the fundamental nature of reality. Though initially confined to a small circle of Romantic thinkers, this new view of music spread far and wide over the subsequent decades – to the extent that its consequences continue to reverberate through to the present day.

What could possibly have driven such a turnaround? Most commentators have assumed that a change so dramatic could only have been inspired by an equally dramatic change in the music of this time. A closer examination, however, shows that this new view of music arose not in response to changes in contemporary composition or performance, but rather in response to – indeed, as part of – changes in contemporary philosophy. More precisely, a revolution in philosophical epistemology – that branch of philosophy concerned with the nature of knowledge – led to a wholesale re-evaluation of what and how human subjects can know. As part of this re-evaluation, thinkers of this period came to believe that music itself could offer a distinctive route to knowledge.

The purpose of this chapter is to show how early Romantic thinkers came to this belief. In what follows, I start by charting some key moments in the philosophical background of the 1780s and '90s. Building on this, I trace the emergence of the Romantic view of music in the works of the two philosophers most closely involved in its earliest formulations: Friedrich Schlegel and Georg Friedrich Philipp von Hardenberg (better known by his pen name Novalis). I conclude with brief examinations of the ways in which this view was elaborated by two now-canonical philosophers of this era, Friedrich Schelling and Arthur Schopenhauer, and with a reflection on its subsequent influence.

The Philosophical Background

The starting point for Schlegel and Novalis – and indeed Schelling and Schopenhauer – was a radically new epistemology proposed by Immanuel Kant in his groundbreaking 1781 *Critique of Pure Reason* (also published in a significantly revised second edition in 1787).[1] The central insight of this work is that the subject – that is, the individual searching for knowledge – can know things only as they appear, rather than as they are in themselves. As such, Kant's philosophy is a form of idealism: the view that the world around us (or our knowledge thereof) is in some fundamental way dependent on the shape of human thought. The *Critique of Pure Reason* is now widely regarded as a masterpiece. Initially, however, it was a bit of a damp squib: long, counter-intuitive, and very badly written, its main effect on its first readers was to confuse them. Kant's fortunes changed only when his younger contemporary, Karl Leonhard Reinhold, took it upon himself to publish a series of public 'letters' that aimed to popularise the Kantian philosophy. These letters, published in the leading literary journal *Der teutsche Merkur* (*The German Mercury*) in 1786–7, met with remarkable success, and catapulted Kant's philosophy straight into the popular imagination.[2]

Reinhold, however, was not content to stop at popularisation. Rather, he took Kant's philosophy as the starting point for a new Idealist philosophical system that he called the *Elementarphilosophie* ('elementary philosophy' or 'philosophy of elements'), and that he set forward in a series of works from the years 1789–91.[3] And 'system' is very much the right word here: Reinhold believed that it should be possible to derive, systematically, the whole of philosophy from a single, self-evident fact. Reinhold's work quickly brought him not just fame, but also a steady income, in the form of the first ever professorship in critical philosophy at the University of Jena, starting in 1787. Stemming in part from Reinhold's appointment, Jena became at this time a hotbed for the latest developments in German philosophy, and was to be the main home of the early German Romantic movement.

In 1794, however, Reinhold gave up this post for a better-paid position at the University of Kiel. His successor was to be the young Kant enthusiast, Johann Gottlieb Fichte. Fichte believed Kant to be correct in his overall orientation to knowledge, but placed even greater emphasis than had Kant on the activity of the thinking subject. And he agreed with Reinhold that philosophy should be wholly and systematically derivable from a single, self-evident proposition, but pursued this goal with even more fervour than had Reinhold. This approach, which can be called *epistemological foundationalism*, was set out by Fichte in a serious of lectures and writings from the mid-1790s, known collectively as the *Wissenschaftslehre*, or the 'Doctrine of Scientific Knowledge'.[4]

Friedrich Schlegel

In his early work from 1793–6, Schlegel accepts wholeheartedly Fichte's epistemological foundationalism. In particular, in his essay 'On the Study of Greek Poetry', written in 1794–5, Schlegel states his intention to expand Fichte's philosophical system to include the realm of aesthetics, something that Fichte himself had failed to address in any depth.[5] Around the summer of 1796, however, Schlegel came to reject Fichte's foundationalism. Reacting specifically against Fichte's foundationalist epistemology, Schlegel established a distinctively *anti-foundationalist* alternative. Specifically, against Fichte's belief that all philosophy can be derived from a single proposition, Schlegel argued that philosophy must start from multiple principles, each of which occupies a place in a system that is coherent, but that has no single foundation.

Against Fichte's belief that philosophy can reach irrefutable and complete conclusions, Schlegel sees philosophy as an infinite task.[6] The task is infinite in two senses: first, it is a quest to search for the infinity of total knowledge; second, as such, it is an endless quest that will never be complete. The human longs for the infinity of knowledge, but this longing will never be fulfilled. There will, rather, be a constant 'longing for the infinite' (*Sehnsucht nach dem Unendlichen*), which will itself forever spur further investigation. Because the nature of the human quest for knowledge is now characterised as longing, that which provides the most insight into the human condition is now, for Schlegel, that which provides the most insight into longing.

Subsequently, Schlegel begins to develop a view of art as equal or superior to philosophy. Years before he came to his post-Fichtean characterisation of the human quest for knowledge as a longing for the infinite, Schlegel had characterised modern poetry (as opposed to ancient poetry) in terms of longing.[7] In his early work, Schlegel had seen this as a weakness of modern poetry, for its restless striving meant that it could not find a stable place in a systematic aesthetics. As Schlegel rejected Fichte's epistemological foundationalism, however, he came to see the longing inherent in modern poetry as a strength, for it allows insight into the epistemological longing that is at the core of the human condition.

With this move, Schlegel also started to refer to modern poetry not simply as modern, but as 'romantic' poetry (*romantische Poesie*). In a fragment from a collection first published in the journal *Athenaeum*, which ran from 1798 to 1800, Schlegel writes that romantic poetry is

in the state of becoming; that, in fact, is its real essence: that it should forever be becoming and never be perfected. It can be exhausted by no theory and only a divinatory criticism would dare try to characterize its ideal. It alone is infinite, just as it alone is free.[8]

Whereas for the early Schlegel, the endless striving of modern poetry leaves it inferior to ancient poetry (whose striving is complete), for the anti-foundationalist Schlegel of 1796 onwards, the longing of romantic poetry joins it to the human quest for knowledge and, as such, is a mark of its superiority.

So what has this to do with music? The answer is simple: for the anti-foundationalist Schlegel, music is poetry. There has been much debate as to the exact nature of Schlegel's *romantische Poesie*, but for several generations of scholars, the presumption has been that it refers to some kind of literature. Drawing on the work of the historian of philosophy Frederick Beiser, however, I would suggest that *romantische Poesie* refers not only to literature, but to all the arts, and indeed to creative work in general.[9] The conclusion that music should be included within *romantische Poesie* is given confirmation by a passage from Schlegel's *Dialogue on Poetry* of 1799–1800, in which three characters discuss the nature of poetry:

AMALIA: If it goes on like this, before too long one thing after another will be transformed into poetry (*Poesie*). Is, then, everything poetry?

LOTHARIO: Every art and every discipline that functions through language, when exercised as an art for its own sake and when it achieves its highest summit, appears as poetry.

LUDOVICO: And every art or discipline which does not manifest its nature through language possesses an invisible spirit: and that is poetry.[10]

Similarly, in his most famous discussion of *romantische Poesie* – the *Athenaeumsfragment* 116 – Schlegel writes that:

Romantic poetry is a progressive, universal poetry . . . It embraces everything that is purely poetic, from the greatest systems of art, containing within themselves still further systems, to the sigh, the kiss that the poeticising child breathes forth in artless song.[11]

In this definition, *romantische Poesie* includes music both implicitly (by including all the arts) and explicitly (by making reference specifically to artless song). Music, however, is more than just one more art within the broad spectrum of romantic poetry, for Schlegel also conceives of music as a distinctive, independent art form. Just as was the case with his broad view of romantic poetry, his thought on music in particular derives from his epistemological anti-foundationalism.

It should be noted that Schlegel's ideas about music at this time are not wholly consistent. Such a situation does not indicate philosophical amateurism on Schlegel's part, but rather reflects Schlegel's general philosophical stance, which, after rejecting the possibility of a single, fixed system of knowledge, embraces contradiction and paradox. Yet Schlegel is decidedly not, as some postmodern interpretations would have it, an anti-systematic thinker. Rather, he aspired to complete systematicity, but also recognised that all human systems will be forever provisional and improvable. As he famously put it: 'it is equally fatal for the mind (*Geist*) to have a system and to have none. It must decide to combine both.' With that in mind, I set out in what follows a systematic overview of Schlegel's thought, yet retain within that overview the deliberate unevenness that characterises Schlegel's reflections on music, art, and philosophy at this time. More precisely, I identify three key themes running through Schlegel's view of music in the years around 1800.

First, Schlegel repeatedly characterises music as a form of longing. This characterisation is especially apparent in his novel *Lucinde* of 1800, in which music is described as becoming 'a dangerous and bottomless abyss of longing and melancholy'. Here, the bottomlessness of music's abyss recalls the infinity of the human subject's longing for knowledge.[12] In what is perhaps the most important reference to longing in the novel, Schlegel uses auditory metaphors to describe his hero's awakening from a deep sleep: 'when with childlike timidity he strives to escape from the mystery of his existence and, sweetly curious, seeks the unknown he hears (*vernimmt*) everywhere only the resonance (*Nachhall*) of his own longing (*Sehnsucht*)'.[13] This passage is a literary paraphrase of Schlegel's philosophical position on knowledge. Just as the philosopher seeks final and certain knowledge of the world as it is in itself but finds only longing, the character at the centre of this passage seeks the unknown but finds only longing. Significantly, this longing is not seen, but heard.

Second, Schlegel believes music to be itself a philosophical art form. Manfred Frank has noted that, with the phrase 'longing for the infinite', Schlegel and his contemporaries believed themselves to have found a new translation of the Greek *filosofiva*, root of the modern word 'philosophy' (in German: *Philosophie*).[14] If music is an embodiment of longing, then music is also, implicitly, an embodiment of philosophy. Schlegel makes this connection explicit at several points, including in a fragment from the *Athenaeum*:

> Many people find it strange and ridiculous when musicians talk about the ideas in their compositions; and it often happens that one perceives they have more ideas in their music than they do about it. But whoever has a feeling for the wonderful affinity of all the arts and sciences will at least not consider the matter from the dull viewpoint of a so-called naturalness that maintains music is supposed to be only the language of the emotions (*Sprache der Empfindung*). Rather, he will consider a certain tendency of pure instrumental music toward philosophy as something not impossible in itself. Doesn't pure instrumental music itself have to create a text? And aren't the themes in it developed, reaffirmed, varied, and contrasted in the same way as the subject of meditation in a philosophical succession of ideas?[15]

This passage explicitly rejects the idea that music should be only a 'language of the emotions', a clear reference to the older, Enlightenment view of music. Rather, the themes in music are 'developed, reaffirmed, varied, and contrasted in the same way as the subject of meditation in a philosophical succession of ideas', even while the passage leaves open the possibility that music might also remain effective at moving the emotions of listeners. The suggestion that there might be a correspondence between musical and philosophical ideas is developed in an entry from the notebooks that Schlegel kept at around this time, in which he associates musical variations with the philosophical thesis, because they involve repetition of a theme, but describes counterpoint as the philosophical antithesis.[16] Schlegel does not provide an association between music and synthesis, the expected third term of the triad, for, he believes, there is no final synthesis, no completion, hence music's longing will never be fulfilled.[17] He does, however, think that there is a unity of being that lies beyond human consciousness but that can occasionally be intuited in finite syntheses that never align fully with each other. Schlegel refers to these syntheses as instances of wit, a term that is often presumed to refer only to a literary device, but which Schlegel explicitly associates with music, writing that 'All wit is musical.'[18]

Third, and most simply, whereas music had long been considered the lowest of the beautiful arts, Schlegel at this time comes to believe, on occasion at least, that music is the highest of the arts. This claim appears in a fascinating fragment from his notebooks:

... beauty ... is the essence of music, the highest among all the arts. It is the most general. Every art has musical principles and, insofar as it is perfected, is music alone. This applies even to philosophy and probably to poetry too, perhaps even to life. Music is love – it is something higher than art.[19]

This brings us back full circle to the observation that music was, for Schlegel, part of romantic poetry. Indeed, Schlegel's remark that poetry probably has musical principles makes clear that not only is music, for Schlegel, contained within romantic poetry, it is also sometimes deemed to be *the essence of* romantic poetry.

Novalis

In his works from around the same time, Novalis puts forward a position on music that is certainly distinct from that of Schlegel but also remarkably similar. As with Schlegel, Novalis's philosophical development grew directly out of his engagement with, and rejection of, Fichte's epistemological foundationalism. In place of this epistemological foundationalism, Novalis developed – as did Schlegel – a notion of philosophy as an infinite task. He built on this notion, however, to develop a unique philosophical position of his own. Novalis was certainly receptive to the idealism of Kant, Reinhold, and Fichte, but sought to combine this idealism with a realism – a belief in the reality of the external world – that he associated with the earlier philosopher Baruch Spinoza. He called the resulting approach to philosophy *magical idealism*, the term 'magical' denoting here the traditional goal of magic to gain control over nature, rather than any adherence to traditions of the occult in particular.[20]

Novalis explains how idealism and realism can be united in a programme for magical idealism given in his unfinished encyclopaedia, the *Allgemeine Brouillon* (1798–9):

if you are unable to transform thoughts into external things, then transform external things into thoughts. . . . Both operations are idealistic. Whosoever has both completely in his power, is a *Magical Idealist*. Shouldn't the perfection of each of these two operations be dependent on the other?[21]

The ability 'to transform thoughts into external things' is a reference to Fichtean idealism, which had suggested, on some readings at least, that the thinking self might somehow create the external world out of itself. Novalis, however, counters this with its polar opposite, the ability to 'transform external things into thoughts'. Novalis refers to this latter operation as 'idealistic', because it is based on the subject's active engagement with the external world. Its philosophical underpinning, however, is thoroughly realist, for it posits a natural world whose existence is not predicated on the subject.

The internal and the external, the ideal and the real, the Fichtean and the Spinozistic all have a distinct meeting point: the human body.[22] As such, the body is at the centre not only of Novalis' philosophy in general, but also of his new, Romantic view of music in particular. In what follows, I present a systematic overview of this new view of music while refusing – mirroring my strategy with that of Schlegel – to iron out the unevenness of Novalis's deliberately fragmentary writings. I identify again three key themes, this time dwelling on the first in particular: a close relationship between music and the body.

The idea that music engages closely with the human body was not new to Novalis. It was indeed foundational for the older, Enlightenment view of music, for theories of musical affect tended to draw specifically on mechanical understandings of the body.[23] One particular way in which they did so was with reference to music's medical potential: to the ways in which music's affective power could prove useful for the treatment of various ailments. Yet Novalis explicitly rejects this older view of music. With regard to art in general, Novalis writes that 'Affects . . . belong to a *lack of virtue* (*Untugend*).'[24] With regard to music in particular, Novalis rejects another idea that had been closely tied up with the older view of music: the idea that music should imitate nature. According to Novalis, 'the musician takes the essence of his art from within himself – not even the slightest suspicion of imitation can apply to him'.[25]

Novalis posits instead a wholly new relationship between music and the body, a relationship that shows itself in a new conception of medicine itself. Drawing on his understanding of the body as meeting point for the internal and the external, Novalis complains that 'common medicine is handiwork. It only has what is useful in mind.' In contrast, 'true therapeutics' forms 'a prescription for the preservation and restoration of [the] special relation and exchange between the [internal and external] stimuli or factors'.[26] Novalis also reconceives death in corresponding fashion, seeing it as 'nothing but an interruption in the *exchange* between the inner and outer stimuli – between the soul and the world'.[27] By preserving the right balance of stimuli, Novalis believes, one could, in principle, extend life indefinitely. The physician who could do this would be an artist:

The artist of immortality practices higher medicine – infinitesimal medicine. – He practices medicine as a higher art – as a synthetic art. He constantly views both factors [internal and external stimuli] simultaneously, as one, and seeks to harmonize them – to unite them into one goal.[28]

At one point, the musician becomes for Novalis the epitome of such an artist. 'Every illness', writes Novalis, 'is a musical problem – the cure is a *musical solution*. The more rapid, and yet the more complete, the solution – the greater the musical talent of the doctor.'[29] The general goal of 'the artist of immortality' – to harmonise inner and outer stimuli – is now the specific goal of the musician. The whole of life is thus figured as musical. Of the traditional elements of music – harmony, melody, and rhythm – harmony would seem to be most closely related to this perceived goal. Novalis, however, stresses not harmony, but rhythm. Seeing the effect of stimuli on the body in terms of 'excitability' (or 'irritability', *Reizbarkeit*), Novalis writes of an 'all-encompassing constitution', that is 'capable of an infinite maximum and infinite minimum of irritability'.[30] This constitution is '*infinite rhythm*' (*unendlicher Rhythmus*). The difficulties of pinning down such a proposition are clear in Novalis's decision to cross out this entry, which occurs in a draft of his *Allgemeine Bouillon*, in a later revision of the same manuscript. Nonetheless, this link raises the question of the role of rhythm in Novalis's philosophy.

The second theme that I wish to identify in Novalis's view of music is, then, an emphasis on rhythm. A few decades before Novalis was writing his *Allgemeine Brouillon*, Enlightenment stalwart Johann Georg Sulzer had developed a new theory of rhythm. Earlier theories of rhythm had believed it to be formed from the combination of discrete units. Sulzer, by contrast, thought rhythm to arise from the breaking down of a continual flow.

This was achieved, thought Sulzer, by placing accents on certain notes.[31] Novalis draws on this understanding of rhythm to develop a broader philosophical position that opposes movement (*Bewegung*) and inertia (*Trägheit*). Inertia functions for Novalis as does the rhythmic accent for Sulzer, punctuating continual movement.[32] Novalis also comes to believe, however, that movement is the essence of all that is, hence all that is becomes rhythmical.

This leads straight into my third theme, a close connection – as we found also in Schlegel – between music and philosophy. The rhythmical outlook identified here certainly suggests such a close connection in itself. This outlook is, however, only one aspect of Novalis's magical idealism, which seeks to combine realism and idealism. In particular, it highlights the idealist side of this pair. In a telling passage from the *Allgemeine Brouillon*, Novalis associates music with (Fichtean) idealism, sculpture with (Spinozistic) realism. Novalis writes that:

Sculptors or atomists require a thrust [*Stoß*] (moving force [*Bewegende Kraft*].) – musicians a modifying body – a *check* [*Anstoß*]. Fichte belongs among the *musicians.*[33]

Here Novalis sees the essence of sculpture and atomism as being rest, whereas the essence of music and Fichtean idealism are movement. (Atomism in Novalis' time was a wide-ranging school of thought whose essential feature, for our purposes here, was that it was thoroughly realist.) Both music and sculpture, however, and both atomism and idealism, take shape only through their contact with their opposing force or body. Fichte had claimed that the thinking subject needs a 'check' against which to strive. Novalis balances this claim by suggesting that matter is equally in need of 'thrust'. Music, however, is associated with the Fichtean, idealist side of the equation, hence Novalis claims that 'Fichte has done nothing else than discover the rhythm of philosophy, and expressed it in a verbal acoustic manner.'[34] Elsewhere, in his novel *Heinrich von Ofterdingen* (1800), Novalis also establishes a clear connection between music and longing.[35]

Both Schlegel and Novalis, then, develop their new views of music out of an engagement with – and ultimately a rejection of – Fichte's philosophy. For Schlegel, the key point was the rejection of Fichte's epistemological foundationalism, to be replaced by an infinite longing for knowledge. Novalis, too, rejects Fichte's epistemological foundationalism, but his view of music rests equally on a new philosophical position – magical idealism – that sought to combine Fichtean idealism with a more common-sensical realism. There can be no denying that Schlegel and Novalis differ in many ways in their conceptions of music, but they agree on two key points. The first is that they both reject the older, Enlightenment view of music, according to which the purpose of music is merely to move the affects of listeners. For sure, they do not deny music's emotional power, or the uses to which this power might be put – but such uses are no longer music's primary purpose. The second key point is that, in response to a shared awareness of the limits of philosophical discourse, they agree that music is able to provide some kind of knowledge or insight that mere philosophy alone cannot provide. This latter belief is the essence of the Romantic view of music.

Schopenhauer and Schelling

Schlegel and Novalis were central to the early German Romantic movement. As such, they can be considered archetypically Romantic thinkers. Their new, Romantic view of music, however, soon spread to thinkers who were less easily straightforwardly 'Romantic' in orientation, yet whose development of the Romantic view of music was to prove of immense historical importance. Two of the most essential of these were Friedrich Wilhelm Joseph Schelling and Arthur Schopenhauer.

Schelling was an associate of Novalis and Schlegel in Jena and accepted some of their core philosophical ideas, yet retained the systematic impulse that had been so central to Reinhold and Fichte. In his *System of Transcendental Idealism* of 1800, Schelling put forward a view of art in general as the synthesis of the real and the ideal.[36] In his lectures on the *Philosophy of Art*, first delivered at the University of Jena in the academic year 1802–3, Schelling developed this position and applied it specifically to music. Here, Schelling makes systematic what was fragmentary in Schlegel and Novalis. '*The forms of music*', writes Schelling, '*are the forms of the eternal things* . . . . the forms of music are necessarily the forms of things in themselves.'[37] The reference to 'things in themselves' is a reference to that which Kant believed to be unknowable: reality apart from its perception in human thought. Music, thinks Schelling, can tell us about the universe as it really is.

Schopenhauer was famously dismissive of his immediate philosophical forebears. Both Fichte and Schelling, for example, are 'windbags'.[38] Yet his view of music comes straight from the work of Novalis, Schlegel, and, especially, Schelling. In his seminal work *The World as Will and*

Representation (1818), Schopenhauer suggested that behind all appearing reality lay a will (*Wille*), a blind striving that remained ever unfulfilled. This is a creative suggestion, but it is also just one more attempt to solve a problem that had lingered since Kant: how to describe reality as it really is, apart from human perception. By naming this more fundamental reality 'will', Schopenhauer thought that he had penetrated the essence of the universe itself. And Schopenhauer believed that music could offer access to this will, in a way that words could not. Hence, he claims that music has a 'serious and profound significance, one that refers to the innermost essence of the world and our self'. Indeed, music is unique amongst the arts in offering 'a direct copy of the will itself'.[39]

As with Kant's *Critique of Pure Reason*, Schopenhauer's *World as Will and Representation* was something of a sleeper hit: it was only with the publication of a volume of short essays, *Parerga and Paralipomena*, in 1851 that Schopenhauer was launched into the philosophical firmament, and interest in his earlier, lengthy tome truly ignited. Schopenhauer's place in musical history was cemented when Wagner first read *The World as Will and Representation* in 1854, a reading that was to have a famously dramatic effect on Wagner's musical and intellectual development.[40]

Schelling and Schopenhauer may not, strictly speaking, have been Romantics. But their views of music grew out of and in dialogue with those of their Romantic contemporaries, and had a mutual impact on more straightforwardly Romantic thinkers. Indeed, to make such blunt distinctions between inside and outside, Romantic and non-Romantic, is itself inimical to the Romantic predilections for multiplicity and universality. (Recall, for example, Schlegel's definition of Romantic poetry as 'forever in a state of becoming' yet a 'universal poetry'.) Whether or not they themselves were Romantics, these two thinkers played a pivotal role in developing and disseminating the Romantic view of music.

There are also other, more typically Romantic, thinkers who could have been given a place in this story. Central amongst them is Wilhelm Heinrich Wackenroder, widely considered to be one of the founders of literary Romanticism, and a famously florid writer on musical affairs. For all the magniloquence of its presentation, however, Wackenroder's core conception of music is more reminiscent of the older, Enlightenment view of music – according to which its purpose is to move the affects of listeners – than it is to the Romantic view discussed in the present chapter. Hence Wackenroder's fictional composer Joseph Berglinger, for example, believes that music is 'created only to move the human heart'.[41]

Another thinker who could have merited attention is the theologian Friedrich Daniel Ernst Schleiermacher, whose *On Religion: Speeches to its Cultured Despisers* of 1799 suggested that art had an 'inner affinity' with religion – and that it could penetrate to the depths of infinity.[42] Unlike that of Schlegel, Novalis, and Schelling, Schleiermacher's work in the years around 1800 had no specific focus on music in particular. In lectures delivered in 1819, 1825, and 1831–2, Schleiermacher discussed music in more detail, setting forward a position that combined affective and epistemological perspectives in unique and pleasantly perplexing ways. The texts of these lectures, however, were available only in limited form until the twentieth century, and so Schleiermacher's discussions of music were of limited historical influence in the later nineteenth century.[43]

The Romantic View of Music

This, then, is the story of the rise of the Romantic view of music. The view first arose in the aphoristic cogitations of Friedrich Schlegel and Novalis in the second half of the 1790s. It was systematised rigorously in Schelling's lectures on the *Philosophy of Art* in 1802–3 and presented in novel form in Schopenhauer's *World as Will and Representation* of 1818. Along the way, Wackenroder presented the older, Enlightenment view of music in Romantic clothing; and in the wake of Schopenhauer, Schleiermacher offered a view of music that was both quintessentially Romantic and unreservedly bound up in a rethinking of music's affective power.

This new, Romantic view of music spread like wildfire through nineteenth-century Europe. It was quickly developed by other philosophers, notably G. W. F. Hegel, and formed a foundational point of engagement for numerous and quite diverse later nineteenth-century thinkers, notably Richard Wagner, Franz Brendel, Eduard Hanslick, and the young Friedrich Nietzsche. This was the case even when these thinkers might have sought to modify this view, or even to reject it altogether. This Romantic view of music infiltrated music criticism with equal speed, underpinning – amongst much else – E. T. A. Hoffmann's famous 1810 review of Beethoven's Fifth Symphony. Further, since many of the figures involved in its creation were also novelists, poets, or essayists – indeed, several were all of these – it swiftly fermented itself in the popular literary imagination of the day. It did not, of course, remain uniform – there were as many variations on this view of music as there were discussions of it – yet at its core remained a rejection (or, at least, a weakening) of the older, more mechanical Enlightenment view of music and the embrace of the belief that music could, and should, offer some kind of knowledge or insight, especially into the fundamental nature of reality.[44]

Even more striking is that this Romantic view of music remains with us to the present day. For sure, few concert audiences are likely to think of music precisely as embodying the philosophical striving that results from epistemological anti-foundationalism. But performers, composers, and audiences across genres retain the belief that music can offer some kind of insight into life's mysteries – insight that simply cannot be put into words. This is a belief that motivates, if not exclusively, so much of contemporary musical life: from the silent listening still customary at classical concerts, to the rapturous critical praise of leading popular musicians, to the practice of music therapy. Perhaps most pertinently of all, this belief helps to underpin the educational and scholarly desire better to understand music, a desire embodied in the time taken by students and scholars to read essays such as this.

Notes

* For extremely helpful comments on earlier versions of this chapter, my thanks go to Mark Evan Bonds, Alexander Wilfing, Elizabeth Swann, and Benedict Taylor. I am grateful also to Anika Babel for invaluable practical assistance in preparing the final version.
1. Immanuel Kant, *Critique of Pure Reason*, trans. and ed. Paul Guyer and Allen W. Wood (Cambridge: Cambridge University Press, 1998).
2. Karl Leonhard Reinhold, *Letters on the Kantian Philosophy*, trans. James Hebbeler, ed. Karl Ameriks (Cambridge: Cambridge University Press, 2005).
3. For a remarkably clear overview of the *Elementarphilosophie* in the context of Reinhold's own philosophical development, see Frederick Beiser, *The Fate of Reason: German Philosophy from Kant to Fichte* (Cambridge, MA: Harvard University Press, 1993), 226–65.
4. The key text of Fichte's *Wissenschaftslehre* in this period is his 1794 *Foundations of the Entire Wissenschaftslehre*, a work even more badly written than Kant's *Critique of Pure Reason*. *Wissenschaftslehre* is a notoriously untranslatable term – to the extent that the best English translations simply leave it in the original German. 'Doctrine of Scientific Knowledge' is the closest English rendering, but 'scientific knowledge' must be taken here in the broadest possible sense, to encompass all branches of (rigorous) learning and scholarship. For an authoritative and remarkably lucid discussion of the *Wissenschaftslehre*, see Daniel Breazeale, *Thinking Through the Wissenschaftslehre: Themes from Fichte's Early Philosophy* (Oxford: Oxford University Press, 2013).

5. Except for references to the *Literarische Notizen*, all references to Schlegel's works are to Friedrich Schlegel, *Kritische Friedrich Schlegel Ausgabe*, ed. Ernst Behler (Munich: Schöningh, 1958–), and are given in the form division: volume, page. I also note the name of the work or fragment collection and, where applicable, the fragment number as given in the collected edition. References to the Literarische Notizen are to *Friedrich Schlegel, Literarische Notizen 1797–1801*, ed. Hans Eichner (Frankfurt: Ullstein Materialien, 1980), and are given in the form fragment number (page). Here, the citation is from I: 1, 357–8 / *On the Study of Greek Poetry*, ed. and trans. Stuart Barnett (Albany: SUNY Press, 2001), 90.

6. The key English-language works on the development of Schlegel's and Novalis' philosophy, in the context of philosophical Romanticism more generally, are Beiser, *The Romantic Imperative: The Concept of Early German Romanticism* (Cambridge, MA: Harvard University Press, 2003); Manfred Frank, *The Philosophical Foundations of Early German Romanticism*, trans. Elizabeth Millán-Zaibert (Albany: SUNY Press, 2003); Andrew Bowie, *Aesthetics and Subjectivity: From Kant to Nietzsche, Music*, 2nd ed. (Manchester: Manchester University Press, 2003); and Elizabeth Millán-Zaibert, *Friedrich Schlegel and the Emergence of Romantic Philosophy* (Albany: SUNY Press, 2007).

7. In *On the Study of Greek Poetry*, for example, Schlegel writes that modern poetry contains a '*restless, insatiable striving after something new, piquant, and striking* despite which, however, longing persists unfulfilled'. I: 1, 228 / *On the Study of Greek Poetry*, 24, translation modified.

8. *Athenaeumsfragmente* 116, I: 2, 182 / *Lucinde and the Fragments*, trans. Peter Firchow (Minneapolis: University of Minnesota Press, 1971), 175.

9. Beiser, *The Romantic Imperative*, 6–22, especially 9–11. It is worth noting in this context that the German word *Poesie* is something of a false friend for English speakers: though 'poetry' is its closest English translation, it naturally indicates a broader sense of 'poetry' than does its English equivalent.

10. I: 2, 304 / *Dialogue on Poetry and Literary Aphorisms*, trans. Ernst Behler and Roman Struc (University Park, PA: Pennsylvania State University Press, 1968), 76.

11. *Athenaeumsfragmente* 116, I: 2, 182 / *Lucinde and the Fragments*, 175.

12. I: 5, 46 / *Lucinde and the Fragments*, 89.

13. Ibid., 60 / 105, translation modified.

14. On this, see Frank, *Philosophical Foundations*, 2.

15. *Athenaeumsfragmente* 444, 1:2, 254 / *Lucinde and the Fragments*, 239, translation modified.

16. Schlegel, *Literarische Notizen*, 859 (101).

17. The terms thesis, antithesis, and synthesis taken together as a philosophical procedure are commonly associated with the work of Hegel, but Hegel himself did not use them. Rather, it was Fichte who, building on Kant, first used them

in their now-customary sense. See Gustav E. Mueller, 'The Hegel Legend of "Thesis-Antithesis-Synthesis"', *Journal of the History of Ideas*, 19 (1958), 413.

18. I: 18, 265.

19. Schlegel, *Literarische Notizen* 1417 (151).

20. Beiser, *German Idealism*, 425.

21. All references to Novalis's works are to Friedrich von Hardenberg [Novalis], *Novalis Schriften*, 6 vols., ed. Paul Kluckhohn, Richard Samuel, Heinz Ritter, Gerhard Schulz, and Hans-Joachim Mähl (Stuttgart: Kohlhammer, 1960–2006). As with Schlegel, I also note the name of the work or fragment collection and, where applicable, the fragment number, as well as the English translation where available. The citation here is from *Allgemeine Brouillon* 338, 3: 301 / *Notes for a Romantic Encyclopaedia*, ed. and trans. David W. Wood (New York: SUNY Press, 2007), 51.

22. See, e.g., *Allgemeine Brouillon* 399, 3: 314 / *Romantic Encyclopaedia*, 61.

23. On this, see Tomás McAuley, 'The Enlightenment', in Tomás McAuley, Nanette Nielsen, and Jerrold Levinson, with Ariana Phillips-Hutton (eds.), *The Oxford Handbook of Western Music and Philosophy* (New York: Oxford University Press, 2020), 181–206.

24. 2: 393 / Novalis, 'Kant Studies', trans. David Wood, *The Philosophical Forum*, 32 (2001), 338.

25. *Logologische Fragmente* 226, 3: 572 / Novalis, *Philosophical Writings*, ed. and trans. Margaret Mahony Stoljar (New York: SUNY Press, 1997), 71.

26. *Allgemeine Brouillon* 399, 3: 315 / *Romantic Encyclopaedia*, 62.

27. Ibid., 3: 314 / 61.

28. Ibid., 3: 315 / 62.

29. *Allgemeine Brouillon* 386, 3: 310 / *Romantic Encyclopaedia*, 58.

30. Ibid. 3: 310 / 58.

31. The theory is first presented in Sulzer's *Allgemeine Theorie der schönen Künste* (Leipzig, 1771, 1774). On this theory and its later influence in Schelling, see Tomás McAuley, 'Rhythmic Accent and the Absolute: Sulzer, Schelling and the Akzenttheorie', *Eighteenth Century Music*, 10/2 (2013), 277–86.

32. Novalis writes: 'Sound seems to be nothing but a broken movement, in the sense that colour is broken light. . . . Sound is connected with movement as if of itself.' *Fragmente und Studien 1799–1800* 43, 3: 561 / *Philosophical Writings*, 154.

33. *Allgemeine Brouillon* 634, 3: 382 / *Romantic Encyclopaedia*, 115, translation modified.

34. *Allgemeine Brouillon* 382, 3: 310 / *Romantic Encyclopaedia*, 57.

35. 3: 214 / Novalis, *Henry von Ofterdingen*, trans. Palmer Hilty (New York: Frederick Ungar, 1964), 36.

36. F. W. J. Schelling, *System of Transcendental Idealism (1800)*, trans. Peter Heath (Charlottesville: University of Virginia Press, 1978).

37. F. W. J. Schelling, *The Philosophy of Art*, ed. and trans. Douglas Stott (Minneapolis: University of Minnesota Press, 1989), 115–16.

38. Arthur Schopenhauer, *The World as Will and Representation*, vol. 1, ed. and trans. Judith Norman and Alistair Welchman (Cambridge: Cambridge University Press, 2010), 14.

39. Ibid., 290.

40. For a more detailed treatment, within a broader Wagnerian context, see Julian Young, *The Philosophies of Richard Wagner* (Lanham, MD: Lexington Books, 2014).

41. See Wilhelm Heinrich Wackenroder, *Wilhelm Heinrich Wackenroder's Confessions and Fantasies*, trans. Mary Hurst Schubert (University Park, PA: Pennsylvania State University Press, 1971). See also Holly Watkins's essay on 'Music and Romantic Interiority' in the present volume (Chapter 12).

42. Friedrich Daniel Ernst Schleiermacher, *On Religion: Speeches to its Cultured Despisers*, 2nd ed., ed. and trans. Richard Crouter (Cambridge: Cambridge University Press, 1996), quotation from 69.

43. Friedrich Daniel Ernst Schleiermacher, *Ästhetik (1819/25). Über den Begriff der Kunst (1831/32)*, ed. Thomas Lehnerer (Hamburg: Felix Meiner Verlag, 1984). On the reception history of Schleiermacher's thought on music, see Gunter Scholtz, 'Schleiermacher', in Stefan Lorenz Sorgner and Oliver Fürbeth (eds.), *Music in German Philosophy: An Introduction*, trans. Susan H. Gillespie (Chicago: University of Chicago Press, 2010), 47–68, at 64–5.

44. Many of the developments in this view of music are discussed elsewhere in this volume. See also Mark Bonds, *Absolute Music: The History of an Idea* (New York: Oxford University Press, 2014).

Further Reading

Beiser, Frederick. *German Idealism: The Struggle Against Subjectivism, 1781–1801* (Cambridge, MA: Harvard University Press, 2002).

    The Romantic Imperative: The Concept of Early German Romanticism (Cambridge, MA: Harvard University Press, 2003).

Bonds, Mark Evan. *Absolute Music: The History of an Idea* (New York: Oxford University Press, 2014).

    Music as Thought: Listening to the Symphony in the Age of Beethoven (Princeton: Princeton University Press, 2006).

Bowie, Andrew. *Aesthetics and Subjectivity: From Kant to Nietzsche*, 2nd ed. (Manchester: Manchester University Press, 2003).

    'Music and the Rise of Aesthetics', in Jim Samson (ed.), *The Cambridge History of Nineteenth-Century Music* (Cambridge: Cambridge University Press, 2002), 29–54.

Chua, Daniel K. L. *Absolute Music and the Construction of Meaning* (Cambridge: Cambridge University Press, 1999).

Gordon, Paul. *Art as the Absolute: Art's Relation to Metaphysics in Kant, Fichte, Schelling, Hegel, and Schopenhauer* (New York: Bloomsbury, 2015).

Hodkinson, James. 'The Cosmic-Symphonic: Novalis, Music, and Universal Discourse', in Siobhán Donovan and Robin Elliot (eds.), *Music and Literature in German Romanticism* (Rochester, NY: Camden House, 2004), 13–26.

McAuley, Tomás. *The Music of Philosophy: German Idealism and Musical Thought, from Kant to Schelling* (New York: Oxford University Press, forthcoming).

Millán-Zaibert, Elizabeth. *Friedrich Schlegel and the Emergence of Romantic Philosophy* (Albany: SUNY Press, 2007).

Morrow, Mary Sue. *German Music Criticism in the Late Eighteenth Century: Aesthetic Issues in Instrumental Music* (Cambridge: Cambridge University Press, 1997).

Pritchard, Matthew. 'Music in Balance: The Aesthetics of Music after Kant, 1790–1810', *Journal of Musicology*, 36/1 (2019), 39–67.

Sorgner, Stefan Lorenz, and Fürbeth, Oliver (eds.). *Music in German Philosophy: An Introduction*, trans. Susan H. Gillespie (Chicago: University of Chicago Press, 2010).

11 | Meaning and Value in Romantic Musical Aesthetics

ALEXANDER WILFING

Questions of aesthetic merit are often tied to questions of (some kind of) utility or meaning. Poems, novels, and plays might prove useful for pedagogic purposes, paintings and sculptures might shed light on the human condition, and buildings – besides having the practical function of housing and shelter – commonly represent the purpose they were built for: governance, spiritual worship, memorialisation, and the like. In the case of much music, its purpose and meaning is as evident as with other arts: church music has the function of uplifting or inspiring the congregation, march music governs the pace of soldiers or parades, and vocal music can readily draw import from a text or *mise en scène*. When it comes to 'pure' music – instrumental compositions without a programme, title, or text – the concept of purpose or meaning becomes more vexing. With the emancipation of instrumental music from functionality, a process usually dated to the eighteenth century,[1] the question of aesthetic merit poses special issues for an art form whose meaning is notoriously problematic to determine, or sometimes considered simply absent. The issue with 'pure' music as an abstract and intricate art form demanding the listener's full cognitive attention, engagement, and participation is captured vividly by the famous outburst of Bernard de Fontenelle, reported by Jean-Jacques Rousseau in 1768: 'Sonate, que me veux-tu?'; that is, 'Sonata, what do you want from me?', or 'Sonata, what do you mean to me?'

In 1790, the essence of Fontenelle's question was restated in a way that continued to dominate the majority of nineteenth-century musical discourse by provoking responses to the growing problem of 'pure' music. In his *Critique of the Power of Judgment*, Immanuel Kant declares a serious dilemma: for him, as for many of his contemporaries, music on its own is considered the 'language of affects'. As it thus does not involve rational concepts or moral ideas akin to the other fine arts and appeals mainly to emotion, it is unclear whether music is to be classified as an agreeable or fine art, the former merely 'intended as momentary entertainment' while the latter 'promotes the cultivation of the mental powers'. Kant proceeds to compare the aesthetic value of each of the fine arts and assigns music without words a double-edged ranking (§53). While poetry takes the first place, music – which 'speaks through mere sensations without concepts' and does not 'leave behind something for reflection' – comes in second if 'charm and movement of the mind' are the deciding features. As soon as it comes to a more intellectual assessment, however, music proves to be 'more enjoyment than culture' and has, 'judged by reason, less value than any other of the beautiful arts'.[2] In Kant's view, music lacks any kind of content, speaking by means of auditory sensations without concepts, and is far too elusive to provide any rational content for intellectual recollection – the hallmark of true fine art. 'Pure' music, put rather simply, has no semantic content and therefore lacks meaning and, by extension, (aesthetic) value.[3]

Kant was by no means alone in his sceptical attitude towards music; indeed, he reflects general problems in grappling with this new phenomenon. Several decades later, Georg Wilhelm Friedrich Hegel's *Lectures on Aesthetics*, compiled from transcripts dating from the 1820s and published posthumously, reflect this Kantian dilemma directly:[4] music without a text to be sung, Hegel purports, forgoes any 'cognitive content and expression', ultimately becoming 'meaningless' so that it must not be counted amongst the fine arts. The 'sensory element' of music, expressing the inwardness of subjectivity, must convey 'intellect'; only then does music rise 'to the rank of true art'.[5] Although regarding the entirety of nineteenth-century musical aesthetics as a response to Kant's charge against music simplifies a complex discourse, many contemporary philosophers, composers, literary figures, and critics in fact came to music's defence. While each writer had their own means of imbuing music with merit and value, I will discuss four main solutions to the problem of musical meaning in roughly the first half of the nineteenth century, all closely linked to 'Romantic' views: (1) a reappraisal of the significance of feeling and emotion, (2) a modified connection between music and words, (3) the use of titles and programmes in instrumental compositions, and (4) a fundamental rethinking of the relationship of content and form. These general strategies and their most important exponents will function as umbrella concepts to be exemplified in the remainder of the current chapter.

Feeling as Content: Hoffmann, Schopenhauer, and the *Affektenlehre*

Relating different kinds of music to feelings is certainly no invention of Romantic aesthetics. Plato, for example, awards music a central place in

Book 3 of *Politeia* or *Republic* (*c.* 375 BC), a dialogue carving out the principles of an ideal city state. As music affects humans profoundly, educators must select modes that improve the morality of pupils, mainly those about to become soldiers: music and instruments categorised as feeble would result in citizens of a similar character and are therefore ostracised (*Politeia, c.* 398–*c.* 400). Derived from this view, modern notions of music were largely shaped by the *Affektenlehre* (the doctrine of affects) as the prevalent approach to music, often based on a mimetic concept of art,[6] which states that music can portray emotions such as pain, joy, and grief by purely musical means that in turn elicit matching sentiments in listeners. Music could reach this goal by imitating actual sounds (birdsong), by emulating the dynamics of natural events (sunrise and sunset), or by retracing expression (the emotional inflections of human speech).[7] This view even produced textbooks specifying which musical features would evoke which affects, exemplified by Johann Mattheson's *Der vollkommene Capellmeister* (1739).[8] The pinnacle of modern mimetic theory is commonly associated with eighteenth-century French writers (e.g., Abbé Dubos and Charles Batteux), who define art as an imitation of nature.[9] This view, which bases the value of music on an emulation of external objects, is ultimately discarded by British theorists such as James Beattie and Adam Smith, who consider musical meaning to be 'complete in itself'.[10]

With the decline of mimetic concepts in general, the nineteenth century saw expression take centre stage in discussions concerning the value of music. Although the *Affektenlehre* gave major weight to emotion and feeling, it did so in terms of a shared lexicon of musical gestures on the part of the composer and emotive arousal on the part of the listener, whereas Romanticism framed this question in terms of individual expression. The Romantic composer was no longer obligated to convey a universally intelligible meaning to his or her audience. Rather, they were expressing subjective emotional states and (in the best of cases) introducing their listeners to hitherto unknown realms of profound experience, culminating in the magical, mystical, and supernatural. Musically speaking, this attitude resulted in the extension of musical material (e.g., intensification of chromaticism and liberal usage of timbral colours), the loosening and exceeding of traditional formal bounds (programmes in instrumental compositions), the blending of distinct genres (the use of choirs in symphonies from Ludwig van Beethoven's Symphony No. 9 to Gustav Mahler's Symphony No. 8), or an emphasis on subjective and inward genres such as piano music and the lied. As E. T. A. Hoffmann and other Romantic writers indicate, however, this shifting attitude towards 'pure' music and its potential for the sublime was for the most part a question of perspective, reflecting primarily a new way of listening,[11] and thus not mirrored directly by changes in musical material or style.

In his famous review of Beethoven's Symphony No. 5 (1810), Hoffmann views music as 'the most romantic of all arts', unlocking an 'unknown realm', a world in which humans 'leave behind all feelings circumscribed by intellect in order to embrace the inexpressible'. While Joseph Haydn's works are the expression of 'childlike optimism', Wolfgang Amadeus Mozart gives us an 'intimation of infinity' by leading us 'deep into the realm of spirits'. Beethoven, finally, sets in motion the 'machinery of awe, of fear, of terror, of pain', and awakes 'that infinite yearning which is the essence of romanticism'.[12] Ten years prior, another pivotal figure of Romantic aesthetics, Ludwig Tieck, had described his experience of attending a staging of *Macbeth*, captured in his brief essay 'Symphonies' (1799). For him, the overture outshone anything the play itself could depict, as the music had already 'voiced the most tremendous and the most excruciating in greater and more poetic ways'. This prelude, capable of manifesting the 'restless, fiercer and fiercer activity of all the psychic forces',[13] was not, however, composed by anyone like Beethoven, but by Johann Friedrich Reichardt in 1795 – a composer certainly not regarded as typically Romantic today. The early stages of Romantic musical aesthetics, as Carl Dahlhaus observed, therefore constitute an ostensible mismatch between Romantic rhetoric and the music it attempts to interpret and 'did not find an adequate object until E. T. A. Hoffmann borrowed Tieck's language in order to do justice to Beethoven'.[14]

Finally, Arthur Schopenhauer's main work *The World as Will and Representation* presents the first full-fledged treatise to declare 'pure' music the central artform because of its capacity to express feelings in their purest form. While the initial edition of 1818 went practically unnoticed in the age of Hegel, the second edition of 1844 proved influential, particularly in music circles, and it deeply shaped composers' philosophical convictions, from Wagner to Mahler, Strauss, and Schoenberg. Schopenhauer's momentous revaluation of music is based on an overarching metaphysics rooted in Platonic and Kantian idealism as well as Indian Vedic philosophy. Schopenhauer distinguishes two aspects of the world: (1) a world of representation, constructed by our peculiar sensory apparatus and mind, and (2) a world apart from any act of perception, that is, the thing-in-itself or noumenon. While Kant treats the thing-in-itself as necessarily unknowable, Schopenhauer calls it Will – a blind force of striving impelling all phenomena, from the plant's growth towards the sun to human volition. As the essential principle of life thus is insatiable striving, humans are torn between volition, temporary fulfilment, and boredom. While grasping the Will as the essence of being itself – thus obliterating the perceived difference between the 'I' and the world – results in the cessation of any volition, art can act as its momentary suppressant by offering objects of contemplation, fleetingly liberating the individual from this 'vale of tears'. In doing so, music attains a special status: while other arts can merely present Ideas (the inner nature of objects), music alone can reveal the Will in totality.[15] Music, states Schopenhauer,

is an *unmediated* objectivation and copy of the entire *will*, just as the world itself is ... This is precisely why the effect of music is so much more powerful and urgent than that of the other arts: the other arts speak only of shadows while music speaks of the essence. ... Therefore it does not express this or that individual and particular joy, this or that sorrow or pain or horror or exaltation or cheerfulness or peace of mind, but rather joy, sorrow, pain, horror, exaltation, cheerfulness and peace of mind as such *in themselves*, abstractly, as it were, the essential in all these without anything superfluous.[16]

Music and Words: Mendelssohn, Wagner, and the Specificity of 'Pure' Music

Romanticism frequently tended towards the ineffable, relating musical works to a 'separate world unto themselves' (Tieck) and to the 'wondrous realm of the infinite' (Hoffmann).[17] The lack of precise content was thus no longer rated as some kind of vice, but was on the contrary perceived as a unique ability of music to approximate the spiritual and absolute. This view also modified the relations between music and words. The old question of the aesthetic priority of music and words in opera – immortalised in Salieri's *Prima la musica e poi le parole* (1786) and posed again in Strauss's *Capriccio* (1942) – had typically been answered in favour of the text, so that Kant in 1798 could claim that music is an art 'only because it serves poetry as a vehicle'.[18] While this debate was usually framed in terms of hierarchy, Felix Mendelssohn restates this problem as one of precision and immediacy. Following a line of thought set out by Johann Gottfried Herder and Wilhelm von Humboldt, Mendelssohn was mindful of the pitfalls of linguistic meaning based on generic, abstract, and highly conventionalised terms, which have different meanings and connotations for different individuals. Music, in contrast, viewed as an immediate expression of the composer's innermost subjectivity, originality, and individuality, can convey precise (emotive) meaning to an audience of like-minded listeners.[19] For him, 'pure' music expresses not 'thoughts too *indefinite* to couch in terms, but on the contrary too *definite*'. He considers any attempt of translating musical thoughts into language to be inadequate in principle and thus also refrained from putting his theoretical convictions into writing, usually a hallmark of Romantic composers: 'If you ask me, what I was thinking of [in writing these pieces], I must say: just this song as it is written.'[20]

This view, reversing the argument against music's vagueness and declaring language too imprecise to do justice to music's import, is an attitude we will come across again in discussing Hanslick's aesthetics, for Hanslick similarly declares 'pure' music to be 'a language that we speak and understand, but are unable to translate'. If we wish to identify the 'content' of a piece or theme for someone, Hanslick continues, 'we have to *play the theme itself* for him. The content of a musical work can therefore never be understood concretely but rather only musically, namely as that which actually resounds in each piece of music.'[21] While Hanslick thereby claimed music's content to be part of 'music itself' and not in need of clarification by language or concepts, other exponents of Romantic aesthetics still used words as a means to achieve musical meaning. Although this notion might, at first glance, seem a relapse into pre-Romantic reasoning, the motivation for introducing words to music had changed markedly. Whereas Baroque authors often treated words as an indispensable prerequisite for giving music merit in the first place, Romantic theorists assumed musical meaning to be intrinsic and self-evident. While this intrinsic meaning was regarded by Mendelssohn as having the utmost immediacy and precision, a second thread of Romantic reasoning considered it transcendent and therefore as exceeding regular human comprehension. Following Hoffmann in linking musical meaning to ineffability, some felt the need to objectify its abstract content by reifying music's absolute meaning through words, thereby linking the universal expression of 'pure' music to concrete human events.

One of these Romantic theorists was Richard Wagner, who, in his Zurich exile (1849–58) following the revolution of 1848, embarked on creating an inclusive concept of art, conceived as a general philosophy including (amongst other things) a critique of the state, society, religion, and capitalist economy, and of the steady decline of art since ancient Greek tragedy.[22] In his key essays from around this time – *Art and Revolution*

(1849), *The Artwork of the Future* (1850), and *Opera and Drama* (1851) – Wagner portrays the historical evolution of art as one of progressive segregation. While Wagner views *mousiké techné* – the unity of song, dance, and music – and the tight link of ancient Greek tragedy to morality, religion, and society as an apex of art, he regards modern art as the result of an 'egoistic' isolation of the arts from each other, ever approximating mere *l'art pour l'art* (art for art's sake). While the fine arts had revelled in their isolated technical progress, they had lost sight of their 'true' purpose: the 'unconditioned, absolute portrayal of perfected human nature' that only the united efforts of all the arts – the *Gesamtkunstwerk* or total work of art – can wholly muster. The autonomous expressive properties of music, Wagner asserts, had reached their limit in Beethoven's symphonies, as testified by the use of Schiller's 'Ode to Joy' in his Ninth, which represents 'the redemption of music from out her own peculiar element into the realm of *universal Art*'. In order to portray the essence of human nature, music's conceptless universality had to be specified, marking the boundary between 'absolute' music and the purely human artwork.[23]

In the Romantic tradition of viewing music as an intimation of the absolute, Wagner treats music as the 'organ of the heart' and 'faculty of uttering the unspeakable'. For the purpose of expressing something more than endless longing, the 'unspeakably expressive language' and 'infinitely soul-full element' of music must focus on tangible objects.[24] This move, however, differs from the question of the aesthetic priority of music and words and is motivated by Wagner's resort to Greek tragedy viewed through the prism of Friedrich Schlegel's universal Romantic poetry, which aimed at fusing philosophy, spirituality, art, and life as such.[25] Wagner, after becoming acquainted with Schopenhauer's metaphysics in 1854, would later award to music an elevated position amongst the fine arts (see his *Beethoven* essay of 1870).[26] His Zurich writings, however, consider words and music as equal in opera, the error of which lay in the fact that 'a Means of expression (Music) has been made the end, while the End of expression (the Drama) has been made a means'. Note that Wagner says that music must serve not the text, but rather the *drama*, the poetic kernel of the total work of art, which all the arts must convey to their fullest extent. Separately, the arts are incapable of fulfilling their expressive potential and need each other to become a universal and undivided art.[27] In deeming music without words unable to portray specific feelings, concepts, and objects, Wagner and Hanslick are still part of Kantian discourse and – although reaching different conclusions – hold 'quite similar' views of music's expressive powers, 'even if they approached the issue of "absolute music" from opposite sides'.[28]

Poetic Music Between the Characteristic and the Programmatic

While words were a tried and tested means of establishing musical meaning, Romanticism brought to fruition another way of defining musical content by creating complete genres still used today: the programme symphony and symphonic poem.[29] The former is frequently considered to have been introduced by Hector Berlioz's *Symphonie fantastique* (1830) and *Harold en Italie* (1834), before being continued effectively in works such as Franz Liszt's *Faust-Sinfonie* (1857) and Pyotr Ilyich Tchaikovsky's *Manfred* Symphony (1885). The symphonic poem, meanwhile, was a theoretical conception introduced by Liszt, whose thirteen specimens presented an exemplary precedent for numerous successors in the later stages of the nineteenth and well into the twentieth century, including well-known pieces by Balakirev, Dvořák, Respighi, Saint-Saëns, Smetana, Sibelius, and Strauss. Using labels or programmes to identify musical meaning was itself hardly an invention of the Romantic era: prominent precedents introducing programmes to instrumental compositions include Antonio Vivaldi's *Le quattro stagioni* (1725), Luigi Boccherini's *Musica Notturna delle strade di Madrid* (1780), Carl Ditters von Dittersdorf's symphonies after Ovid's *Metamorphoses* (1783), or Beethoven's Symphony No. 6 (*Pastoral*, 1808).[30] But it is the belief that music could be imbued with poetic import through the use of fully developed programmes derived from novels, plays, and other forms of stimuli that most of all sets the programme symphony and symphonic poem apart from earlier examples.

It is this very distinction that differentiates such programmatic music from another typical and equally central Romantic development in music in the 1820s and 1830s, the 'characteristic' or 'poetic' piano piece, overture, or symphony, in which 'extra-musical' content is indicated by such means as titles and evocative or topically allusive musical material. This category is epitomised by Mendelssohn's independent concert overtures – *Sommernachtstraum* (1826), *Meeresstille und glückliche Fahrt* (1828), *Die Hebriden* (1832), and *Das Märchen von der schönen Melusine* (1834) – Schumann's piano cycles of the 1830s (e.g., *Carnaval*, *Kinderszenen*, and, inspired by Hoffmann's writings, *Kreisleriana* and *Fantasiestücke*), and to an extent the symphonies of both these composers. In many cases, the boundary between the programmatic and the musically evocative is rather fuzzy: some of Mendelssohn's earlier pieces flirt with more patently programmatic content,[31] whereas several of Liszt's symphonic poems originated as concert overtures or other pieces and profess a tenuous or retrospective association with their expressly declared programme.[32] A work like Louis Spohr's Symphony No. 4, *Die Weihe der Töne* (1832), a 'characteristic tone-painting' based on a poem by Carl Pfeiffer and ending unusually in a measured *Larghetto* movement, shows how easily the programmatic and characteristic became blurred in the symphony after Beethoven.[33] Moreover, the division between the two positions hardened around mid-century, with lines drawn around ideological and political agendas that bury the fluid usage of literary content from the delicately evocative to the categorically programmatic.

By 1850, though, the degree to which music was supposed to conform to 'external' literary templates was proving a matter of heated debate. Composers disagreed as to what extent such literary models were part of 'music itself'. Schumann, for instance, had adopted an attitude that allowed for perspectivist assessments – one and the same work 'as poetry' and 'as a composition' – and regularly used headings as depictions a posteriori, clarifying the 'content' of any given piece. Poetry and music, Schumann asserts, coincide in essence: 'the aesthetics of one art is the same as that of all the other arts; only the material is different'.[34] Liszt, however, regarded the retrospective use of programmes as 'childish'[35] (at least in theory if not in actual practice), as for him, the plot or idea is an integral element of programme music, which simply *is* 'pure' music with definite spiritual content and not a composite of music and words, thus meeting Hegel's demands for 'real' art.[36] The definiteness of programmes was a further matter of dispute: Schumann, for example, regarded an exhaustive programme as obstructing the free flow of imagination. For him, art was life and life was art, expressing the personality, ferventness, and emotions of the creator directly. Liszt, however, endorsed guiding the listener by way of fully developed plots, at least when it came to his theoretical deliberations, which were not always realised in practice. As Franz Brendel, Schumann's successor as editor of *Neue Zeitschrift für Musik*, put the matter: while music's ability to 'express the ineffable' embodies its 'loftiest aspect', the 'completely unspecified' realm of music had to be 'fixed by a programme directing the vagabond imagination towards a definite object'.[37]

Hanslick, Aesthetic Autonomy, and 'Absolute' Music

Whereas Romantic writers largely agreed that any given piece of music might be perceived poetically, irrespective of the creator's intention, defining the relation between the literary subject and music's formal features proved a divisive problem. Rather than acting merely as poetic stimuli, ideas, plots, and entire stories could govern music on the level of structural organisation, justifying harmonic 'oddities' by virtue of literary cohesion. The harmonic ventures of the witches' sabbath in the *Symphonie fantastique* and the final part of *Eine Faust-Sinfonie*, pushing the limits of tonality, were thus explained by their plots: while they might not 'make sense' musically, they were warranted by their poetic topics. Brendel, for instance, held that extraordinary musical progressions are 'legitimised not by technical harmonic analysis, but by the [poetic] *subject directly*'.[38] This opinion, however, did not remain unchallenged amongst Romantic writers, as August Wilhelm Ambros shows: while upholding Schumann's poetic notion of music, he at the same time asserts that literary subjects could never justify a deviation from music's organic unfolding as 'each detail of a piece of music must, according to purely musical logic, allow itself to be entirely derived from and justified by the mere formal element'.[39] This issue is related directly to questions of aesthetic autonomy and the nature of music, ultimately resulting in opposing schools of thought around 1850: the 'New German School', rallying around Wagner and Liszt with Brendel as their main journalistic mouthpiece, and the more 'conservative' Romanticist camp of Brahms, Hanslick, and Joseph Joachim.[40]

While Liszt and Wagner argued for the coherence of different art forms, united in respect of common expressive purposes, Hanslick and like-minded individuals remained sceptical towards music's poetic ambitions. This discord, however, was not based simply on dogmatic appeals to music's purity and the general rejection of poetic music but was derived chiefly from the perceived tendency of programmatic compositions to disregard the 'inherent' principles of music, which were suspended for the purpose of depicting extra-musical content. For Hanslick, music had 'sense and logic' like other arts, but '*musical* sense and logic', which might allow for literary stimuli but must not adhere to external precepts that could compromise an aesthetic autonomy only recently attained.[41] While this idea might appear less 'Romantic' than Wagner's position, it should be viewed as the flipside of Romantic aesthetics: although many Romantics were invested in creating tangible musical content, the purely musical is, as Benedict Taylor observes, an invention of Romanticism as well.[42] Hegel posits three classes of art: symbolic, classical, and Romantic art, the last-named including painting, music, and poetry in order of merit. Romantic musicians, however, went one step further by calling music 'Romantic as such'[43] and stipulating that 'when music is spoken of as an independent art the term can properly apply only to instrumental music, which scorns all aid, all admixture of other arts, and gives pure expression to its own peculiar artistic nature. It is the most romantic of all arts – one might almost say the only one that is *purely* romantic.'[44]

This notion of music as essentially instrumental instead of vocal, although common in certain circles today, marks a profound conceptual shift carried into effect by Romantic aesthetics. Eduard Hanslick, whose *On the Musically Beautiful* probably presents the most significant musical aesthetics of nineteenth-century discourse, develops his approach from this idea: 'only what can be asserted about instrumental music is valid for music as such ... Whatever *instrumental music* cannot do, can never be said that *music* can do it. For only instrumental music is pure, absolute *music*'. Although Hanslick refrains from allotting priority to 'pure' music – he calls this move an 'unscientific procedure' – he asserts against the 'New German School' that 'the unification with poetry extends the power of music, but not its boundaries'.[45] He therefore repudiates Schumann's universal aesthetics and rather insists on a particular approach to music, which 'holds firmly to the maxim that the laws of beauty of each art are inseparable from the characteristics of its material, of its technique'.[46] By defining musical content as 'sonically moved forms',[47] he leaves behind the customary distinction between these factors, thereby turning beauty as well as emotional expression into intrinsic features of 'music itself'.[48] Music thus does not have any purpose beyond itself, nor does it need to arouse affects or present 'external content' in order to have merit, as beauty 'resides solely in the tones and their artistic connection': music, he states, is 'an end unto itself' and not merely 'a means of or material for representing feelings and thoughts'.[49]

While this view is commonly considered the origins of formalist aesthetics and 'traditional' musicology grounded in technical analysis, Hanslick's defence of 'absolute' music – a term he uses only once – clearly derives from Romanticism. What turns 'pure' music into true art for Hanslick besides formal beauty is an essentially Romantic idea: *Geist*, that is, mind, spirit, intellect. Conforming to (historically arbitrary) principles of regularity, symmetry, and perfection is not enough for music to be considered beautiful; composing, Hanslick contends, is 'an operation of the intellect in material of intellectual capacity', which utilises existing musical material to 'invent new, purely musical features'.[50] The original Romantic setting of Hanslick's aesthetics gets lost in translation quite literally, as the English-language renditions of *On the Musically Beautiful* are based on revised editions. The initial 1854 edition of Hanslick's treatise shows the early Romantic leanings of its author most clearly in the concluding paragraph, omitted from later editions, and thereby reveals how both formalism and expressivism are deeply rooted in Romanticism:

In the psyche of the listener, furthermore, this intellectual substance [i.e. *Gehalt* (intellectual substance) in contrast to *Inhalt* (content)] unites the beautiful in music with all other grand and beautiful ideas. Music affects the psyche not merely and absolutely by means of its own particular beauty, but rather simultaneously as a sounding reflection of the great motions of the cosmos. Through profound and covert relationships to nature, the significance of tones increases far above themselves, and allows us at the same time always to feel the infinite in the work of human talent. Because the elements of music – sound, tone, rhythm, forcefulness, gentleness – exist in the entire universe, so does man rediscover the entire universe in music.[51]

Notes

* I want to thank Mark Evan Bonds, Thomas S. Grey, Tomás McAuley, Meike Wilfing-Albrecht, and especially Benedict Taylor for productive criticism on earlier sketches of this text. The writing of this chapter was supported financially by the Austrian Science Fund (FWF, project number P30554-G30).

1. John Neubauer, *The Emancipation of Music from Language: Departure from Mimesis in Eighteenth-Century Aesthetics* (New Haven: Yale University Press, 1986).

2. Immanuel Kant, *Critique of the Power of Judgment*, ed. Paul Guyer and Eric Matthews (Cambridge: Cambridge University Press, 2000), 184–5 and 205–6.

3. Tomás McAuley, 'Immanuel Kant and the Downfall of the *Affektenlehre*', in Stephen Decatur Smith, Judy Lochhead, and Eduardo Mendieta (eds.), *Sound and Affect: Voice, Music, World* (Chicago: University of Chicago Press, 2021).

4. For the essentials of Hegel's notion of music, see Richard Eldridge, 'Hegel on Music', in Stephen Houlgate (ed.), *Hegel and the Arts* (Evanston: Northwestern University Press, 2007), 119–45.

5. My translation. Cf. G. W. F. Hegel, *Aesthetics: Lectures on Fine Art by G. W. F. Hegel*, trans. T. M. Knox (Oxford: Clarendon Press, 1975), vol. 2, 901–2.

6. Stephen Halliwell, *The Aesthetics of Mimesis: Ancient Texts and Modern Problems* (Princeton: Princeton University Press, 2002); and Roger Matthew Grant, *Peculiar Attunements: How Affect Theory Turned Musical* (New York: Fordham University Press, 2020).

7. Peter Kivy, *Sound and Semblance: Reflections on Musical Representation* (Ithaca: Cornell University Press, 1984); and Bruce Haynes and Geoffrey Burgess, *The Pathetick Musician: Moving an Audience in the Age of Eloquence* (Oxford: Oxford University Press, 2016).

8. Johann Mattheson, *Johann Mattheson's 'Der vollkommene Capellmeister':
   A Revised Translation with Critical Commentary*, trans. Ernest C. Harris (Ann
   Arbor: UMI Research Press, 1981).

9. Edward Lippman, *A History of Western Musical Aesthetics* (Lincoln, NE:
   University of Nebraska Press, 1992), 82–98.

10. Adam Smith, *Essays on Philosophical Subjects*, ed. W. Wightman, J. Bryce, and
    I. S. Ross (Oxford: Clarendon Press, 1980), 205.

11. Mark Evan Bonds, *Music as Thought: Listening to the Symphony in the Age of
    Beethoven* (Princeton: Princeton University Press, 2006), ch. 1.

12. E. T. A. Hoffmann, *E. T. A. Hoffmann's Musical Writings: Kreisleriana, The
    Poet and the Composer, Music Criticism*, ed. David Charlton, trans.
    Martyn Clarke (Cambridge: Cambridge University Press, 1989), 236–8.

13. W. H. Wackenroder, *Phantasien über die Kunst, für Freunde der Kunst*, ed.
    Ludwig Tieck (Hamburg: Friedrich Perthes, 1799), 266–7.

14. Carl Dahlhaus, *The Idea of Absolute Music*, trans. Roger Lustig (Chicago:
    University of Chicago Press, 1989), 90.

15. Lawrence Ferrara, 'Schopenhauer on Music as the Embodiment of Will', in
    Dale Jacquette (ed.), *Schopenhauer, Philosophy, and the Arts* (Cambridge:
    Cambridge University Press, 1996), 183–99.

16. Arthur Schopenhauer, *The World as Will and Representation*, ed. and trans.
    Judith Norman, Alistair Welchman, and Christopher Janaway (Cambridge:
    Cambridge University Press, 2010), 285 and 289.

17. Mark Evan Bonds, 'Idealism and the Aesthetics of Instrumental Music at the
    Turn of the Nineteenth Century', *Journal of the American Musicological
    Society*, 50/2–3 (1997), 392 and 407.

18. Immanuel Kant, *Anthropology from a Pragmatic Point of View*, trans. Robert
    B. Louden (Cambridge: Cambridge University Press, 2006), 145. Cf.
    Peter Kivy, *Antithetical Arts: On the Ancient Quarrel Between Literature and
    Music* (Oxford: Clarendon Press, 2009).

19. Thomas Schmidt, *Die ästhetischen Grundlagen der Instrumentalmusik Felix
    Mendelssohn-Bartholdys* (Stuttgart: Metzler, 1996), ch. 4, esp. 171–81.

20. Letter of 15 October 1842, in Felix Mendelssohn Bartholdy, *Sämtliche Briefe*, ed.
    Helmut Loos, Wilhelm Seidel et al. (Kassel: Bärenreiter, 2008–17), vol. 9, 74.

21. *Eduard Hanslick's 'On the Musically Beautiful': A New Translation*, trans.
    Lee Rothfarb and Christoph Landerer (New York: Oxford University Press,
    2018), 44 and 113.

22. Julian Young, *The Philosophies of Richard Wagner* (Lanham: Lexington, 2014),
    ch. 1–3.

23. Richard Wagner, *The Art-Work of the Future and Other Works*, trans. William
    Ashton Ellis (Lincoln, NE: University of Nebraska Press, 1993), 88 and 126.

24. Wagner, *Art-Work of the Future*, 110 and 122; and *Opera and Drama*,
    trans. William Ashton Ellis (Lincoln, NE: University of Nebraska Press,
    1995), 316.

25. Friedrich Schlegel, *Philosophical Fragments*, trans. Peter Firchow (Minneapolis: University of Minnesota Press, 1991), 31.

26. *Richard Wagner's 'Beethoven' (1870): A New Translation*, trans. Roger Allen (Woodbridge: Boydell Press, 2014).

27. Wagner, *Opera and Drama*, 17; *Art-Work of the Future*, 97–8.

28. Thomas S. Grey, 'Wagner, the Overture, and the Aesthetics of Musical Form', *19th-Century Music*, 12/1 (1988), 4. Also see his *Wagner's Musical Prose: Texts and Contexts* (Cambridge: Cambridge University Press, 1995), ch. 1.

29. James Hepokoski, 'Program Music', in Stephen Downes (ed.), *Aesthetics of Music: Musicological Perspectives* (New York: Routledge, 2014), 62–83.

30. Richard Will, *The Characteristic Symphony in the Age of Haydn and Beethoven* (Cambridge: Cambridge University Press, 2002).

31. Thomas S. Grey, 'Deformed Beauty? Narrative and Musical Form in Mendelssohn's *Overture to the Tale of the Fair Melusina*, Op. 32', in Benedict Taylor (ed.), *Rethinking Mendelssohn* (New York: Oxford University Press, 2020), 9–37.

32. Richard Kaplan, 'Sonata Form in the Orchestral Works of Liszt: The Revolutionary Reconsidered', *19th-Century Music*, 8/2 (1984), 142–52.

33. On Beethoven as a symphonic landmark, see Mark Evan Bonds, *After Beethoven: Imperatives of Originality in the Symphony* (Cambridge, MA: Harvard University Press, 1996).

34. Robert Schumann, *Gesammelte Schriften über Musik und Musiker*, 2nd ed. (Leipzig: Georg Wigand, 1871), vol. 1, 91 and vol. 1, 24.

35. Franz Liszt, *Aus den Annalen des Fortschritts: Konzert- und kammermusikalische Essays*, trans. L. Ramann (Leipzig: Breitkopf und Härtel, 1882), 50.

36. Jee-Weon Cha, '*Ton* Versus *Dichtung*: Two Aesthetic Theories of the Symphonic Poem and Their Sources', *Journal of Musicological Research*, 26 (2007), 397.

37. Franz Brendel, 'F. Liszt's symphonische Dichtungen', in *Neue Zeitschrift für Musik*, 49 (1858), 86.

38. Ibid., 122.

39. A. W. Ambros, *The Boundaries of Music and Poetry: A Study in Musical Aesthetics*, trans. J. H. Cornell (New York: Schirmer, 1893), 179.

40. James Deaville, 'The Controversy Surrounding Liszt's Conception of Programme Music', in Jim Samson and Bennett Zon (eds.), *Nineteenth-Century Music: Selected Proceedings of the Tenth International Conference* (Aldershot: Ashgate, 2002), 98–124.

41. *Hanslick's 'On the Musically Beautiful'*, 43–4.

42. See the opening chapter of the present volume.

43. Schumann, *Gesammelte Schriften*, vol. 1, 24.

44. *Hoffmann's Musical Writings*, 236.

45. *Hanslick's 'On the Musically Beautiful'*, 23–4.

46. Ibid., 2. For an introduction to Hanslick's aesthetics in general, see Alexander Wilfing and Christoph Landerer, 'Eduard Hanslick (1825–1904)', *Internet Encyclopaedia of Philosophy* (2019), esp. ch. 3b, www.iep.utm.edu /hanslick.

47. *Hanslick's 'On the Musically Beautiful'*, 40–1.

48. On Hanslick's complex approach to musical expression, see Alexander Wilfing, 'Tonally *Moving* Forms: Peter Kivy and Eduard Hanslick's "Enhanced Formalism"', *Principia*, 63 (2016), 5–35.

49. *Hanslick's 'On the Musically Beautiful'*, 40. On establishing the autonomy of 'pure' music and Hanslick's role in this process, see Thomas S. Grey, 'Absolute Music', in Downes, *Aesthetics of Music*, 42–61.

50. *Hanslick's 'On the Musically Beautiful'*, 45 and 51.

51. Ibid., 120. Cf. Mark Evan Bonds, *Absolute Music: The History of an Idea* (New York: Oxford University Press, 2014), 183–209; and Christoph Landerer and Nick Zangwill, 'Hanslick's Deleted Ending', *British Journal of Aesthetics*, 57/1 (2017), 85–95.

Further Reading

Bowie, Andrew. *Music, Philosophy, and Modernity* (Cambridge: Cambridge University Press, 2007).

Bent, Ian (ed.). *Music Theory in the Age of Romanticism* (Cambridge: Cambridge University Press, 1996).

Bonds, Mark Evan. *Absolute Music: The History of an Idea* (New York: Oxford University Press, 2014).

Chapple, Gerald, Hall, Frederick, and Schulte, Hans (eds.). *German Literature and Music in the Nineteenth Century* (Lanham: University Press of America, 1992).

Chua, Daniel K. L. *Absolute Music and the Construction of Meaning* (Cambridge: Cambridge University Press, 1999).

Dahlhaus, Carl. *The Idea of Absolute Music*, trans. Roger Lustig (Chicago: University of Chicago Press, 1989).

Daverio, John. *Nineteenth-Century Music and the German Romantic Ideology* (New York: Schirmer, 1993).

Donovan, Siobhán and Elliott, Robin (eds.). *Music and Literature in German Romanticism* (Rochester, NY and Woodbridge: Camden House, 2004).

Fubini, Enrico. *The History of Music Aesthetics*, trans. Michael Hatwell (London: Macmillan, 1990).

Garratt, James. *Music, Culture, and Social Reform in the Age of Wagner* (Cambridge: Cambridge University Press, 2010).

Pederson, Sanna. *Enlightened and Romantic German Music Criticism, 1800–1850* (PhD dissertation, University of Pennsylvania, 1995).

Ruiter, Jacob de. *Der Charakterbegriff in der Musik: Studien zur deutschen Ästhetik der Instrumentalmusik, 1740–1850* (Stuttgart: Steiner, 1989).

Samson, Jim (ed.). *The Cambridge History of Nineteenth-Century Music* (Cambridge: Cambridge University Press, 2001).

Sorgner, Stefan Lorenz, and Fürbeth, Oliver (eds.). *Music in German Philosophy: An Introduction* (Chicago: University of Chicago Press, 2010).

Stegbauer, Hanna. *Die Akustik der Seele: Zum Einfluss der Literatur auf die Entstehung der romantischen Instrumentalmusik und ihrer Semantik* (Göttingen: Vandenhoeck & Ruprecht, 2006).

Tadday, Ulrich. *Das schöne Unendliche: Ästhetik, Kritik, Geschichte der romantischen Musikanschauung* (Stuttgart: Metzler, 1999).

12 | Music and Romantic Interiority

HOLLY WATKINS

Das Gemüt, die Seele, das Innere, die Tiefen: these and other words connoting heart, soul, and the inner depths of the self are the lexical landmarks of German Romantic thinking about interiority. In writings on music, such words map the shadowy inner arena of music's impact on attentive listeners. The listening posture that accompanied the rise of Romantic musical aesthetics in the late 1790s valorised interior response over external circumstance, the inner sensation of transport over the discharging of functional purposes. In states of rapt attention, perhaps with eyes closed, Romantic listeners desired to be carried away by tones, to be swept up into a world that, as E. T. A. Hoffmann insisted, had nothing to do with everyday concerns or conventional sociality.[1] Contemporary accounts suggest that such experiences could be had in the home, at a concert, or in church. No matter where listeners were located, though, the world into which music transported them was one of both feeling and imagination, a world that stretched inward through the ear to the affective wellsprings of human existence and outward to the realm of nature, whose dynamism served as a frequent point of comparison for musical processes. Listening to a symphony, Wilhelm Heinrich Wackenroder surmised, entailed confronting 'an entire world' as well as an 'entire drama of human emotions'.[2] Wackenroder's breathless commentary on the genre of greatest interest to Romantics indicates that the defining quality of instrumental music was its fertile production of metaphor. Music, in short, carried Romantic listeners across some indefinable inner boundary into novel regions of emotion and fantasy. Music's pertinence for Romantic notions of interiority arises largely from its capacity to induce such transport, a capacity that many witnesses considered unparalleled amongst the arts.

The most voluble contributors to the transformation of musical values between about 1800 and 1830 tended to be German speakers.[3] The historical and cultural reasons for this were many, and they include the growing fascination with symbols of darkness and obscurity (such as dense forests, deep waters, and ruined castles); an Enlightenment-rejecting hostility to the perceived superficiality of France, that politically and culturally powerful nation to the west of the fragmented Germanic lands; an unusually high dissemination of mining lore into the popular imagination, abetted by the underground exploits of authors such as Novalis (Friedrich von Hardenberg) and Johann Wolfgang von Goethe; and the inward-facing tradition of religious devotion that sprang from seventeenth-century Pietism, itself a disillusioned variation of Lutheranism.[4] Following the debilitating losses of the Thirty Years' War (1618–48), which disproportionally affected Germans, God seemed to have abandoned humans to a world replete with violence and suffering. All the better to seek divinity within through prayer or the cultivation of mystical feelings. Indeed, turning away from the world to pursue private contemplation or reflection presupposes that active immersion in everyday social, political, or mercantile life was antithetical to certain human pursuits. Even the pivotal Enlightenment philosopher Immanuel Kant took his own inward path in the three *Critiques* – namely, an epistemological turn that redirected thought to the very process of knowing itself, to the hidden constraints that organised human cognition from within. For aesthetes and thinkers frustrated by a lack of sympathy for their enthusiasms, solitary study, creative activity, or even private musical performance offered an escape from mundane reality.

Hoffmann's fictional musician Johannes Kreisler was one such aesthete, and he will serve as the tour guide for our excursion into the terrain of German Romantic interiority. Composer, keyboardist, music teacher, and all-round eccentric, Kreisler is the central figure of Hoffmann's music-themed essays *Kreisleriana* (1814) and a key protagonist in his novel *Kater Murr* (*Tomcat Murr*, 1820–1). It might be objected that a fictional character should not be considered a trustworthy guide to Romantic principles. However, not only is Hoffmann's Kreisler semi-autobiographical, but it would also be quite artificial to insist on a strict separation of truth from fiction in Romantic writings. The very word *romantic* originally meant novelistic, and Romanticism generally sought to make life artistic and art lifelike; witness, for example, Bettina von Arnim's semi-fictionalised versions of her correspondence with Goethe and her close friend Günderode. Wackenroder's best-known essays on music, furthermore, were written as if from the pen of the fictional composer Joseph Berglinger. Without further ado, then, let us turn to the second essay of *Kreisleriana* ('Ombra adorata'), which recounts Kreisler's experiences at a concert of instrumental and vocal music. Its very first lines comprise a suitable point of departure for a study of Romantic aesthetics:

What an utterly miraculous thing is music, and how little can men penetrate its deeper mysteries! But does it not reside in the breast of man himself and fill his heart with its enchanting images, so that all his senses respond to them, and a radiant new life transports him from his enslavement here below, from the oppressive torment of his earthly existence?[5]

Three guiding principles can be extracted from Hoffmann's words: that music is inscrutably deep or profound, that musical sounds penetrate into and change the listener's inner world, and that music is capable of transporting listeners to some more ideal, and markedly spiritual, state of being. This essay will show how each of these principles undergirds broader Romantic convictions about the relationship between music and interiority. I draw for support on the writings of Hoffmann, Wackenroder, and Bettina von Arnim; the philosophers Georg Wilhelm Friedrich Hegel and Arthur Schopenhauer; and the author and champion of women's rights Malwida von Meysenbug. Finally, the essay will close with some reflections on how the Romantics' much-vaunted inwardness, for all its apparent self-absorption, engages in a dialogue with the natural world through the boundary-defying powers of metaphor and analogy.

Hidden Depths

At issue for Romantic thinkers was not simply the influence music exerted over the inner life, but the way that music seemed to harbour its own inner depths by virtue of its occult efficacy, mathematical foundations, and physical origin in vibration. In particular, commentators on music wondered how (or even if) the sensuous rapture and spiritual transport occasioned by music were related to the art's numerical and proportional bases, whose rational character seemed so out of step with its affective sway. Hoffmann's suspicion that music's 'deeper mysteries' could not really be elucidated was shared by Wackenroder, who encapsulated the enigma as follows: 'Between the individual, mathematical, tonal relationships and the individual fibres of the human heart an inexplicable sympathy has revealed itself, through which the musical art has become a comprehensive and flexible mechanism for the portrayal of human emotions.'[6] With these words, Wackenroder effectively placed something essential about music, something he called its 'dark and indescribable element', in a permanent state of obscurity.[7]

Where explanation is lacking, myth steps in. Wackenroder speculated that before music could advance beyond the 'screaming and the beating of drums' of ancient peoples (modelled, one assumes, on Eurocentric notions of allegedly uncivilised contemporaries), 'wise men first descended into the oracle caves of the most occult sciences, where Nature, begetter of all things, herself unveiled for them the fundamental laws of sound. Out of these secret vaults they brought to the light of day the new theory, written in profound numbers.'[8] Several senses of mystery and depth converge in these remarks. First, knowledge must be obtained by way of a penetration into the nature of things analogous to the descent into a cave (here, the image is less geological or mineralogical than evocative of the underground oracle at Delphi). Knowledge is then gained only when nature 'unveils' herself to inquiring human minds. Finally, the fruits of knowledge – the 'profound numbers' of modern music theory – retain an aura of depth indebted to their recondite origins. While the rational underpinnings of music theory may seem to supply the 'objective' counterpart to music's 'subjective' impact, both were connected to domains (natural law, interior feeling) marked as inward or deep.

That sound was not a visible property of objects but was caused by physical vibration only added to music's mystique. Voices emerged from the depths of the vocal cavity, instrumental sounds (in many cases) from a resonance-producing chamber. Just as musical sounds emerged from such inner spaces, so too did they enter the hidden passages of the ear and, by some obscure pathway, find their way to the seat of feeling and emotion. In his writings on aesthetics, Hegel posited that the 'world of sounds, quickly rustling away, is directly drawn by the ear into the inner life of the heart and harmonizes the soul with emotions in sympathy with it'.[9] Hegel sought to explain the peculiar effect that music exercises on inner feeling by recourse to two factors: the inward nature of tones (what the *Introductory Lectures on Aesthetics* calls the 'earliest inwardness of matter') and the fleeting character of music, which, by neither occupying nor persisting in space, mirrors the fluidity and non-specific location of 'inwardness as such'.[10]

While it is easy to understand how the sound of the voice (either as uttered or merely imagined) could be considered a medium for mental inwardness, it is nothing short of remarkable that the sounds of inanimate objects fulfil the same purpose in Hegel's account. This supposition hints at a human readiness to hear sound, whether or not it is produced by living things, as evidence of animation. Confronted with the fragile tones emanating from vibrating bodies, Romantic listeners felt as though they were hearing secret messages transmitted from one soul to another. Hegel's one-time friend and colleague Friedrich Wilhelm Joseph Schelling contended that tone is 'nothing other than the intuition of the soul of the material body itself', a phrase that speaks to the borderline animism of Romantic *Naturphilosophie*.[11] Indeed, the liveliness of sound helps to account for much of the intimacy Romantic thinkers intuited between music and the natural world. The narrator of *Kreisleriana*'s final instalment praises music as a 'universal language of nature' that 'speaks to us in magical and mysterious resonances', while *Kater Murr* features a scene in which Kreisler reports that, during an excursion into the countryside, he 'listened to the voices of the forest and of the brook that spoke to me in comforting melodies'.[12] As only one member of a wider community of jostling, vibrating entities, music exhibits affinities with both living and non-living modes of expression, at least for those skilled in the category-defying, soul-extending perception demanded by Romanticism.[13]

Music Is Inwardness Is Music

Music, Kreisler says, harbours inscrutable mysteries, yet it also resides 'in the breast of man himself' and 'fill[s] his heart with its enchanting images'. Kreisler's references to the breast and heart might lead one to expect a paean to the feelings music either expresses or awakens. Yet Hoffmann's take on the expressivist tenets of conventional music aesthetics was rather unusual, as his famous review of Beethoven's Fifth Symphony, and its reworking in *Kreisleriana*, demonstrates. In contrast to earlier theories that focused on the isolated, nameable emotions (such as joy or sorrow) purportedly conveyed by music, Hoffmann argues that, when listening to contemporary symphonic works, one 'leaves behind all precise feelings' and experiences only 'an inexpressible longing'.[14] Hoffmann's commentary traces a progression in which instrumental music gradually penetrates inward, moving from the 'humanity in human life' (Haydn) to the 'superhuman, magical quality residing in the inner self' (Mozart) to the 'infinite yearning which is the essence of romanticism' (Beethoven).[15] Curiously, the further inward one goes, the less personal one gets, with interior exploration ultimately opening out onto the infinite reaches of the sublime.

Beethoven, who in Hoffmann's view penetrated to the 'innermost nature' of instrumental music, revealed that music was essentially both vague and deeply affecting, a peculiar confluence of qualities that distinguished it from representational arts such as poetry and sculpture.[16] Thanks to its non-specific semiotic character, instrumental music was the only 'genuinely romantic' art for Hoffmann, 'since its only subject-matter is infinity'.[17] Even as he rejected the idea that music expresses particular feelings, though, Hoffmann attached specific images to Beethoven's music as well as to that of his predecessors. Haydn's symphonies 'lead us through endless, green forest glades, through a motley throng of happy people', while Mozart 'leads us deep into the realm of spirits', where we 'hear the gentle spirit-voices of love and melancholy'. Beethoven's music, finally, 'unveils before us the realm of the mighty and immeasurable', where 'shining rays of light shoot through the darkness of night and we become aware of giant shadows swaying back and forth'.[18] The point of listening, it seems, is not simply to swoon in hazy yearning but to revel in the imagery music spontaneously engenders. In the phase of Romanticism that followed the waning of Enlightenment aesthetics but preceded the rise of programme music later in the nineteenth century, music was considered more an occasion for intensely 'subjective' experiences of feeling and the generation of mental images than a vehicle for the 'objective' expression of emotion or the representation of events such as sunrises, storms, or battles (all of which Hoffmann rejected as topics of musical discourse).

Wackenroder fell somewhere in the middle of Enlightenment and Romantic aesthetic positions. On the one hand, he hewed to a fairly traditional mimetic theory of music when he stated that 'no art portrays the emotions in such an artistic, bold, such a *poetic* ... manner', and he listed a whole gamut of emotions that music might represent, from 'masculine, exulting joy' to the 'sweet, ardent yearning of love' to 'deep pain'.[19] On the other hand, Wackenroder discounted the power of language truly to capture such feelings, whereas music, so much more akin to the 'secret river in the depths of the human soul', streams feelings out before our very ears.[20] And not just any feelings, but explicitly *musical* feelings. Musical sounds, he wrote, teach us to feel emotion and 'enrich our souls with entirely new, bewitching essences of feeling'.[21] These remarks suggest that music does not merely reflect emotions that would exist without it, but inducts listeners into an alternative zone of affect, one whose contents ultimately resist linguistic translation. 'Why do I strive to melt words into tones?' Wackenroder asks at the end of his essay, 'It is never as I feel it.'[22] Music represents what is unrepresentable by other means – and thus coaxes feelings from us that could not exist by other means.

Experiences in which one listens to a symphony and undergoes all the feelings of its protagonist-like 'resounding soul' (as Wackenroder called it) inspired Hegel to ask how music could so closely resemble or even replace the listener's own sense of interiority. In addition to the 'inward' quality of tone discussed above, Hegel located the key to music's power in the temporal and insubstantial character music shared with the feelings he understood to be its content. What music 'claims as its own', Hegel wrote, 'is the depth of a person's inner life as such'.[23] In taking inwardness as its point of departure, music adopts a subject matter that is not cleanly distinguishable from the observer, as, say, a painting of a tree can be said to hang on that wall over there. When we experience emotions, Hegel claims, the distinction between the 'I' who experiences and the feelings experienced is 'not yet explicit'. Instead, emotions are 'interwoven with the inner feeling as such, without any separation between them'.[24] Because of this, music, which constitutes (he says) feelings in the form of tones, wields a power over the heart that does not so much come to consciousness as reside in the 'undisclosed depth' of feeling.[25] Even though music can be considered a form of sensuous existence independent of the listener, the inherently expressive nature of musical tones and music's failure to establish a stable existence in either space or time mean that this inescapably mobile art 'penetrates the arcanum of all the movements of the soul'. 'Therefore', Hegel continues, music 'captivates the consciousness which is no longer confronted by an object and which in the loss of this freedom is carried away itself by the ever-flowing stream of sounds.'[26]

Though Hegel's ascription of music's content to determinate feelings was perhaps not as sophisticated as Hoffmann's hypothesis of music's fundamental indeterminacy, Hoffmann would surely have agreed with the philosopher's account of music's uncanny ability to take possession of its listeners.[27] Indeed, Hoffmann's alter ego Kreisler epitomises the figure of the listener (and, in his case, performer) routinely possessed by music. For Kreisler, music went so far beyond Kant's notion of a meaningless 'play with sensations' as to threaten the very integrity of his personality.[28] The preface to *Kreisleriana* notes that singing had an 'almost fatal effect' on its main character, because 'his imagination became overstimulated and his mind withdrew into a realm where nobody could follow him without danger'.[29] Whether co-opting the listener's feelings or calling forth a tumult of mental imagery, music issued directives to the self so irresistible as to become a surrogate inwardness. Where the self 'goes' in such moments is a question for the next section.

Transported, Within and Beyond

> What would have become of me if, almost overwhelmed by all the earthly misery continuously seething around me in recent times, Beethoven's

mighty spirit had confronted me, and seized me as if with arms of red-hot metal, and carried me off to the realm of the mighty and the immeasurable that is revealed by his thunderous sounds?[30]

Had Beethoven's Fifth Symphony not been omitted from the concert that included 'Ombra adorata', Kreisler imagines that he would have been transported to a sublime realm that seems thoroughly overpowering, if not outright unfriendly. Much of Kreisler's language derives from Hoffmann's earlier review of the Fifth. While the experience Kreisler envisions is unusually violent – he is, after all, immoderately susceptible to music – the sense of being catapulted to the beyond that the passage describes falls squarely within what music's devotees expected of their favourite art. Even Hegel's casual reference to being 'possessed' by music confirms that, by the 1820s, transport was considered an indispensable feature of Romantic musical experience.

Describing the rich musical life of her childhood in the 1820s and '30s, Malwida von Meysenbug recalled that she preferred listening over playing because she could give herself up wholly to the music. Otherwise, she had to spend too many dull hours practising the piano in order to achieve the results she had in mind. As an able singer, however, she could play a more active role in bringing about the distinctly musical mood of being 'transported from the world' (*weltentrückter*).[31] Meysenbug considered music a requirement of the soul, and her memoirs describe a powerful instance of transport she experienced at the funeral of a close friend's mother. In the midst of the ceremony, she recounts, 'a power suddenly arose from the beautiful, earnest singing that elevated me above myself. I broke the fetters of grief, full of pride and energy; I raised up my head and eyes, for wings carried me far above fate and death, into the ranks of free spirits.'[32] Meysenbug's account suggests that music affords an inward sensation of soaring spirits, of a virtual inner movement that transports the self beyond its apparent limits. Her impressions had plenty of antecedents: the rapt Berglinger, for example, feels his soul 'soaring up to the radiant Heavens' when he listens to music in church, while Kreisler's 'soul flies with rapid wing-beats through shining clouds' as he drinks in the melismas of 'Ombra adorata'.[33]

These and other evocations of flight, along with the vocabulary of soul, spirit, and heavenly motion that frequently accompanies them, indicate that for Romantic listeners, music was a fundamentally spiritual affair. Yet the nature of the spirit involved varied considerably amongst commentators, a situation further complicated by the multivalence of the

German word *Geist*, with its range of sacred and secular meanings. For some listeners, the spiritual import of music was explicitly religious. Wackenroder wrote that music's raw material (tone) is 'already impregnated with divine spirit', while Kreisler maintained that through music, humans are 'suffused by a divine power'.[34] As a self-described idealist, Meysenbug nonetheless refused to relegate spirit to an entirely otherworldly realm. Objecting to the tenets of Christian asceticism, she held that 'the senses are not the enemies of the spirit, but rather its instruments'.[35] In portraying spirit as a partner to sensation rather than its negation, Meysenbug concurred with one of her heroines, Bettina von Arnim, who wrote that music was a 'medium of the spirit, whereby the sensuous becomes spiritual'.[36] For these listeners, the sense of transport was induced by the transmutation of sensuous input into spiritual intimations, a process whose obscurity only further burnished music's reputation for mystery.

While Romanticism's spiritual aspirations were undeniably lofty, sometimes transport was just as much about what one was fleeing as where one was going. Kreisler, for example, finds that music opens up a 'radiant new life' and offers consolation for the 'torment' of everyday reality. Kreisler's desire for transcendence by way of music arises in large part from the philistinism of the respectable but unimaginative society folk who employ him, while Berglinger complains of the indifferent audiences to whom he pours out his soul in sound. Even as a youth, Berglinger suffered from the 'bitter conflict between his inborn ethereal striving and the claims of everyday life', and he would become depressed upon returning from his musical feasts in church to the world of 'normal, happy, jovial people'.[37] Literary portrayals of music as both cause of and panacea for disappointment, as the temporary vehicle of an existence more exalted than that of everyday life, suggest that Romantic ideals thrived best in middle-class settings. Why, indeed, would the well-to-do patrons who employed musicians such as Kreisler (not to mention countless real-life figures) need to be transported to a world beyond the everyday? Servants, farm workers, and other manual labourers, on the other hand, had little leisure time in which to indulge in musical or other artistic pursuits, let alone to bask in what Hoffmann called the 'purple shimmer of romanticism'.[38]

A final scene of transport from Hoffmann's novel *Kater Murr* illustrates the class-related tensions attendant upon the practising musician's career. In his capacity as the local Kapellmeister, Kreisler has become entangled with two young friends, Julia and the Princess Hedwiga, daughter of Fürst Irenäus. The Princess has taken offence at Kreisler's unpredictable behaviour but is also jealous of his musical instruction of Julia (and its successful results). Julia's mother, the Rätin Benzon, has persuaded the Princess to attend a party where Kreisler will be present, and she urges her not to avoid him just because he 'behaved now and then in a bizarre way'.[39] Just as the Princess makes a halting overture to the Kapellmeister, the partygoers demand music from him and Julia. The two sing an impassioned duet of his own composing that concludes with a graphic climax, one in which both voices 'founder[ed] in the roaring stream of chords until ardent sighs announced imminent death and the last *addio* burst forth in a wild cry of pain from the lacerated heart like a fountain of blood'.[40] Many of the listeners are moved to tears.

The Princess, by contrast, is not amused, and she upbraids Kreisler, saying, 'Is it right, is it proper that in a pleasant gathering where friendly conversation should prevail ... that such extravagant things are served up which lacerate the soul and whose powerful, destructive effect cannot be mastered?' She continues, 'Is there then no Cimarosa, no Paisiello whose compositions are written for social gatherings?' Falsely apologetic, Kreisler retorts, 'Is it not a violation of all manners and neatness in dress to appear in society with the breast with all its sorrow, all its pain, all its rapture, without a heavy wrapping of the muslin of good manners and propriety?'[41] Increasingly frenzied, Kreisler enjoins Julia to sing several pieces of lighter fare (Paisiello amongst them), an imposition that makes her angry in turn. Stating that she cannot understand his wild lurching from one affect to another, Julia cries, 'I beg you, dear Kreisler, do not again demand that I sing something comic, no matter how charming and pretty, when I am deeply agitated, and when the sounds of deepest sorrow are echoing in my soul.'[42] Like Rameau's nephew in Diderot's story, Kreisler exchanges his interior states for those of music at the drop of a hat – Julia, however, is too earnest for such aesthetic play. Kreisler's duet has transported her into a state of spiritual unrest, and she cannot simply forfeit that affect in favour of another. While Kreisler's susceptibility to music seems to go hand in hand with his unstable personality, Julia's love of the art arises from her capacity for enduring, authentic feelings. If musical transport takes Kreisler to a place where 'nobody could follow him without danger', it does so to the detriment of his mental integrity. For Julia, music sends her more deeply within and strengthens her sense of self. Yet for both, the transport occasioned by music erodes tolerance for the demands of polite society. Transport, it seems, is a dish best served in solitude.

Conclusion: What Is Inward?

The three principles of Romantic musical aesthetics I have elucidated in this essay – that music harbours hidden depths, that it is intimately entwined with inwardness, and that it induces a sense of transport – might be better called impressions or intuitions since the boundaries between them are porous. Ponder one long enough, and it is liable to turn into another: the special qualities of tone, for example, are what allow it to become a vehicle for human inwardness; the inner identification with music is what creates the sensation of being transported; and so on. In this regard, the mutability of Romantic thought, once again, finds its most fitting emblem in music.[43]

I would like to close by considering one further transformation that music encouraged in the minds of Romantic listeners. While music potentially can be heard in relation to many aspects of human and non-human existence, it is surely no coincidence that so much Romantic commentary on the impact of music resorts to nature imagery. Music may have resembled the flux of feeling, but it also resembled torrents of water, massing clouds and storms, even violent upheavals of the earth. Wackenroder's description of the images that come to him upon listening to a symphony blends emotive, martial, and natural occurrences into a single dramatic unfolding; his account culminates with distorted shapes falling upon one another like 'a mountain range come alive'.[44] The wave-upon-wave unfolding of music seems to have called especially for water imagery. Recall Hegel's depiction of being carried away by a stream of tones, or Wackenroder's image of music causing the 'secret river in the depths of the human soul' to flow past us in audible form. That music conjures up both 'an entire world' and an 'entire drama of human emotions', as Wackenroder put it, points not just to music's capacity to create metaphor, but to a more fundamental relatedness between music, the dynamic nature of the self, and the world in which both are embedded.[45]

Shortly before Hegel began offering lectures on aesthetics, Arthur Schopenhauer located the source of that relatedness in what he termed the will, a blind, eternal striving that courses through inanimate matter and living creatures alike. For Schopenhauer, music's power over the inner life was so great not because it represented the will that presents itself as feelings and desires, but because it was a directly audible manifestation of will, one whose expressive import could be understood just as immediately as feeling itself.[46] Nor was that import restricted to the human realm: in

musical polyphony, Schopenhauer found an analogue to the world's strati-
fied 'grades' of existence, with soprano, alto, tenor, and bass parts corresponding to human, animal, plant, and mineral registers of being. With very
few exceptions, Schopenhauer suggested, human interiority shares in the
tendencies and strivings found everywhere else in the universe, a thesis for
which music, in his view, offered a strange kind of confirmation. Even as it
simulates human (read: linguistic) consciousness through the freedom of
melodic invention, music also turns the analogy-prone listener's attention
to the supporting layers of animal, vegetal, and mineral existence meta-
phorised by the multiple voices of musical texture.

However idiosyncratic Schopenhauer's perspective, and however reluc-
tant we may be today to believe that music of any sort is immediately
comprehensible, Schopenhauer's conviction that we can hear an echo of
ontological totality in music remains a source of inspiration, at least for
those inclined to dispense with the customary understanding of music as
primarily a matter of human emotions. It may be that, as Hoffmann put it
in one of *Kreisleriana*'s falsely satirical moments, only 'madmen' think that
music allows them to 'perceive the sublime song of – trees, flowers, animals,
stones, water!'[47] It would nonetheless be fittingly Romantic if the inward
journey inspired by music ended up taking us outward once more, transporting us beyond ourselves by effectively turning our minds inside out.

Notes

1. See Hoffmann's review of Beethoven's Fifth Symphony in *E. T. A. Hoffmann's
   Musical Writings: Kreisleriana, The Poet and the Composer, Music Criticism*, ed.
   David Charlton, trans. Martyn Clarke (Cambridge: Cambridge University
   Press, 1989), 236.
2. Wilhelm Heinrich Wackenroder, 'The Characteristic Inner Nature of the
   Musical Art and the Psychology of Today's Instrumental Music', in *Confessions
   and Fantasies*, trans. Mary Hurst Schubert (University Park: The Pennsylvanian
   State University Press, 1971), 193.
3. Of the considerable literature on this transition, see especially Mark Evan Bonds,
   Music as Thought: Listening to the Symphony in the Age of Beethoven (Princeton:
   Princeton University Press, 2006); and Carl Dahlhaus, *The Idea of Absolute Music*,
   trans. Roger Lustig (Chicago: University of Chicago Press, 1989).
4. For more on these aspects of German culture, see my *Metaphors of Depth in
   German Musical Thought: From E. T. A. Hoffmann to Arnold Schoenberg*
   (Cambridge: Cambridge University Press, 2011); see also Isaiah Berlin, *The
   Roots of Romanticism*, ed. Henry Hardy (London: Chatto & Windus, 1999).

5. Hoffmann, *E. T. A. Hoffmann's Musical Writings*, 88.
6. Wackenroder, *Confessions and Fantasies*, 188.
7. Ibid.
8. Ibid.
9. G. W. F. Hegel, *Aesthetics: Lectures on Fine Art*, vol. 2, trans. T. M. Knox (Oxford: Clarendon Press, 1975), 894.
10. G. W. F. Hegel, *Introductory Lectures on Aesthetics*, ed. Michael Inwood, trans. Bernard Bosanquet (London: Penguin Books, 1993), 95; Hegel, *Aesthetics*, 902.
11. See the excerpt 'Schelling. *Vorlesungen über die Philosophie der Kunst* (1802–03)', trans. Edward A. Lippman, in Lippman (ed.), *Musical Aesthetics: A Historical Reader*, vol. 2: The Nineteenth Century (Stuyvesant, NY: Pendragon Press, 1988), 69 (translation altered).
12. Hoffmann, *E. T. A. Hoffmann's Musical Writings*, 164–5; Hoffmann, *Selected Writings of E. T. A. Hoffmann*, ed. and trans. Leonard J. Kent and Elizabeth C. Knight, vol. 2: The Novel (Chicago: University of Chicago Press, 1969), 213.
13. For more on these aspects of Romantic musical thought, see my *Musical Vitalities: Ventures in a Biotic Aesthetics of Music* (Chicago: University of Chicago Press, 2018).
14. Hoffmann, *E. T. A. Hoffmann's Musical Writings*, 96.
15. Ibid., 98.
16. Ibid., 97.
17. Ibid., 96.
18. Ibid., 97.
19. Wackenroder, *Confessions and Fantasies*, 191–2.
20. Ibid., 191.
21. Ibid.
22. Ibid., 194.
23. Hegel, *Aesthetics*, 891.
24. Ibid., 904.
25. Ibid., 905.
26. Ibid., 906.
27. Hegel's claim is undermined by his remark that, although music is normally heard as an expression of the inner life, it can also be the source of 'delight, without any movement of emotion, in the purely sensuous sound and its melodiousness' or inspire us to 'follow with purely intellectual consideration the course of the harmony and melody by which the heart itself is no further touched or led' (*Aesthetics*, 906).
28. See Kant's discussion of music in section 51 of the *Critique of Judgment*. Immanuel Kant, *Critique of Judgment*, trans. Werner S. Pluhar (Indianapolis: Hackett Publishing Co., 1987).
29. Hoffmann, *E. T. A. Hoffmann's Musical Writings*, 80.
30. Ibid., 88.

31. Malwida von Meysenbug, *Memoiren einer Idealistin*, vol. 1, 9th ed. (Berlin and Leipzig: Schuster & Loeffler, 1905), 152.

32. Ibid., 272.

33. Wackenroder and Ludwig Tieck, *Outpourings of an Art-Loving Friar*, trans. Edward Mornin (New York: Frederick Ungar Publishing Co., 1975), 105.

34. Wackenroder, *Confessions and Fantasies*, 189; Hoffmann, *E. T. A. Hoffmann's Musical Writings*, 88.

35. Meysenbug, *Memoiren*, 116.

36. Roman Nahrebecky, *Wackenroder, Tieck, E. T. A. Hoffmann, Bettina von Arnim: Ihre Beziehung zur Musik und zum musikalischen Erlebnis* (Bonn: Bouvier Verlag Herbert Grundmann, 1979), 199.

37. Wackenroder and Tieck, *Outpourings of an Art-Loving Friar*, 106–7.

38. Hoffmann, *E. T. A. Hoffmann's Musical Writings*, 96. On class aspects of Romanticism, see Berlin, *The Roots of Romanticism*, ch. 2.

39. Hoffmann, *Selected Writings of E. T. A. Hoffmann*, vol. 2, 115.

40. Ibid., 117.

41. Ibid., 118.

42. Ibid., 120.

43. See Bonds, *Music as Thought*.

44. Wackenroder, *Confessions and Fantasies*, 193.

45. For more on this topic, see my *Musical Vitalities*.

46. Schopenhauer's discussions of music can be found in *The World as Will and Representation*, trans. E. F. J. Payne (New York: Dover, 1958), vol. 1, section 52 and vol. 2, section 39.

47. Hoffmann, *E. T. A. Hoffmann's Musical Writings*, 94.

Further Reading

Berlin, Isaiah. *The Roots of Romanticism*, ed. Henry Hardy (London: Chatto & Windus, 1999).

Bonds, Mark Evan. *Absolute Music: The History of an Idea* (New York: Oxford University Press, 2014).

   Music as Thought: Listening to the Symphony in the Age of Beethoven (Princeton: Princeton University Press, 2006).

Dahlhaus, Carl. *The Idea of Absolute Music*, trans. Roger Lustig (Chicago: University of Chicago Press, 1989).

Hegel, Georg Wilhelm Friedrich. *Aesthetics: Lectures on Fine Art*, trans. T. M. Knox, 2 vols. (Oxford: Clarendon Press, 1975).

Hoffmann, E. T. A. *E. T. A. Hoffmann's Musical Writings: Kreisleriana, The Poet and the Composer, Music Criticism*, ed. David Charlton, trans. Martyn Clarke (Cambridge: Cambridge University Press, 1989).

Selected Writings of E. T. A. Hoffmann, vol. 2: *The Novel*, ed. and trans. Leonard J. Kent and Elizabeth C. Knight (Chicago: University of Chicago Press, 1969).

Kant, Immanuel. *Critique of Judgment*, trans. Werner S. Pluhar (Indianapolis: Hackett Publishing Co., 1987).

Lippman, Edward A. *Musical Aesthetics: A Historical Reader, vol. II: The Nineteenth Century* (Stuyvesant, NY: Pendragon Press, 1988).

Meysenbug, Malwida von. *Memoiren einer Idealistin*, 3 vols. (Berlin and Leipzig: Schuster & Loeffler, 1905).

Rosen, Charles. *The Romantic Generation* (Cambridge, MA: Harvard University Press, 1995).

Schopenhauer, Arthur. *The World as Will and Representation*, trans. E. F. J. Payne, 2 vols. (New York: Dover, 1958).

Wackenroder, Wilhelm Heinrich. *Confessions and Fantasies*, trans. Mary Hurst Schubert (University Park, PA: Pennsylvanian State University Press, 1971).

Watkins, Holly. *Metaphors of Depth in German Musical Thought: From E. T. A. Hoffmann to Arnold Schoenberg* (Cambridge: Cambridge University Press, 2011).

Musical Vitalities: Ventures in a Biotic Aesthetics of Music (Chicago: University of Chicago Press, 2018).

13 | Music, Expression, and the Aesthetics of Authenticity

KAREN LEISTRA-JONES

> Right in the middle of the first Allegro, there was a passage that I knew must please, and all the hearers were quite carried away – and there was a great burst of applause – but I had known when I wrote it what kind of effect it would make, so I brought it back again at the close – when there were shouts of Da capo.
>
> – W. A. Mozart, letter to Leopold Mozart, 3 July 1778[1]

> In writing as in playing . . . Field was intent only on expressing his inner feelings for his own gratification. It would be impossible to imagine a more unabashed indifference to the public than his . . .

> But it is directly to this total disregard of anything that aims merely at effect that we owe the first attempts – and what perfect ones! – to infuse the piano with feelings and dreams . . .
>
> – Franz Liszt, Über John Fields Nocturne, 1859[2]

When Mozart was commissioned to write a symphony for the Concert Spirituel in Paris in 1778, he made a point of learning about the tastes and expectations of his audience. As his letter to his father details, he composed his 'Paris' Symphony, No. 31 (K. 297) with an eye to their response, writing particular passages to delight and astonish them, and taking immense satisfaction in their applause. In doing so, he was following his father's tried-and-true advice: as Leopold Mozart had written to his son just a few months earlier regarding another work, 'you will do well to follow the taste of the French. If one can only win applause and be paid well, the rest is not important.'[3]

According to Liszt, the Irish pianist-composer John Field, born only a generation after Mozart, had a completely different attitude towards his music and his public. He was 'unabashedly indifferent' to his audience, relying only on his own interior experience (his 'inner feelings' and 'dreams') for inspiration. Not only was there no question of an audience's tastes and expectations influencing his compositions, but Liszt emphasised that the 'feelings and dreams' that infused Field's piano music were possible only because of the composer's complete autonomy and independence from the public.

214

To be sure, caveats can be added to both of these accounts. Mozart's relationship to his audience was often more ambivalent and complex than what he described in this letter, and Liszt's essay on Field probably says as much about Liszt's own creative ideals (or the ideals with which he wanted to be associated) as it says about Field's views and creative process. Nevertheless, the differences between the two reflect a sea change in ideas about music that occurred in the early decades of the nineteenth century, particularly in Germany and Britain. Under the influence of the Romantic movement, these years saw a rethinking of the aesthetics and ethics of musical expression, and Liszt's remarks distil several important features of the new orientation. As Liszt described it, Field's music was valuable not only because it stemmed from his innermost 'feelings and dreams', but also because it was authentic. Authenticity, as it is colloquially used, often denotes the quality of being 'true to oneself'. But for Liszt and other Romantics, the concept meant more. Being true to oneself was contingent on the ability to hold oneself apart from the external world, to resist its influence, to compose (and live) almost as though it did not exist. The reasons for this shift in priorities are multiple and complex, and as we shall see, the concept of authentic self-expression was not without internal tensions and contradictions. Nevertheless, it was one of the core ideals of musical Romanticism, and as such, it contributed to new expectations for composers, performers, and audiences, as well as significant changes in the status of music as an art form.

For much of Western history, the concept of mimesis (imitation, or 're-presentation') provided a foundation for understanding music's effects.[4] At a basic level, mimetic theories hold that music's expressive power derives from its capacity to imitate something observable and definable in the world – often (although not always) human passions. Mimesis was a particularly important concept in eighteenth-century aesthetics. Discussions varied as to what exactly music imitated (the impassioned rhetoric of a skilled orator; the internal motions of bodily humours and passions; the pre-articulate cries of early humans, etc.) and the techniques by which this imitation was accomplished. Nevertheless, many eighteenth-century writers on musical aesthetics assumed that: (1) *what* music imitated was a recognisable phenomenon in the world around it; (2) the musician, through a combination of skill, training, and judgement (including reliance on known techniques and past models), could somehow re-present this phenomenon in the medium of music; and (3) if the music was successful, it would produce the desired effect (often a sympathetic emotional resonance, delighted recognition, or pleasure) on the part of the listener. This last part is crucial: in this paradigm, the work of art is directed towards an audience. It is a means to an end, and can be evaluated according to its success at eliciting the intended response. We can observe this view in the Mozart letter quoted above. Although there is no consensus about which passage Mozart was describing in his letter to his father (and he seems to have been aiming for delight and astonishment rather than a more specific imitation of emotion through music), he makes it clear that he viewed his symphony as a success because of the audience's strong reaction.

In the later decades of the eighteenth century, though, mimetic theories of music gradually ceded ground to what has sometimes been termed an 'expressive' or 'expressivist' orientation.[5] The extent to which Romantic thinkers rejected earlier audience-centred paradigms can be seen in an essay by E. T. A. Hoffmann, 'On a Remark of Sacchini's, and on so-called Effect in Music', which first appeared in 1814.[6] Hoffmann, one of the foundational figures in Romantic music criticism, bemoaned what he saw as a tendency amongst contemporary opera composers to heed 'the eternal braying of theatre-directors for "Effect! Only effect!" in order to pull in the audience'. According to Hoffmann, because the goal of so many composers was 'effect', they set about composing in exactly the wrong way. Studying the works of past composers, they 'became preoccupied with technical resources, seeing them as the means whereby effect was obtained'. With Mozart as a model, for example, they might observe that 'striking modulations' and 'his frequent use of wind instruments' produced strong emotional effects on the audience. (Notably, Hoffmann viewed Mozart as a 'Romantic' composer and did not find him guilty of the same 'composing for effect' as his successors.) But by mechanically imitating the features they observed in Mozart, composers could only produce 'curious compositions in which without any motivation ... crude changes of key and blaring chords from every conceivable wind instrument follow in rapid succession, like garish colours that never coalesce into a picture'. Ironically, because of their overemphasis on 'effect', the music of these composers failed to move the audience.

Instead, Hoffmann outlines a creative process for would-be opera composers in which the key to writing 'effective' music, paradoxically, is not thinking about its effect at all:

In order to move us, in order to stir us profoundly, the artist must be affected deeply within his own heart; and the art of composing effectively is to employ the highest possible skill to capture ideas unconsciously conceived in a state of ecstasy, and to write them down in the hieroglyphs of musical sound (notation). If a young artist asks, therefore, how he should set about composing an opera with the maximum effect, one can only give him the following reply. 'Read the libretto, concentrate your mind on it with all your strength, enter into the dramatic situations with all the resources of your imagination; you live in the characters of the drama, you yourself are the tyrant, the hero, the lover; you feel the pain and the joy of love, the humiliation, fear, horror, even the nameless agony of death, and the blissful ecstasy of transfiguration; you brood, you rage, you hope, you despair; your blood races through your veins, your pulse beats faster; from the fire of inspiration that inflames your breast emerge notes, melodies, chords, and the drama flows from within you translated into the magical language of music.'[7]

The passage encapsulates several Romantic ideas about musical expression. First, the content comes not from the external world, but from deep within the composer ('deep within his own heart' or 'the fire of inspiration that inflames [his] breast').[8] This is not to say that this inner experience cannot be stimulated by something external, such as the characters and situations of the libretto, but rather that these external stimuli need to be internalised, processed, *lived* by the composer, and that this inner process, rather than the external stimulus, is the true source of the composition that results.

Furthermore, the process of composition that Hoffmann describes seems to preclude any rationalised calculation; it happens 'unconsciously' and 'in a state of ecstasy' as the composer's 'inner music' flows outward. While his musical training has a role to play, at no point does he consciously wield technique. Instead, all of his previous training only gives him the ability to 'grasp hold of the music that would otherwise rush past him'. Indeed, such a description evokes the etymological origins of the word 'express': to 'push' or 'press' out. Hoffmann's understanding was predicated on the Romantic conviction that within the artist there lay mysterious, untapped depths, an inner spiritual domain that could never definitively be articulated or rationally understood, but that nevertheless could be accessed or intuited through art. Yet crucially, the originality and depth of inner experience that this process required was not available to just anyone. Hoffmann ended his account of the creative process by noting, 'admittedly all this is tantamount to saying: just make sure, my dear fellow, that you are a musical genius, and then the rest will take care of itself.'[9]

Hoffmann's concept of the composer's autonomy hinged on following inner inspiration and renouncing the objective of creating an 'effect' on an audience. Other writers cast this autonomy in even more stringent terms, attempting to bracket out any awareness of an audience from the creative process. This principle was explored at length in the British philosopher

John Stuart Mill's essay, 'What Is Poetry?' from 1833. Mill, for whom the work of the Romantic poet William Wordsworth had been personally transformative, drew a strict hierarchical distinction between 'poetry' and what he called 'eloquence', and he believed that this distinction applied not only to the written word, but also to music.[10] 'Eloquence', Mill wrote, 'is *heard*; poetry is *over*heard.' He continued:

Eloquence supposes an audience; the peculiarity of poetry appears to us to lie in the poet's utter unconsciousness of a listener. Poetry is feeling confessing itself to itself, in moments of solitude . . . Eloquence is feeling pouring itself forth to other minds, courting their sympathy, or endeavouring to influence their belief, or move them to passion or to action.[11]

Mill recognised that it was a tall order to ask poets to remain unaware of the eventual readers of their work, that their poems would eventually be 'printed on hot-pressed paper, and sold at a bookseller's shop'.[12] Still, he maintained that the creative process and product should be uncontaminated by this knowledge: 'No trace of consciousness that any eyes are upon us must be visible in the work itself', and the poet must 'succeed in excluding from his work every vestige of such lookings-forth into the outward and every-day world, and can express his feelings exactly as he has felt them in solitude, or as he feels that he should feel them, though they were to remain for ever unuttered'.[13]

   In short, Romantic theories of expressive authenticity frequently emphasised the need to erect boundaries against the external social world. Their concern was that becoming too porous, too subject to the influence ('in-flowing') of society would corrupt or fragment the artist's unique sense of being – the inner source from which all true art springs. A host of philosophical, social, and economic developments contributed to this shift in priorities. As early as the mid-eighteenth century, the French *philosophe* Jean-Jacques Rousseau had argued that human nature was essentially good, but became corrupt through participation in society, which required artifice and posturing in pursuit of status and esteem. This valuing of 'inner' nature over 'outer' social relations was amplified as the bourgeoisie replaced the aristocracy as the primary patrons and consumers of music and other cultural products in the nineteenth century. As has been well documented, a reconfiguration of social space (and the modes of subjectivity and relationship cultivated within that space) accompanied the ascendancy of these middle classes.[14] The bourgeois individual cultivated his or her inwardness most assiduously within the private sphere of the home, where the sense of being sheltered from the demands of public and economic life was thought to enable a kind of idealised, 'purely human' form of relationship unmarred by pretence or artifice – an ideal to which the many earnest, confessional letters written during this time period vividly attest.[15] The supposedly unmannered intimacy of this space was defined in contrast to the pomp and artifice of the noble court, where ritual, ceremony, and display (often involving music and other arts) served to convey distinctions of wealth, power, and status.[16]

At the same time, increased social, economic, and geographic mobility during the nineteenth century meant that individuals frequently found themselves in unfamiliar social settings and amongst strangers. This social reality required the ability to interpret others, and present oneself, in situations where a system of shared social codes (the meanings ascribed to comportment, speech, dress, and other forms of behaviour) could no longer be assumed. In this context, the moralising tone accompanying exhortations to personal authenticity also betrays an anxiety, both about misinterpreting (or worse, being deliberately misled about) the essential character of someone else, or about being misinterpreted oneself. The ideal of the authentic individual arose partly in response to these circumstances: a virtuous person was cast as someone in whom there was complete harmony between inner nature and outward behaviour, who remained the same no matter the social circumstances, who resisted the temptation to alter his or her behaviour in different settings, in a word, who refused to *perform*.[17]

There was a continuity, then, between ethical demands placed on individuals and aesthetic standards applied to the arts. Amongst the arts, the ideal of authenticity was perhaps most pronounced within music. In the early nineteenth century, music and lyric poetry were seen as the art forms most conducive to self-expression, and music in particular was thought to offer the most pure, direct, and unmediated access to the inner life. As many Romantic writers pointed out, even poetry relied on the seemingly arbitrary symbols and syntax of language, and thus inserted a layer of artifice and convention between subjective experience and its artistic expression. Music, on the other hand, was known as the least representational medium, and instrumental music in particular was defined by its absence of clear signifiers, and was thus best suited to expressing the 'inexpressible'. Indeed, in some Romantic thought music did not merely 'represent' this deeper reality, but rather embodied or manifested it.[18] As Wilhelm Heinrich Wackenroder wrote (in language reminiscent of Hoffmann's later image of music 'flowing out' of the composer), 'with the mysterious stream in the depths of the human spirit – speech reckons and names and describes its changes in a foreign material; music streams out before us as it is in itself'.[19]

Nevertheless, at the same time that music was idealised as the purest, most immediate expression of interiority, it also entered into a series of expanded contexts in public life. In the nineteenth century, public concerts became widespread, mass market publishing made printed music more readily available than ever before, and a burgeoning music criticism industry produced accounts of new compositions and events that were consumed by a diverse reading public.[20] These contexts placed strain on the ideal of expressive authenticity, making it difficult to ignore the centrifugal forces of outward performance and other-orientedness that inevitably accompany the social practice of music.[21] In an era in which expressive authenticity had become a moral and aesthetic standard, musicians found themselves in the paradoxical position of needing to perform an authentic self through music – to convince audiences and critics of this authenticity – in order to achieve any degree of success or critical esteem. Even the most idealistic composers found it difficult to operate outside this logic. Robert Schumann, writing to his fiancée Clara Wieck in 1838, told her that she had made the right choice in not performing his *Études symphoniques* in one of her concerts: 'they do not suit the public – and it would be lame if I later wanted to complain that they had not understood something that was not intended for applause; it was not intended for anything at all and exists only for its own sake'. Nevertheless, in the next sentence, he wrote, 'But I confess that it would make me very happy if something of mine were successful sometime, that is, if you played it and the audience ran up the walls from excitement; we composers are vain, even if we have no reason to be.'[22]

Due in no small part to these inherent tensions, then, in practice expressive authenticity was not a stable quality. Instead, it functioned as what has sometimes been termed a 'regulative' ideal in nineteenth-century musical life: broadly and intuitively understood and valued, and frequently evoked as a way of conferring aesthetic legitimacy and prestige, yet employed in ways that were inconsistent and complex.[23] Because of this function, it is important to ask not only *what* it was, but also *how* it worked. How did nineteenth-century musical practice (including composing, performing, listening, and criticism) orient itself towards the ideal of expressive authenticity? What were the practical consequences of adherence to this ideal? And how did it create or reinforce hierarchies and power relationships in musical culture? The remainder of this essay will explore how these questions played out in several interrelated areas of musical practice in which questions of expression and authenticity came into the foreground.

In nineteenth-century criticism, efforts to discern the authenticity of a composition often hinged on evaluating the extent to which certain technical features emanated from a point at the centre – the composer's inner subjectivity, or more specifically, an inner experience that manifested outwardly as music. For many nineteenth-century listeners and critics, Beethoven's music came to represent a gold standard in this respect, as a veritable industry of biographical and myth-making initiatives encouraged listeners to experience his music as the sonic record of his inner experiences and struggles, and analytical criticism by Hoffmann, A. B. Marx, and others drew attention to the integration between whole and parts in his music, and argued for an organic relationship between individual features and essential, spiritual content (in Marx's terms, the *Idee* of a work).[24]

Such a division of works of art into inner essence and external form was indebted to the Idealist philosophy that dominated German intellectual life in the early nineteenth century.[25] And indeed, in his *Lectures on Aesthetics*, the philosopher G. W. F. Hegel had considered the question of authenticity in art. Hegel drew a contrast between what he termed the 'ideal style', which 'hovers in between the purely substantive expression of the topic [*Sache*] and the complete emergence of what pleases', and the 'pleasing' artistic style, whose primary aim was to produce an effect on the spectator:

[In the pleasing style], it is no longer the one topic [*Sache*] itself to which the whole external appearance refers; consequently in this way the particular details of this appearance become more and more independent, even if at first they still proceed from the topic itself and are necessitated by it. We feel that they are adduced and interpolated as decorations or contrived episodes. But just because they remain accidental to the topic itself and have their essential purpose solely in relation to the spectator or reader, they flatter the person for whom they have been devised.[26]

The notion that particular details can become detached from inner content and turn towards an audience provides an indication of how certain musical characteristics and practices emerged as flashpoints in discussions of authenticity in music. Many critics, for example, viewed piquant orchestral sonorities with some degree of suspicion. Timbre was often cast as a way of using instrumental effects to 'dress up' the more enduring content of a musical work (usually thought to reside in such elements as pitch, rhythm, and harmony) with ephemeral sound effects that played directly on listeners' senses.[27] Because timbre seemed to fall into the category of 'external appearance', it was at risk of becoming independent of the 'topic' and existing solely 'in relation to the spectator'. Indeed, the abuse of orchestral effects ('blaring chords from every conceivable wind instrument') was exactly what Hoffmann lambasted in the essay cited above, when he admonished composers for pandering to audiences at the expense of their inner inspiration.

In practice, composers responded to the discourse on timbre in varying ways. When the British composer Ethel Smyth lived and studied amongst Brahms and his friends in the 1870s, her impression was that they viewed orchestration with a high-minded disdain: 'in that circle what you may call the *external*, the merely pleasing element in music, was so little insisted on that its motto really might have been the famous "take care of the sense and the sounds will take care of themselves"'.[28] Other composers, of course, fully embraced the creative possibilities offered by timbre. But it is noteworthy that even Berlioz, a composer famous for his innovative orchestral effects, regularly emphasised that such effects were only justified when they were 'motivated' by some deeper expressive purpose.[29] When discussing Wagner's *Der fliegende Holländer* in his memoirs, for example, he praised the overall 'sombre colouring' and 'certain stormy effects perfectly appropriate to the subject', yet censured Wagner for his 'abuse of the *tremolo*' in passages that contained no other 'striking ideas'.[30] The implication was that such passages might appeal to listeners' senses and emotions with their wash of shimmering sound, but because they expressed nothing, they were effects without a cause; in fact, they may even disguise a lack of invention or authentic content on the composer's part.

For similar reasons, virtuosity represented another flashpoint in nineteenth-century discussions of self-expression and authenticity. Rooted in the physical process of singing or playing an instrument and the spectacle of performers displaying their technique, virtuosity brought forward several familiar dichotomies. Could virtuoso showpieces be the expression of a composer's deep interiority, or were they merely a hodgepodge of impressive techniques and figures designed to impress audiences? To what extent did virtuoso performers allow the 'mysterious stream in the depths of the human spirit' to flow forth 'as it is in itself' (to paraphrase Wackenroder), and to what extent were they merely skilled technicians, compromised by a desire to gain applause, acclaim, and commercial success? Many of these recurring questions can be observed in an anonymous 1834 review of Sigismund Thalberg's *Grande fantaisie sur 'I Capuleti e Montecchi'* that appeared in Schumann's *Neue Zeitschrift für Musik*. Describing the work's alternation between learned contrapuntal writing and brilliant virtuosity, the reviewer discerned no inner expressive necessity, but rather a desire to 'adorn itself with different colours for each person': 'One sees very clearly how the composer wanted to make the variations pleasing for the connoisseur as well as the layperson, how he thinks to satisfy the former with pretty fugued or four-voice passages, and for the latter, to compensate for their boredom with brilliant and elegant passages. ... A piece like this', he concluded, 'whose highest and only tendency is to seek admiration ... we cannot possibly call good'.[31]

Scattered throughout the review are suggestions about how Thalberg should approach composing: 'A young composer, if like Herr Thalberg he possesses knowledge in addition to natural talent, does not need to fear that he will become ordinary if he only renders simply and transparently what is inwardly felt.' The reviewer's conviction that Thalberg had not achieved this goal derived from an analysis of the piece's technical bravura and frequent stylistic shifts. Yet tellingly, the reviewer describes authenticity in both absolute and strikingly personal terms, perceiving a continuity between Thalberg's compositional choices and his essential character: 'If he mistakes this principle, if he senses it not even once, if he worships the fashion of the day as his God, and if he subordinates his talent to the applause of the masses, then everything that he wants to do to preserve a deeper individuality is a vain effort.'[32]

Such identification between the musical ('the piece' seeks admiration) and the personal (the composer is unable to preserve his 'deeper individuality') were typical in nineteenth-century criticism. In an age of musical celebrity, listeners and critics consumed reports, biographies, and images of famous musicians coterminously with their music; each informed the other. But this emphasis on the identity of the composer could combine in troubling ways with the assumption (as articulated above by Hoffmann) that only a unique individual – a genius – would possess both the inner depth and creative power to produce authentically expressive music. Increasingly over the course of the nineteenth century, such an individual was assumed to have a gender (male) and a nationality (German). For musicians who did not fit this profile, it was often the case that even the most compelling music was suspected of inauthenticity, of meeting the surface requirements of form and technique but lacking expressive depth.

Of this strain of criticism, Wagner's invective against Meyerbeer and Mendelssohn in *Das Judenthum in der Musik* (1850/1869) is only one of the most well known and pernicious examples. Wagner's argument was that an artist's inner inspiration could only be nurtured through membership in a historical community: the German *Volk*, which Wagner defined in racialised terms that excluded even German-born converted Jews such as Mendelssohn. In Wagner's view, a Jewish composer, a perpetual outsider, could never obtain 'so intimate a glimpse into our essence: ... he merely listens to the barest surface of our art, but not to its life-bestowing inner organism'.[33] In Mendelssohn's case, Wagner wrote, his music might appeal to audiences when it is confined to 'the presentment, stringing together and entanglement of the most elegant, the smoothest and most polished figures';[34] indeed, it may mimic the music of other great German composers with 'quite distressing accuracy and deceptive likeness'.[35] But it had no centre; it could not contain the 'deep and stalwart feelings of the human heart', all external appearances to the contrary.[36] In a word, it was inauthentic.

It is here that we can observe how the Romantic ideal of authentic self-expression, while nurturing artists' 'feelings and dreams', also enabled many of the ideologies of exclusion that have become deeply embedded in the Western musical canon. Within an aesthetic framework valuing skilful imitation and demonstrable effect, the kind of argument advanced by Wagner lacked power. Yet with the composer's inner experience as the yardstick, inauthenticity became one of the most damning charges to level at music. It was also one of the most difficult to counter: Wagner's evidence for his claims lay in common knowledge about Mendelssohn's Jewish identity and social background, and descriptions of what Wagner felt or failed to feel when listening to Mendelssohn's music. Wagner warns his readers not to be deceived, to question the music's authenticity. But he leaves it to 'professional critics' to 'prove' his claims with 'specimens of Mendelssohn's art-products'.[37] Yet even if someone attempted to 'disprove' Wagner's allegations using the tools of musical analysis, the essay's distrust of musical surfaces – Wagner's assertion that they can bear a deceptive, even indistinguishable similarity to the 'real thing' – would to some extent defang such a defence. The success or failure of the argument depended on its appeal to readers' existing prejudices and their acceptance of the writer's authority as someone who *is* able to discern authentic from inauthentic music. As even the most cursory look at much music criticism of the last 200 years shows, the logic underlying this kind of critical gatekeeping has proved remarkably tenacious despite its speciousness.[38]

Yet Wagner was hardly the dominant voice on Mendelssohn's music, and a final example shows in a more general sense how the Romantic aesthetics of authenticity opened up new modalities of musical experience that have remained influential. When Mendelssohn was away from Berlin on his Grand Tour in 1829, his sister Fanny often consoled herself for his absence by engaging with his music, and recorded a particularly intense experience one evening: 'I've been alone for two hours, at the piano, which sounds especially nice today, playing the *Hora* [Felix's motet *Hora est*]. I get up from the piano, stand in front of your picture, and kiss it, and immerse myself so completely in your presence that I – must write you now.'[39] In some intangible way, Fanny felt her brother's spirit to be there in his music, accessible to her under the right conditions; while her description may seem uncanny, even extreme, belief in this possibility guided many nineteenth-century approaches to listening, performance, and criticism. The fact that this belief can still be observed informing these practices today, albeit sometimes in altered ways, testifies to the flexibility and capaciousness of expressive authenticity as a critical concept.

Notes

1. Quoted in Stanley Sadie, *Mozart: The Early Years, 1756–1781* (Oxford: Oxford University Press, 2006), 473.
2. Quoted in Pietro Weiss and Richard Taruskin (eds.), *Music in the Western World: A History in Documents* (New York: Simon & Schuster, 1984), 368–9.
3. Quoted in M. Range, 'The "Effective Passage" in Mozart's "Paris" Symphony', *Eighteenth-Century Music*, 9/1 (2012), 109–19, at 119.
4. For further reading on mimetic theories of art, see M. H. Abrams, *The Mirror and the Lamp: Romantic Theory and the Critical Tradition* (New York: Oxford University Press, 1953), 3–45; for discussions specific to music, see Mark Evan Bonds, *Absolute Music: The History of an Idea* (New York: Oxford University Press, 2014), 69–78, and Edward Lippman, *A History of Western Musical Aesthetics* (Lincoln, NE: University of Nebraska Press, 1992), 83–136.
5. See Abrams, *The Mirror and the Lamp*, and Charles Taylor, *Sources of the Self: The Making of the Modern Identity* (Cambridge, MA: Harvard University Press, 1989), 368–90.
6. 'On a Remark of Sacchini's, and On So-Called Effect in Music', in *E. T. A. Hoffmann's Musical Writings: Kreisleriana, The Poet and the Composer, Music Criticism*, ed. David Charlton, trans. Martyn Clarke (Cambridge: Cambridge University Press, 1989), 152–9.
7. Ibid., 155.
8. On the concept of depth in Romantic musical discourse, see Holly Watkins, *Metaphors of Depth in German Musical Thought, from E. T. A. Hoffmann to Arnold Schoenberg* (Cambridge: Cambridge University Press, 2011).

9. Ibid., 155.

10. As applied to music, Mill's binary became 'poetry' versus 'oratory'.

11. J. S. Mill, 'What Is Poetry?', in *Early Essays by John Stuart Mill* (New York: George Bell & Sons, 1897), 208–9.

12. Ibid., 209.

13. Ibid., 209.

14. See Jürgen Habermas, *The Structural Transformation of the Public Sphere: An Inquiry into a Category of Bourgeois Society*, trans. T. Burger (Cambridge, MA: MIT Press, 1991), 43–50. For a recent discussion of how musical practices responded to these developments, see Jennifer Ronyak, *Intimacy, Performance, and the Lied in the Early Nineteenth Century* (Bloomington: Indiana University Press, 2018), esp. 1–20.

15. Habermas, *The Structural Transformation*, 48.

16. And, it should be noted, in contrast to the lower classes who lacked the means, both economic and educational, to cultivate such inwardness. See David Gramit, *Cultivating Music: The Aspirations, Interests, and Limits of German Musical Culture, 1770–1848* (Berkeley: University of California Press, 2002).

17. Two classic explorations of this authenticity ideal are Lionel Trilling, *Sincerity and Authenticity* (Cambridge, MA: Harvard University Press, 1972) and R. Sennett, *The Fall of Public Man* (New York: Penguin Books, 2002).

18. In philosophy, Arthur Schopenhauer's *Die Welt als Wille und Vorstellung* (first published in 1818 and then in expanded editions in 1844 and 1859), provided the fullest and most influential articulation of this idea.

19. Quoted in Abrams, *The Mirror and the Lamp*, 93.

20. The rise of the authenticity ideal was in fact inseparable from these contexts; just as greater social mobility led to increased exhortations to personal authenticity, so music's growing presence in public and commercial spheres produced similar demands on music.

21. Indeed, as has often been noted, Romantic inwardness contains within itself a certain paradox, namely that it needed outward expression in order to be fully realised. In the words of philosopher Charles Taylor, our inner nature 'cannot be known outside of and prior to our articulation/definition of it'. This involves making 'what was hidden manifest for both [ourselves] and others'. See Taylor, *Sources of the Self*, 374–6.

22. Robert Schumann to Clara Wieck, March 1838, in *The Complete Correspondence of Clara and Robert Schumann, vol. 1*, ed. E. Weissweiler, trans. H. Fritsch and R. L. Crawford (New York: Peter Lang, 1994), 129–30. On Robert's conflicted relationship to the 'public' for his early piano pieces, see David Ferris, 'Public Performance and Private Understanding: Clara Wieck's Concerts in Berlin', *Journal of the American Musicological Society*, 56/2 (2003), 351–408.

23. Recent scholarship has fruitfully applied this concept to several other cherished ideals (many of them closely related to the ideal of expressive authenticity)

within nineteenth-century musical culture, including the work-concept, aesthetic autonomy, and absolute music. See Lydia Goehr, *The Imaginary Museum of Musical Works: An Essay in the Philosophy of Music* (Oxford: Oxford University Press, 2002); Richard Taruskin, 'Is There a Baby in the Bathwater?', *Archiv für Musikwissenschaft*, 63/3 (2006), 163–85, 309–27; and Bonds, *Absolute Music*.

24. See Scott Burnham, 'Criticism, Faith, and the "Idee": A. B. Marx's Early Reception of Beethoven', *19th-Century Music*, 13/3 (1990), 183–92.

25. See Mark Evan Bonds, 'Idealism and the Aesthetics of Instrumental Music at the Turn of the Nineteenth Century', *Journal of the American Musicological Society*, 50/2–3 (1997), 387–420; and *Music as Thought: Listening to the Symphony in the Age of Beethoven* (Princeton: Princeton University Press, 2006), esp. 5–28.

26. *Hegel's Aesthetics: Lectures on Fine Art*, trans. T. M. Knox, 2 vols. (Oxford: Oxford University Press, 1988), vol. 2, 618.

27. Emily Dolan, *The Orchestral Revolution: Haydn and the Technologies of Timbre* (Cambridge: Cambridge University Press, 2013), 256–7.

28. Ethel Smyth, *The Impressions that Remained*, vol. 1 (London: Longmans, Green, and Co., 1923), 286.

29. As F. Reckow has shown, the notion of musical 'effect' had different meanings in French and German Romanticism, an important context for understanding the heated debates (and often censure) that Berlioz's music engendered in German music criticism. F. Reckow, '"Wirkung" und "Effekt". Über einige Voraussetzungen, Tendenzen und Probleme der deutschen Berlioz-Kritik', *Die Musikforschung*, 33/1 (1980), 1–36.

30. Hector Berlioz, *Memoirs*, trans. R. Holmes and E. Holmes, vol. 2 (London: Macmillan & Co., 1884), 67.

31. 'Grande Fantaisie et Variations . . . par S. Thalberg', *Neue Zeitschrift für Musik*, 1/2 (7 April 1834), 6–7. Translations of some of the above passages are from Alexander Stefaniak, *Schumann's Virtuosity: Criticism, Composition, and Performance in Nineteenth-Century Germany* (Bloomington: Indiana University Press, 2016), 40.

32. Ibid.

33. R. Wagner, 'Judaism in Music', in *Richard Wagner's Prose Works*, vol. 3, trans. W. A. Ellis (London: Kegan Paul, Trench, Trübner & Co., 1907), 92.

34. Ibid., 93.

35. Ibid., 89.

36. Ibid., 94.

37. Ibid., 94.

38. Indeed, there is some poetic justice in the fact that Nietzsche, and later Adorno, accused Wagner's music of the same falseness and deception that Wagner claimed to hear in Mendelssohn. See K. Leistra-Jones, 'Staging Authenticity:

Joachim, Brahms, and the Politics of *Werktreue* Performance', *Journal of the American Musicological Society*, 66/2 (2013), 397–436.

39. Fanny Mendelssohn to Felix Mendelssohn, 29 June 1829, in *The Letters of Fanny Hensel to Felix Mendelssohn*, ed. and trans. M. J. Citron (Stuyvestant, NY: Pendragon Press, 1987), 57.

Further Reading

Abrams, M. H. *The Mirror and the Lamp: Romantic Theory and the Critical Tradition* (Oxford: Oxford University Press, 1953).

Bernstein, Susan. *Virtuosity of the Nineteenth Century: Performing Music and Language in Heine, Liszt, and Baudelaire* (Stanford: Stanford University Press, 1998).

Bonds, Mark Evan. *Absolute Music: The History of an Idea* (New York: Oxford University Press, 2014).

'Idealism and the Aesthetics of Instrumental Music at the Turn of the Nineteenth Century', *Journal of the American Musicological Society*, 50/2–3 (1997), 387–420.

Burnham, Scott. 'Criticism, Faith, and the "Idee": A. B. Marx's Early Reception of Beethoven', *19th-Century Music*, 13/3 (1990), 183–92.

Gay, Peter. *The Naked Heart* (New York: Norton, 1995).

Gooley, Dana. 'The Battle Against Instrumental Virtuosity in the Early Nineteenth Century', in Christopher H. Gibbs and Dana Gooley (eds.), *Franz Liszt and his World* (Princeton: Princeton University Press, 2006), 75–112.

Leistra-Jones, Karen. 'Staging Authenticity: Joachim, Brahms, and the Politics of *Werktreue* Performance', *Journal of the American Musicological Society*, 66/2 (2013), 397–436.

Lippman, Edward A. *A History of Western Musical Aesthetics* (Lincoln, NE: University of Nebraska Press, 1992).

Ronyak, Jennifer *Intimacy, Performance, and the Lied in the Early Nineteenth Century* (Bloomington: Indiana University Press, 2018).

Stefaniak, Alexander. 'Clara Schumann's Interiorities and the Cutting Edge of Popular Pianism', *Journal of the American Musicological Society*, 70/3 (2017), 697–765.

Taylor, Charles. *Sources of the Self: The Making of the Modern Identity* (Cambridge, MA: Harvard University Press, 1989).

Trilling, Lionel. *Sincerity and Authenticity* (Cambridge, MA: Harvard University Press, 1972).

Watkins, Holly. *Metaphors of Depth in German Musical Thought: From E. T. A. Hoffmann to Arnold Schoenberg* (Cambridge: Cambridge University Press, 2011).

PART IV

Practices

14 | Romantic Languages

JULIAN HORTON

Introduction

Applying linguistic analogies to music is inevitably a precarious activity. The idea that we can usefully characterise a composer's musical 'language' is a musicological commonplace; the analogy has variously encompassed melodic style, harmony, approaches to form and genre, and expressive means and objectives, as well as more ambitious claims that music and language are somehow synonymous. Yet few commentators accept the functional synonymy of music and language uncritically. Research in the fields of musical semiotics, expression, and narrativity has not established any precise linguistic function for music; and linguistic models of musical meaning of the sort attempted by Deryck Cooke seem doomed to failure.[1]

This analogy is nevertheless crucial to any consideration of music and Romanticism. As Benedict Taylor makes clear in this volume's opening chapter, a new interest in the relationship between music and literature and a belief that music can fulfil poetic, dramatic, and narrative aspirations without the need for written language are defining factors of music's Romantic turn. These convictions rely on a complex mediation of musical and extra-musical factors. In one sense, Romantic music is marked by a retreat from extra-musical meaning: Beethoven, above all, comes to be associated with the concept of autonomy, by which is generally meant the liberation of music from textual and social dependencies and a consequent freedom to pursue its own self-reflective ambitions.[2] At the same time, autonomy facilitates a perception of music as the purveyor of higher meanings: precisely because instrumental music coheres without textual support, it can convey conceptual essences without the intervention of written or spoken language. This is absolute music's aesthetic precept: textless music accesses narrative and poetic ideas directly, without recourse to language.

This chapter offers three case studies of Romanticism's musical 'language', understood as the melodic, harmonic, and formal means that

231

composers deployed to expressive ends. The first and second case studies – melody in Beethoven and Field, and harmony from Schubert to Brahms – deal with aspects of what could, by analogy, be called Romanticism's vocabulary and grammar, paying attention to compositional materials, the logic of their employment, and the sources from which they arise. The third – the Finale of Schumann's Symphony No. 2 – turns to matters of form specifically to address the relationship with literature, and therefore isolates narrative as well as purely formal strategies (questions of Romantic form are addressed by Steven Vande Moortele in Chapter 15). Connecting these studies is the common theme of Romanticism's new-found musical self-awareness. The thematic habits of Beethoven's middle period betray a degree of overt intellectual self-reflection in excess of eighteenth-century precedent; harmonic experimentation develops alongside an emerging theoretical understanding of music's systems as well its practices; and Schumann's symphonic-literary sensibility is enabled by reflection on the idea of a symphony as well as its generic requirements.

Melody, Theme, and Texture

Romanticism's attitude towards melody is characterised by contrasted, if not contradictory, tendencies. Composers accorded new importance to lyric and rhapsodic styles, emphasising a degree of freedom that went beyond classical conventions and devising novel vehicles for its expression. At the same time, they also placed a heightened value on thematic and motivic coherence, pursuing cyclical integration and developmental processes in instrumental compositions especially. To an extent, these tendencies evidence the polarised priorities of vocal and instrumental music, which Carl Dahlhaus housed under the contentious 'style dualism' of Rossinian opera and Beethovenian instrumental music.[3] Yet this duality conceals a more nuanced reality: composers in Beethoven's shadow found new ways of imitating vocality; and lyrically inclined genres emerged, which are impossible to classify into straightforward national schools.

That the lyric strain of Romantic melody evades simple explanation is aptly demonstrated by the development of the nocturne. Credit for its invention as an instrumental genre is invariably given to John Field, whose sixteen contributions were published between 1812 and 1836, but this origin myth masks complex circumstances: Field did not 'invent' the nocturne in an act of Romantic innovation. Many of the pieces he eventually published as nocturnes began life under other titles, which sometimes indicate a debt to the eighteenth-century *notturno* ('serenade') and sometimes do not ('pastorale', 'romance').[4] In some cases, stand-alone nocturnes migrated from other genres entirely: the Nocturne No. 12 in G is, for example, also a slow episode in the first movement of Field's Piano Concerto No. 7. More properly, we can see the piano nocturne as coalescing from various generic and stylistic sources. Its melody-and-accompaniment idiom derives from the high-classical singing style, crucially augmented by the pedalling technology that allowed pianists to displace the bassline from the interior texture by more than an octave.[5] Vocal precedents are folded into the genre – the operatic serenade and bel canto fioritura are often cited – but in Chopin's hands especially, the title accommodates a broad range of implied genres.[6]

The nocturne's Romantic credentials, and Field's status as its progenitor, were secured by Franz Liszt, whose preface to the first collected edition nominated the pieces as seminal for musical Romanticism. For Liszt, it was to Field's unique sensibility that 'we owe the first essays which feeling and revery ventured to make on the piano, to free themselves from the constraints exercised over them by the regular and official model imposed until that time on all compositions'. Before Field, 'It was formally necessary that they should be either Sonatas or Rondos etc.; Field was the first to introduce a species which belonged to none of the established classes, and in which feeling and melody reigned alone, liberated from the fetters and encumbrances of a coercive form.'[7] Liszt's claims are hard to categorise within Dahlhaus's dualism. Field's style is clearly vocal, but also distant from Rossinian opera's formulae and overt display. Liszt subsequently emphasises Field's lyricism, thereby associating him more closely with Schubert; but there is nothing in Field that suggests poetic dependency or an anchorage in art song. And Liszt's Field is even more distant from the instrumental style that Dahlhaus valorised in Beethoven. Field also falls outside Dahlhaus's geographical remit, as a representative of the so-called 'London pianoforte school', the influence of which was both widespread and distinct from both Austro-German and Franco-Italian genealogies. Nevertheless, as a progenitor of Romanticism, Field is arguably more important than any of these precursors, since, for Liszt, it is to Field that Romanticism owes all of those genres that are specifically post-classical.

Brief comparison of Field's Nocturne No. 1 in E flat of 1811 with the first movement of Beethoven's 'Tempest' Sonata, Op. 31 No. 2 of 1801 makes clear the sheer distance between Field's aesthetic and Beethoven's motivic style. The first movement of the 'Tempest' has become an exemplar of Beethoven's middle-period intellectualism. Dahlhaus repeatedly observed the novelty of its opening, shown in Ex. 14.1, which moves from

Example 14.1 Beethoven, 'Tempest' Sonata, Op. 31 No. 2 (1801), i, bb. 1–41

Example 14.1 (Cont.)

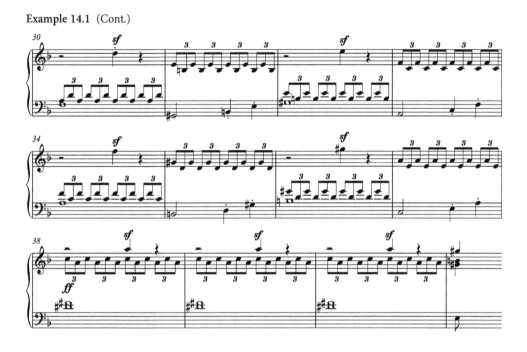

introduction to transition without ever establishing a stable main theme.[8]
More recently, Janet Schmalfeldt has explained this as an example of
'becoming', or the retrospective reinterpretation of formal function. On
first hearing, bar 21 seems to initiate a main theme, because it is the first
unequivocal downbeat, which establishes a root-position tonic. By bar 41,
however, it has become clear that bar 21 initiates a transition, not a theme,
which means that we have to mentally revisit bars 1–21 and reinterpret
them as thematic.[9]

　　Dahlhaus and Schmalfeldt consider Beethoven's innovation here to be
the creation of a dialectical formal concept, which collapses formal function into process. The material's identity is not confirmed with its presentation; instead, Beethoven forces his listener to reconsider and discard
perceptions of formal function as the music proceeds. Because we have to
convert a main theme into a transition, we also have to convert an introduction into a main theme. All of this happens retrospectively and speaks
to a kind of form, in which the listener is an active participant. As a result,
the 'Tempest' transforms the formal functions of sonata form from genre
markers ('I know we are listening to a piano sonata, because I hear a main
theme and transition') into objects of conscious reflection ('I am invited to

participate in the construction of the main theme and transition as I hear them, as well as acknowledging their generic circumstances'). Both Dahlhaus and Schmalfeldt are quick to point out the parallels with contemporaneous philosophy. The notion of a consciously critical art was central to Friedrich Schlegel's idea of the Romantic fragment; and it is easy to see resonances with Hegel's coming-to-self-consciousness of the spirit, as narrated in the *Phenomenology*.[10] In effect, Beethoven's 'Tempest' composes the coming-to-self-consciousness of sonata form, as a musical experience that folds the form's identity into the listener's emerging consciousness of it.

As Dahlhaus points out, Beethoven compensates for the resulting loss of formal stability by retaining a single, concise motive across the passage (the arpeggiated figure with which the piece begins). More important than the development of this motive, however, is the new status that its formal context attains. There is an important sense in which Beethoven composes music which is *about the idea of first-movement form* more it is about confirming those features that the genre requires. In Beethoven's music, this is what autonomy means: the music's meaning resides in what it has to say about musical composition in sonata form, in addition to its expressive and generic responsibilities.

Numerous scholars have since identified this notion of becoming as a crucial feature of Romantic music; but even cursory appraisal of Field's Nocturne (Ex. 14.2 shows bars 1–21; Table 14.1 appraises its form) reveals its distance from both Beethovenian and classical frames of reference.[11] The piece's form is ternary, to the extent that bars 1–19 form a closed unit, which is reprised in bars 43–66, between which new music is inserted. All three of the Nocturne's sections however culminate with perfect-cadential closure in the tonic, violating William Caplin's precondition that classical ternary forms should conclude their contrasting middle sections half-cadentially.[12] Moreover, the second section offers only limited material contrast, since it sustains the A section's texture and loosely varies its

Table 14.1 Field, Nocturne No. 1, form

Bars:	1	15	20	43	57
Form:	A	(codetta)	B	A^1	Coda
Keys:	I		V→ii→I	I	
Cadences:	PAC		PAC	PAC	

Example 14.2 Field, Nocturne No. 1 in E flat (1811), bb. 1–22

Example 14.2 (cont.)

material in V and ii. The music's self-containment bespeaks lyricism, but the form is not strophic in a way that encourages poetic analogies, and its recursive features occasion neither variation in any strict classical sense nor simple recurrence.[13]

Crucially, what Field offers is in the first instance a *texture*, not a theme; or rather, the theme gives architectonic substance to the texture. The first few bars establish a melody-and-accompaniment division of labour, which is maintained throughout, and the left-hand triplet figuration remains consistent for the entire piece, in its rhythmic patterning and internal division into registrally disjunct bass and registrally invariant inner voices. Details of Field's voicing are classically aberrant but have clear textural motivation. This is apparent in bar 2, where, as Ex. 14.2 shows, the alto doubles the soprano's leading note at the octave, while clearly supplying a distinct voice. This is contrapuntally obtuse, but texturally intelligent, since the net effect, especially taken in conjunction with the pedalling, is to create a specifically resonant sonority.[14] Above this, the melody trades in free, fioritura elaboration, which is not variation as such, because the accompaniment never changes, but a kind of bel canto improvisation. The results are undeniably vocal, to the extent that they resemble a cantabile topic, but Field's germinal source of material is the instrument itself, and more specifically the fashioning of texture from sonority, and of melody from texture. To this extent, the vocal analogy is fortuitous rather than essential: the music is about the piano, not about the piano imagined as a voice.

There is an enticing dualism here, which is quite different from the dichotomy of the dramatic and the lyric usually observed between Beethoven and Schubert, or the style dualism of Beethoven and Rossini conjured by Dahlhaus. Beethoven's germinal idea is abstract and, in a sense, pianistically indifferent: the initial arpeggio could in principle occur on any instrument. In Field's case, the instrument's sonority generates the material: the piece's 'idea' is not the progress of a theme, but the elaboration of a texture. In this respect at least, Liszt is right to see Field's nocturnes as the ancestors of Romanticism's post-classical, poetic forms, but what he misses is a preoccupation with sonority, which tracks through Chopin to Fauré and Debussy, and on into the twentieth century.

Harmony and Tonality

A further, critical feature of Romanticism's musical language is its attitude towards tonality. The very idea that harmony can be classified within an evolving tonal system is an early nineteenth-century invention. The term itself ('tonalité') was first coined by Alexandre Choron in 1810 in his 'Sommaire de l'histoire de la musique', the introduction to Volume I of his *Dictionnaire historique des musicien*, in order to describe the practice, originating with Monteverdi, of establishing a tonic in relation to its dominant and subdominant triads.[15] The idea that music is based on an historically evolving tonal system was further elaborated in François-Joseph Fétis's *Traité complet de la théorie et de la pratique de l'harmonie* of 1844. Fétis interpreted musical history in terms of tonality's evolution, splitting the period from the Renaissance to his own time into four tonal 'orders', from the 'unitonic', non-modulatory tonality of the sixteenth century through the 'transitonic' tonality established by Monteverdi – which replaces the modal system with modulation between diatonic keys – and the eighteenth century's 'pluritonic' elision of major and minor modes, to the nineteenth century's 'omnitonic' order, which 'frustrates' tonal unity by permitting complete chromatic modulation.[16]

This theoretical self-consciousness supplies both a context and a pre-requisite for harmonic diversity. Romanticism's most overt innovations involve the unseating of classical conventions, above all the cadence's syntactic primacy. William Caplin has noted Romantic composers' tendency to favour non-cadential phrase endings, usually by replacing classical cadential progressions with what he terms 'prolongational closure'.[17] Ex. 14.3 shows an instance in the 'Valse Allemande' from

Example 14.3 Robert Schumann, 'Valse Allemande', from *Carnaval*, Op. 9 (1835)

Schumann's *Carnaval* . The excerpt is in rounded binary form, but neither the A nor A^1 sections end with a conventional cadence. Bars 5–8 are weakly cadential at best, comprising a V_3^4–V^7–I progression in the dominant, the security of which is immediately undone by the alto D♭ in bar 8. The end of A^1 secures the tonic but is not cadential at all. Schumann alights on IV$_3^6$ in bar 21 as a potential predominant, but before V is attained in bar 23, the music passes through three potential chromatic predominants – an Italian augmented sixth, an inversion of vii/V, and V^7/V – only the last of which resolves in an orthodox way (to V). Having reached V, Schumann then progresses to I via a bass arpeggiation, thereby undermining any sense of cadential root motion. There is closure on the tonic, but no authentic-cadential confirmation.

Schubert's 'Ihr Bild' from *Schwanengesang* (Ex. 14.4) adjusts other aspects of classical practice. The mixture of major and minor modes penetrates the music to an extent that unseats classical orthodoxy, even though Schubert's harmonic palette is overwhelmingly classical in its details. Modal mixture emerges in the interaction of cadential and pre-cadential harmony. In the setting of stanza 1 in bars 1–12, Schubert slips between an initially established B flat minor and a B flat major secured by a perfect authentic cadence (PAC) in bars 11–12, a setting that recurs verbatim in the final stanza, thereby securing a ternary design, in which stanzas 1 and 3 enfold a middle section in G flat, which sets stanza 2. The pianist's postlude however undoes the voice's ostensibly decisive tonic-major PAC, completed by bar 34, by returning to B flat minor, in which mode the song concludes. The methods of prolongation and cadence Schubert employs are wholly classical, but the balance of modes is such that arbitrating between them becomes virtually impossible. If we think that B flat minor is the tonic, then we have to confront the problem that no structural cadence establishes it. If we think B flat major is the tonic, then we need to discount the fact that the song neither begins nor ends in this mode. The frame qualifies the cadences, and the cadences qualify the frame.

The return to B flat minor for stanza 3 in bars 23–4 moreover discloses a harmonic detail, boxed in Ex. 14.4, which clearly signals Schubert's post-classical intent. Schubert deploys a chord in bar 23 which has the pitch content of a German augmented sixth but is arranged with B♭ rather than G♭ in the bass, creating an augmented fourth chord defined by the interval between B♭ and E♮. In orthodox circumstances, this chord would resolve onto a cadential 6–4, which then corrects to V. Schubert instead holds the B♭ bass as a common tone and propels the E♮ upwards to F, producing a strongly implied root-position triad of B flat minor, which, however,

Example 14.4 Schubert, 'Ihr Bild', from *Schwanengesang*, D. 957 (1828)

Example 14.4 (cont.)

contains no third. No dominant of B flat minor is subsequently forthcoming: stanza 3 reprises the music of stanza 1 directly in the minor mode. Schubert's innovation here is not the sonority itself, but its contextual treatment: the augmented sixth is rethought and so, in consequence, is the retransitional approach to the tonic.

By the mid-century, the reconception of classical means had annexed other sonorities. The opening of Liszt's *Faust-Symphonie*, first performed in 1857 and quoted in Ex. 14.5, famously liberates the augmented triad from its diatonic constraints. The initial twelve-note theme, comprising the statement and three descending semitonal transpositions of an augmented triad, is, like Schubert's augmented fourth, radical not because of the triad's presence, but because of its de-contextualisation. In common-practice usage, augmented triads are formed from the motion either of a chromatic passing note or a suspension, which temporarily generates a triad comprising two major thirds. Ex. 14.6 shows an instance in Mendelssohn's *Lied ohne Worte*, Op. 30 No. 3. This is really a progression from V_2^4/ii to ii^6 in E, but Mendelssohn delays the leading note's resolution, creating a downbeat suspension, which temporarily emphasises the augmented triad A-C♯-E♯, before the E♯ moves correctly to its note of resolution, F♯. This is not a triad in its own right, but

Example 14.5 Liszt, *Eine Faust-Symphonie* (1857), i, bb. 1–11

Example 14.6 Mendelssohn, *Lied ohne Worte*, Op. 30 No. 3 (1834), bb. 7–11

a sonority formed contrapuntally from the motion of parts between two functional chords.

Liszt's augmented triads, however, have no diatonic anchorage. They descend in stepwise sequence; and at no point is any pitch revealed as a passing note or suspension in search of resolution towards a major or minor triad. More than this, one particular augmented triad – that founded on E, on which the opening material comes to rest in bar 2 – is effectively the centre of gravity for the introduction's first thematic paragraph. As Ex. 14.5 reveals, this triad is prolonged, with elaboration, from bar 2 to bar 11, as a simultaneity until bar 7, and then in descending arpeggiation thereafter. Liszt in effect makes a dissonance (the augmented triad) perform a role analogous to the tonic triad in the diatonic common practice.[18]

The diversity of practices after *Faust* is clarified by comparison of passages from Brahms's Violin Sonata, Op. 100, and Mussorgsky's *Boris Godunov*, completed in 1887 and 1872, respectively. Opus 100's first theme (Ex. 14.7) confirms Dahlhaus's perception that Brahms 'enriches' rather than endangers diatonic tonality.[19] A major's tonic status is never in dispute and none of the progressions employed would be out of place in a Mozart sonata. And yet the theme's idiom is incomprehensible in late-classical terms. Its opening statement, bars 1–5, initiates an entirely ortho-dox ascending step progression from I to ii; V/ii anticipates a B-minor harmony, which duly arrives at the start of the response phrase in bar 6. Bar 7 finds B minor's Neapolitan, C major; by bar 8, this has been treated pivotally as IV of G, which is confirmed via its V_2^4 on the last beat of bar 7. The step progression, which at the start was mobilised to produce a I–ii progression, now returns us to A, V of which is attained in bars 9–10. Within ten bars, and without ever threatening A's stability, Brahms has moved through an interior region of G major which has no close diatonic connection to the tonic.

Example 14.7 Brahms, Violin Sonata in A major, Op. 100 (1886), i, bb. 1–10

The Coronation Scene from *Boris Godunov*'s Prologue contrasts with Brahms in almost every respect. The entire orchestral introduction, totalling some thirty-eight bars, consists of the alternation of two chords, quoted in Ex. 14.8. According to the notation, these chords are V_2^4 of G, or at least a D dominant seventh chord in its last inversion, and a German augmented sixth chord in C major, spelled with its third in the bass, that is, as an augmented fourth chord. With effort, we could hear this progression in C major, as the alternation of a secondary dominant and an augmented sixth; but nothing in the progression's context supports this reading. The harmonic oscillation robs both chords of their functional identities; after a while, any expectation that V_2^4/V should resolve to V disperses, as does the perception that the augmented fourth should resolve to V_4^6 in C.

Two factors cause the progression to cohere in the absence of a functional *milieu*. The first is the common-tone C, which sits beneath the entire passage as a pedal point. The second is the two chords' membership of the same octatonic collection; as Ex. 14.8 explains, although tritonally distant – their roots are D and A♭ – they both derive from octatonic Collection II, applying Pieter van den Toorn's terminology, and together comprise a six-note subset of the Collection.[20] In a sense, we do not hear this music as diatonically tonal at all, but as projecting a single sonority over time, which is a six-note octatonic surrogate. The music breaks out of this oscillation at bar 40 and becomes wholly triadic, but the sense of diatonic indeterminacy persists, because the progression (E major, C major, A major, E major) favours third relations over any attempt to confirm a tonic via V–I motion.

Taken together, the habits of these composers instantiate many of Romanticism's major harmonic innovations. Schubert merges major and minor modes; Schubert, Liszt, and Mussorgsky decontextualise common-practice sonorities; Liszt and Mussorgsky liberate dissonances (the augmented triad and the dominant seventh) from tonal functionality; Liszt and Mussorgsky seek alternative foundations for triadic harmony (octatonic and hexatonic); and Brahms exploits diatonic harmony's multivalence to create chromatic relationships. This new harmonic language is of course also aesthetic, feeding the nineteenth century's appetite for poetic and programmatic representation and its concern for sonority over functionality. Like Beethoven's motives and Field's textures, it instantiates a strikingly post-classical self-reflective musical consciousness, which in this case is a consciousness of tonal harmony as a system subject to historical change.

Example 14.8 Mussorgsky, Coronation Scene from *Boris Godunov* (1872), bb. 1–45

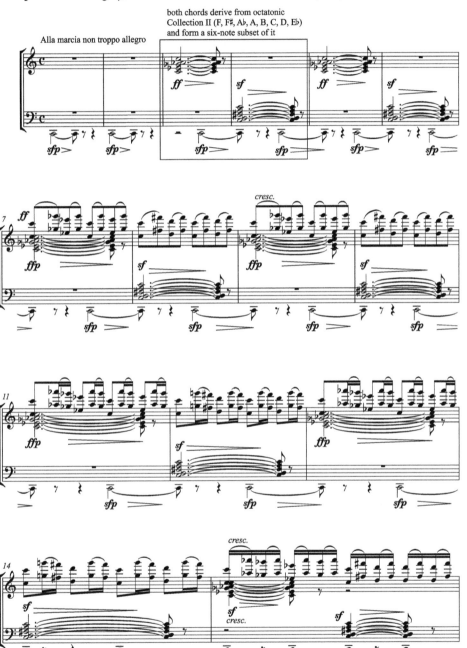

Example 14.8 (Cont.)

Form and Narrative

Romanticism's formal and tonal self-consciousness merges with its literary aspirations in the adaptation of classical forms and genres to poetic and narrative ends. This is especially clear in the development of programme music, most obviously the programme symphonies of Berlioz, which reimagine classical precedents in order to portray the progress of a central protagonist, and Liszt's symphonic poems, in which he professed to subordinate classical form to the conveyance of a poetic idea.[21] Literature's influence is, however, more pervasive than this: the idea that classical forms could function in analogy with literary or dramatic narratives is, for example, widespread in nineteenth-century symphonies, which nevertheless shun overt programmatic intent. The literary ambitions Schumann nursed for his instrumental forms are especially well documented; as John Daverio argues, the single factor relating all of his output, from the piano cycles of the 1830s to the *Faust* music and the 'Rhenish' Symphony in the 1850s, is 'the notion that music should be imbued with the same intellectual substance as literature'.[22] Daverio sees this mentality emerging in the *Papillons* of 1831, which rethink the piano cycle as a vehicle for expressing aspects of Jean-Paul Richter's novel *Flegeljahre*. As Daverio explains: '*Papillons* shows us a young composer in the process of construing music as literature.'[23]

In Schumann's Symphony No. 2, composed in 1845, poetic and narrative impulses jostle with the work's generic inheritance, resulting in a dense web of musical and extra-musical references. The finale has attracted particular attention in this respect, prompted by its chequered reception history and the difficulty of explaining its form in terms of any one classical paradigm. Anthony Newcomb sought to restore the Symphony's reputation by pointing out the finale's narrative implications. For Newcomb, attempts to describe its form in terms of any one model inevitably fail, because they overlook its narrative as well as formal hybridity: 'the mistake comes in wanting to claim that the finale is in any *single* form. It starts as one thing and becomes another, and this formal transformation is part of its meaning.'[24]

Newcomb contends that the movement's two halves, described in Table 14.2, align with two plot archetypes as well as two possible forms. At the start, the main theme wrong-foots the narrative expectations established by the first, second, and third movements, by moving straight from the tragedy voiced by the C-minor Adagio to an uncomplicated happy

Table 14.2 Schumann, Symphony No. 2, Finale, form (after Newcomb)

Bars:	1	46	63	84	105	118	191	272
Form: Rondo	Exposition				⇒Development			
	A	TR	B	RT	A¹	⇒pre-core (no C)?	core	'collapse'
Key:	(V) I	→	V/V	V/I	I	V/I →	v →	i
Cadence:	PAC		HC		V:PAC (reinterpreted HC)	prolongational closure (no PAC)	PAC	

Bars:	280	301	359	394	453	475	493
Form: Sonata (emergent)	chorale adumbrated (*An die ferne Geliebte*)		⇒RT	A (chorale)	Contrasting middle (first-movement recall)	A¹	Coda
Key:	♭III→V→	V/I →	V/I	I			
Cadence:		HC	V:HC MC effect	PAC	PAC	PAC	

ending or *lieto fine* in C major. Having tended increasingly towards the struggle–victory narrative currency of Beethoven's Symphony No. 5, Schumann seems at the finale's outset to have moved to an affirmation of structural security before any moment of overcoming has occurred:

> If the plot archetype is that of Beethoven's Fifth – suffering finding its way to strength and health – Schumann's beginning here may seem an unsatisfactory way of making the crucial move. To bring the strands so carefully together at the end of the third movement only to break them, it seems, with the sharp reversal that greets us at the beginning of the last is much less subtle even than Beethoven's obvious transition from ghostly lack of vigor at the end of his third movement to triumph at the beginning of the finale.[25]

In Newcomb's reading, Schumann's strategy is to undo the *lieto fine* as the movement progresses, replacing it with a grand summative finale in Beethoven's manner. The development sinks to an expressive low point in C minor, recalling the Adagio's main theme as well as its key, after which the finale's refrain and its associated rondo form are rejected in favour of a recapitulation and coda dwelling more substantially on the chorale introduced from bar 280, which simultaneously quotes the sixth song of Beethoven's *An die ferne Geliebte* and the first movement of Schumann's own *Fantasie*, Op. 17. As Newcomb argues: 'This thematic replacement is paralleled by a formal and generic one. Formally, in the process of the development, rondo elements retreat into the background, and weightier sonata elements ... replace them. Generically, the last movement as modest-sized *lieto fine* becomes the last movement as weighty, reflective summary.'[26]

Crucial to Newcomb's reading is the vital role narrativity plays in grasping Schumann's finale. It is not enough to hear a contribution to the symphony as a *musical* genre; we have also to hear it as a *quasi-literary* genre, which engages its generic history in part as a system of plot archetypes. Schumann assumes that his audience will hear the piece in this pseudo-novelistic or dramatic way: as the story of a protagonist, whose ultimate fate can be grasped as the outcome of a narrative. The quotation from *An die ferne Geliebte* is critical in this respect because it performs several tasks at once. By citing Beethoven, Schumann acknowledges his symphonic precedent; but the fact that his Beethovenian source is a song not a symphony connects the work to a lyric rather than a symphonic heritage, on which Newcomb does not dwell. It is telling in this respect that the Symphony's other major precedent is Schubert 'Great' C major, a piece in the revival of which Schumann played a critical role. Schubert's model is apparent across Schumann's Symphony, being evident in the tonality itself, the first movement's lengthy slow introduction, the focal role played by dance rhythms in the outer movements, and the presence of a minor-mode processional slow movement. The Beethovenian plot archetype to which Newcomb refers coexists with a Schubertian paradigm, the aesthetic of which is 'lyric-epic' rather than dramatic, as Dahlhaus says.[27] Schumann's Symphony, in other words, is both a dramatic Beethovenian symphony and a lyric-epic Schubertian symphony; it conflates these two precedents and attempts their synthesis. The quotation from *An die ferne Geliebte* makes this explicit: Beethoven, Schumann tells us, is a source for the lyric as well as the dramatic. A symphonic transformation of Beethoven's song is the agent of the Symphony's formal salvation. It is through the lyric's intervention that the premature *lieto fine* is undone.

The song reference allows Schumann to address another precedent, on which Newcomb is also mute. The Symphony No. 2 has an instrumental finale, but its vocal resonances inevitably raise the spectre of Beethoven's Symphony No. 9. Like Brahms's Symphony No. 1 thirty years later, Schumann alludes to a vocal Beethovenian source in order to legitimise a purely instrumental finale. The lyric, Schumann suggests, is the means by which the instrumental symphony can transcend Beethoven's transcendence of the instrumental in his Ninth. At a single stroke, Schumann fuses Beethovenian and Schubertian precedents in a strategy that also confirms the instrumental symphony's aesthetic legitimacy. This manoeuvre is confirmed in bars 544–51 in the coda, where, as Douglass Seaton notes, the falling thirds with which Beethoven twice sets 'alle Menschen' towards the end of the Ninth's finale are retrieved as purely instrumental material.[28]

Conclusions

Of course, Romanticism's heightened awareness of means and meaning is attended by broader historical discourses, which it is now commonplace to treat with scepticism, if not outright condemnation. Schoenberg's argument for the historical necessity of atonality is perhaps their most well-known outcome. Its problematic Hegelianism has long been acknowledged: Richard Taruskin dismisses it as a kind of myth-making, in which 'ontogeny' (the development of Schoenberg's musical style) is mistaken for 'phylogeny' (the development of Western music in general).[29] More controversial still in light of recent decolonial scholarship is the intersection of music and race in nineteenth-century discourse. Fétis's tonal theory was, for example, partnered with a conception of history which qualitatively differentiated musical practices according to 'innate' racial capacities. By this argument, European music emerged as superior, thanks to the superior cranial and mental capacities of 'Aryan' peoples.[30] The Romantic tendency to historicise and taxonomise music in a racially hierarchical way supplies an epistemic context in which accelerating experimentation with music's 'language' takes place. As Gary Tomlinson has stressed, this context is ultimately grounded in Europe's developing tendency to perceive its culture and polity as 'unique and superior', a self-perception that also underwrote its burgeoning colonialism.[31]

Respectively problematic and repugnant as these modes of thought now seem, the wholesale critique of Romantic music on decolonial grounds is hard to sustain, because its cultural diversity resists classification under a monolithic notion of imperialism. The Bonn into which Beethoven was born was an electorate of the Holy Roman Empire, a loose polity at best, which had dissolved by the time of Beethoven's death in 1827 in Vienna, itself the capital of a wholly European empire that had little in common with the colonial trading empires of Britain, France, and the Netherlands. The duress of French imperialism was a recurrent feature of Beethoven's adult life. The threat of French invasion hung over Bonn in 1792, when Beethoven left for Vienna, and the city was incorporated into the First French Empire in 1794; Vienna was twice captured by Napoleon while Beethoven lived there, in 1805 and 1809. Field, in contrast, was born in Dublin in 1782, during a period of increasing parliamentary independence from England, but left Ireland for London in 1793 and London for St Petersburg in 1802, remaining in Russia until his death in 1837, by which time the Acts of Union had quashed fledgling Irish independence. There is no binding concept of 'empire', which contains Beethoven and Field, notwithstanding a reception history that sees Beethoven especially as *the* world-historical Western European composer. And it is very unclear how Field's Anglo-Hibernian/Russian contexts and Beethoven's Hapsburg context could be merged with that of Fétis, whose *Traité* was published in 1844 during the period of the July Monarchy in France.

Even if Beethoven, Field, Schubert, Liszt, Brahms, Mussorgsky, and Schumann could all be ramified within an encompassing imperialism, an awareness of this context does not help us to decode the particularity of Romanticism's musical languages, because the connections between ideology and technique are associative, not causative: historical research will never demonstrate that Fétis's European supremacism or any comparable ideology motivates all Romantic harmonic, formal, or textural innovations beyond classical precedent. We can and should recognise the complicity of musical Romanticism's discourses with colonialism where it is manifest. But the sheer diversity of Romanticism's musical languages frustrates explanation in terms of any totalising disciplinary imperative.

Notes

1. Deryck Cooke, *The Language of Music* (Oxford: Clarendon Press 1989).
2. On autonomy and music's Romantic turn, see, e.g., Lydia Goehr, *The Imaginary Museum of Musical Works: An Essay in the Philosophy of Music* (Oxford: Clarendon Press, 1994), and more recently Mark Evan Bonds, *Absolute Music: The History of an Idea* (New York: Oxford University Press, 2014).
3. Carl Dahlhaus, *Nineteenth-Century Music*, trans. J. Bradford Robinson (Berkeley and Los Angeles: University of California Press, 1989), 8–15 and see also Benjamin Walton and Nicholas Mathew, *The Invention of Beethoven and Rossini* (Cambridge: Cambridge University Press, 2013).
4. On which subject, see Nicholas Temperley, 'John Field and the First Nocturne', *Music & Letters*, 3/4 (1975), 335–40 and specifically 337 on the generic variability of these pieces.
5. This crucial aspect of the genre is considered in Temperley, 'John Field and the First Nocturne', 337–8.
6. On which subject, see Jeffrey Kallberg, 'The Rhetoric of Genre: Chopin's Nocturne in G Minor', *19th-Century Music*, 11/3 (1988), 238–61.
7. Franz Liszt, 'Prämium-Beigabe zu John Field, Nocturnes', trans. Julius Schuberth in Franz Liszt (ed.), *John Field: 18 Nocturnes* (J. Schuberth: Leipzig, 1859), 1–8, at 5.
8. For example, in Carl Dahlhaus, *Ludwig van Beethoven: Approaches to His Music*, trans. Mary Whittall (Oxford: Clarendon Press, 1991), 171, and *Nineteenth-Century Music*, 10–15.
9. Janet Schmalfeldt, *In the Process of Becoming: Analytic and Philosophical Perspectives on Form in Early Nineteenth-Century Music* (New York: Oxford University Press, 2011), 23–58.
10. Schlegel's most famous expression of this is found in the *Athenaeumsfragment* 116, which advocates a Romantic poetry that 'fuses poetry and prose, inspiration and criticism, the poetry of art and the poetry of nature; and makes poetry lively and sociable, and life and society poetical'; see Friedrich Schlegel,

Philosophical Fragments, trans. Peter Firchow (Minneapolis: University of Minnesota Press, 1991). I also have in mind Georg Wilhelm Friedrich Hegel, *Phenomenology of Spirit*, trans. A. V. Miller (Oxford: Oxford University Press, 1977).

11. See, e.g., Carissa Reddick, 'Becoming at a Deeper Level: Divisional Overlap in Sonata Forms from the Late Nineteenth Century', *Music Theory Online*, 16/2 (2010), 1–5; Steven Vande Moortele, 'In Search of Romantic Form', *Music Analysis*, 32 (2013), 404–31; Nathan Martin and Steven Vande Moortele, 'Formal Functions and Retrospective Reinterpretation in the First Movement of Schubert's String Quintet', *Music Analysis*, 33 (2014), 130–55; and Julian Horton, *Brahms's Piano Concerto No. 2, Op. 83: Analytical and Contextual Studies* (Leuven: Peeters, 2017).

12. William E. Caplin, *Classical Form: A Theory of Formal Functions for the Instrumental Music of Haydn, Mozart, and Beethoven* (Oxford: Oxford University Press, 1998), 75–81 and 225.

13. On the use of poetic forms in Schubert's instrumental music, see Su-Yin Mak, 'Schubert's Sonata Forms and the Poetics of the Lyric', *Journal of Musicology*, 23/2 (2006), 263–306.

14. Again, there are precedents for thinking about piano resonance in Schubert scholarship; see Robert Hatten, 'Schubert the Progressive: The Role of Resonance and Gesture in the Piano Sonata in A, D. 959', *Intégral*, 7 (1993), 38–81.

15. Alexandre Choron, *Dictionnaire historique des musiciens* (Paris: Falade and Lenormant, 1810), xi–xcii; Monteverdi's practice is considered at xxxix.

16. François-Joseph Fétis, *Traité complet de la théorie et de la pratique de l'harmonie* (Paris: Schlesinger, 1844), trans. Peter Landey as *Complete Treatise on the Theory and Practice of Harmony* (Hillsdale, NY: Pendragon Press, 2008). For the progression of tonal orders, see the latter, 149–94. Fétis describes the 'anéantissement de l'unité tonale' as the defining characteristic of nineteenth-century omnitonic tonality: see *Traité complet*, 183, and *Complete Treatise*, 180, where Landey translates 'anéantissement' as 'annihilation'.

17. William E. Caplin, 'Beyond the Classical Cadence', *Music Theory Spectrum*, 40/1 (2018), 1–26, at 14–16.

18. Robert Morgan calls this practice 'dissonant prolongation'; see 'Dissonant Prolongation: Theoretical and Compositional Precedents', *Journal of Music Theory*, 20/1 (1976), 49–91.

19. Carl Dahlhaus, *Between Romanticism and Modernism: Four Studies in the Music of the Later Nineteenth Century*, trans. Mary Whittall (Berkeley and Los Angeles: University of California Press, 1980), 65.

20. Pieter van den Toorn, *The Music of Igor Stravinsky* (New Haven: Yale University Press, 1997).

21. On the genesis of Liszt's symphonic poems, see Joanne Cormac, *Liszt and the Symphonic Poem* (Cambridge: Cambridge University Press, 2017).

22. John Daverio, *Robert Schumann: Herald of a New Poetic Age* (Oxford: Oxford University Press, 1997), 19.

23. Ibid., 79.

24. Anthony Newcomb, 'Once More "Between Absolute and Programme Music": Schumann's Second Symphony', *19th-Century Music*, 7/3 (1984), 233–50, at 240. On the form of this movement, see also Lauri Suurpää, 'Endings without Resolution: The Slow Movement and Finale of Schumann's Second Symphony', in David Beach and Su-Yin Mak (eds.), *Explorations in Schenkerian Analysis* (Rochester, NY: University of Rochester Press, 2016), 123–41.

25. Newcomb, 'Once More "Between Absolute and Programme Music"', 243.

26. Ibid., 245–6.

27. Carl Dahlhaus, 'Sonata Form in Schubert: The First Movement of the G Major String Quartet Op. 161 (D. 887)', trans. Thilo Reinhard, in Walter Frisch (ed.), *Schubert: Critical and Analytical Studies* (Lincoln, NE: University of Nebraska Press, 1986), 1–12.

28. Douglass Seaton, 'Back from Bach: Schumann's Symphony No. 2 in C Major', in Gregory G. Butler, George B. Stauffer, and Mary Dalton Greer (eds.), *About Bach* (Chicago: University of Illinois Press, 2008), 191–206, at 197–8.

29. Richard Taruskin, *The Early Twentieth Century, volume 5 of The Oxford History of Western Music* (New York: Oxford University Press, 2005), 358–61.

30. François-Joseph Fétis, 'Préface' (26 August 1868), in *Histoire générale de la musique depuis les temps les plus anciens jusqu'à nos jours* (Paris: Fermin Didot Frères, 1869), i–viii, at i, trans. in Jann Pasler, 'The Utility of Musical Instruments in the Racial and Colonial Agendas of Late-Nineteenth-Century France', *Journal of the Royal Musical Association*, 129/1 (2004), 24–76, at 26–7. See also Nina Sun Eidsheim, 'Race and the Aesthetics of Vocal Timbre', in Olivia Bloechl, Melanie Lowe, and Jeffrey Kallberg (eds.), *Rethinking Difference in Music Scholarship* (Cambridge: Cambridge University Press, 2015), 338–65.

31. Gary Tomlinson, 'Musicology, Anthropology, History', in Martin Clayton, Trevor Herbert, and Richard Middleton (eds.), *The Cultural Study of Music: A Critical Introduction* (London: Routledge, 2003), 31–44, at 40.

Further Reading

Caplin, William E. 'Beyond the Classical Cadence', *Music Theory Spectrum*, 40/1 (2018), 1–26.

Dahlhaus, Carl. *Between Romanticism and Modernism: Four Studies in the Music of the Later Nineteenth Century*, trans. Mary Whittall (Berkeley and Los Angeles: University of California Press, 1980).

Nineteenth-Century Music, trans. J. Bradford Robinson (Berkeley and Los Angeles: University of California Press, 1989).

Daverio, John. *Robert Schumann: Herald of a New Poetic Age* (Oxford: Oxford University Press, 1997).

Horton, Julian. *Brahms's Piano Concerto No. 2, Op. 83: Analytical and Contextual Studies* (Leuven: Peeters, 2017).

Newcomb, Anthony. 'Once More "Between Absolute and Programme Music": Schumann's Second Symphony', *19th-Century Music*, 7/3 (1984), 233–50.

Schmalfeldt, Janet. *In the Process of Becoming: Analytic and Philosophical Perspectives on Form in Early Nineteenth-Century Music* (New York: Oxford University Press, 2011).

Walton, Benjamin and Mathew, Nicholas. *The Invention of Beethoven and Rossini* (Cambridge: Cambridge University Press, 2013).

15 | Romantic Forms

STEVEN VANDE MOORTELE

'On the whole', Robert Schumann wrote in a review of a number of newly published sonatas in 1839, 'it would seem that [classical] form has run its life course, and this is surely in the order of things, for we should not repeat the same things for centuries but rather have an open mind to what is new'.[1] Schumann, the arch-Romantic, is presenting here *in nuce* his view of what a responsible composer should do: something 'new'. In doing so, he pitches the Romantic (the 'new') against the classical ('the same things' that should not be repeated forever), casting the Romantic as non-classical, perhaps even as anti-classical. This familiar rhetoric is common amongst Schumann's contemporaries; about a decade and a half later, for instance, Liszt would similarly insist on 'new forms for new ideas, new skins for new wine'.[2]

This anti-classical rhetoric, however, contrasts starkly with what actually happens in Romantic music, including Schumann's and (at least until 1860) even Liszt's. Much of what composers wrote between, say, 1820 and 1890 shows a surprisingly high level of continuity with the formal language of earlier generations. One wouldn't want to go so far as to claim, with the mid-twentieth-century German musicologist Friedrich Blume, that classicism and Romanticism are 'no[t] discernible styles', but 'just two aspects of one and the same musical phenomenon'; when taken literally this verges on the nonsensical – there obviously *are* stylistic differences between classical and Romantic music.[3] Yet when Blume later elaborates that 'genres and forms are common to both and subject only to amplification, specialization, and modification', then that opens a much more nuanced perspective.[4] The picture of Romantic music that comes into focus here is of something that is not anti-classical, but post-classical: rather than abandoning what existed before, it engages in a creative dialogue with the classical tradition, especially the one often associated with the works of Haydn, Mozart, and Beethoven.

When it comes specifically to musical form, classical formal types by and large survive throughout the nineteenth century. This applies to both the large and the smaller scale – from the form of an entire movement to the internal organisation of one of its themes. In this sense, the musical forms of Romanticism are often the same as those of classicism: sonata form or sonata-rondo, small ternary or sentence, and so on. Those same forms are, however, treated differently in the nineteenth century than they were in the late eighteenth century – and, in fact, treated differently at different times and places in the nineteenth century as well. Indeed, although Romantic form obviously is a nineteenth-century phenomenon, it would be wrong to equate it with nineteenth-century form as such. For the purposes of this chapter, Romantic form is understood narrowly as a set of practices that is especially prevalent in the works of a group of composers working in Germany between 1825 and 1850, commonly termed the 'Romantic Generation', and that survives in the music of selected composers until the final years of the century. Formal practices at other times and places in the nineteenth century (for instance in *primo ottocento* Italian opera) are often very different from the ones described here. Using examples drawn from vocal and instrumental works by five different composers (in chronological order: Felix Mendelssohn, Robert Schumann, Richard Wagner, Clara Schumann, and Antonín Dvořák), this chapter explores some of these typically Romantic formal tendencies as well as the ways they relate to theoretical models that have been developed for classical music. The chapter is organised in two sections. The first addresses matters of formal syntax, that is, the construction and interrelation of musical phrases, under the rubric 'Proliferation, Expansion, and Form as Process'; the second ('Fragments and Cycles') explores issues of formal incompleteness as well as connections that go beyond the single-movement level.

Proliferation, Expansion, and Form as Process

When looking closely at Romantic music, the analyst with a working knowledge of recent theories of classical form will find that many of its building blocks are similar to those in the music of earlier composers.[5] This is true for all levels of musical form. For two- or four-bar units no less than for passages of several dozen bars long, it is often immediately obvious what their formal function is – their role in the larger form, for example the basic idea of a sentence, or the subordinate theme of a sonata-form exposition. The way in which different levels of form are related in Romantic music, however, can be quite different from what one finds in classical form.

One way this manifests itself is in more complex thematic structures. An instructive (even though perhaps unexpected) example of a Romantic theme comes from the fast portion of the Dutchman's aria 'Die Frist ist um' from Wagner's 'Romantic opera' *Der fliegende Holländer* (1840–1, see Ex. 15.1). The theme begins with an eight-bar sentence that could hardly be

Example 15.1 Wagner, 'Die Frist ist um', from *Der fliegende Holländer*, Act 1 (1840–1), bb. 1–34

Example 15.1 (Cont.)

Example 15.1 (Cont.)

clearer in its internal organisation (even though its tonal organisation may seem quite outlandish): a two-bar basic idea and its repetition, together prolonging tonic harmony, followed by four bars of continuation (with contrasting material and a faster harmonic rhythm) that lead to a perfect authentic cadence (PAC) in the dominant minor. In the next eight bars, this sentence is restated, now with its continuation modified so that it modulates to flat-V. In classical form, the only common situation in which a modulating sentence is combined with its parallel restatement is in a compound period, where the former, leading to a weaker cadence (usually in or on the dominant), functions as an antecedent and the latter, leading to a stronger cadence, as a consequent. But such a reading is difficult to support here: the cadence in the dominant at b. 16 is in the minor mode, thus resisting automatic reinterpretation as a half cadence (HC) in the tonic, and the consequent, rather than returning to the home key, moves even farther away from it. Instead, the two parallel sentences function as the presentation of a much larger overarching sentence. The following sixteen bars indeed take the form of a continuation, starting with a repeated four-bar fragment and closing with a four-bar cadential unit (note the cadential progression V^6/iv – iv – V^7 – i) that is also repeated and leads to a PAC in the supertonic. Echoing the internal formal structure of each of the two halves of the presentation, this continuation can itself be heard as loosely sentential, with its first eight bars taking the place of a presentation and the next eight as a double continuation.

What this analysis shows is that there is little in this theme at the two-, four-, or eight-bar level that we cannot accurately describe with a concept familiar from classical form, and that those concepts are readily applicable with only minimal modifications. The larger constellations in which those building blocks appear, however, are different. They illustrate a mode of formal organisation characteristic of much Romantic music and for which Julian Horton has coined the term 'proliferation'.[6] Units of the length of a simple classical theme (i.e., of approximately eight bars in length) are nested within relatively long and hierarchically complex thematic units. In Wagner's theme, the eight-bar sentence appears at the lowest level of formal organisation. It is not the whole theme (as in a simple sentence); it is not at the level of the antecedent and consequent (as in a compound period); it is at the level of the basic idea – that is, what in classical practice is the two-bar level. This degree of hierarchical complexity is virtually non-existent in classical music. And the form-functional proliferation that leads to the hierarchical complexity is itself a form of expansion: a technique used to generate larger structures. In one respect Wagner's theme is somewhat atypical. In spite of its expansion and hierarchical complexity, it maintains a classical balance in its internal proportions, so that there is something architectonic about it. On the basis of its first building block (the opening eight-bar sentence), one can accurately predict the length of the entire thirty-two-bar theme, just like in a textbook classical sentence.

More often than not, expansion in Romantic music distorts a theme's internal proportions. An example of what this can look like is the finale of Mendelssohn's Piano Sonata in E major, Op. 6 (1826). This movement juxtaposes classical and Romantic modes of formal organisation with almost didactic clarity. The exposition stands out for its formal transparency. Both its interthematic layout and its cadential structure could hardly be more straightforward: main theme in bb. 1–16 concluding with a PAC in the tonic; modulating transition (bb. 16–38) leading to an HC in v; subordinate theme group in bb. 39–69 ending with a PAC in V, codetta turning into a link to the development (the exposition is not repeated) in bb. 69–76. The recapitulation, by contrast, is much more formally adventurous. Rather than by and large replicating the exposition's modular succession, it thoroughly recomposes it. This recomposition itself as well as the specific techniques Mendelssohn uses are highly characteristic of Romantic form.

Nowhere is this clearer than in the recapitulation's subordinate theme. In the exposition, the subordinate theme group consisted of two distinct thematic units: a highly regular compound period concluding with a PAC (bb. 39–54) and its repetition, structurally identical but with the right and left hands exchanging roles (bb. 55–69). In the recapitulation, by contrast, there is only a single, but hugely expanded, subordinate theme. At b. 154, the compound period from bb. 39–54 returns, with one crucial difference: in the very last instant, the PAC that concluded the theme in the exposition is evaded (note the telltale V_2^4–I^6 in bb. 169–70). This evaded cadence (EC) launches a process of expansion that postpones the eventual arrival of the PAC by no fewer than seventy-three bars all the way to b. 243.

The expansion happens in several steps, shown in Ex. 15.2. The EC at b. 170 is immediately followed by two renewed approaches to the cadence.

Example 15.2 Mendelssohn, Piano Sonata in E major, Op. 6 (1826), iv, cadential approaches between bb. 167 and 243

The first (bb. 170–3) is swift but abandons the cadential progression before ever reaching the required dominant in root position. The second (bb. 174–86) proceeds in broader strokes and does lead to a PAC. As if to reinforce the arrival of the cadence, the progression leading up to it is immediately repeated. Yet the repetition instead undoes the closure that was previously achieved when the expected PAC is evaded at b. 190. The next attempt at a cadence (now using material derived from the main theme) does not lead to a PAC either, but to a deceptive cadence (DC, b. 199). The DC is elided with a full-on return of the main theme that culminates in a very long and promising expanded dominant at b. 206. Instead of resolving to the tonic, however, the dominant goes into over-drive (note the change in time signature and tempo at b. 217) before losing steam. Only the unexpected return of the main theme from the first movement leads to a successful cadence, first an imperfect authentic cadence (IAC; b. 232), then a PAC (b. 243).[7]

The cadence at b. 243 is the end point of the thematic process that started at b. 155. The subordinate theme in Mendelssohn's recapitulation is thus considerably longer than expected – both in comparison to the original subordinate theme from the exposition, and measured against the dimensions the beginning of the subordinate theme in the recapitulation suggest. In contrast to Wagner's theme, it is impossible to predict how long it will be; rather than architectonic, the expansion in Mendelssohn's theme presents itself as a process that unfolds over time. Step by step, the theme grows longer, before the listener's ear, as it were.

It would be too simple to call all of the music between bb. 155 and 243 a subordinate theme, however. Especially the change in tempo and metre, as well as the return of material from the first movement, are distinct features of a coda. Yet the structural position of a coda is, by definition, post-cadential. It comes 'after the end', when the recapitulation, and with it the sonata form as a whole, has achieved structural closure by means of a PAC in the home key at the end of the subordinate theme. What is remarkable about the end of Mendelssohn's movement is that the coda begins before the subordinate theme has ended; both functions, which normally appear consecutively, temporarily overlap. The technical term for this is 'formal fusion': subordinate theme and coda are fused together within one formal unit, without it being possible to determine where one ends and the other begins. A listener attuned to formal functions may perceive this fusion as a gradual transformation from one function to another, a 'process of becoming', to use the phrase coined by Janet Schmalfeldt.[8]

Proliferation, expansion, and processual form remain important characteristics of Romantic form throughout the nineteenth century. The
procedures used in the subordinate theme in the first-movement recapitulation of Dvořák's Piano Quintet in A major, Op. 81 (1888) are strikingly
similar to the ones Mendelssohn used more than half a century before. The
subordinate theme begins with a large-scale antecedent in bb. 335–52 (this
unit is also another example of proliferation, since it consists of two smaller
parallel phrases that each have the structure of an antecedent). At b. 353,
the large-scale antecedent is answered by a parallel consequent that initially
seems to be compressed, heading for a PAC already at b. 356. The anticipated cadence is, however, evaded, and only materialises thirty-five bars
later, at b. 391 (the PAC in the piano is covered by the first violin). Yet being
in the submediant rather than the tonic, the cadence at b. 391 cannot be the
structural end point of the recapitulation. A PAC in the home key arrives
only at b. 422, well into coda territory. A process that would normally take
place within the recapitulation (the attainment of structural closure) thus
spills over into the coda. Like in the Mendelssohn movement, the recapitulation and coda are fused.

A difference between Mendelssohn's and Dvořák's movements is that in
the latter, expansion is not limited to the recapitulation, but plays a role in the
exposition as well, most notably in the main theme. After a two-bar introductory vamp, the exposition begins with a broadly proportioned periodic
hybrid (compound basic idea+continuation) leading to a PAC at b. 17. The
sudden changes in thematic-motivic content, dynamics, mode, and texture
at the moment the cadence arrives all suggest the beginning of a transition.
This impression is confirmed when an HC in the dominant arrives at b. 37,
followed by a standing on the dominant and a medial caesura; it is not hard
to imagine how the unison caesura-fill in the piano right hand could have
served as an extended pickup to a subordinate theme in the dominant
around b. 47. But this is not what happens. Instead the music makes a volte-
face, turning the tonic of the dominant back into the dominant of the tonic
and leading, via a dreamy transformation of the opening theme, to a full
restatement of bb. 3–17. Like the one at b. 17, the PAC at b. 75 is elided with
a transition (again there is a change of mode, texture, thematic-motivic
content, and, to an extent, dynamics) that first leads to an HC in the tonic
and then, in the last instant, to an HC in iii, the key in which the subordinate
theme finally enters at b. 93.

The first ninety-two bars of Dvořák's exposition are an example of the
specific type of processual form that Schmalfeldt calls 'retrospective
reinterpretation': the listener who initially interpreted the unit starting at

b. 17 as a transition is forced to reinterpret that same unit as part of a complex main theme when it is not followed by a subordinate theme but by a return of the opening melody. Like in the subordinate theme, the scope of the form is enlarged before the listener's ears, in real time. The initial impression is that of a modestly sized main theme, and a 'sonata-form clock' – the speed at which we move through the different way stations along the sonata-form trajectory – that is ticking fast.[9] The reinterpretation of the seeming transition turns the clock back, as it were: we are not yet where we thought we were, and the main theme group is much larger than we initially thought it was. The expansion thus emphatically takes the form of a process that plays out over time, and that is difficult to capture in a schematic overview (this is true of much music, but it has been argued that it is especially characteristic of Romantic form).

Fragments and Cycles

The most remarkable feature of Clara Schumann's song 'Die stille Lotosblume' (the final of the *Sechs Lieder*, Op. 13, from 1844, see Ex. 15.3) is its ending: a dominant seventh chord with a double $\hat{9}$–$\hat{8}$ and $\hat{4}$–$\hat{3}$ appoggiatura.[10] Its second most remarkable feature is its beginning: the same dominant seventh chord, the same appoggiatura. An unusual emphasis on dominant harmony permeates the song. The opening of its vocal portion takes the form of the antecedent of a compound period: bb. 3–4 function as a basic idea that groups together with a contrasting idea into a simple (four-bar) antecedent, which is in turn complemented by a four-bar continuation phrase to form a higher-level eight-bar antecedent ending with an HC at b. 10. This eight-bar antecedent sets the first textual strophe, and when the second strophe is set to a near-identical repetition of the same antecedent (the HC at b. 18 now followed by a brief post-cadential expansion in the piano), the song starts to unfold as a simple strophic form. This impression is initially confirmed at the beginning of the third strophe, until an inspired move into the region of flat-III at b. 26 completely abandons the strophic plan. Yet even though the song's second half is more freely organised than the first, the cadential behaviour remains constant. In the second half, too, each unit ends with an HC: the move to the flat side leads to an HC in flat-III at b. 33, and when the music moves back to the home key, it again leads to two HCs, first in the piano at b. 35, then in the voice at b. 43 (replicating the cadential formula from the original compound antecedent).

Example 15.3 Clara Schumann, 'Die stille Lotosblume', from *Sechs Lieder*, Op. 13 No. 6 (1844), bb. 1–10, 42–7

'Die stille Lotosblume' thus remains curiously incomplete, literally open-ended. In the same way that the dominant at the end never resolves to a tonic chord, the entire song consists of a series of antecedents that are never answered by a parallel consequent – or even a concluding authentic cadence. The form, moreover, is circular: its end is like its beginning. Applied to this song, the terms 'beginning' and 'end' are in fact already problematic. Theories of musical form consider a complete formal utterance at any level (a theme, section, or movement) to consists of a beginning, a middle, and an end.[11] Each of those temporal functions is expressed by a specific combination of formal and harmonic characteristics. At the level of the theme, for instance, a beginning takes the form of a basic idea with tonic-prolongation, whereas an ending takes the form of a cadential progression. In that sense, the song's first two bars are not a beginning, and its last two not an ending. And whereas one could argue that the song's real beginning is at b. 3, with the first two bars as an introductory or anacrustic gesture, the sense of openness at the end is irreducible: an HC is a possible ending function at the intermediate level, but not at the end of a complete form.

Forms that, like 'Die stille Lotosblume', are left intentionally incomplete are called fragments, and they constitute one of the most characteristic ways in which Romantic composers treated form differently than did their classical counterparts.[12] In addition to incompleteness, the term fragment also implies a larger whole to which the fragment belongs (and of which it is, literally, a fragment). The openness of a fragment can be a way to create connections between different songs, pieces, or movements that belong together. Because of its inherent incompleteness, the fragment makes sense only in the context of the larger whole. When that is the case, the level of coherence between those songs, pieces, and movements transcends that of the mere 'collection': they form a cycle.

In 'Die stille Lotosblume', the relation between the fragment and the whole of the song set it concludes is not so clear. To be sure, the song immediately before ends on a tonic chord in the same key, to which the dominant at the beginning orients itself; in context, the opening bars sound significantly less puzzling than in isolation. But since 'Die schöne Lotosblume' comes at the end of the set, the dominant in the final bars does not obviously establish a connection to a larger whole – or, if it does, then it would be to a whole that is abstract or implied rather than concrete.[13]

In what is perhaps the most cited example of a Romantic fragment in music, 'Im wunderschönen Monat Mai' (composed in 1840 by Clara Schumann's husband Robert as the opening of the song cycle *Dichterliebe*, Op. 48), the formal openness more obviously serves to connect the individual song to the cycle as a whole. Like 'Die stille Lotosblume', 'Im wunderschönen Monat Mai' ends on a dominant seventh chord, and as in that song, the last two bars are identical to the first (see Ex. 15.4). And here as well, those first two bars are, form-functionally speaking, not

Example 15.4 Robert Schumann, 'Im wunderschönen Monat Mai', from *Dichterliebe*, Op. 48 No. 1 (1840), bb. 1–13, 23–5

a beginning. Moreover, they cannot be explained as an introduction either. Considered by themselves, they constitute a half-cadential gesture (iv^6–V^7 in F sharp minor), and therefore an (intermediary) ending function, that is immediately repeated. As the music theorist Nathan Martin has shown, that apparent cadential function is recast as a continuation when in bb. 5–6 the piano produces a stronger cadential gesture, a PAC in A major, using the same motivic material.[14] At the same time, b. 5 clearly stands out as a new beginning, if only because this is where the voice enters. From this perspective, bb. 5–6 form a basic idea that is immediately repeated and then gives way to a continuation, thus suggesting a sentence. Yet at the end of the continuation that sentence slips back into F sharp minor and into a return of the opening four bars, which now effectively function as the half-cadential conclusion to the theme. This entire process then starts over, so that the song is circular on two levels: the individual strophe and the song as a whole.

The song's formal openness is compounded by a fundamental (and much commented upon) ambiguity between the keys of F sharp minor and A major – the key on the dominant of which the song begins and ends, and the key of the song's only (but, as we saw, qualified) PACs. The combination of formal openness and tonal ambiguity contributes to the almost seamless connection between the cycle's opening song and the next, 'Aus meinen Thränen'. On the surface of it, the second song is in A major. Upon closer inspection, however, its opening wavers between the two keys that were at play in the first song: in isolation, it is impossible to tell whether the first three harmonies prolong A or F sharp. And coming from the dominant at the end of the first song, the song's beginning arguably sounds like (or at least can be heard in) F sharp minor; only at the end of b. 1 does it settle in A major.

Tonal instability does not end here: at b. 12, the second song seems temporarily to lapse back into F sharp, with the HC at the end of the contrasting B section reconnecting with the cadence at the end of the first song. And while the beginning of the A′ section (bb. 13–17) returns to A major, the tonic appears as V^7 of IV. Tonicisations of vi and IV are, of course, hardly unheard of. Yet here they gain additional significance because of their connection to the surrounding songs: the HC in F sharp at b. 12 reconnects with the cadence at the end of the first song, and the tonicisation of IV in the final section in turn looks forward to the third song ('Die Rose, die Lilie'), which is in D major. Even though 'Aus meinen Thränen' is formally closed – much more so, at least, than the previous two examples – it can still be considered a fragment, not only because it is so short that a performance in isolation would make little sense, but also because its internal details are intimately connected to the larger whole of which it is part.

One characteristic the songs discussed so far have in common is their small scale. They are, in addition to fragments, also miniatures: apart from the missing beginnings and endings, their basic formal structure is relatively classical but would, within the classical style, be part of a larger form rather than a complete piece or movement. This is particularly clear in 'Aus meinen Thränen': the song is easily recognised as quatrain (or AABA') form, not fundamentally different from the way in which that theme type would have appeared in a late eighteenth or early nineteenth-century composition except for a few harmonic details. But whereas there, it would have acted as a theme within larger form, here it forms the complete song.

While such miniatures (usually grouped into collections or cycles) are indeed characteristic of Romantic music, and while many fragments are indeed miniatures, it would be wrong to conclude that fragments cannot have larger proportions. Schumann's Fourth Symphony (originally composed in 1841, here discussed in its 1851 revision) is a good counterexample. This piece is often cited as an example of a 'cyclic' symphony in the sense that a high number of thematic ideas and their variants recur across its various movements.[15] This unusually dense thematic cyclicism, however, works in tandem with an equally uncommon degree of formal cyclicism. The first three of the symphony's four movements are all fragments, remaining formally incomplete and thus creating an openness towards the larger whole of which they are part.

The most obviously open-ended movement is the third, which begins in D minor and ends in B flat major. Initially the movement unfolds as a standard scherzo form, with a scherzo proper (bb. 1–64), a trio (bb. 65–112), and a complete recapitulation of the scherzo (bb. 113–76). When the trio begins a second time at b. 177, this increases the dimensions of the form: instead of a ternary format, we now seem to be dealing with a five-part scherzo, in which the second appearance of the trio would normally be followed by a final recapitulation of the scherzo proper. Yet this concluding scherzo section never materialises, so that the movement as a whole remains a fragment that is connected by an eight-bar link to the slow introduction to the finale.

The slow second movement (Romanze) is a large ternary form. Its A section (bb. 1–26), itself in the form of a small ternary (a bb. 3–12, b bb. 13–22, a' bb. 23–6) is in the tonic A minor, its contrasting B section (bb. 27–42) in the subdominant major. When the A' section arrives in bb. 43–53, it is curtailed, preserving only the *a* section of the original small ternary. This in itself is hardly unusual: compressed reprises in ternary forms are common both in the eighteenth and the nineteenth centuries. What is noteworthy is that the A' section is transposed up a perfect fourth, and thus starts in D minor. The result of this subdominant reprise is that the same modulation that in the original *a* section led away from the tonic (i.e., from A minor to E minor/major) now leads back to it (from D minor to A minor/major). From the local perspective of the slow movement, the form may therefore appear to be closed. Within the broader context of the symphony as a whole, however, the final harmony of the Romanze functions not as a concluding tonic, but as the dominant of the D minor in which the next movement begins.

The most complex fragment is the first movement. It comprises a slow introduction (bb. 1–29), a compact exposition (bb. 29–86), and a comparatively sprawling development (bb. 87–296), the end of which is signalled by the pedal point on the dominant A in bb. 285ff. The return of the tonic major that follows, however, is not accompanied by anything that comes even close to a formal recapitulation, and what little recapitulation there is is not the recapitulation that goes with the exposition from earlier in the movement. Phrase-structurally, bb. 297–337 are most reminiscent of the final stages of a subordinate theme, leading to the cadence that concludes the recapitulation that is, as such, largely missing; and the thematic material in these bars is derived not from the exposition, but from the second of two new themes that were first presented in the development (bb. 121ff. and 147ff., respectively). Only at b. 337 does motivic material from the exposition's main theme return, now clearly with post-cadential function (i.e., as a codetta or coda). The formal openness of the first movement is answered in the finale, the exposition of which begins, paradoxically, with a recapitulatory gesture: its main theme combines a close variant of the first new theme from the first movement's development (the one from bb. 121ff.) with the head motive of the first movement's main theme, thus to a certain extent providing compensation for the missing recapitulation of these themes in the first movement.

***

As all these examples illustrate, Romantic form does not exist in a universe separate from classical form, but rather maintains a state of perpetual dialogue with it. Forms both small and large are, to repeat Blume's words cited above, 'common to both' even if they are 'subject . . . to amplification, specialization, and modification'.[16] From the perspective of the music analyst, there are obvious advantages to this: if duly modified, established theories of classical form – theories that are at least somewhat familiar to most undergraduate music students – can go a long way in explaining what happens in this music. But there is also a drawback. Because theories of classical form are so readily applicable to Romantic music, the risk is to treat them as a standard – a norm – to which everything that is different (and in Romantic music, a lot is different) relates as a deviation. Yet in the context of Romantic music, that which by classical standards would be a deviation can be the norm, rather than the exception, and should be interpreted accordingly. Finding a balance between the continuing presence of classical formal types and the self-sufficiency of the Romantic style is perhaps the greatest challenge to the analyst of Romantic form.

Notes

1. Robert Schumann, 'Sonaten für das Klavier', *Neue Zeitschrift für Musik*, 10 (1839): 134–5, 137–8; this quotation 134.
2. Franz Liszt, 'Berlioz und seine Harold-Symphonie' [1855], in Lina Ramann (ed.), *Aus den Annalen des Fortschritts. Konzert- und kammermusikalische Essays*, vol. 4 of *Gesammelte Schriften von Franz Liszt* (Leipzig: Breitkopf und Härtel, 1882, repr. Hildesheim and New York: Olms, 1978), 3–102, at 60.
3. Friedrich Blume, *Classic and Romantic Music: A Comprehensive Survey*, trans. M. D. Herter Norton (New York: Norton, 1970), vii–viii.
4. Ibid., 146.
5. The standard modern theories of classical form are William E. Caplin, *Classical Form: A Theory of Formal Functions for the Music of Haydn, Mozart, and Beethoven* (Oxford: Oxford University Press, 1998) and James Hepokoski and Warren Darcy, *Elements of Sonata Theory: Norms, Types, and Deformations in the Late-Eighteenth-Century Sonata* (New York: Oxford University Press, 2006). Most technical terms used in this chapter are drawn from these two books.
6. See Julian Horton, 'Formal Type and Formal Function in the Postclassical Piano Concerto', in Steven Vande Moortele, Julie Pedneault-Deslauriers, and Nathan John Martin (eds.), *Formal Functions in Perspective: Studies in Musical Form from Haydn to Adorno* (Rochester, NY: University of Rochester Press, 2015), 85–103.
7. On the inter-movement connections in Mendelssohn's sonata, see Benedict Taylor, *Mendelssohn, Time and Memory: The Romantic Conception of Cyclic Form* (Cambridge: Cambridge University Press, 2011), 103–25.

8. Janet Schmalfeldt, *In the Process of Becoming: Analytic and Philosophical Perspectives on Form in Early Nineteenth-Century Music* (New York: Oxford University Press, 2011). For a further development of Schmalfeldt's theory, see Nathan John Martin and Steven Vande Moortele, 'Formal Functions and Retrospective Reinterpretation in the First Movement of Schubert's String Quintet, D. 956', *Music Analysis*, 33 (2014), 130–55.

9. On the sonata-form clock, see William E. Caplin and Nathan John Martin, 'The Continuous Exposition and the Concept of Subordinate Theme', *Music Analysis*, 35 (2016), 4–43.

10. Compare the analysis in Schmalfeldt, *In the Process of Becoming*, 241–4.

11. See, e.g., William E. Caplin, 'What Are Formal Functions?', in William E. Caplin, James Hepokoski, and James Webster, *Musical Form, Forms & Formenlehre: Three Methodological Reflections*, ed. Pieter Bergé (Leuven: Leuven University Press, 2009), 21–40.

12. On Romantic fragments, see Charles Rosen, 'Fragments', in *The Romantic Generation* (Cambridge, MA: Harvard University Press, 1995), 41–115; Beate Perrey, *Schumann's Dichterliebe and Early Romantic Poetics: Fragmentation of Desire* (Cambridge: Cambridge University Press, 2002); Nathan John Martin, 'Schumann's Fragment', *Indiana Theory Review*, 28 (2010), 85–109.

13. It is worth noting that in nineteenth-century performance practice, stand-alone performances of songs were the norm, even when they were published as part of a larger set.

14. Martin, 'Schumann's Fragment', 104–5.

15. Compare Julian Horton, 'Cyclical Thematic Processes in the Nineteenth-Century Symphony', in Julian Horton (ed.), *The Cambridge Companion to the Symphony* (Cambridge: Cambridge University Press, 2013), 203–6. See also the more extended discussion along the same lines in Steven Vande Moortele, *Two-Dimensional Sonata Form in Germany and Austria between 1850 and 1950: Theoretical, Analytical, and Critical Perspectives* (PhD dissertation, University of Leuven, 2006), 72–6.

16. Blume, *Classic and Romantic Music*.

Further Reading

Caplin, William E. *Classical Form: A Theory of Formal Functions for the Instrumental Music of Haydn, Mozart, and Beethoven* (Oxford: Oxford University Press, 1998).

Davis, Andrew. *Sonata Fragments: Romantic Narratives in Chopin, Schumann, and Brahms* (Bloomington: Indiana University Press, 2017).

Hepokoski, James, and Darcy, Warren. *Elements of Sonata Theory: Norms, Types, and Deformations in the Late-Eighteenth-Century Sonata* (New York: Oxford University Press, 2006).

Horton, Julian. *Brahms' Piano Concerto No. 2, Op. 83: Analytical and Contextual Studies* (Leuven: Peeters, 2017).

Rodgers, Stephen. *Form, Program, and Metaphor in the Music of Berlioz* (Cambridge: Cambridge University Press, 2009).

Schmalfeldt, Janet. *In the Process of Becoming: Analytic and Philosophical Perspectives on Form in Early Nineteenth-Century Music* (New York: Oxford University Press, 2011).

Taylor, Benedict. *Mendelssohn, Time and Memory: The Romantic Conception of Cyclic Form* (Cambridge: Cambridge University Press, 2011).

Vande Moortele, Steven. *The Romantic Overture and Musical Form from Rossini to Wagner* (Cambridge: Cambridge University Press, 2017).

16 | Romanticism and the Ideal of Song

LISA FEURZEIG

Expression as the Purpose of Song

On first hearing a typical eighteenth-century German song, perhaps by Christian Gottfried Krause or Beethoven's early teacher Christian Gottlob Neefe, and comparing it to a Romantic song by a composer such as Schubert or Fauré, one might first be struck by their differences. The earlier work would be short and simple, designed for an amateur performer, requiring only a small vocal range and minimal accompaniment, while the later one might be longer, more taxing for both singer and pianist, and much more sophisticated in melody, harmony, and musical design. Despite these differences, in some ways the earlier piece would hold the kernel of what came later: the goal of expressing human experience through sung poetry.

During the eighteenth century, aesthetic preferences shifted away from the intricacy of late baroque style. Philosophers such as Jean-Jacques Rousseau (who was also a novelist and composer) asserted the value of simple expressive art that was closer to nature. Intellectuals began to value and seek out folk culture (however unclearly that was defined). Music was seen as an important tool for educating and shaping children, and hence it was important to provide mothers with singable material for that purpose. All these factors combined to encourage the production of songs that could be performed by amateurs, as exemplified in collections such as *Oden mit Melodien*, published in Berlin in the early 1750s. Somewhat later in the century, composers such as Carl Friedrich Zelter and Johann Friedrich Reichardt began to write songs that blended the simple folk-like tone with virtuosity, creating a hybrid style: for example, a relatively simple melody might conclude with a cadenza reminiscent of opera.

Broadly acknowledged as the master whose *oeuvre* redefined art song, the Viennese composer Franz Schubert (1797–1828) developed a new approach to the genre. While Schubert was well aware of earlier models and wrote many strophic songs with folk-like melodies, he also used other musical forms. He was a master of modified strophic form, in which significant variation is added to the basic strophic structure. 'Im Frühling' (D. 882, 1826), on a poem by Ernst Schulze, provides a powerful example. A wistful but calm first stanza portraying springtime is followed by one with a more florid accompaniment, and then by a mini-storm scene that accompanies the same melody – but in the minor mode – for the third stanza, expressing the poetic character's despair over lost love. The final stanza brings a return to major with new ornamentation. In through-composed songs modelled in part on ballads by Johann Rudolf Zumsteeg (1760–1802), Schubert abandoned strophic repetition altogether in favour of new music to go along with shifting poetic situations.

Schubert was frequently hailed for his ability to internalise and repro-duce a poet's intention, as though he could magically convert verbal into musical meaning. His friend Joseph von Spaun commented that 'Whatever filled the poet's breast Schubert faithfully reflected and transfigured. ... Every one of his song compositions is in reality a poem on the poem he set to music.'[1] Schubert used many musical techniques to express what he found through his sensitive readings of poetry. He made the piano an equal partner to the singer, often writing figurations to represent something about the outward scene, such as rippling water or a galloping horse, while the vocal part portrayed the inward experience of the poetic persona. He employed many kinds of musical nuance – altering harmonies, rhythms, phrase lengths, and more – to bring out particular words or moments of change in the text.

Schubert altered and deepened the art song in many ways – yet even as the means of musical expression grew more complex, the central goal of song remained the same: to convey textual meaning through music. Song was still idealised as being natural and unaffected, portraying the charac-ter's experience in a direct way in order to arouse empathy and under-standing in listeners.

Nevertheless, some literary figures, notably Johann Wolfgang von Goethe, did not like to see the symmetrical qualities of their verbal cre-ations altered to fit new musical structures, which might seem to obscure the lyric voice. Goethe seemingly preferred the compositions of Zelter (a personal friend of his) to those of the young Schubert – at least, the poet never replied when Spaun, in 1816, sent him a carefully copied group of Schubert's settings of his poems. Goethe's taste reflected Weimar Classicism even as the literary world had already begun its shift towards Romanticism. Already in the 1790s, the young Friedrich Schlegel, leader of the Jena Romantic circle, had sought Goethe's approval while also teasing and mocking some aspects of Weimar Classicism.

The genre of art song came into its own in the nineteenth century, becoming valued as a worthy art form on a par with larger works such as operas. This development paralleled the rise of the stand-alone character piece for piano. It is no coincidence that Felix Mendelssohn chose the title *Lieder ohne Worte* (*Songs without Words*) for several collections of piano works, paying a sort of backhanded compliment to the vocal genre by implying that music did not need a sung text to express something equivalent to poetry.

Early Romantic Concepts: Interdisciplinarity, Symphilosophy, the Fragment, and Subjectivity

Friedrich Schlegel (1772–1829) was the guiding intellect of the early Romantic movement in Germany, or *Frühromantik*. This movement took shape during the 1790s in intellectual and social circles of Berlin and the small university city of Jena, not far from Weimar. The early Romantic ideas were intertwined with the intense personal relationships of those who first expressed them. Other key members of these Romantic circles included Schlegel's brother August Wilhelm; Friedrich's wife, Dorothea (a daughter of the important Jewish thinker Moses Mendelssohn; Felix Mendelssohn was her nephew) and August Wilhelm's wife, Caroline; Friedrich von Hardenberg, who wrote poetry under the name Novalis; and the theologian and translator Friedrich Schleiermacher. The group placed high value on what Schlegel called 'Symphilosophy', meaning ideas that grew from shared interdisciplinary creativity.

The early Romantics were pioneers in the study of drama, literature, and the visual arts, though they had little to say about music. Moving away from the sole emphasis on ancient classics, they looked closely at European literature from the Middle Ages and beyond, disseminating their thoughts through lecture series and translations. While they deeply appreciated art in various styles, the Romantics strove to escape whatever they found overly self-contained and conventional; in their own time, they advocated what Schlegel labelled 'Romantic irony', meaning a kind of self-awareness within the artwork that both acknowledges and breaks away from artificiality.

Schlegel pioneered a genre he called the fragment. He wrote many of these pithy comments, and also recruited his friends as contributors, publishing fragments in sets without revealing who had written which ones (though later editors have worked out attributions). This mix of materials, ideas, and authors was intended to symbolise the interconnectedness of the universe. One of Schlegel's fragments stated that 'A fragment, like a miniature work of art, has to be entirely isolated from the surrounding world and complete in itself like a hedgehog.'[2] Yet he also made a point of grouping fragments, creating a clear sense of relationship amongst them. This opposition between independence and connectedness was later mirrored in the art-song genre.

One of the most influential fragments was a fairly long one by Friedrich Schlegel himself on the nature of Romantic poetry. He begins by writing that

Romantic poetry is a progressive universal poetry. . . . It tries to and should mix and fuse poetry and prose, inspiration and criticism, the poetry of art and the poetry of nature; and make poetry lively and sociable, and life and society poetical . . . .

Schlegel emphasises the universality of Romantic poetry by showing how it unites opposites. Later in the passage, he focuses on the progressiveness of Romantic poetry by showing it to be an ongoing process rather than a finished product.

Other kinds of poetry are finished and are now capable of being fully analyzed. The romantic kind of poetry is still in the state of becoming; that, in fact, is its real essence: that it should forever be becoming and never be perfected.[3]

On first encounter, these ideas may seem contradictory. How can something called a fragment be complete in itself? What does it mean for a work of art to be a process rather than a thing? All these apparent contradictions, though, are conscious and deliberate, and they reflect the central Romantic idea of infinite striving or yearning (*Sehnsucht* in German). This conception of constant growth and development as a goal was drawn from other late-eighteenth-century thinkers. Immanuel Kant's moral philosophy, rather than laying out a set of rules, concludes that what humans should do is continually to seek the moral law. In Goethe's drama *Faust*, Mephistopheles sets conditions stating that Faust will forfeit his soul only when he expresses complete satisfaction with a particular moment and wants to remain there rather than quest eternally onward. The belief that the answer consists of more questions was central to early Romantic thought.

These central Romantic ideas – interdisciplinarity, shared intellectual work, and the interplay between fragment and larger structure – should help clarify why, as explained in the opening chapter to this volume, Romantic aesthetics preferred art to be 'incomplete, fragmentary, open, evolving, [and] stylistically heterogeneous, in contrast to the perceived formal unity of the works of classical antiquity'.[4]

Romantic poetry also strongly emphasised individual experience expressed in the first person, known as the 'lyric I'. It should be noted that this 'I' can but does not always represent the poet in an autobiographical sense. A poet may write in the first person while presenting the experiences of some other character. For this reason, the phrase 'poetic persona' is often used to stand for the character represented by this lyric I.

Paradoxically, the individual experience portrayed in Romantic literature was frequently understood as universal. While the scenes and events of a novel or poem belong in a narrow sense to its story and main character, those particulars partake in broader archetypal experiences that were assumed to be universal, such as leaving home, falling in love, growing old, and so on. This perspective strongly contrasts the idea of our time that literature should emphasise difference and identity, showing how various individuals are set apart through their gender, class, ethnicity, race, or place of origin, and thus may experience the world in vastly different ways. The Romantic assumption of universality helps to explain why both poetry and song were intended and expected to arouse understanding and empathy.

As songs expanded beyond comfortable domestic music suitable to be sung and played by amateurs, various song types developed, ranging from tiny vignettes just a page or two long to lengthy episodic ballads. Although most were settings of lyric poetry, there were song texts in the category of epics told by a narrator, and even occasional dramatic scenes. Some songs embraced the ideal of fragmentariness by presenting a moment with no broader plot or context, while others were joined into longer sets or song cycles. Like one of Schlegel's fragments, a song could exist in its own prickly self-sufficiency or could be combined with others into a larger collection that might or might not present a connected narrative.

Poets and Subject Matter

Schubert's approach to song composition became a model for many Austrian and German composers, including Robert and Clara Schumann, Felix Mendelssohn and his sister Fanny Hensel, Robert Franz, Johannes Brahms, Hugo Wolf, and Gustav Mahler. Works by dozens of poets were set to music, including writers who were famous in their own right and minor literary figures whose works became renowned through their use for music. Some German poets whose works were frequently set to music were the two central figures of Weimar Classicism, Goethe (1749–1832) and Friedrich Schiller (1759–1805); others included Heinrich Heine (1797–1856), and Friedrich Rückert (1788–1866). Wilhelm Müller (1794–1827) is significant as the poet of Franz Schubert's two song cycles *Die schöne Müllerin* and *Winterreise*. Some composers, such as Robert Schumann and Hugo Wolf, preferred poetry at the most elevated level. For others, including Schubert, Mendelssohn, and Brahms, literary acclaim was not the primary concern. Both Schubert and Mendelssohn set some poems by the most renowned poets and others written by their personal friends.

Eventually, as German songs were translated and performed elsewhere, Romantic song based on these models developed in other countries. Significant composers included Gabriel Fauré, Henri Duparc, and Ernest Chausson in France; Edvard Grieg in Norway; Jean Sibelius in Finland; and Modest Mussorgsky in Russia. These later composers selected poetry that reflected the middle and late nineteenth century. For example, some French poets often used in song included Victor Hugo (1802–85), Théophile Gautier (1811–72), Charles Marie René Leconte de Lisle (1818–94), Charles Baudelaire (1821–67), Sully Prudhomme (1839–1907), and Paul Verlaine (1844–96).

One inexhaustible source of poetic subject matter was nature as viewed by the lyrical subject. In his *Naturphilosophie*, Jena circle member Friedrich Wilhelm Schelling (1775–1854) proposed a model in which natural entities, such as rocks, mountains, or trees, are governed by something like consciousness or a soul. Just as a poetic character wandering through a natural landscape experiences it through the subjective lens of his or her own experiences and emotions, the birds or flowers also perceive that person through their own subjectivities. This is particularly evident in poetry by Heine, in which natural beings voice their own thoughts and emotions. (See, e.g., the poem 'Ich wandelte unter den Bäumen', set by Robert Schumann in his Heine *Liederkreis*, Op. 24.) Romantic poets sometimes present nature as a mirror of the poetic character's emotional state, sometimes as an ironic contrast.

Romantic poets also addressed philosophical issues, one significant theme being the unquenchable *Sehnsucht* mentioned earlier. The quintessential figure of the Romantic wanderer, often represented in Romantic literature and visual art, symbolises this eternal quest, represented in poems such as Schiller's 'Der Pilgrim' (The Pilgrim) and Schmidt von Lübeck's 'Der Wanderer' (The Wanderer). Another topic addressed in poetry was the fleeting nature of time, linked to the notion that any moment is also eternal; this theme is found in Friedrich Leopold Stolberg's 'Auf dem Wasser zu singen' (To Be Sung on the Water) and Friedrich Schlegel's 'Der Fluß' (The River). The Petrarchan paradoxes of love – mixing joy and sorrow, pleasure and pain – also preoccupied poets, for example in Rückert's poem 'Du bist die Ruh' (Thou art Rest). All the poems mentioned in this paragraph were set by Schubert.

Many intellectuals of the period were inspired by the ideas of the American and French revolutions, so it is not surprising to find political texts and subtexts in poetry. Political commentary could be expressed openly at times – for example, nationalistic German poetry was common during the Napoleonic Wars – but for most of the nineteenth century dissent was dangerous, and political content had to be disguised to appear innocent and uncontroversial. Another important tendency was a growing interest in folk culture, grounded in the work of Johann Gottfried Herder (1744–1803) and reflected in publications of folk-song texts and folk tales. *Des Knaben Wunderhorn* (*The Boy's Magic Horn*), a significant collection of German folk poetry, was published by Achim von Arnim and Clemens Brentano in 1805 and 1808. Influenced by these writers, the Brothers Grimm (Jacob and Wilhelm) published a set of 200 German folk tales, inspiring similar collections in other countries.

Metaphorical Uses of Nature in Three Songs

The following case studies explore three songs, along with the cycle from which one is drawn. Each poem uses a natural scene in both a descriptive and metaphorical way. Through these examples, one can absorb some of the central elements of how the Romantics understood and experienced the world around them.

Schubert's 'Am See', D. 746: Pantheistic Reflections on Nature

This song, composed around 1822 or 1823, is on a poem by Schubert's friend Franz Ritter von Bruchmann (1798–1867). Though not primarily a poet, here Bruchmann invents an ingenious two-layered metaphor combined with a play on words. The poem evidently captured Schubert's imagination, as shown by his evocative musical response.

In des Sees Wogenspiele	Into the lake's waveplay
Fallen durch den Sonnenschein	Fall through the sunshine
Sterne, ach, gar viele, viele,	Stars, ah, so many, many,
Flammend leuchtend stets hinein.	Ever flaming and glowing.
Wenn der Mensch zum See geworden,	When man has become lake,
In der Seele Wogenspiele	Into the soul's waveplay
Fallen aus des Himmels Pforten	Fall from heaven's gate
Sterne, ach, gar viele, viele.	Stars, ah, so many, many.

Note first that lines 1–3 of the first stanza are very similar to lines 2–4 of the second, with two changes. The word 'See' (lake – here in the possessive form) is replaced by 'Seele' (soul). In German, these two words sound very similar, so there is a play on words (*Wortspiel*) to match the poem's playing waves (*Wogenspiele*). Second, instead of falling 'through the sunshine', the stars are described as falling 'from heaven's gate'. These three lines and their varied repetition set up a developing metaphor in two layers. The 'stars' that fall into the sparkling water in the first four-line stanza are not actual stars, which cannot be seen in the daytime. Instead, the word 'stars' stands for the dancing particles of light that bounce off the lake's rippling water, something most people have experienced when at the shore. While grounded in the physical world, this image strongly hints at some kind of deeper significance, which is offered by the second quatrain. Beginning with the mysterious phrase 'When man has become lake', this stanza sets up a spiritual metaphor parallel to the earlier physical one: just as the reflected light pours into the lake, so do heaven's stars fall into the transmuted soul.

The phrase 'when man has become lake' might mean all humans merging together into a single consciousness, like the drops of water in a lake, or might represent the idea that when we die, our souls join the natural world. There are other possible interpretations as well; Bruchmann leaves this open for each reader to interpret. No matter what specific meaning one reads into the poem, the image of human souls flowing into the cosmos is closely linked with a religious outlook dating back to ancient times. Pantheism – the belief that the divine is distributed throughout the world, rather than only in a god or gods – fit very naturally into the Romantics' perspective and their strong bond with nature. Just as the arts became somewhat of a substitute for formal religion in the nineteenth century, so did the beauties of nature, and this poem's implication that a human soul can merge into the lake is part of this outlook.[5]

In Schubert's musical setting, the piano accompaniment replicates the lake's waves in a way that is both visible and audible. In each of the first eight bars, a wave begins low in the left hand, arches up through an arpeggio continued by the right hand, and then crests, falling by a tritone as another wave begins in the left hand. This figuration aptly represents the unceasing pattern of waves: as each one crashes onto the shore, its successors are already growing and approaching from farther away.

The vocal line also mimics the arching pattern of waves and uses descending tritones in two inverted forms: Ab_3–D_3 and D_4–Ab_3. The repetition of this dissonant interval creates a sense of yearning that is especially poignant when D, the leading tone, descends by a tritone rather than ascending a half-step to the tonic. Schubert sets up a drive towards ascent when the voice part leaps a third up to F_4 (a seventh above the bass) on the expressive word 'ach', preceding an overall descent to the tonic Eb_3 at the end of the phrase (see Ex. 16.1).

Example 16.1 Schubert, 'Am See', D. 746 (1822/3), bb. 1–13

In the middle section (not shown), there are two more arrivals on F_4, which remains the highest pitch of the vocal line. In the song's final eight bars, as the word 'ach' sounds once more, an upward leap of a perfect fourth lands on G_4, bringing a gratifying sense of culmination. The first quatrain's physical metaphor about light on the lake presses upward as far as F (scale degree 2); the metaphysical metaphor of stars penetrating the soul alights on G (scale degree 3), which reveals itself to be the aural goal (see Ex. 16.2). Schubert chooses to repeat the final line of text, though – and to finish off the song, he twice repeats the stepwise descent from F_4 to $E\flat_4$ on the word 'viele', so that the song's final expressive declaration returns from that great climax to the earlier experience of incompleteness and *Sehnsucht*.

Example 16.2 Schubert, 'Am See', bb. 29–36

Fauré's 'La Lune Blanche': Nature as a Setting for Love

This song is part of the cycle *La Bonne chanson* (*The Good Song*, composed 1892–4), which sets nine poems by Paul Verlaine, but it will be discussed on its own for the purposes of this chapter. Here, nature is a setting for intimacy, bliss, and fulfilment. This song differs greatly from 'Am See' in both musical and poetic language. The poem is divided into three parts, each with two layers. In each part, a set of five lines describes the outward scene, followed by a single line addressed directly to the poet's beloved. Those three separated lines make up their own brief poem describing the subjective experience of the lovers.

La lune blanche	The white moon
Luit dans les bois;	Gleams in the woods;
De chaque branche	From every branch
Part une voix	There comes a voice
Sous la ramée . . .	Beneath the boughs . . .
Ô bien-aimée.	O beloved.
L'étang reflète,	The pool reflects,
Profond miroir,	Deep mirror,
La silhouette	The silhouette
Du saule noir	Of the black willow
Où le vent pleure . . .	Where the wind weeps . . .
Rêvons, c'est l'heure.	Let us dream, it is the hour.
Un vaste et tendre	A vast and tender
Apaisement	Consolation
Semble descendre	Seems to fall
Du firmament	From the sky
Que l'astre irise . . .	That the moon illuminates . . .
C'est l'heure exquise.	It is the exquisite hour.[6]

Whereas the piano prelude to 'Am See' introduces those falling tritones that prefigure the vocal line, Fauré begins here with shimmering, static triplets played *pianissimo*. Along with the key of F sharp major, this opening establishes a sense of nature's fragile beauty, preparing us for the lovers' expectation and readiness for this ecstatic experience. The triplet motif, moving through various chords, continues for much of the song, tapering off only in the last stanza, soon after the metre changes from 9/8 to 3/4. Both piano and voice live in a world of constantly shifting harmony. Shifting accidentals and enharmonic reinterpretation of notes (e.g., B♭ respelled as A♯) reinforce the musical ambiguity and evanescence. Subtle shifts in accidentals and chords create slight alterations in atmosphere. As Graham Johnson writes, '[t]he deep mirror of the pool glints with the colours of many different changing harmonies ... a kaleidoscope of sound'.[7] We find a remarkable example of this in the song's last twelve bars (see Ex. 16.3). Focusing simply on the melodic line in the right hand, we see the same basic figure four times: a stepwise line ascending from F_3 or $F\sharp_3$ to D_4 or $C\sharp_4$. Each of the first three melodies is slightly different, though, until the last occurrence finally repeats what we have just heard. Analysis of the specific chords and 'reasons' for these variants would be of some interest, but ultimately the kaleidoscope exists for its own sake rather than that of some larger harmonic plan.

Except through pauses and a shift of metre the first time, Fauré does not clearly separate the two poetic layers. (For the sixth song in *La Bonne chanson*, 'Avant que tu ne t'en ailles', whose text also presents two separate and converging stories, he made a different choice, using changes of both key and metre to distinguish the layers.) In 'La Lune blanche' the composer

Example 16.3 Fauré, 'La Lune blanche', from *La Bonne chanson*, Op. 61 No. 3 (1892–4), bb. 38–49

unites the two layers of text, as if to show how their contemplation of external beauty intensifies the intimate experience of the two lovers.

Like 'Am See', this song illustrates the Romantic affinity with nature. It might be argued that the song and poem together also demonstrate the ambiguous potential of the fragment. While Verlaine separates the poem into two layers that could be thought of as intersecting fragments, Fauré transforms them through his music into a more unified experience.

Schumann's *Eichendorff* Liederkreis, *Op. 39: An Assemblage of Fragments – Nature as Soulmate*

This set of twelve songs, dating from 1840, is linked through the authorship of Joseph von Eichendorff. Many of the poems were originally written for various characters in Eichendorff's fictional works, making this a very clear example of how the 'lyric I' is not necessarily equivalent to the poet. Eichendorff later published them in a poetry collection in 1837, separated from the specific circumstances of the fiction – but even so, Schumann's decision to combine them into a set to be performed together altered their intent and meaning. Any connectivity or narrative in the set originates primarily from Schumann – and also from a shared tone and spirit belonging to Eichendorff's work. Barbara Turchin, citing critics Theodor Adorno and Karl Wörner, writes of a 'poetic structure based on mood and feeling' that ties the *Liederkreis* together, offering the idea of 'two expressive arches', songs 1–6 and 7–12, that unfold in parallel ways.[8] Benedict Taylor proposes, on the other hand, that the lack of clarity as to whether these songs are connected or separate is a central part of our experience: 'the tension between the two alternatives is the most crucial factor in coming to an aesthetic understanding of the work'.[9] This quality of being separate yet linked can be tied to Schlegel's ideal of the fragment and his practice of grouping fragments and publishing them as sets. While each poem and song has autonomy, it is also presented within a set, enticing and perhaps compelling listeners to seek relationships amongst the individual members. The following discussion points out a few possible connections.

One strong factor that may predispose listeners to seek a narrative trajectory in the set is that the persona of the first song is melancholy and isolated, while the persona of the last song is in a joyful partnership. In each of these poems, metaphors drawn from nature express the situation. In the first poem, a threatening storm symbolises the persona's alienation and separation from home, and in the final one the poet declares that a group of natural entities (moon, stars, grove, and nightingales) is crying out that 'she is yours!' Also, the cycle is framed by a tonal bond between these two, as the first song is in F sharp minor and the last in F sharp major. These correlations encourage the idea that the set tells a story about moving from loneliness to a fulfilling love, even though it is difficult to account for some of the intervening songs.

The songs are held together in shifting combinations through a network of related themes, ideas, and musical qualities. For example, song 7, 'Auf einer Burg' (In a Fortress), shares a contrapuntal, fugue-like texture with song 10, 'Zwielicht' (Twilight), while its text seems more related to song 3, 'Waldesgespräch' (Forest Conversation) and song 11, 'Im Walde' (In the Forest). 'Zwielicht' warns that twilight is a dangerous time when no one can be trusted. Reflecting the Romantic interest in folklore, the other three songs (3, 7, and 11) depict legends and traditions with a mix of nostalgia and dread. 'Waldesgespräch' tells of a man who rescues a lost woman in the forest, only to discover that she is a witch; she calls herself 'Lorelei', referring to a related story of a mermaid or siren in the Rhine River. This song is in the ballad tradition; to conjure up a sense of narration, Schumann constructs a lulling piano part that combines octaves and fifths in the left hand with horn calls in the right. 'Auf einer Burg' describes a knight turned to stone who silently witnesses events of the present time; it refers to the legend that Friedrich Barbarossa, a Holy Roman Emperor in the twelfth century, is sleeping in a cave and will awake in Germany's hour of need. The poem ends ominously with a picturesque wedding at which the bride is weeping, suggesting that modernity has spoiled the old sacred rituals. 'Im Walde' also questions traditional customs: after describing a wedding and a merry hunt with bouncy, fanfare-like piano figurations, it ends slowly and legato, in the first person, on the line 'Und mich schauert's im Herzensgrunde' (And I shuddered in the depths of my heart).[10]

For a closer look, consider the song 'Mondnacht', the fifth in the *Liederkreis*. Like 'La Lune blanche', this song describes a moon-illuminated landscape, but here there is only one viewer rather than two.

Mondnacht	Moonlit Night
Es war, als hätt der Himmel	It was as if the sky
Die Erde still geküsst,	Had silently kissed the earth,
Dass sie, im Blütenschimmer	So that she, in the blossoms' radiance,
Von ihm nur träumen müsst.	Must now only dream* of him.
Die Luft ging durch die Felder,	The breeze passed through the fields,
Die Ähren wogten sacht,	The grain swayed gently,

(*cont.*)

Es rauschten leis die Wälder,	The woods murmured quietly,
So sternklar war die Nacht.	The night was so starry clear.
Und meine Seele spannte	And my soul spread
Weit ihre Flügel aus,	Its wings out widely,
Flog durch die stillen Lande,	Flew through the silent lands
Als flöge sie nach Haus.	As if it flew toward home.[11]
	*or 'dream only'

This atmospheric poem is typical of Eichendorff, combining his interests in the special qualities of particular landscapes and times of day. After two stanzas of third-person description, the text suddenly reveals the existence of a lyric I who shifts from being an observer to a participant in the exquisitely tranquil scene. Eichendorff also creates compound words, as one can easily do in German: the expressive quality of 'Blütenschimmer' (blossom-shimmer) and 'sternklar' (star-clear) cannot be fully rendered in normal English.

For Schumann, the poem inspired a structure based largely on variants of one phrase:

$$P - AA - P - A'A'' - BA''' - P'$$

The phrase P represents the piano prelude, interlude, and postlude, while A and B are phrases for voice and piano together. Each poetic stanza is presented in two musical phrases, with five of these six phrases being very similar (here marked 'A' in various forms). After the first stanza, each iteration of A adds harmonic notes that thicken the texture. Stanza 3 begins with the new B phrase – this significant arrival of unexpected new music reflects the presence of the lyrical subject – and then returns to the central phrase of the song with yet another version of the accompaniment. Just as the poem begins with the personified earth and sky and then adds specific elements of fields, woods, and so on, the harmonic landscape is similarly altered and enriched by new chord tones.

Example 16.4 shows the P and A phrases. Schumann begins with an unusual five-bar phrase that should perhaps be considered as four bars of action followed by a held breath that suspends time. The left hand plays B_1, followed by a $C\sharp_6$ in the right hand: two notes, just over four octaves apart, that symbolise the earth and the sky; the descending melodic lines then suggest the sky leaning far down to kiss the earth even before that text has been sung. In b. 5, the right hand begins a repeated semiquaver pedal tone on B that continues for much of the song, though occasionally replaced by

Example 16.4 Robert Schumann, 'Mondnacht', from the Eichendorff *Liederkreis*, Op. 39 No. 5 (1840), bb. 1–22

the notes on either side, A and C♯. It is also noteworthy that Schumann pairs the B with those two adjacent notes, creating gentle dissonances that may signify the 'shimmer' of the flowers. This impressionistic depiction is only intensified by his addition of chord tones as the song progresses.

Conclusion: Song as Mystic Unity

In the eighteenth-century model of song, the addition of music supported the expression of a poetic text without overshadowing the original. During the nineteenth century, Romantic composers deepened the expressive qualities of the genre. They devised many ways to go beyond simple supportive depiction of the poetry, adding new layers of meaning. A Romantic song might develop musical symbols and processes to illustrate and intensify poetic metaphors. It might reshape our understanding of a poem in a way the poet did not foresee. It might draw on chords and pitches that are easier to understand intuitively than to explain through a music-theoretical model. Romantic song epitomises the intermingling of the verbal and musical realms, bringing out the interconnectedness of the universe that the *Frühromantiker* celebrated. Whether standing alone in its prickly individuality or combined with others into a cycle, any Romantic song embodies the mystic unity of thought, image, and sound.

Notes

* This chapter, which I completed on her birthday, is dedicated to the memory of my mother, Nanni Kahn Feurzeig, who loved poetry.
1. Otto Erich Deutsch, *The Schubert Reader*, trans. Eric Blom (New York: W. W. Norton, 1947), 886.
2. Athenaeum Fragment No. 206, trans. David Firchow, in *Friedrich Schlegel's Lucinde and the Fragments* (Minneapolis: University of Minnesota Press, 1971), 189; I have changed Firchow's translation from 'porcupine' to 'hedgehog'.
3. Ibid., Athenaeum Fragment No. 116, 175.
4. Chapter 1, p. 10.
5. Despite its subjective way of presenting the topic, the poem may be referring to one of the scientific controversies of that time: the nature of light as either a wave or a particle. Bruchmann refers to the waves on the lake (*Wogenspiele*), but his imagery implies that light is a particle. Schubert set other poems as well that emphasised the idea of light reflecting off water: 'Auf dem Wasser zu Singen' (mentioned above), 'Der liebliche Stern' by Ernst Schulze, and 'Des Fischers

Liebesglück' by Carl Gottfried von Leitner. He also set poetry related to scientific topics of the day. Two songs in *Winterreise* refer to unusual phenomena of light: the will-o'-the-wisp in 'Irrlicht' and parhelia or sun dogs in 'Die Nebensonnen'. 'Aufenthalt', on a poem by Ludwig Rellstab, refers to the unchanging nature of rock, at the very time that geologists were beginning to consider theories of how the earth moves.

6. Adapted from Graham Johnson and Richard Stokes, *A French Song Companion* (Oxford: Oxford University Press, 2000), 191.
7. Graham Johnson, *Gabriel Fauré: The Songs and Their Poets* (Farnham: Ashgate/The Guildhall School of Music and Drama, 2009), 232.
8. Barbara Turchin, 'Schumann's Song Cycles: The Cycle Within the Song', *19th-Century Music*, 8/3 (1985), 231–44, at 237.
9. Benedict Taylor, 'Absent Subjects and Empty Centers: Eichendorff's Romantic Phantasmagoria and Schumann's *Liederkreis*, Op. 39', *19th-Century Music*, 40/3 (2017), 201–22, at 205.
10. Translation by Celia Sgroi. Her full text and translation of the *Liederkreis* are available online at www.kanevas.be/lieder/translations/schumann_039.pdf.
11. Ibid.

Further Reading

Ferris, David. *Schumann's Eichendorff Liederkreis and the Genre of the Romantic Cycle* (New York: Oxford University Press, 2000).

Feurzeig, Lisa. *Schubert's Lieder and the Philosophy of Early German Romanticism* (Farnham: Ashgate, 2014).

Hallmark, Rufus (ed.). *German Lieder in the Nineteenth Century*, 2nd ed. (New York: Routledge, 2010).

Hirsch, Marjorie W. *Romantic Lieder and the Search for Lost Paradise* (Cambridge: Cambridge University Press, 2007).

Johnson, Graham. *Gabriel Fauré: The Songs and Their Poets* (Farnham: Ashgate/The Guildhall School of Music and Drama, 2009).

Johnson, Graham and Stokes, Richard. *A French Song Companion* (Oxford: Oxford University Press, 2000).

Muxfeldt, Kristina. 'Schubert's Songs: the Transformation of a Genre', in Christopher Gibbs (ed.), *The Cambridge Companion to Schubert* (Cambridge: Cambridge University Press, 1997), 121–37.

Parsons, James (ed.). *The Cambridge Companion to the Lied* (Cambridge: Cambridge University Press, 2004).

Rosen, Charles. 'Mountains and Song Cycles', in *The Romantic Generation* (Cambridge MA: Harvard University Press, 1995), 116–236.

Rushton, Julian. 'Music and the Poetic', in Jim Samson (ed.), *The Cambridge History of Nineteenth-Century Music* (Cambridge: Cambridge University Press, 2001), 157–77.

Taylor, Benedict. 'Absent Subjects and Empty Centers: Eichendorff's Romantic Phantasmagoria and Schumann's *Liederkreis*, Op. 39', *19th-Century Music*, 40/3 (2017), 201–22.

Youens, Susan. *Heinrich Heine and the Lied* (Cambridge: Cambridge University Press, 2007).

   '"So tönt in Welle Welle": Schubert and Pantheism in Song', in Andreas Dorschel (ed.), *Verwandlungsmusik: Über komponierte Transfigurationen* (Vienna: Universal Edition, 2007), 153–83.

17 | Music Staged and Unstaged

SARAH HIBBERD

E. T. A. Hoffmann's 1810 review of Beethoven's Symphony No. 5 has become emblematic of music's arrival at the very top of the hierarchy of the arts. Music had risen from a merely mimetic artform (in the conception of German Romantic thinkers) to an autonomous, ineffable, transcendent force: 'Beethoven's instrumental music unveils before us the realm of the mighty and the immeasurable . . . . [it] sets in motion the machinery of awe, of fear, of terror, of pain, and awakens that infinite yearning which is the essence of romanticism.'[1] Hoffmann roots this power in the symphony's internal motivic and tonal relationships and its instrumentation. Although he relies on simile to convey the music's particular effects ('like a friendly figure moving through the clouds', 'like the voice of a propitious spirit'),[2] his approach has been recognised as a landmark in music criticism, capturing the non-representational 'absolutism' of instrumental music that was to be cast in opposition to programmaticism later in the century.[3]

Hoffmann's description also captures the way in which the act of listening was reconceived by the early Romantics. The artwork's essence was grasped through the imagination, which mediated between sensory and spiritual realms. In other words, aesthetic contemplation was a creative process that realised the work's emotional effect.[4] Appreciation of music's evocative and representational qualities remained prominent in this conception. In fact, Edward Dent claims that the roots of musical Romanticism and its evocative power lay not in the Beethoven symphony, but rather in the Parisian *opéras comiques* of the 1790s. The noisy, effect-driven music of Luigi Cherubini and others stimulated 'a general Romantic phraseology' that was common to most German composers in the first decades of the new century.[5] Dent's implicit embracing of musical Romanticism's theatrical and political as well as philosophical roots encourages us to follow Carl Dahlhaus in acknowledging its simultaneous emergence in different intellectual centres around 1790, and the co-existence of multiple 'cultures of music'.[6] In what follows, I therefore move beyond the primarily German, elite context in which Hoffmann's review was initially received to consider musical Romanticism in its broader European (and in particular, French) context. In so doing, I highlight three expressive modes in which music was understood as operating in partnership with real and imagined visual stimuli: the melodramatic tableau, the unsung voice, and symphonic scenography. These modes pervaded European culture and offer a perspective on musical Romanticism that acknowledges its breadth and the social diversity of its audiences, as well as the variety of listening experiences.

The Melodramatic Tableau

René-Charles Guilbert de Pixerécourt's 'mélodrame à grand spectacle', a theatrical genre created in the 1790s, has commonly been understood as satisfying the new demand for thrilling stories of tyrannical oppression that mirrored real-life experiences during the French Revolution. Music, speech, gesture, stage action, and special effects combined to produce a clear narrative and heighten the emotional charge of its twists and turns. The audience was drawn into the unfolding drama, experiencing those same emotions. Key to the effect of such works was the spectacular conclusion, typically a tableau in which a sensory assault first overwhelmed the spectator and then offered space for critical reflection on the drama's moral resolution.

Despite its ultimate dispersion across the popular stages of Europe and beyond, melodrama's roots lay in the private and court theatres of the 1770s.[7] Jean-Jacques Rousseau's *scène lyrique*, *Pygmalion* (1770), is generally understood as the first example, and although it had limited exposure, it became a model for further experiments in a similar vein: the alternation of music and spoken text (with pantomime) to create a new expressively discursive medium inspired by ancient Greek declamation.[8] Georg Anton Benda's staged melodramas on classical themes for the French-influenced Gotha court (*Ariadne auf Naxos* and *Medea*, 1775) each featured a heroine at their heart, whose monologue invited the audience into her disturbed psyche. In a similar fashion, fragmented speech alternated with colourful musical passages deploying bold juxtaposition, repetition, and harmonic ambiguity to lead the spectator through the psychodrama and heighten the emotional effect. Reminiscence motifs were used, often with psychological associations, bound closely to changes of affect. Most significantly, the climatic moments in these dramas – Ariadne's suicide, Medea's murder of her children – were not represented on stage. Instead, they unfolded in darkness – in the music and in the imagination. Thus, when Medea enters the palace, dagger in hand, and then disappears from sight, a passage of *allegro furioso* is heard. As Jacqueline Waeber has argued, 'in its horror,

Medea's crime goes not only beyond speech, but beyond any form of visual representation'.[9] In other words, music takes on the burden of expression.

Such scenes of apparently unrepresentable horror proved an irresistible challenge on Parisian stages in the revolutionary decade and during the Napoleonic Wars.[10] In the 'denouement à grand fracas' that concludes Pixerécourt's melodrama *La Citerne* (1809), a fierce conflagration takes hold of the stage, and the tyrannical Spalatro orders the death of the heroine Séraphine and her little sister Clara. The stage directions detail the horror in the tableau before the audience, but also point to the underlying hope of rescue:

All flee, crying out in horror and throwing themselves in front of the spiral staircase that will carry them to certain death. At the same moment, a terrible explosion is heard. The wall crumbles; the ramps of the staircase break; the gallery (no longer supported) collapses with a horrible fracas, carrying with it Spalatro and his men. At the back of the stage we see the castle lit by torches and flames and packed with fighting men . . . . The workers attach ropes to trees and slide into the cistern, suspended from the branches and stonework . . . .

The musical accompaniment provided by house composer Alexandre Piccinni responds in kind to convey the emotional affect, echoing the language of Benda's melodramas, albeit in more restrained harmonic terms. The score is also reminiscent of the programmatic battle and hunting symphonies that were so popular in the 1780s, mirroring the movement on stage – the falling masonry and bodies and the general confusion – with teeming descending scales and sequenced and fragmented motifs.[11] Furthermore, as contemporary accounts suggested, the overwhelming, visceral effect of the combined audiovisual spectacle served to blur the distinction between dramatic and lived experience, thereby enhancing its emotional charge.[12] But hope and horror tend to be held in tension in these revolutionary melodramas. The reiterated tonic and dominant chords which gradually come to underpin the passage signal the eventual happy ending, and lead the spectator out of the chaos, into a cathartic conclusion where good triumphs over evil. Such scenes freeze the moment of crisis: the effect is magnified and discharged through visual and musical excess, and space is thereby created for reflection on the moral consequences of the narrative.

A similar musico-dramatic language often characterised the climactic tableaux of *opéras comiques*, in which spoken dialogue, song, orchestral writing, gesture, and visual effects worked together. In Cherubini's *Lodoiska* (1791), for example, the heroine is rescued from a burning castle, with a musical accompaniment very similar in style and affect to that of *La Citerne*. Melodrama and *opéra comique* were staples of the Viennese theatres, and Beethoven's *Fidelio* (1814) and its earlier *Leonore* incarnations (1805, 1806) are often cited as variations on the archetypal 'rescue' plot. But the shared lineage of their musico-dramatic effects is also evident. The orchestrally punctuated declamation ('Melodram') before the duet between Leonore and the jailer Rocco (as they dig the grave for their prisoner Florestan in Act II) makes tangible the physical environment and reveals the emotional states of the three characters. Following a scalic descent that accompanies the pair down to the dungeon, landing on a (tremolo) diminished seventh chord, the spoken exchange between Leonore ('halb laut') and Rocco is punctuated and occasionally underscored by a flow of unstable harmonies, suspensions, and changing tempi; Florestan's dream is revealed to the audience by the fleeting recall of a lyrical phrase from his earlier aria. In this manner the hidden thoughts and the uncertainties of the situation are conveyed almost subliminally, and the cold dark dungeon is vividly evoked (especially in the earlier *Leonore* incarnations).

German Romantic opera also absorbed French revolutionary opera's use of innovative stage machinery and lighting to create its special effects. *Opéras comiques* created for the Théâtre Feydeau (recognised across Europe for its innovative staging design) formed the backbone of the repertory that Carl Maria von Weber introduced as director of opera in Prague (1813–16). The Wolfsschlucht scene in *Der Freischütz* (1821) attests to the influence of this scenic ambition, and matches it with equally daring orchestral innovation.[13] The casting of magic bullets at midnight takes place within a multi-section second-act finale that mixes melodrama, song, chorus, and what John Warrack has termed 'raging orchestral description', as well as wide-ranging sound effects.[14] A series of extravagant visions reproduced the effects of a phantasmagoria – from flapping birds, to ghostly hunters, to a furious tempest.[15] By this means, the fantastical narrative was conveyed through evocative musical realisation and explicit visual representation that together overwhelmed the senses.

The power of such audiovisual spectacle was further developed in the French grand operas of the 1830s and '40s, but with renewed political relevance. The cataclysmic tableau that concludes Giacomo Meyerbeer's *Le Prophète* (1849), for example, was modelled on John Martin's 1821 panoramic painting of Belshazzar's feast. When the palace of Münster explodes, consuming the entire cast in flames, the counterpoint between visual and musical techniques again amplifies the physical confusion and the horror and invites reflection on its implications. Tremolo strings, repeating motifs, swirling scales, and a powerful downward chromatic thrust together capture the physical activity on stage, the interior drama of the characters and their peril. But this is shot through with elegiac rising arpeggios that invite the spectator to consider higher forces as the protagonists look to the heavens, and sing out as joyful martyrs, 'Ah! viens divine flamme, / Vers Dieu qui nous réclame, / Ah! viens portes notre âme, /Au ciel, au ciel' [Ah! Come divine flame, towards God who reclaims us, ah! Come carry our soul to heaven, to heaven!].[16] Reviewers took this as a cue to contemplate the failure of revolution in the theatre in relation to the events of 1848–9 in Paris.

The destructive but ultimately transcendental melodramatic tableau was to become a regular feature in later nineteenth-century operas.[17] It arguably reaches its zenith in the final scene of Wagner's *Götterdämmerung* (1876), the final part of *Der Ring des Nibelungen*: moments from the preceding drama are recalled through a dense web of leitmotifs, and as the gods are consumed in the flames, the audience hears the redemption motif ring out. John Deathridge points to the lineage back through Meyerbeer's *Robert le diable* (1831) and Daniel Auber's *La Muette de Portici* (1828): in the original 1848 version of Wagner's libretto, in the wake of the Dresden revolution, the focus is on the heroic optimism of Siegfried, but twenty years later the emphasis has shifted to Wotan's tragic resignation. For Heinrich Heine, as Deathridge reminds us, the two French operas offered the model for such a reversal, with their vacillation between desire for revolution and acceptance of the end – hope and horror – captured in their cataclysmic and multisensory denouements.[18]

Unsung Voices

In addition to magnifying emotion and providing access to a transcendental realm, music was also employed as a mediator: translating gestures and representing voices of the dead and the supernatural. A variety of tools were deployed: familiar tunes were quoted (their remembered words or dramatic significance clarified meaning in their new settings); the sound of the speaking voice was ventriloquised by an instrument in the orchestra; and striking timbres were chosen to evoke character and create an aura of the otherworldly.

Ballet-pantomime emerged as an independent theatrical art at the end of the eighteenth century – from the same soup of hybrid musico-dramatic genres from which melodrama sprang – and began to evolve from a series of mimes interspersed with dancing to a more continuous discourse of expression. A rich and nuanced gestural language was explained in such manuals as Gilbert Austin's *Chironomia: A Treatise in Rhetorical Delivery* (1806) and Carlo Blasis's *The Code of Terpsichore* (1828). These gestures were supported by scores that were typically assembled from well-known pre-existing melodies whose unsung words would relate to the stage action and 'translate' and further clarify the narrative and the emotional state of the characters. As Marian Smith has explained, the language of ballet-pantomime flowed into opera, as the two genres were performed on the same stage, often on the same night, at the Paris Opéra.[19]

Perhaps the best-known embodiment of this genre fusion is Fenella, the mute, dancing heroine of Auber's opera *La Muette de Portici*, whose voicelessness stands in the opera for that of the oppressed revolutionaries of southern Italy.[20] The critics marvelled at the orchestra's ability to 'translate' the dancer's gestures by recalling significant motifs from earlier in the opera and by imitating speech-rhythms. Thus, for example, in conversation with her brother Masaniello, the identity of her mysterious lover is signalled by quotation of the chorus 'Du prince objet de notre amour' from the first act (Act II scene 4). In a previous scene when she points him out, the orchestra mimics her imagined (iambic) cry 'C'est lui!' with a fortissimo upbeat semiquaver followed by a semibreve (Act I scene 5). Her pantomime was often interspersed with the recitative of a singing character, to confirm its meaning, so the challenge for the audience was not too demanding. At another level, Fenella's desperation and emotional turmoil in the final scene of the opera is represented in the orchestra. To accompany her decisive leap into the lava of an erupting Vesuvius, Auber uses the same language of teeming, descending scales and repeating motifs that we encountered in *La Citerne*. By this means both her narrative and emotional state are conveyed in a heightened expressive musical language working in partnership with her pantomime and the stage design.

In contrast, the fairy-tale opera-ballet *La Tentation* (1832), with music by Fromental Halévy and Casimir Gide, is closer to a ballet-pantomime than an opera, with more dancing characters in major roles, and longer passages of music intended to support actions and gestures. It was more challenging for audiences to understand the narrative with fewer linguistic clues from singing characters, and so musical memory was enlisted more forcefully. A recurring melody identified with the temptation of the central character is heard in different guises, as too are quotations from

Beethoven's Piano Sonata, No. 8 Op. 13 (*Pathétique*), 'Voi che sapete' from Mozart's *Le nozze di Figaro*, and other familiar works that provided short-cuts to narrative clarification.[21]

Tolerance for pantomime and its often rather laborious musical transla-tion in such genres began to wane amongst audiences, however. After 1830 more homogenous newly composed scores became the norm. The display element of dance in the emerging Romantic ballet was more important than pantomime, and fairy tales had become common source material. Music was frequently enlisted here to create an otherworldly atmosphere and to represent characters speaking from beyond the grave. Meyerbeer's opera *Robert le diable* (1831) features a plethora of such voices: offstage demons shouting through megaphones, resurrected nuns, and the hero's dead mother.[22] During the infamous Act III ballet, nuns rise from their tombs to seduce Robert into plucking a sacred branch. The staging and lighting designed by Louis Daguerre created the effect of moonlight using subtle new techniques: gas jets were hung from a batten above the stage, allowing greater concentration onto the stage floor and finer gradations of light. The dancing nuns in this half-light appeared insubstantial, their movements unearthly and weightless.[23] The music offered a similarly veiled listening experience: brass and lower strings suggested the deep shadows of the cloister, low woodwinds the stirrings of life, and the new technology of the ophicleide – the conical-bore keyed instrument akin to a tuba, heard the previous year sounding the Dies Irae motif in the *Symphonie Fantastique* – opened up a channel between past and present as the voice of Robert's demon father, Bertram. Hector Berlioz wrote about the effect at some length in his review of the opera and similar techniques were deployed in many subsequent pieces.[24] Meyerbeer's new approach to orchestration – original combinations of timbres to create precise, nuanced effects – complemented Daguerre's experimentation with lighting, and during the 1830s visual and sonic arts nourished each other at the Paris Opéra.

Towards the end of Meyerbeer's opera, another new orchestral sound is introduced: the *trompette à clef*, or keyed bugle, with its raw, oddly archaic sound. Robert is paralysed by indecision: whether to follow his father to the underworld forever or heed his saintly mother's warning and embrace this world. A pair of *trompettes* suggest his mother's voice as he reads a letter from her: a tonally ambiguous seven-bar melody is supported by three horns, two trombones, an ophicleide, and timpani – the same shadowy sound-world associated with Bertram, here suggesting both his distant union with Robert's mother and his attempt to silence her now. But time runs out before Robert makes his decision, and as midnight strikes Bertram alone is swallowed up into the underworld. The uncanny evocation of his mother's disembodied voice seems to transfix Robert, and ultimately prevents him from leaping into hell. Critics were impressed by the way in which Meyerbeer's orchestration drew the audience to the edge of this world: 'transported to the limit of this life and eternity, having before you heaven and hell, your heart struggles between terror and hope ... until the illusion is broken'.[25] Music's power to awaken 'infinite yearning' was apparently felt by audiences as well as by the opera's protagonists.

The imagined interlocutors in Italian operatic mad scenes of the 1820s and '30s are another manifestation of the uncanny voice. Most famously, the glass harmonica that Donizetti initially envisaged for Lucia's mad scene suggests a hallucinated voice – that of her lover Edgardo – in its recall of the theme from their earlier love duet. As Heather Hadlock has argued, '[Lucia's] perilous vocalizing, following the armonica into ever higher and more distant registers, charts her progress out of the realm of human utterance' – and in the cadenza, woman and instrument merge 'in ecstatic flights'.[26] For Emilio Sala, the instrument is like 'a tonal Doppelgänger, at once evanescent and disquieting'.[27] Although the glass harmonica was replaced by a flute before the premiere, the otherworldliness of the duet texture endured, accentuated by the elaborate coloratura, the remembered melody, and the uncanny voice-instrument sonority.[28]

Such projections of an imagined voice by the orchestra are an important facet of musical Romanticism: new instruments and technologies offered novel ways to channel both spirit and matter. They made tangible the uncanny voices lurking at the edges of consciousness, supporting singers in timbral high definition. Meyerbeer was at the heart of such experimentation. For Emily Dolan and John Tresch, he created auditory experiences that, in partnership with dazzling lighting and staging effects, overwhelmed the senses and became 'vessels of the transcendent and divine'.[29]

Symphonic Scenography

Audio-visual tableaux in which the emotional drama was heightened and magnified, and the expansion of temporal and imaginative space by means of orchestral voices are examples of ways in which early nineteenth-century composers expanded their expressive palates in the theatre. During the 1830s and '40s, two composers were particularly invested in developing such an approach in concert works: Berlioz and Mendelssohn.

Berlioz famously conceived his orchestral works as quasi-theatrical pieces. He termed *Roméo et Juliette* (1839) a 'symphonie dramatique', and its seven movements together challenge generic categorisation: some are vocal (in the form of arias, recitatives, and choruses), some are purely instrumental. Consideration of the work's position in his *oeuvre* helps to clarify his evolving attitude to representation. It comes after the 'mélologue' *Lélio* (1832), which borrows from the techniques of melodrama, and the 'symphonie à programme' *Harold en Italie* (1834), in which the viola is understood as the work's main protagonist, but before his 'légende dramatique' *La Damnation de Faust* (1846), which feels like an unstaged opera. These are not merely programmatic pieces, but operatic in their ambitions.[30]

Roméo et Juliette, although a concert work, has precise staging instructions: the performers are distributed between the stage and a platform in front of the stage.[31] Violaine Anger argues that the work evinces a gradual shift from the 'visible but impersonal singers' to whom we are introduced at the beginning of the work, through the climactic 'purely orchestral dream sequence' – the love scene – to the conclusion 'in the style of a grand opera, but without the *mise-en-scène*'.[32] In this way, Berlioz seems to be feeling his way through different temporalities and spaces. He claimed that the pivotal 'Scène d'amour' (the third movement) required a different mode of expression: 'the composer has had to give a latitude to his fantasy that the exact sense of sung words would not allow, and has had recourse to the language of instruments which is richer, more varied, less limited, and by its very vagueness, infinitely more powerful'.[33] In many ways this sentiment echoes Benda's predilection for representing the climactic moments of his dramas purely with the orchestra, and this part of the work is delivered as a sort of operatic duet without singers. Its subtitle reads like a stage direction ('Serene night – The Capulets' garden is silent and deserted. The young Capulets leaving the ball, pass by while singing reminiscences of the music of the ball'), and the use of offstage music helps to create a sense of scenic space.[34] The movement itself is set in a free-flowing form using themes that had been associated with the lovers earlier in the work. For Berlioz, the listener's knowledge of Shakespeare would have supplied the underpinning information about the scene, even if its precise relationship to the balcony scene that inspired it is not easily discernible.

The sixth movement, 'Roméo au tombeau des Capulets', relies on the audience's awareness that Juliet wakes at the moment when the poison Romeo has taken begins to take its effect – in line with the Parisian performances of the play in 1827–8 by the visiting English troupe that had included Harriet Smithson. In contrast to Shakespeare's lovers, they get the chance to speak before they die.[35] Atmosphere and emotion are conveyed by the orchestra in a manner familiar from melodrama: the dark emptiness of the tomb (ponderous augmented chords), Romeo's sadness (conveyed by cor anglais, bassoons and horn). But implied conversation between the lovers and graphic representation of the action feel closer to pantomime (without staging) and require some background knowledge from the audience. Thus: a *crescendo molto* as Romeo drains his cup of poison, orchestral exclamations (and recall of the love theme) as they find each other, stumbling strings heralding Romeo's collapse, and finally four tutti chords and a descending scale as Juliet stabs herself.

Felix Mendelssohn's orchestral writing also enlists the mind's eye. Rather than evoking shared memories of a specific theatrical production, however, his works might, for Thomas Grey, 'be construed as a kind of figurative musical *tableau vivant*' that arises from a shared middle-class culture.[36] 'Mental pictures' are conjured up by Mendelssohn from the landscape paintings, dioramas, and panoramas of the period, with which contemporary audiences would have been familiar. In other words, his orchestral writing evokes the *mise en scène* rather than the individual narratives and emotional dramas we have found elsewhere. The 'Italian' Symphony, Grey argues, is a series of musical tableaux suggested by landscape and genre paintings; the 'Scottish' Symphony imbues its landscapes with imagined events, inspired by contemporary history painting; and the *Hebrides* Overture and its evocation of Ossianic myth suggests the spectral projections of the phantasmagoria. Such images are animated by musical designs that invoke sounding analogues to light, shade, colour, character.

The pictorial listening that Berlioz and Mendelssohn arguably activated in their audiences in such works flowed directly from the cultural environments in which they worked. In Paris in particular it was the theatre that shaped visual literacy: its gestural language and special lighting effects informed the development of painting itself.[37] For Mendelssohn, the middle-class culture of the salon and its mix of sociable and performative traditions were a productive stimulus. Though the relationship between listening and watching was rarely straightforward, and the interpretation particular to the individual listener, it is difficult to envisage any concert-going in Europe as a purely aural experience.

* * *

One of the tensions running through the works discussed in this chapter centres on the apparent opposition of narrative and spectacle, and the potential incompatibility of temporal and spatial experiences. The tension comes more clearly into focus in one of the less successful hybrid experiments of 1830s Paris: Louis Jullien's 1837 'nocturnorama' for the Jardin Turc, in which a series of paintings of Martin's *Belshazzar's Feast* were unfurled, with lighting playing across them, to the accompaniment of a quadrille that told the story.[38] It drew complaints from music and art critics alike. Comprehension of the (repeating) image, which captured the entire story at a glance, was confused if one tried to concentrate simultaneously on the musical narrative that necessarily unrolled through time; equally, enjoyment of the musical flow was disturbed if one tried to focus on the story encapsulated by the painting. The relation between painting and music was rather different from that enacted in the concluding tableau of Meyerbeer's *Prophète*, discussed above, where the painting itself remained in the mind's eye, offering a less explicit reference point rather than a competing artwork. Nevertheless, such protests resonate with the most common complaint about grand opera: that audiences were so dazzled by the visual effects that they forgot to listen to the score.

Yet, as this chapter has demonstrated, music and visuals (and the fault line for dissatisfaction) do not always map neatly onto temporal versus spatial planes. Indeed, Emilio Sala has claimed, in the context of melodrama, that music can negotiate a path through this contradictory experience, 'gluing' spectators to the stage, while simultaneously guiding and orienting their emotions.[39] And contemporary accounts frequently attest to an engagement with musical works that was not merely supported by a real (or imagined) visual component, but also demanded one. James Q. Davies has outlined the ways in which concert audiences in London in 1829 were fascinated by the physical movements of the players and the emerging pantomimic figure of the conductor, how vocal music and poetic interpolations featured on programmes, and how stage and lighting effects were added to orchestral music.[40] Beethoven's Symphony No. 6, for example, was rendered as a ballet-pantomime, *La Symphonie pastorale*, by Robert Bochsa and a team of French performers at the King's Theatre (Berlioz saw it a year later in Lyons). Davies views this now-forgotten oddity as representative of the 'ballet-concert exchange' that characterised artistic trends of the moment, and of the tendency to hear music as a dance-like picture. Both critical and novelistic writing of the period offers further evidence: analogies with paintings and poetry were often drawn to convey the essence of the listening experience. Berlioz likened the slow movement of the *Eroica* Symphony to the funeral cortège of Pallas in Virgil's *Aeneid*, for example, and quoted lines from some English poetry to capture the effect produced in the Andante of the Seventh Symphony; in response to the Sixth Symphony, he sought to engage the full sensorium: 'these speaking images! these perfumes! this light! this eloquent silence! those vast horizons! those enchanted forest glens! those golden harvests!'[41]

Ultimately, then, the listening experiences of early nineteenth-century audiences bear witness to a multisensory kind of attention, flickering between memories, what will happen next, and absorption in the pleasure of the moment. Such events were nourished by experiences of different musical and dramatic genres, and bear witness to audiences that were ready to expand their horizons. In this way, musical Romanticism set in motion a 'machinery' of emotions, as Hoffmann asserted, and perception was indeed a truly creative force.

Notes

1. *Allgemeine musikalische Zeitung*, xii, 4 and 11 July 1810, cols. 630–42, 652–9; *E. T. A. Hoffmann's Musical Writings: Kreisleriana, The Poet and the Composer, Music Criticism,* ed., annot., intro. David Charlton, trans. Martyn Clarke (Cambridge: Cambridge University Press), 234–51, at 238.

2. Ibid., 242, 244.

3. See, e.g., Carl Dahlhaus, *The Idea of Absolute Music*, trans. Roger Lustig (Chicago: University of Chicago Press, 1989), viii. This topic is discussed in Alexander Wilfing's chapter in this volume.

4. See Mark Evan Bonds, 'Idealism and the Aesthetics of Instrumental Music at the Turn of the Nineteenth Century', *Journal of the American Musicological Society*, 50/2–3 (1997), 387–420, at 393–4.

5. Edward Dent, *The Rise of Romantic Opera*, ed. Winton Dean (Cambridge, 1976). Cherubini's influence on Beethoven has been acknowledged more widely, though it is usually his commissioned revolutionary works rather than his *opéras comiques* that are viewed as the principal source of inspiration.

6. Carl Dahlhaus, *Nineteenth-Century Music*, trans. J. Bradford Robinson (Berkeley: University of California Press, 1989), 19.

7. For a stimulating transnational examination of melodrama at the turn of the eighteenth century, see Katherine Hambridge and Jonathan Hicks (eds.), *The Melodramatic Moment: Music and Theatrical Culture, 1790–1820* (Chicago: University of Chicago Press, 2018).

8. Jacqueline Waeber, *En Musique dans le texte: Le mélodrama, de Rousseau à Schoenberg* (Paris: Van Dieren, 2005).

9. Ibid., 66–7.

10. For an assessment of melodrama's parallel development on the German stage, see Austin Glatthorn, 'The Legacy of *Ariadne* and the Melodramatic Sublime', *Music & Letters*, 100/2 (2019), 233–70.

11. Richard Will, *Characteristic Symphony in the Age of Haydn and Beethoven* (Cambridge: Cambridge University Press, 2002).

12. Imaginative interplay between the perceiving subject, the 'hors texte', and the drama had been an important facet of the aesthetic of revolutionary theatre. Mark Darlow, 'History and (Meta-)Theatricality: The French Revolution's Paranoid Aesthetics', *Modern Language Review*, 105 (2010), 384–400.

13. John Warrack has noted the influence of French operas on Weber's style in *German Opera: From the Beginnings to Wagner* (Cambridge: Cambridge University Press, 2001), 304–5.

14. Ibid., 306.

15. Anthony Newcomb, 'New Light(s) on Weber's Wolf's Glen Scene', in Thomas Bauman and Marita Petzoldt McClymonds (eds.), *Opera and the Enlightenment* (Cambridge: Cambridge University Press, 1995), 61–88.

16. Eugène Scribe, *Le Prophète* [libretto] (Paris: Brandus [1849]), Act V scene 6.

17. See, e.g., Mary Ann Smart on the conclusion to *Aida* in *Mimomania: Music and Gesture in Nineteenth-Century Opera* (Berkeley: University of California Press, 2004), ch. 5: 'Uneasy Bodies: Verdi and Sublimation'.

18. John Deathridge, *Wagner Beyond Good and Evil* (Berkeley: University of California Press, 2008), 74. For more on the multisensory nature of such scenes, rooted in French practice, see Gundula Kreuzer, *Curtain, Gong, Steam: Wagnerian Technologies of Nineteenth-Century Opera* (Berkeley: University of California Press, 2019).

19. Marian Smith, 'Three Hybrid Works at the Paris Opéra, circa 1830', *Dance Chronicle*, 24/1 (2001), 7–53. See also, Smith, *Ballet and Opera in the Age of Giselle* (Princeton: Princeton University Press, 2000).

20. Sarah Hibberd, *French Grand Opera and the Historical Imagination* (Cambridge: Cambridge University Press, 2009), ch. 2.

21. Smith, 'Three Hybrid Works at the Paris Opéra', 35–42.

22. For a more detailed discussion of these otherworldly voices in *Robert*, see Sarah Hibberd, '"Stranded in the Present": Temporal Expression in *Robert le diable*', in Roman Brotbeck, Kai Köpp, Laura Möckli, Anette Schaffer, and Stephanie Schroedter (eds.), *Image and Movement in Music Theatre* (Bern: Argus, 2018), 156–68.

23. Rebecca S. Wilberg, 'The *mise en scène* at the Paris Opéra – Salle Le Peletier (1821–1873) and the Staging of the First French Grand Opéra: Meyerbeer's *Robert le Diable*' (PhD dissertation, Brigham Young University, 1990).

24. Hector Berlioz, *Gazette musicale de Paris*, 2/28 (12 July 1835), 231.

25. Joseph d'Ortigue, *Revue de Paris*, 33 (4 December 1831), 26.

26. Heather Hadlock, 'Sonorous Bodies: Women and the Glass Harmonica', *Journal of the American Musicological Society*, 53/3 (2000), 507–42, at 534–5.

27. Emilio Sala, 'Women Crazed by Love: An Aspect of Romantic Opera', trans. William Ashbrook, *Opera Quarterly*, 10/3 (1994), 19–41, at, 40 n. 39; cited in ibid., 535.

28. Mary Ann Smart, 'The Silencing of Lucia', *Cambridge Opera Journal*, 4/2 (1992), 119–41, at 128–30.

29. Emily Dolan and John Tresch, 'A Sublime Invasion: Meyerbeer, Balzac, and the Opera Machine', *Opera Quarterly*, 27/1 (2011), 4–31, at 5. See further Tresch's chapter in this volume (Chapter 7).

30. For more on the especially French operatic resonances in *Roméo et Juliette*, and its 'mixed-genre' qualities, see Jeffrey Langford, 'The "Dramatic Symphonies" of Berlioz as an Outgrowth of the French Operatic Tradition', *Musical Quarterly*, 69/1 (1983), 85–103.

31. The details are published with the score, and discussed in Violaine Anger, 'Berlioz's *Roméo au tombeau*: Melodrama of the Mind', in Sarah Hibberd (ed.), *Melodramatic Voices: Understanding Music Drama* (Farnham: Ashgate, 2011), 185–96, at 186.

32. Ibid., 187.

33. Preface to *Roméo et Juliette*, cited in Langford, 'The "Dramatic Symphonies" of Berlioz', 93.

34. Cited and translated in Jeffrey Langford, 'The Symphonies', in Peter Bloom (ed.), *The Cambridge Companion to Berlioz* (Cambridge: Cambridge University Press, 2000), 53–68, at 63.

35. Anger describes in detail the orchestral commentary in this scene and argues for it as 'melodrama of the mind' in 'Berlioz's *Roméo au tombeau*'.

36. Thomas S. Grey, 'Tableaux vivants: Landscape, History Painting, and the Visual Imagination in Mendelssohn's Orchestral Music', *19th-Century Music*, 21/1 (1997), 38–76, at 41. See further Thomas Peattie's chapter in this volume (Chapter 4).

37. See, e.g., Beth S. Wright, *Painting and History during the French Restoration: Abandoned by the Past* (Cambridge: Cambridge University Press, 1997).

38. Sarah Hibberd, '*Le Naufrage de la Méduse* and Operatic Spectacle in 1830s Paris', *19th-Century Music*, 36/3 (2013), 248–63.

39. Emilio Sala, 'Musique et dramatisation dans la "pantomime dialogue": le cas de L'Homme au masque de fer (1790)', in Jacqueline Waeber (ed.), *Musique et geste en France de Lully à la revolution* (Bern: Peter Lang, 2009), 215–31, at 216; he uses the phrase 'adhésion du public à la scène'.

40. James Q. Davies, 'Dancing the Symphonic: Beethoven-Bochsa's Symphonie Pastorale, 1829', *19th-Century Music*, 27/1 (2003), 25–47.

41. Hector Berlioz, *A Critical Study of Beethoven's Nine Symphonies*, trans. Edwin Evans, intro. D. Kern Holoman (Urbana: University of Illinois Press, 2000), 44, 88; *The Art of Music and Other Essays [A travers chant]*, ed. and

trans. Elizabeth Csicsery-Rónay (Bloomington: Indiana University Press, 1994), 25.

Further Reading

Brittan, Francesca. *Music and Fantasy in the Age of Berlioz* (Cambridge: Cambridge University Press, 2017).

Charlton, David. 'Storms, Sacrifices: The "Melodrama Model" in Opera', in *French Opera 1730–1830: Meaning and Media* (Aldershot: Ashgate, 2000), 1–61.

Dolan, Emily, and Tresch, John. 'A Sublime Invasion: Meyerbeer, Balzac, and the Opera Machine', *Opera Quarterly*, 27/1 (2011), 4–31.

Grey, Thomas S. '*Tableaux vivants*: Landscape, History Painting, and the Visual Imagination in Mendelssohn's Orchestral Music', *19th-Century Music*, 21/1 (1997), 38–76.

Hambridge, Katherine, and Hicks, Jonathan (eds.). *The Melodramatic Moment: Music and Theatrical Culture, 1790–1820* (Chicago: University of Chicago Press, 2018).

Hibberd, Sarah. *French Grand Opera and the Historical Imagination* (Cambridge: Cambridge University Press, 2009).

Loughridge, Deirdre. *Haydn's Sunrise, Beethoven's Shadow: Audiovisual Culture and the Emergence of Musical Romanticism* (Chicago: University of Chicago Press, 2016).

Sala, Emilio. *L'opera senza canto: il mélo romantico e l'invenzione della colonna Sonora* (Venice: Marsilio, 1995).

Smith, Marian. *Ballet and Opera in the Age of Giselle* (Princeton: Princeton University Press, 2000).

Waeber, Jacqueline. *En Musique dans le texte: Le mélodrama, de Rousseau à Schoenberg* (Paris: Van Dieren, 2005).

18 | Romanticism and Performance

DANA GOOLEY

Romanticism originated in Germany and England as a philosophical and literary movement, not a musical one. It took music into its orbit only in the early decades of the nineteenth century, when Friedrich Rochlitz wrote fantastical essays for the *Allgemeine musikalische Zeitung* – one of the earliest music periodicals of the modern sort – and when the popular writer E. T. A. Hoffmann published his stories and novellas, where music is aligned with eccentric or irrational minds, psychological states of exaltation or brooding melancholy, and with supernatural, divine, or otherwise transcendent presences. The principal medium of the movement, literature – whether fictional, moral, philosophical, religious, historical, or journalistic – is important to keep in mind when considering its relation to performers and performance. For it is very difficult to say that *any* performer was 'Romantic' by virtue of anything specifically performative. To a significant degree, performers became 'Romantic' not by what they did on stage, but by actions of writing and literary interpretation. Older studies of Romanticism struggled to delineate its consistent 'traits' and 'characteristics', but it is more useful to concentrate, as more recent scholars have, on Romanticism in terms of the reader's or spectator's disposition, attitude, and sensibility. Romanticism might be defined in these terms as an orientation towards the perception and interpretation of things – an attunement to, and drive to discover qualities of mystery, irrationality, fantasy, psychological complexity, and fervent expression. This orientation was formed by literary authors, and burned into the receptive dispositions of readers before musicians ever took Romanticism as a stimulus to any particular manner of performing music. The whole notion of a 'Romantic' performer, in other words, could only come about through the entwining of literary and musical worlds, an entwining greatly favoured by the growth of musical periodicals in the nineteenth century. The Romantic artist became a viable identity because public concert life was expanding alongside a dramatic growth in journalism and popular print culture. Audiences came to concerts equipped with notions and expectations shaped by popular fiction, which depicted the lives and creative work of artists, and by

311

journalism, which circulated anecdotes and reports about touring musicians to an international readership.

In fiction, the most influential shapers of Romantic images of musical performance were E. T. A. Hoffmann and Sir Walter Scott, both of whose works travelled widely in translation. Hoffmann's most famous musical character, appearing in several of his stories and novellas of the 1810s, is Kapellmeister Johannes Kreisler. Kreisler is an archetype of the creative artist – completely devoted to his art and fully committed to transcending the limitations of quotidian experience through a surrender to music's sentimental or sublime power. The stories revolve around the tension between his musical life – lived in an otherworldly orbit, 'the Ideal' – and his everyday life, which is full of banal conventions and prosaic characters that perpetually impede access to the Ideal. As he struggles to negotiate this tension Kreisler manifests eccentric behaviour and bitterly ironic outbursts. Not least amongst the social impediments are rigid class barriers that prevent Kreisler from attaining his true beloved. In a representative scene from the fantastic novel *Life and Opinions of Tomcat Murr*, Kreisler is in love with an upper-class woman, Julia, whose parents object to his lower social status and seek to prevent a marriage. Their love can find realisation only in the anti-real, fantastical realm of musical performance:

Without a word Kreisler abruptly seated himself at the piano, and played the first chords of the duet as though seized and transfixed by a strange disturbance. Julia began: *Ah che mi manga l'anima in si fatal momento.* – – It is important to note that the words of this duet spoke quite simply, in the usual Italian manner, about the parting of a pair of lovers . . . . Kreisler had accordingly set these words in a state of highest agitation, with a great ardour, so that when performed it would irresistibly transport anyone to whom heaven had given even mediocre ears. The duet was the most passionate in the genre, and since Kreisler only strove for the highest expression of the moment, and did not take up Julia's calm, collected manner, his intonation went off quite badly. And thus it came about that Julia commenced hesitantly, with an almost uncertain voice, and that Kreisler entered hardly more felicitously. But soon both voices elevated themselves onto the waves of song like gleaming swans, now rising toward the golden, radiant clouds with whooshing wings, then dying away in sweet embraces of love in the rustling river of chords, until a deep sigh of exhalation announced approaching death and the final *Addio* gushed from the breast of the torn hearts like a bleeding fountain.[1]

Several motifs in this passage became central to the Romantic idea of performance: the sudden inspiration, the expressive immediacy, the feeling of otherworldly transcendence at the end. Most distinctive to Hoffmann is the process narrated: Kreisler does not warm into the performance gradually, as if by graduated steps, but is caught unexpectedly by his inspiration, as if another world has stolen upon his mind. And the singing pair has to work through practical, material problems – misalignments of feeling and tuning – before launching their erotic flight in song. In these ways Hoffmann accents the irreconcilable difference between social-material reality and art-mediated ideality, clearly privileging the latter as the locus of fulfilment, perfection, and social harmony.

Hoffmann's Romanticisation of music did not always centre on per-formers or performance. His famous essay on Beethoven's Fifth Symphony, for example, concentrated on the score, and particularly the recurring musical motive, not its performance. His celebrations of church polyphony stressed pure, disembodied sound.[2] Nonetheless, his fictions disseminated influential images of the optimally inspired, impassioned performer, of the musician whose performances perfectly reflect his inner life, and of the performer who is as interesting to watch as to hear because he seems so removed from conventional society and behaviour.

The fiction of Sir Walter Scott, too, gave forth influential Romantic images of musical performance, but without the psychological and ironic tinges characteristic of Hoffmann. Scott suffused his novels with the atmos-phere of the Scottish Highlands, imagined as a premodern, tribal society regulated by chivalrous and martial heroism, yet miraculously still alive in the backwaters of 'civilised' eighteenth-century Europe. In this more organic, 'natural' Highland world music is inseparable from poetry, and poetry is the carrier of *Volksgeist* – an original 'spirit of the people' uncorrupted by civilising influences.[3] And because the people in this world do not have printed literature, poetry exists only as performance: song and bardic recitation accompanied by music. The eponymous hero of the novel *Waverley* is an English gentleman who ventures out into the Scottish territory and discovers a tribal society led by chieftain Mac-Ivor. In a representative scene, Waverley encounter's Mac-Ivor's sister Flora in a sylvan setting:

Here, like one of those lovely forms which decorate the landscapes of Poussin, Waverley found Flora, gazing on the waterfall. Two paces further back stood Cathleen, holding a small Scottish harp. . . . Edward thought he had never, even in his wildest dreams, imagined a figure of such exquisite and interesting loveliness. The wild beauty of the retreat, bursting upon him as if by magic, augmented the mingled feeling of delight and awe with which he approached her. . . . [Flora] led the way to a spot at such a distance from the cascade, that its sound should rather accompany than interrupt that of her voice and instrument, and, sitting down upon a mossy fragment of rock, she took the harp from Cathleen. . . . [T]he wild feeling of romantic delight with which he heard the first few notes she drew from her instrument, amounted almost to a sense of pain. He would not for worlds have quitted his place by her side; yet he almost longed for solitude, that he might decipher and examine at leisure the complication of emotions which now agitated his bosom. . . . Flora had exchanged the measured and monotonous recitative of the bard for a lofty and uncommon Highland air, which had been a battle-song in former ages. A few irregular strains introduced a prelude of a wild and peculiar tone, which harmonized well with the distant waterfall, and the soft sigh of the evening breeze in the rustling leaves of an aspen which overhung the seat of the fair harpess. The following verses convey but little idea of the feelings with which, so sung and accompanied, they were heard by Waverley . . . .[4]

What is characteristically Romantic in this account is not just the integration of the singer with the natural world around her, but the particular type of 'beauty' it celebrates: the 'wild beauty' of the natural scene resounds through the 'wild and peculiar' tones of the harp prelude and stimulates in Waverley 'wild feeling of romantic delight'.[5] This fantastical music is in many respects the negative image of 'civilised' European music. Just a few decades earlier, the learned music historian Charles Burney had criticised as 'barbaric' the dissonances of seventeenth-century composers such as Henry Purcell, which modern composers had normalised through consonant contrapuntal solutions. From the Romantic viewpoint, however, such moments of musical alterity are valued for their unfamiliarity, surprise, and mystery; they generate unaccountable feelings that make Waverley want to 'decipher and examine at leisure the complication of emotions'. And in another Romantic trope, the narrator underlines the insufficiency of the printed page in representing the full power of Flora's song; only in performance, and only in its reception, does music attain its full meaning.[6]

In very different ways, then, Hoffmann and Scott celebrated the vital energy and communicative intensity of 'live' performance. A similar impetus gave rise to the Romantic celebration of poetry improvisers, who were particularly numerous in Italy in the decades around 1800. The celebrity of extemporaneous poets such as Rosa Taddei and Tomassi Sgricci, as well as Germaine de Staël's heroine Corinne, advanced a poetic aesthetic privileging performance over textual transmission. At the same time, these improvisers were greeted with widespread suspicion, which suggests that Romanticism was only partially committed to performance as such, or was committed to it only in rhetoric.[7]

I have dwelled on literary constructions of performance because there was very little impetus within musical life itself for the emergence of figures such as Niccolò Paganini and Franz Liszt, the paradigmatic Romantic instrumentalists. Most virtuoso instrumentalists of Paganini's and Liszt's time continued to self-present as gentlemen, with polished social manners and a collected, detached onstage demeanour. Paganini was fully forty-six years of age when he left Italy in 1828 and began the European concert tours that made him so famous, and there is very little evidence that a 'Romantic' aura surrounded him before then. It was only when German, French, and English writers, steeped in Romantic ideas and Romantic journalistic tropes, poured out articles and essays about the violinist that Paganini acquired an image as a 'Romantic' artist. Outside Italy Paganini appeared otherworldly and fantastical for a number of reasons. He did not have a European network of professional and personal connections prior to his tours, and was in this sense truly unfamiliar. In private society he was reserved and introverted, giving the impression he had dark secrets to conceal. He was visibly in compromised health – gaunt and with sunken cheeks – as if paying for some transgression. He did not hold the violin in a standard 'noble' manner but held it close to his chest, pointing more downward, as if cradling it.

All of these elements combined to make Paganini a mysterious, exotic, and compelling personality and opened him to Romantic appropriation. But it was above all his astonishing instrumental bravura that made him seem to be 'from another world'. The speed, density, and complexity of his violin playing was so far beyond the norm that it disorientated spectators, dissolving normative perception altogether. Not everyone welcomed the feeling of being overwhelmed or crushed by a player's generative and creative power, an effect sometimes described in Romantic terms as the ascendancy of the 'sublime' over the 'beautiful'. But the extremely enthusiastic responses of audiences everywhere attest that the European public found such disturbing, excessive, and irrational sensations pleasurable and desirable. And to this extent, at least, Paganini opened up a quite new, nominally 'Romantic' world of musical experience.

These sensations were not the result of Paganini's technical instrumental command alone. They were also the product of his distinctive handling of the violin. In the most complex bravura passages, he treated the violin polyphonically, leaping across the strings and assigning each string a distinctive sound or sound-figure. He presented listeners with a melange of pizzicatos, harmonics, and arco sounds, all intermingled in such a manner that it sounded like two or three performers or, indeed, different instruments. He was a master imitator of voices, both animal and human. Entire passages in harmonics – still very rare in the 1830s – could sound like old or ghostly presences. Entire passages on the G string alone, also a Paganini trademark, evoked the deep pathos of a tragic opera heroine. With the use of 'illegitimate' scratchy bowing techniques and 'grotesque' vibrato he conjured the sounds of mocking, demonic laughter and the voices of damned souls. Altogether, his playing offering up a charivari of singing and chattering voices, thoroughly disrupting the dominance of regular figuration and 'singing tone' in violin aesthetics.[8]

The predominant reception of Paganini as 'Mephistophelean', 'demonic', and 'diabolical' represents the influence of E. T. A. Hoffmann's popular musical stories, particularly those characters, usually outsiders of some sort, who seem to be 'normal' on the surface but give forth a 'darker' second self beneath the surface.[9] It is important to remember, in this connection, that Paganini was just as admired for his melodic playing – heard in slow movements, cantabile introductions, and variations played on the G string – as for his bravura. This playing rendered plaintive, passionate, and 'noble' sentiments that offset the demonic playing and stylised his playing into this sharp duality – a performance of incommensurables.

Franz Liszt, often considered the paradigmatic Romantic pianist, was directly inspired by Paganini, first witnessing him in performance at the Paris Opéra in 1832. The experience spurred him on to the superhuman levels of instrumental virtuosity for which he is well known, and Paganini doubtless also served as an example of how a concert instrumentalist can, through the force of a theatrical stage presence, turn a public concert into a supercharged dramatic ritual. While Liszt picked up his 'Mephistophelean' mode from Paganini, his personas and postures did not resolve into the normal/diabolical polarity. Rather he performed a multitude of personas and affective modes – military, pastoral, patriotic, mocking, dreamy, priestly – and fascinated audiences by transitioning, metamorphically, from one to the other within a single extended concert piece. This required little more, and nothing less, than fully engaging his facial and bodily expressions to mimic the characters and scenes that furnished the material of his concert fantasies, a majority of which were based in popular contemporary opera, such as his transcription of Rossini's *William Tell* overture, or the *Reminiscences of Don Juan*. Virtuosos had long been playing fantasies based on opera tunes and popular folk songs, but they had always adopted the role of 'musical professional', a gentleman and skilled artisan. Liszt alone approached such fantasies as a template for role-play and dramatic acting – he 'became' what he played, became whatever the music signified.

Liszt's performance model was radically new and provoked a great deal of professional and critical opposition. But this opposition was impotent in the face of Liszt's seemingly limitless popularity. The boundless enthusiasm that greeted him everywhere ushered in a distinctively modern sort of celebrity. Reports of his 'victories' over audiences circulated widely in the international press and shaped him into living legend. Biographical pamphlets written by close associates from the Romantic circle, like Marie d'Agoult and George Sand, expanded the anecdotal penumbra hovering around him. The legend accrued various levels of meaning through widely reported episodes of demonstrative patriotism, political resistance, heroic charity, and private romance that seemed to fuse his private and public selves, and convinced people that Liszt's life and his art were seamlessly joined.[10] In this he was anticipated only by Lord Byron – the poet, Romantic adventurer, and passionate advocate for Greek independence. Byron was the Romantic personality to whom Liszt professed the greatest debt, and it can appear as though Liszt's compelling, idealistic, and self-fashioned persona occupied the void left by the poet's premature death in 1824. Liszt, however, added to the Byronic image a pronounced spiritual and religious dimension. He published religion-themed compositions, and apprenticed himself to the poet, priest, and political theorist Abbé Lamennais. He published essays arguing that the modern artist must be like a priest, leading the public towards a brighter future by regenerating its sense of the ideal and the spiritual.[11] Although a composer might have fulfilled this role, it seems clear that Liszt was modelling this kind of artist in his own image – entrancing his audiences with inspired pianistic sermons and lifting them into states of ecstasy.

The interplay of live performance and print culture so central to Liszt's Romantic image was equally as important, if not more important, in the case of Chopin. Chopin spent most of his time teaching and composing, and he performed in public only rarely. The dissemination of his public reputation was thus mainly the work of the Romantic authors with whom he circulated, including George Sand, Heinrich Heine, and indeed Liszt. Such writers accentuated his Polish national origins, his pained feelings of exile (from politically 'repressive' Poland), his innate, introverted melancholy, and his deeply nuanced, 'poetic' sensibility. They rarely described Chopin's music without imagining Chopin himself playing it. They often wrote of his 'improvisations' as if the score or the piece in question did not matter, so fully and directly did the art emanate from within the artist's soul. The impression that he was improvising was doubtless enhanced by his distinctive rubato approach to time – inspired as much by bel canto singing as by the greater sustaining power of the latest pianos – which made far greater room for accelerating or retarding the motion of a phrase and lingering on melodic details for a sense of freedom and expressive nuance.[12] The notion of Chopin as a 'Romantic' pianist thus crystallised quite exclusively around his performance of poetic inferiority and noble melancholy, filtering out the heroic bravura that other, more publicly active virtuosos highlighted. While he was not 'cold' and 'objective' like Kalkbrenner (with whom he seriously considered studying), his playing had nothing of Liszt's dramatic mimesis or metamorphic transformability, and he did not invite poetic fantasy into the titles or genres of music he wrote, the Ballades possibly excepted. And as Charles Rosen has underlined, the predominating construction of Chopin as a 'Romantic' obscures his considerable debt to classical ideas and particularly the constructive refinement of J. S. Bach's music.[13] This side of his musical temperament exerted some restraint upon the Romantic influences that might otherwise have overtaken him more completely.

Also found in the circle of Liszt and Chopin was Hector Berlioz. Berlioz is normally thought of as a composer first and foremost, yet his conducting played no small part in establishing his reputation within and beyond France. He was moreover a talented writer who turned to journalism for extra income, and his writing betrays the influence of Romantic literature. His symphonic works announced an alliance with literary Romanticism by taking impetus from Sir Walter Scott, Goethe, Shakespeare, Victor Hugo, and fantastical authors. The orchestral scores inspired by these works were so novel, detailed, and complex by the standards of their day that only Berlioz himself was capable of conducting the rehearsals and performances. It was a role he appears to have relished, in spite of the formidable logistical and administrative challenges it imposed. He had never mastered an instrument, and he craved the visibility, power, and acknowledgement conducting could bring him. His dedication to conducting won him public status and audience connection that compensated, to a degree, for the profound sense of alienation he felt as a composer. Indeed, a shortage of opportunities and income at home prompted him to undertake risky, exceedingly laborious tours to various European countries, where he became known as both conductor and composer – and as a personality.

But was Berlioz a 'Romantic' conductor? Perhaps no conductor was ever as Romantic as virtuosos like Liszt and Paganini, or actors like Charles Kean and Marie Dorval. The role of the orchestra leader demanded too much in terms of leadership and 'service' – to the coordination of the ensemble, to the engagement of the public, to the sponsors of the concert enterprise – to sustain performances of interiority, wild fantasy, or poetic reverie commonly associated with Romantic performers. (It appears that Liszt, in his role as Kapellmeister in Weimar in the 1850s, was the first conductor to embody the evolving musical passions with facial and bodily mimicry after the fashion of Romantic virtuosos.) Yet 'service' itself could be Romantic, as long as the conductor's activity was directed towards 'art' and the creative 'genius', not royal patrons or frivolous aristocrats. Berlioz was perhaps the most important figure to rethink the conductor's role in this way. 'There are two quite distinct parts to the task of the conductor', he wrote in his memoirs: 'the first (the easier) consists solely in leading the execution of a work already known to the players'.

In the second, on the contrary, it is his business to direct the study of a score unknown to the performers, to help reveal the thought of the author, render it clear and salient, eliciting from the players qualities of fidelity, ensemble and expression without which there is no music; and, having mastered the practical difficulties, to identify himself with them [the players], warm them with his ardour, animate them with his enthusiasm, in a word, to transmit his inspiration.[14]

Here the conductor is an exceptional, superior figure – an artist – possessing exclusive insight into the composer's intention and gifted with fiery enthusiasm he can channel outwards. Berlioz embodied this new model with meticulous attention to detail, generally high standards, his insistence on fidelity to the score, and his demonstrative reverence for the 'great' works of Beethoven, Gluck, Halévy, and others. This curatorial attitude towards modern and older classics – essentially the 'interpreter' role as it is understood today – is often falsely presented as the opposite of that of the 'Romantic' performer, the latter understood as a charismatic, egotistical celebrity playing his or her own music.[15] The interpreter identity, insofar as it cast the performer as a priest, medium, or messenger, emerged out of Romanticism every bit as much as did the radically individual heroic virtuoso. Liszt, who played both roles with considerable success, is the proof.

Berlioz's conducting was also capable of signifying Romanticism in more direct, embodied ways. Between his oversized coif, dress, and purposeful gesturing he had an arresting persona from the podium – a heroic stance contrasting sharply with the more conventional, self-effacing demeanour of orchestral leaders (as seen in a famous 1846 illustration).[16] He also exploited the potential of larger performing ensembles to generate experiences of terror and sublimity that are distinctly Romantic (and represented, respectively, in two of his most-programmed works, the

'March to the Scaffold' and his arrangement of the 'Rákócsy March'). At the conclusion of the 1844 industrial exposition in Paris, for instance, he had the idea of putting on a grand 'monster' concert at the exposition hall. The concert would include vast performing forces and a lengthy programme of choral, orchestral, and operatic works, the majority of them from the repertoire of the Paris opera houses. He envisioned the concert as a performance of massive, sublime power, in which the conductor is a radiant centre of energy, sending his energy out to the public through a network of subsidiary conductors, instruments, and voices. From the moment the introduction to Spontini's *Vestale* began, he recalled,

the majesty, power, and ensemble of this enormous mass of instruments and voices became more and more remarkable. My thousand and twenty-two artists moved in unity as if they were the members of an excellent quartet. I had two secondary conductors ... In addition, five choral conductors, one placed in the middle of the others at the corners of the choral mass, were in charge of transmitting my movements to the singers .... Thus there were seven time-keepers, who never lost eye-contact with me, and our eight arms, though placed a great distance from each other, rose up simultaneously with the most unbelievable precision. It was this miraculous ensemble that astonished the public so much.[17]

The key word here is 'miraculous'. The Romantic conductor only succeeds if he transcends the 'achievement' to arrive at the 'miracle'. Later in the concert, when the 'Benediction of the Swords' from *Les Huguenots* played, 'I was taken, while conducting, by a nervous trembling such that my teeth chattered, as if in a violent feverish rush .... This terrifying piece, which one would think written with electric fluid by a gigantic battery of Volta, seemed to be accompanied by lightning strokes and sung by storm winds.'[18] In passages like this Berlioz was both describing his performance and summoning the literary tropes of Romanticism – tropes he commanded as a professional-level writer and journalist.

As influential as Liszt, Paganini, and Berlioz were, most instrumental virtuosos and orchestra leaders in the nineteenth century continued to self-present as gentlemen – persons of refined manners and disciplined self-possession. Liszt's students were generally less 'Romantic' in their performance manner than their teacher, and Berlioz the conductor only found a spiritual successor later in the century, in the figure of Gustav Mahler. Playing habits associated with Romanticism – free, flexible approaches to rhythm and time, the fetishisation of varied tonal colours, use of strong contrasts of dynamics and tempo, and an emphasis on the momentary impetus as against the composer's letter – persisted well into the twentieth century, and continue to exert a profound influence on classical music performance.[19] After the Second World War a profoundly anti-Romantic reaction set in, and it was in this context that the term 'Romantic' became an overall designation for 'nineteenth-century' performance. The renewed literalism and emphasis on textual fidelity after the war prompted Vladimir Horowitz to declare 'I'm a 19th-century Romantic. I am the last. I take terrible risks . . . . The score is not a bible, and I am never afraid to dare. The music is behind those dots. You search for it, and that is what I mean by the grand manner. I play, so to speak, from the other side of the score, looking back.'[20]

In today's discourse, performers are typically called 'Romantic' if they fall on the more emotive or passionate side of the spectrum, with 'cerebral' or 'intellectual' at the opposite pole. The regulating ideals of today's classical music culture appear to favour moderate balance between the Romanticism of the later nineteenth century and the more severe, structure-oriented modernism of the mid-twentieth. And yet every so often there appears a new performer – a Gidon Kremer or Nigel Kennedy, an Ivo Pogorelich or Lang Lang or Lucas Debargue – who disturbs the peace, throws conventional expectations out of balance, and reminds us of the wilder, disruptive energies that Romanticism unleashed into the musical world in the early nineteenth century.

Notes

1. E. T. A. Hoffmann, *Lebensansichten des Katers Murr* (Hamburg: Hamburgische Hausbibliothek, 1912), 120.
2. On this lesser-known aspect of musical romanticism, see James Garratt, *Palestrina and the German Romantic Imagination: Interpreting Historicism in Nineteenth-Century Music* (Cambridge: Cambridge University Press, 2002), particularly ch. 2.
3. See Matthew Gelbart, *The Invention of Folk Music and Art Music: Emerging Categories from Ossian to Wagner* (Cambridge: Cambridge University Press, 2007).
4. Sir Walter Scott, *Waverley* (Edinburgh: Robert Cadell, 1842), 144.
5. Early Romantic discourse developed an aesthetic of 'the picturesque' centred on the interplay between wild, fantastical proliferation and underlying rational order. See Annette Richards, *The Free Fantasia and the Musical Picturesque* (Cambridge: Cambridge University Press, 2001).
6. For English translations and commentary see *E. T. A. Hoffmann's Musical Writings: Kreisleriana, The Poet and the Composer, Music Criticism*, ed.

David Charlton, trans. Martyn Clarke (Cambridge: Cambridge University Press, 1989).

7. Angela Esterhammer, *Romanticism and Improvisation, 1750–1850* (Cambridge: Cambridge University Press, 2009). On musical improvisers in this period see Dana Gooley, *Fantasies of Improvisation: Free Playing in Nineteenth-Century Music* (Oxford: Oxford University Press, 2017).

8. Dana Gooley, '"La Commedia del Violino": Paganini's Comic Strains', *Musical Quarterly*, 88/3 (2005), 370–427.

9. For an analysis of these narratives see Maiko Kawabata, *Paganini, the 'Demonic' Virtuoso* (Woodbridge: Boydell & Brewer, 2013).

10. Adrian Williams (ed.), *Portrait of Liszt: By Himself and His Contemporaries* (New York: Oxford University Press, 1990).

11. Charles Suttoni (ed. and trans.), *Franz Liszt, an Artist's Journey: Lettres d'un bachelier ès musique, 1835–1841* (Chicago: Chicago University Press, 1989).

12. Jean-Jacques Eigeldinger (ed. and trans.), *Chopin: Pianist and Teacher, as Seen by His Pupils* (Cambridge: Cambridge University Press, 1986).

13. Charles Rosen, *The Romantic Generation* (Cambridge, MA: Harvard University Press, 1995). See especially ch. 5.

14. *Mémoires de Hector Berlioz, membre de l'Institut de France: comprenant ses voyages en Italie, en Allemagne, en Russie et en Angleterre*, 2 vols. (Paris: Calmann-Lévy, 1878), vol. 2, 247.

15. See Mary Hunter, '"To Play as if from the Soul of the Composer": The Idea of the Performer in Early Romantic Aesthetics', *Journal of the American Musicological Society*, 58/2 (2005), 357–98.

16. See https://commons.wikimedia.org/wiki/Category: Caricatures_of_Hector_Berlioz#/media/File:Berlioz_conducting.jpg

17. *Mémoires de Hector Berlioz*, vol. 2, 268.

18. Ibid., 169.

19. Kenneth Hamilton, *Romantic Pianism and Modern Performance* (New York: Oxford University Press, 2008).

20. Bernard Holland, 'Vladimir Horowitz, Titan of the Piano, Dies', *New York Times*, 6 November 1989, section A, 1.

Further Reading

Berlioz, Hector. *Memoirs of Hector Berlioz, from 1803 to 1865, Comprising His Travels in Germany, Italy, Russia, and England*, trans. R. Holmes and E. Holmes, ann. Ernest Newman (New York: Dover Publications, 1960).

Eigeldinger, Jean-Jacques (ed. and trans.). *Chopin: Pianist and Teacher, as Seen by His Pupils* (Cambridge: Cambridge University Press, 1986).

Esterhammer, Angela. *Romanticism and Improvisation, 1750–1850* (Cambridge: Cambridge University Press, 2009).

Garratt, James. *Palestrina and the German Romantic Imagination: Interpreting Historicism in Nineteenth-Century Music* (Cambridge: Cambridge University Press, 2002).

Gelbart, Matthew. *The Invention of 'Folk Music' and 'Art Music': Emerging Categories from Ossian to Wagner* (Cambridge: Cambridge University Press, 2007).

Gooley, Dana. *Fantasies of Improvisation: Free Playing in Nineteenth-Century Music* (New York: Oxford University Press, 2017).

'"La Commedia del Violino": Paganini's Comic Strains', *Musical Quarterly*, 88/3 (2005), 370–427.

The Virtuoso Liszt (Cambridge: Cambridge University Press, 2004).

Hamilton, Kenneth. *Romantic Pianism and Modern Performance* (New York: Oxford University Press, 2008).

Hunter, Mary. '"To Play as if from the Soul of the Composer": The Idea of the Performer in Early Romantic Aesthetics', *Journal of the American Musicological Society*, 58/2 (2005), 357–98.

Kawabata, Maiko. *Paganini, the 'Demonic' Virtuoso* (Woodbridge: Boydell & Brewer, 2013).

Richards, Annette. *The Free Fantasia and the Musical Picturesque* (Cambridge: Cambridge University Press, 2001).

Suttoni, Charles (ed. and trans.). *Franz Liszt, an Artist's Journey: Lettres d'un bachelier ès musique, 1835–1841* (Chicago: Chicago University Press, 1989).

Williams, Adrian (ed.). *Portrait of Liszt: By Himself and His Contemporaries* (New York: Oxford University Press, 1990).

PART V

Histories

19 | Musical Romanticism as a Historiographical Construct

NICOLE GRIMES

> Your song came over me like a lullaby, he says. Like the unconscious has
> a language it can speak in. The unconscious, the subconscious, I've never
> known the difference. What I mean is, it sounded like one of them was
> singing.
>
> I know what you mean very well, but it's a conscious and everyday and
> very real language, Alda says. What'll we call it? Romanticism, I suppose.[1]

From Classicism to Romanticism

One of the truisms of twentieth-century music history textbooks is that
there is a clear distinction between classicism and Romanticism in music,
with each term allotted a specific historical period and associated style. Yet
there is little evidence of this distinction in nineteenth-century practice or
writings. Instead, it is only when musical Romanticism is ostensibly over
that the concept of a Romantic era starts being crystallised.

The earliest references to these two terms in a musical context actually
undermine any notion of strict historical periodisation. To avoid what he
perceived to be the flawed binary opposition between the classical (i.e., 'the
expression of the Greek character') and the Romantic (i.e., 'the expression
of the Christian religious idea'), Karl August Kahlert, in an 1848 essay
called 'On the Concepts of Classical and Romantic in Music', suggested
opposing Romanticism with antiquity, which would thereby allow for the
word 'classic' to refer to 'that which is excellent, exemplary in its kind or
genre'.[2] He conceded, however, that musical categories had grown up
around the terms 'classical' and 'Romantic', with the former designating
the music of composers preoccupied with the laws of musical form, and the
latter designating composers who wish 'to assert the freedom of the spirit'
against such formal musical laws. For Kahlert, notably, each of these two
categories was populated by post-Beethovenian composers: in the classical,
there is Hummel and Spohr, in the Romantic Schumann, Loewe, Berlioz,
and Paganini, amongst others.

Over half a century later, in 1911, Guido Adler (1855–1941) discerned a clear division between the 'classical style' and the 'Romantic school', though again he uses the two primarily as categories that can operate flexibly throughout history and are not confined to one specific age. In *Der Stil in der Musik* (*Style in Music*) the 'classical' style is characterised as an aesthetic and historical concept which embraces, first, the a cappella music of the sixteenth century; second, the polyphonic music from the time of Bach and Handel (which he designates as 'alt-klassische'); and third, the Viennese classical composers (the 'neu-klassische') with their main focus on the form of the sonata.[3] Contrasted with this, in Adler's schematisation, is the 'Romantic school', the music of which exhibits a 'blurring of form' ('Verschwemmung der Form') which is bound up with 'disorder and excess' ('Regellosigkeit und Ausschweifung'), and a preference for colour and sound-painting.[4] Much like his 'classical style', the 'Romantic school' also 'begins with the heyday of a cappella music', but it rapidly extends beyond this 'with the use of chromaticism by the madrigalists', and it is once again found in the 'eccentricity' of the music of those composers he refers to with his singular use of the term 'neo-Romanticists' for the nineteenth century.[5]

In places, however, Adler seems to point to the historical usage more familiar to us now. Certain late works by Mozart, for instance, fall in the category of a 'transition' to Romanticism, and he also speaks of Romanticism without obvious reference to his transhistorical aesthetic scheme, for instance, 'the Romantic opera of the nineteenth century', or Paris as a 'breeding ground for instrumental virtuosity around 1830, which had a lasting impact on the Romantic style'.[6] And other writers around this time were similarly reducing what might have originally been considered open aesthetic categories to historical periods.[7]

This growing sense of a distinct Romantic period following an age of musical classicism was widely taken up in subsequent twentieth-century histories. The writings of Alfred Einstein (1880–1952) provide an influential example, from his *Geschichte der Musik* of 1917 to *Music in the Romantic Era* thirty years later.[8] Yet even while the periodisation solidified, the boundaries between the two categories were nevertheless still often blurred. This is exemplified in a classic 1942 study by Paul Henry Lang (1901–91). In Lang's view, 'Romanticism should not be taken as the antithesis of classicism, nor was it a mere reaction to it, but rather a logical enhancement of certain elements which in classicism were inherent and active, but tamed and kept in equilibrium.'[9] For him, the subjectivity that characterised Romanticism was not new, but instead had become increasingly more pronounced since the end of the seventeenth century.[10] Lang also argues that late classicism and early Romanticism did not necessarily alternate, but, instead for a time ran concurrently. He counts Goethe and Beethoven amongst 'the last giants of classicism, already affected by early Romanticism', and identifies a pivotal historical moment when 'in Hegel, Schelling, and Schleiermacher, classicism and Romanticism met, in Beethoven classicism became romantic, and in Schubert romanticism became classic'.[11]

In 1958, Friedrich Blume (1893–1975) also conceived of a continuum of musical Romanticism running from the eighteenth to the twentieth century. For him, the structural foundations of most Romantic music can be found in late eighteenth-century classical practice. According to this argument, 'Classicism and Romanticism' are 'two aspects of the same musical phenomenon'. There is 'no "Romantic style" as such, the way there are definable and delimitable styles for other periods of music history'. Instead, for Blume, 'there is only a slow transforming of the stylistic type that had taken shape at the beginning of the Classic-Romantic age'.[12] The elasticity of Blume's periodisation is evident when he speaks of 'the romanticism of J. S. Bach' in the same breath as he discusses the Infinite in relation to form and content in Stravinsky's *Poetics of Music*. Romanticism, in Blume's formulation, is a 'reaction against the aesthetics of the Enlightenment', one that nonetheless continues to contain much of the Enlightenment and to be 'a variant of musical Classicism'.[13] He argues that the 'unity of the [Romantic] period' was battered to pieces around the time of the First World War such that 'the generation that came on the scene around 1910–1920 found itself faced with the ruins'.[14] Whereas Blume's Romanticism embraces an extended periodisation, it is bound by stylistic limitations he draws at the 'classicistic, thoroughly anti-Romantic musical theater of Bellini, Donizetti, Rossini, and the young Verdi'.[15]

Despite the fluidity allowed by writers like Lang and Blume, it is nevertheless clear that in the century that separates them from Kahlert the idea of Romanticism in music has solidified from an aesthetic capable of broad historical application (witnessed already in E. T. A. Hoffmann's use of the term some three decades before) to a more or less definitely circumscribed historical-stylistic category concentrated on the nineteenth century.

Romanticism and the Caesura of 1848

If the origins of the idea of a Romantic period in music are less clear than popularly supposed, its end point is no less subject to debate. In many accounts, the year 1848 is considered to be a symbolic moment for the end of Romanticism (and musical Romanticism). At a purely musical level, there are sound reasons for this division. A generation of composers died or else stopped composing around mid-century, including Mendelssohn, Hensel, Schumann, and Chopin, amongst others. At this time, Wagner, Berlioz, and Liszt enjoyed increased notoriety and a younger generation of composers including Brahms were on their way to their first compositional maturity. Historiographical writings also emphasise the sociopolitical context for 1848 as a symbolic year of division. The failed revolutions put an end to the era of political liberalism of the late eighteenth and early nineteenth centuries that had 'projected an idealised image of what the world is'.[16] 'It would certainly be naïve', as Jim Samson notes, 'to identify the political turning point of 1848 as a precise divider of nineteenth-century music history. But it would be equally misguided to ignore the evidence of a caesura around that time', not least because of the abundant evidence that writers in 1848 articulated such an aesthetic break.[17]

Franz Brendel (1811–68), a proponent of the 'New German School' of Liszt and Wagner, recognised 'modern musical romanticism' as taking a direction that 'does not have the capability to penetrate and uplift the masses or to wield its power over all'. With its focus on inner subjectivity, he deemed Romanticism to be incompatible with 'the demands of the community' after the 1848 revolutions. Rather than 'seizing hold of reality', this autonomous art, which is so often 'inaccessible and unpalatable', offers only a negation of it.[18] Appealing like Brendel to a Hegelian framework, Kahlert argued that both the classical and Romantic styles were now superseded, for 'the political gravity of the present has thoroughly defeated the romantic worldview. There is no longer time in which to lose oneself in dreams.'[19] He traced the antecedents for this revolutionary thought back to the writings of the political activists Arnold Ruge and Georg Gottfried Gervinus a decade earlier who had argued that Romanticism 'had sapped the political energy of the German nation'.[20] Carl Kretschmann (1826–97), also writing in 1848, dismissed Romanticism as an aesthetic that led to inward contemplation rather than outward change.[21]

Drawing on these primary sources from 1848, Sanna Pederson argues convincingly for 'a period of musical anti-Romanticism' following the revolutions, noting a tendency to 're-conceptualise music at the most basic level of perception in order to disavow romantic affiliation'.[22] Her historical framework appeals to the lasting and profound legacy of Hegel's sceptical, anti-Romantic attitude towards music (viewed by him as a highly Romantic art), particularly his argument that 'amongst all the arts music has the maximum possibility of freeing itself from any actual text as well as from expression of any specific content'.[23] For Hegel, this freedom came at a price, for in liberating itself from the text, music lost its 'function as bearer of spirit'.[24]

Later authors have often taken their cue from such pronouncements. Lang, writing in 1942, considered 'the rekindled liberal movements of 1848' to have 'pushed romanticism into the background and it has never again come to life in its original guise'.[25] In keeping with Kahlert's categorisation of 1848, Lang argued that if Romanticism had been bound up with a Kantian expression of the self that revealed a mode of intuitive knowledge of the world through the work of the individual artist, then a return to formal convention, and the resulting prominence of form extinguished the spirit of Romanticism:

> The woods and groves, the fairylands and gnomes of early romanticism, waned; the domain of the romanticist became his innermost soul, his sentiments. No vestiges of a real world remained, and nothing coarse disturbed the spiritual quality of the music. This was a true idealism, but it, in its turn, had to give way. The worshippers of 'form' killed it. The priests of l'art pour l'art crippled art, for the form they championed was merely a pleasing arrangement of surfaces, not an inner necessity striving for articulation.[26]

Musical Romanticism in the Later Nineteenth Century: Neo-Romanticism, Realism, and Modernity

The Hegelian argument that music could no longer serve as a bearer of spirit, but only as an occasion for regressive subjectivity, has powerfully influenced the bifurcated view of music in the nineteenth century that informs twentieth-century writings. As Walter Frisch frames it, 'the term [Romanticism] is less well suited to the latter part of the [nineteenth] century'.[27] Arnold Whittall similarly argues that music was 'in a sense anachronistic' at this time.[28] Within the vast periodic expanse of his concept of musical Romanticism explored above, Lang's distinction between the terms Romantic and Romanticism underlines the same bifurcation, and posits that the discovery of 'the romantic' by 'the romanticists' was 'merely a rediscovery, a reawakening of an ageless human quality under a new name'. 'The romantic was still living in the second half of the nineteenth century', he claims, 'though not in its erstwhile ampleness, for life in itself is romantic and always has been; but it was no longer romanticism.'[29] With distinct echoes of Hegel, Lang refers to Romantic music after 1848 as 'artistic atheism', devoid of its former spirit,[30] explaining that 'there is little of the profound preoccupation with the problems of romanticism of Chopin or Schumann in Grieg or Tchaikovsky'. For the latter composers, 'romanticism was no longer an ideal to them, only an artistic metier'.[31] Carl Dahlhaus summarises the situation:

Early nineteenth-century music could be said to be romantic in an age of romanticism, which produced romantic poetry and painting and even romantic physics and chemistry, whereas the neo-romanticism of the later part of the century was romantic in an unromantic age, dominated by positivism and realism. Music, the romantic art, had become 'untimely' in general terms, though by no means unimportant; on the contrary, its very dissociation from the prevailing spirit of the age enabled it to fulfil a spiritual, cultural, and ideological function of magnitude which can hardly be exaggerated: it stood for an alternative world.[32]

Musical manifestations of Romanticism in the years after 1848 are hence sometimes termed 'neo-Romantic' to distinguish them from the Romanticism of the preceding decades, but other terms are also encountered in accounts of this period. Just as a classical period is now popularly supposed to have given way to a Romantic one around the early decades of the nineteenth century, so the concept of 'Romanticism' is itself regularly positioned as a precursor to the concept of 'realism' in music historical writings, with the two being considered to overlap in the second half of the century. For Paul Henry Lang, the shift 'from romanticism to realism' was bound up with social consciousness and the labour movement, played out in 'a clash between Christian ideals and those of capitalism'. The 'urge toward the proletarian' after 1848 did not mean 'that the romantic root had died, it merely stopped growing upward and continued to spread on the flat ground, for romanticism is not altogether opposed to realism; the social orientation had its beginnings in the romantic movement and subjective moments cannot be denied in nascent realism'.[33] Mark Evan Bonds defines 'the formalist realism that would come to dominate thinking about music from the second half of the nineteenth century until well into the twentieth' to be a reaction against the 'empty dreams' of Romanticism.[34] Again appealing to a Hegelian framework, Dahlhaus argues that the 'notion of a romantic art flourishing in a realist age contradicts the idea of a Zeitgeist which is of the same nature in all the arts'.[35] Critiquing the tendency to view the music of the entire century as the output of Romanticism, he adds that 'the problem represented by that contradiction will not be solved satisfactorily if it is crudely conceived in terms simply of a confrontation between romantic music and realist literature'.[36]

Realism was also understood to be bound up with the impact of science on the world of ideas. As a result of the industrial and scientific revolutions, realism was simultaneously seen as inaugurating 'an art of "scientific" analysis and observation', and as marking 'a loss of idealism and subjectivism'.[37] Writing in 1937, Ernst Bücken (1884–1949) questioned whether 'the breakthrough of realism into the art of sound really happened so much later and in a fundamentally different way than in the fields of the visual arts and poetry'. He suggested that the term plays a very minor role in musical terminology, as far as it can be understood for certain, as it cannot be attached to musical features per se. This, he notes, is also true of the concept of Romanticism.[38]

If it is disputed as to what extent music after 1848 should be considered 'Romantic', the issue is only exacerbated when it comes to the question of how a later generation of composers such as Debussy, Elgar, Mahler, Nielsen, Puccini, Rachmaninov, Sibelius, Strauss, and Wolf, who all came to prominence around the end of the nineteenth and turn of the twentieth centuries, ought to be categorised. James Hepokoski neatly encapsulates the issues at stake in this debate over what he terms 'the generation of the 1860s':

> That these composers thought of themselves as the first modernists – as something of a youth movement, not as 'late Romantics' – has now been clearly established. The pejorative label late Romanticism (or 'post-Romanticism'), with its faded pressed-flower connotations, was a polemical term of reproach affixed to them only by the next generation of high modernists, supporters of the dissonant 'new music' in the years before and after the First World War.[39]

Still, in concert programmes and popular accounts, many of these composers are invariably described as 'late-Romantic'; the term is unlikely to die any time soon, and has been resurrected by some scholars.[40]

Instrumental versus Vocal Music

Perhaps the most important primary source for recent constructions of musical Romanticism is E. T. A. Hoffmann (1776–1822) and his passionate plea that music is 'the most Romantic of all the arts'. This phrase is famously used in his 1810 review of Beethoven's Fifth Symphony, but is also repeated throughout Hoffmann's writings, where it does not always refer to the metaphysics of instrumental music or to German composers of recent times. Those twentieth- and twenty-first-century authors who extract this phrase as a trope of German Idealist thought overlook a wealth of Hoffmann's writings that extol vocal music as the true embodiment of the Romantic ideal. They also fixate on the notion that Romantic music is inherently German. There are abundant examples in Hoffmann's writings that contradict these stereotypes, for instance his writings on Palestrina and ancient church music, or his identification of Spontini and opera as the true source of the impact of Romantic music.[41] This aspect of Hoffmann's writings, moreover, is consistent with Adler's conception of the 'Romantic School' as being concerned with the a cappella music of the sixteenth century. In fact, Hoffmann's target of critique in the Beethoven review, as Matthew Riley attests, was not vocal music, but the battle symphony.[42] Contrary to the well-worn view of Hoffmann and his Beethoven review put forward in recent musicological writings, it was Mozart, and not Beethoven, whom the critic considered to be the greatest composer (he did, after all, adopt the middle name 'Amadeus'), and it was the Italian traditions of *commedia dell'arte* and *opera buffa* that he considered to be the most important genres for the development of character and narrative structure in music.[43] Indeed, Hoffmann considered the voice itself as a mechanism through which we are offered spiritual transcendence.[44]

Nonetheless, Hoffmann's famous phrase is given its most emphatic expression in 'Beethoven's Instrumental Music', where he qualified it to make the case that instrumental music is superior to vocal music.[45] Carl Dahlhaus's description of Hoffmann's Beethoven review as 'the founding document of Romantic music aesthetics'[46] has stuck, for better or worse, and it continues to inform a branch of scholarship that has become increasingly essentialist in its reading of music history. Over time, the name Hoffmann has shifted from evoking a figure who promoted music as a pre-eminent art form with the potential to allow us to reach the ineffable, to the 'chief spokesman' for the absolute in the programme/ absolute music debate that was played out in German music journals in the 1850s, long after Hoffmann's death in 1822.[47] Thus Blume, for example, places Hoffmann squarely in relation to 'absolute music':[48] The performer's

utmost subjectivity becomes the high-priestly service to the Infinite. Every admixture of other motives – contemplative ideas, pictorial presentations, descriptive paintings, narration – every program, in short, but also in the end every *literary text*, besmirches the work of art, which in the most exalted cases becomes 'absolute' music (Hoffmann). For this reason, now for the first time in history, pure instrumental music stands above every other.[49] (Emphasis added.)

This stereotype of Hoffmann's view of Romanticism, divorced from literary texts, has become a dubious truism of music history.[50]

Romanticism and Its Home(s)

As touched on here, one of the major considerations in writings on musical Romanticism is the question not only of when it arose, but where it belongs. Romanticism, as Arthur Locke attests, 'dominated the intellectual current of all Europe'.[51] Arnold Whittall traces Romanticism throughout Italy, France, Poland, Scandinavia, Britain, and America. Rey Longyear asserts that 'this movement was an international manifestation strongest in Germany, quite influential in England, France, and Russia, but also evident in Bohemia, Poland, Spain, and Italy'.[52] Katharine Ellis argues that Romanticism was widely considered to be a pejorative term in France, one that indicated smeared harmonies and an over-reliance on literature or programmaticism.[53] Whereas the centre of gravity in Blume's chapter on 'the Romantic concept in music' is the Germanic realm, he gives brief consideration to Romanticism in France and Eastern Europe.[54] In his *Music in the Nineteenth Century*, Walter Frisch notes that 'Romanticism was originally defined and self-consciously practiced' in the German-speaking realm, 'and secondarily in France and Italy'.[55]

For many other commentators writing in the genre of the music textbook, however, musical Romanticism is routinely presented as a concept that is dominated by German thought and German music. In Donald J. Grout's conception of Romanticism in *A History of Western Music*, Chopin, for instance, barely features. He is relegated to a single mention in a sentence that contrasts the grandiose creations of Meyerbeer, Berlioz, Wagner, Strauss, and Mahler with the 'lyrical effusions of Schumann's Lieder [and] Schubert's, Mendelssohn's and Chopin's short piano pieces'.[56]

Few scholars have accepted René Wellek's invitation to transcend national boundaries and to explore instead the unity of European Romanticism as it applies to music.[57] John Michael Cooper is perhaps the only scholar to have done so convincingly. He disputes 'the notion that Romanticism was a predominantly European force whose leaders were all or mostly French, German, Italian and Russian males'. He draws an important distinction between Romantic music and 'the latter-day canon of Romantic music' which, he asserts, 'is itself a culturally and politically self-affirming construct whose cult of "masters" and "masterworks" either implicitly or explicitly excluded composers, ideas, and repertoires that it deemed alien or (in the verbiage of the 19th century itself) "inferior" or "primitive"'.[58]

Such a latter-day canon referred to by Cooper firmly underpins Grout's broader conception of Romanticism, which is governed by a series of dualities: between words and music; between the strong literary orientation of nineteenth-century music and pure instrumental music; and between the mass audience and the solitary composer. The weight of Grout's oppositions invariably falls to the latter. For him, instrumental music is conceived of as 'a vehicle for the utterance of thoughts which, though they may be hinted in words, are ultimately beyond the power of words to express'.[59] This passage from 'Classicism and Romanticism' exemplifies Grout's tendency to paint over a great variety of difference in music of the period:

The great bulk of the music written from about 1770 to about 1900 constitutes a single period, with a common limited stock of usable musical sounds, a common basic vocabulary of harmonies, common basic principles of harmonic progression, rhythm, and form, and a common intention, namely to communicate meaning exclusively through music without extraneous symbolism from composer to performer to listener, starting from an exact and complete notation. From Mozart to Mahler, all tentative departures, individual modifications, experiments, developments along special lines – all take place within one tradition and with references to one common basic set of principles. If Mozart could have heard Mahler's music he might or might not have liked it, but he would not have found it utterly strange. The experience for him would have been more like flying from Vienna to Peking than from Vienna to the moon.[60]

The vastness of Grout's lunar imagery is grounded by the geographical narrowness of his account of 'Classicism and Romanticism', which, in turn, is firmly entrenched in earth and restricted to composers in a German-speaking realm. The depiction of this realm, moreover, is devoid of the ethnic and political diversity that characterised the Habsburg Empire, and of the music-stylistic diversity contained therein.

Romanticism and Diversity

Women are largely conspicuous by their absence in the constructions of musical Romanticism sketched in this chapter. As a general rule, throughout the twentieth century women tended to be safely siphoned off from any serious discussion of musical Romanticism, their contributions to that artistic concept and movement found only in those spaces clearly marked out for women. We must turn to *The Norton/Grove Dictionary of Women Composers* to learn of Bettina von Arnim (née Brentano), for instance, that 'her versatility, intellect and enthusiasm reveal one of the most accomplished women of German Romanticism'.[61] There are some notable and welcome exceptions to this, such as Charles Rosen's *Romantic Generation* where Clara Wieck is given sustained attention, albeit within a discussion of Robert Schumann.[62] But the broader trend to marginalise women in the discourse on musical Romanticism is intricately related to the 'devaluation of the feminine' that Alan Richardson observes in relation to literary Romanticism.[63]

Closely related to this is the degree to which Romanticism was gendered feminine in the nineteenth century, reports of which are ubiquitous throughout the twentieth century, such as Pederson's account of Kretschmann's framing of 'the manly side, to which "character" and history belonged and the feminine side, sentimental and nature-loving'. In Kretschmann's conception, an 'over-reliance on the feminine in artistic production had resulted in romantic music'.[64] Indeed, Hoffmann satirised this very gender stereotype in characters such as Olimpia in the novella 'Der Sandmann' (1815).[65]

Gendered readings of Romanticism were given renewed strength after the Second World War, when books such as Thomas Mann's *Doktor Faustus* and Georg Lukács's *The Destruction of Reason* implicated German Romanticism as a progenitor of fascism. Such literary depictions of Romanticism, as Erik Levi has shown, had a firm basis in historical events repositioning Romanticism within the masculine realm of heady ideas. Consider, for instance, this passage, from Goebbels's opening address of the Reich's Chamber of Culture, which embraces the view that the Nazi revolution was 'inspired by the rebirth of a national romantic art':

Gone was the nervous flaccidity which surrendered before life's seriousness, which denied it or fled from it and forward strode the heroic view of life which today resounds from the marching steps of brown shirted columns. ... it is a kind of romanticism of steel that has made German life worth living once again, a romanticism that does not hide from the harshness of existence ... a romanticism which has the mettle to face ruthless problems and look them unflinchingly in the eye.[66]

'Because the nineteenth-century lied embodies romanticism', Edward F. Kravitt argues, 'enthusiasm for the genre declined in postwar years.'[67]

What the *New York Times* referred to in 1988 as 'The vanishing Lieder ritual' in the mid-twentieth century went hand in hand with the enduring tendency to see Romanticism in music as being bound up with pure, instrumental music.[68] Grout exemplifies the point by considering art song to be just one of a number of genres in which the text is entirely incidental. According to his account, the degree to which 'the Romantics reconciled music with words is reflected in the importance they placed on the instrumental accompaniment of vocal music, from the *Lieder* of Schubert to the symphonic orchestra that enfolds the voices in Wagner's music dramas'.[69] Musicologists such as Jim Samson, who argues convincingly to the contrary that 'art song might sustain a claim to be the quintessential Romantic genre',[70] provide hope for the twenty-first century. We might yet recover a fuller understanding of musical Romanticism, one that restores the relationship between music and language. Rather than privileging modes of thought that stifle the (literary) imagination, we can instead – in the spirit of Ali Smith and her focus on Beethoven's 'An die Hoffnung' in the novel *Spring* – allow musical Romanticism to celebrate its multifaceted richness.

Notes

1. Ali Smith, *Spring* (London: Penguin, Random House, 2019), 253.
2. Karl August Kahlert, 'Ueber den Begriff der klassischen und romantischen Musik', *Allgemeine musikalische Zeitung*, 50 (3 May 1848), 289–95, at 295. See also Hans Lenneberg, 'Classic and Romantic: The First Usage of the Terms', *Musical Quarterly*, 78 (1994), 610–25. Unless otherwise noted, translations from German texts are by the author.
3. Guido Adler, *Der Stil in der Musik* (Leipzig: Breitkopf & Härtel, 1911), 225–6.
4. Ibid., 228.
5. Ibid., 228.
6. Ibid., 122, 45, 166.
7. See, for instance, Hubert Parry (1848–1918), whose *Style in Musical Art*, published the same year as Adler's study, reveals the author's evolutionary view of music as progressing from the classicism of the late-eighteenth century to the Romantic music of the nineteenth century, in which Beethoven, predictably, forms the pivotal figure of change. C. Hubert H. Parry, *Style in Musical Art* (London: Macmillan and Co., 1911).
8. Alfred Einstein, *Geschichte der Musik* (Leipzig: B. G. Teubner, 1917), *Music in the Romantic Era: A History of Musical Thought in the 19th Century* (New York: W. W. Norton & Co., 1947).

9. Paul Henry Lang, 'The Confluence of Classicism and Romanticism', in *Music in Western Civilization* (London: Dent, 1942), 740.

10. Ibid., 740.

11. Ibid., 745, 746.

12. Friedrich Blume, *Classic and Romantic Music: A Comprehensive Survey* (New York: Norton, 1970), 124. (First published in German in 1958.)

13. Ibid., 115.

14. Ibid., 123.

15. Ibid., 121.

16. Jim Samson, 'The Musical Work and Nineteenth-Century History', in Jim Samson (ed.), *The Cambridge History of Nineteenth-Century Music* (Cambridge: Cambridge University Press, 2001), 3–28, at 22.

17. Jim Samson, 'Music and Society', in Jim Samson (ed.), *The Late Romantic Era: From the Mid-19th Century to World War I* (New York: Palgrave Macmillan, 1991), 1–49, at 1.

18. Franz Brendel, *Die Musik in der Gegenwart*, as cited in James Garratt, *Music, Culture, and Social Reform in the Age of Wagner* (Cambridge: Cambridge University Press, 2010), 179.

19. Kahlert, 'Ueber den Begriff', 295, cited in Mark Evan Bonds, *Absolute Music: The History of an Idea* (New York: Oxford University Press, 2014), 129.

20. Ibid., 129.

21. Carl Kretschmann, 'Romantik in der Musik', *Neue Zeitschrift für Musik*, 29 (1848), cited in Bonds, *Absolute Music*, 129.

22. Sanna Pederson, 'Romantic Music under Siege in 1848', in Ian Bent (ed.), *Music Theory in the Age of Romanticism* (Cambridge: Cambridge University Press, 1996), 57–74, at 59, 71–2.

23. G. W. F. Hegel, *Aesthetics: Lectures on Fine Art*, trans. T. M. Knox, cited in Pederson, 'Romantic Music', 59.

24. Pederson, 'Romantic Music', 61.

25. Lang, 'The Confluence of Classicism and Romanticism', 739.

26. Ibid., 748.

27. Walter Frisch, *Music in the Nineteenth Century* (New York: Norton, 2013), 14.

28. Arnold Whittall, *Romantic Music: A Concise History from Schubert to Sibelius* (London: Thames and Hudson, 1987), 13.

29. Lang, 'The Confluence of Classicism and Romanticism', 739.

30. Ibid., 739.

31. Ibid., 746.

32. Carl Dahlhaus, *Between Romanticism and Modernism: Four Studies in the Music of the Later Nineteenth Century*, trans. Mary Whittall (Berkeley and Los Angeles: University of California Press, 1980), 5.

33. Lang, 'From Romanticism to Realism', in *Music in Western Civilization*, 844.

34. Bonds, *Absolute Music*, 209, 225.

35. Dahlhaus, *Realism in Nineteenth-Century Music*, trans. Mary Whittall (Cambridge: Cambridge University Press, 1985), 12.

36. Ibid., 12.

37. Jim Samson, 'Music and Society', 22.

38. Ernst Bücken, 'Romantik und Realismus. Zur Periodisierung der "romantischen" Epoche', in Helmut Osthoff, Walter Serauky, and Adam Adrio (eds.), *Festschrift Arnold Schering* (Berlin: A. Glas, 1937), 46–50, at 46.

39. James Hepokoski, 'Beethoven Reception: The Symphonic Tradition', in Jim Samson (ed.), *The Cambridge History of Nineteenth-Century Music* (Cambridge: Cambridge University Press, 2001), 424–59, at 456.

40. See further Sebastian Wedler's chapter in this volume (Chapter 20).

41. See James Garratt, *Palestrina and the German Romantic Imagination: Interpreting Historicism in Nineteenth-Century Music* (Cambridge: Cambridge University Press, 2002).

42. Matthew Riley, 'E. T. A. Hoffmann Beyond the "Paradigm Shift": Music and Irony in the Novellas 1815–1819', in Phyllis Weliver and Katharine Ellis (eds.), *Words and Notes in the Long Nineteenth Century* (Woodbridge: Boydell Press, 2013), 119–43, at 121.

43. Ibid.

44. Examples of the latter include Hoffmann's *Rat Krespel* (1816) and *Don Juan* (1812).

45. '[Instrumental music] is the most romantic of all arts, one might almost say the only one that is genuinely romantic, since its only subject-matter is infinity.' E. T. A. Hoffmann, 'Beethoven's Instrumental Music', in *E. T. A. Hoffmann's Musical Writings: Kreisleriana, The Poet and the Composer, Music Criticism*, ed. David Charlton, trans. Martyn Clarke (Cambridge: Cambridge University Press, 1989), 96.

46. Carl Dahlhaus, *Die Idee der absoluten Musik* (Leipzig: Deutscher Verlag für Musik, 1979), 47.

47. Riley, 'E. T. A. Hoffmann', 120.

48. On the changing conceptions of 'absolute music' over time, see Nicole Grimes, 'Introduction', in Nicole Grimes, Siobhán Donovan, and Wolfgang Marx (eds.), *Rethinking Hanslick: Music, Formalism, and Expression* (Rochester NY: University of Rochester Press, 2013), 5; and Bonds, *Absolute Music*.

49. Friedrich Blume, *Classic and Romantic Music*, 112–13.

50. This stems from Carl Dahlhaus, for instance *Nineteenth-Century Music*, trans. J. Bradford Robinson (Berkeley and Los Angeles: University of California Press, 1989), 18. See, e.g., Richard Taruskin, *The Seventeenth and Eighteenth Centuries, volume 2 of The Oxford History of Western Music* (New York: Oxford University Press, 2005), 649–50. Taruskin's fixation on the post-1800 paradigm of instrumental music is part of a well-worn trope in Anglophone musicology.

51. Arthur W. Locke, 'The Background of the Romantic Movement in French Music', *Musical Quarterly*, 6/2 (1920), 257–71, at 259.

52. Rey Longyear, *Nineteenth-Century Romanticism in Music* (Englewood Cliffs, NJ: Prentice Hall, 1988), 8.

53. Katharine Ellis, *Music Criticism in Nineteenth Century France: La revue et gazette musical de Paris 1834–80* (Cambridge: Cambridge University Press, 1995).

54. Friedrich Blume, *Classic and Romantic Music*, 118.

55. Frisch, *Music in the Nineteenth Century*, 14.

56. Donald Jay Grout, *A History of Western Music* (New York: Norton, 1973), 542.

57. René Wellek, 'The Concept of Romanticism in Literary History', in Robert F. Gleckner and Gerald E. Enscoe (eds.), *Romanticism: Points of View* (Detroit: Wayne State University Press, 1974), 181–206.

58. John Michael Cooper (with Randy Kinnett), *Historical Dictionary of Romantic Music* (Lanham, MD: Scarecrow Press, 2013), 10.

59. Grout, *A History of Western Music*, 541.

60. Ibid., 538.

61. Julie Anne Sadie and Rhian Samuel (eds.), *The Norton/Grove Dictionary of Women Composers* (New York and London: Norton, 1994), 84. An exception is found in Longyear, *Nineteenth-Century Romanticism in Music*, 17.

62. Charles Rosen, *The Romantic Generation* (Cambridge, MA: Harvard University Press, 1995), 658ff.

63. Alan Richardson, 'Romanticism and the Colonization of the Feminine', in Anne Mellor (ed.), *Romanticism and Feminism* (Bloomington, IN: Indiana University Press, 1988), 13–25, at 14.

64. Kretschmann, 'Romantik in der Musik', cited in Pederson, 'Romantic Music', 68.

65. E. T. A. Hoffmann, 'Der Sandmann', *Sämtliche Werke*, ed. Wulf Segebrecht, Hartmut Steinecke, Gerhard Allroggen, and Ursula Segebrecht, 6 vols., vol. 3: *Nachtstücke*, Klein Zaches: Prinzessin Brambilla. Werke 1816–1820 (Frankfurt: Deutscher Klassiker Verlag, 1985), 11–49.

66. Erik Levi, *Music in the Third Reich* (New York: Palgrave Macmillan, 1994, Repr. 1996), 88.

67. Edward F. Kravitt, *The Lied: Mirror of Late Romanticism* (New Haven: Yale University Press, 1996).

68. Donal Henehan, 'Music View: The Vanishing Lieder Ritual', *New York Times*, 3 April 1988.

69. Grout, *A History of Western Music*, 541.

70. Jim Samson, 'Romanticism', in Stanley Sadie (ed.), *The New Grove Dictionary of Music and Musicians*, 29 vols. (London: Macmillan, 2001), vol. 21, 596–603.

Further Reading

Blume, Friedrich. *Classic and Romantic Music: A Comprehensive Survey* (New York: Norton, 1970).

Cooper, John Michael (with Randy Kinnett). *Historical Dictionary of Romantic Music* (Lanham MD: Scarecrow Press, 2013).

Dahlhaus, Carl. *Between Romanticism and Modernism: Four Studies in the Music of the Later Nineteenth Century*, trans. Mary Whittall (Berkeley and Los Angeles: University of California Press, 1980).

   Nineteenth-Century Music, trans. J. B. Robinson (Berkeley and Los Angeles: University of California Press, 1989).

Einstein, Alfred. *Music in the Romantic Era: A History of Musical Thought in the 19th Century* (New York: W. W. Norton & Co., 1947).

Frisch, Walter. *Music in the Nineteenth Century* (New York: Norton, 2013).

Lang, Paul Henry. *Music in Western Civilization* (London: Dent, 1942).

Longyear, Rey. *Nineteenth-Century Romanticism in Music* (Englewood Cliffs, NJ: Prentice Hall, 1988).

Mellor, Anne (ed.). *Romanticism and Feminism* (Bloomington, IN: Indiana University Press, 1988).

Pederson, Sanna. 'Romantic Music under Siege in 1848', in Ian Bent (ed.), *Music Theory in the Age of Romanticism* (Cambridge: Cambridge University Press, 1996), 57–74.

Samson, Jim (ed.). *The Cambridge History of Nineteenth-Century Music* (Cambridge: Cambridge University Press, 2001).

   The Late Romantic Era: From the Mid-19th Century to World War I (London: Macmillan, 1991).

Whittall, Arnold. *Romantic Music: A Concise History from Schubert to Sibelius* (London: Thames and Hudson, 1987).

20 | The End(s) of Musical Romanticism

In Lieu of an Introduction: An Anecdote

Arnold Schoenberg had been receiving unreserved support from Richard Strauss for years, in the form of much-needed scholarships and copying work, when in July 1909 he asked the elder composer for help in finding a performance opportunity for a new set of orchestral pieces (later to become his Five Pieces for Orchestra, Op. 16). Writing with a tinge of enticement, Schoenberg expressed 'great hopes' for the affective qualities that he imagined would radiate from their sound world, describing the pieces as an uninterrupted flow of 'varied colours, rhythms and moods'.[1] In his response, Strauss, by that time general musical director at the Berlin State Opera and still closely connected with the Berlin Philharmonic (as whose principal conductor he had served in 1895–6), seemed interested and invited Schoenberg to send him the scores.[2] It would not have been the first time that Strauss had given Schoenberg a leg up. Only two years earlier, Schoenberg had succeeded in getting his First String Quartet Op. 7 performed at the Tonkünstlerfest in Dresden, after Gustav Mahler had put in a good word for him to Strauss, who, in his capacity as honorary president of the General German Musical Society, thereupon seems to have arranged to cover the Rosé Quartet's expenses.[3] This time, however, the situation turned out very differently. Strauss replied in the negative, and returned the scores accompanied with the explanation that, although generally 'happy to help' and also willing to act with 'courage', he found that the pieces comprised 'experiments of such an audacious character, both on the level of content and presentation', that he 'dare not introduce them to the extremely conservative Berlin public'.[4]

While there is little reason to doubt that Strauss did genuinely fear the public response and possible damage to his reputation – especially if he were to conduct the pieces himself, as Schoenberg had probably hoped – this external reasoning likely reveals only part of the picture. It is quite conceivable that looming behind his rejection was a much more personal,

343

internally rooted scepticism concerning Schoenberg's latest creative direction, as a well-known letter he sent to Alma Mahler in 1914 suggests. Although still signalling his general support for Schoenberg's application for a scholarship endowed in memoriam of Gustav Mahler, on a personal note Strauss did not hide his more recent reservations against Schoenberg, railing that 'it would be better for him to be shovelling snow than scrawling on music paper'.[5] Curiously enough, Schoenberg seems to have learned about Strauss's disparaging comment shortly thereafter, through indiscretion. When in the same year he was approached by Strauss's later biographer Richard Specht to write an essay on the occasion of the elder composer's fiftieth birthday, he turned the offer down, referencing this condemning remark in nearly its exact wording.[6] In fact, Strauss's remark seems to have sent tangible shockwaves through Schoenberg's inner circle, as evinced by both Alban Berg and Anton Webern's biographical documents. Berg was somehow able to copy out the precise quotation from Strauss's letter to Alma Mahler into one of his notebooks. And in a letter to Schoenberg featuring one of his numerous anti-Strauss bouts during that time, Webern alludes to Strauss's aspersion in quotation marks, ranting and raving that it was Strauss himself who 'should be "shovelling snow"', before continuing with vehemence that '[t]his chap should really have to clear the snow from all of his Bavarian mountains as a punishment'.[7] These glimpses provide an idea of the extent to which, by 1914, Strauss's reservations against the path that Schoenberg had embarked upon had created a deep rift between the two composers on a personal level. Even though Schoenberg maintained a degree of admiration for Strauss and his music, the two of them would never fully reconcile.

Three Different Historiographical Interpretations

With anecdotes like these, the waters of music historiography begin to part. Interpreted through the Adornian lens of the 'historical dialectic of musical material'[8] and the teleological narrative of history as progress therein embedded, Schoenberg's bitter disappointment about Strauss's distancing from him shines forth as heroic, self-asserting defiance, the testament of a man unwilling to compromise his vision of emancipating harmony, form, and timbre into the new idiom of 'high modernism'.[9] In contrast, Strauss stands revealed as a kind of regressive, old 'neo-Romantic' beyond hope – in Carl Dahlhaus's words, as an 'about-face from modernism'[10] – who, for opportunistic reasons, merely ingratiates himself with the philistine masses, assumed to be relentlessly ignorant of high art and ever liable to overshadow performances with riots and turmoil. Cast in this polarising light, Strauss's rejection gains the veneer of a sheer, unshatterable adherence to the 'Romantic' tradition (in some textbooks simply moulded into the problematic rubric of the 'survival of tonality' beyond Schoenberg's 'atonal revolution'[11]), as much as it marks the ultimate confirmation that Schoenberg, during these years, was breaking through to a new stage of history for which, to speak after Webern's well-known turn of phrase, the time 'wasn't yet ripe'.[12] When understood in these terms, the alienation between the two men encapsulates in the private sphere the ostensible break between Romanticism and Modernism in the public-cultural sphere (which may justify the use of capitalised letters for these terms).

This being said, the same anecdote could also be interpreted in a very different light. It has been well observed that Schoenberg – the 'anti-bourgeois bourgeois'[13] – continued to rely heavily on 'conservative' tenets and ideas, in his own way. For a start, it is possible to argue that Schoenberg's resistance to making any aesthetic concessions grows out of the aesthetics of inwardness and expressive authenticity deeply rooted in nineteenth-century thought. Holly Watkins speaks rightly about 'inner-ness, the unconscious, necessity, and organicism' as belonging to 'an essentially Romantic set of concepts' that 'still governed attitudes toward artistic creation' amongst the members of the Schoenberg circle.[14] Moreover, as Richard Taruskin has argued – playing the heretic with palpable joy in heralding Erik Satie, Claude Debussy, and eventually Igor Stravinsky as the 'real' figureheads of modernism, contra Adorno and Dahlhaus – Schoenberg can be denied entrance into the pantheon of modernists on the grounds of, for example, the seemingly uncritical use of high-classical formal types in his dodecaphonic works.[15] Indeed, the project of 'remaking the past', to mention the title of Joseph N. Straus's important study on the topic,[16] is so deeply ingrained in Schoenberg's musical imagination that it is of little surprise to find, in some of his sketches, the primary row and its tritone transposition referred to by the letters 'T' and 'D' respectively, the designations for 'tonic' and 'dominant'. Approached from this perspective, the grand historiographical narrative of nineteenth-century music advocated by Adorno as a 'history of emancipation' culminating with Schoenberg's accomplishments is thus outflanked by a 'history of continuity' – or, in Taruskin's idiosyncratic term, 'maximalization'.[17]

Then again, it is possible to read the same anecdote in a way that, refreshingly, defies any Procrustean temptation to categorise it along the progressive–regressive axis. To this end, we may wish to attend to a detail that at first glance seems somewhat negligible: the fact that Schoenberg, in the cited letter to Strauss, claims that his set of orchestral pieces conjures up a distinctive mood or atmosphere – he uses the existential term *Stimmung* (twice). By this claim, he can be taken to situate his pieces within the horizon of *Stimmungsmusik*, a new aesthetic trope of musical composition that, as Erik Wallrup has shown, crystallised towards the end of the nineteenth century across Europe as a musical genre in its own right, giving rise to such works as – notably – Strauss's *Stimmungsbilder*, Op. 9.[18] If we dismiss the idea that Schoenberg might have cast his orchestral pieces in the light of *Stimmungsmusik* for purely sycophantic reasons, it seems not implausible to see both works alike, despite their undeniably different stylistic physiognomies, as contributions to one and the same philosophical discourse: the formation of a new phenomenological epistemology, pivoting on notions of presence, immediacy, and ephemerality. As Daniel M. Grimley pointed out, the critical impulse ascribed to *Stimmung* at the post-linguistic turn related to 'breaking down a monistic sense of autonomy or individual being into a more blended understanding of space, place, and time, one that dissolves or suspends the familiar subject-object distinction that underpins much nineteenth-century writing on music'.[19] Considered against this backdrop, Schoenberg's orchestral pieces can be construed as sharing the same aesthetic vision as that expressed in some of Strauss's early works (which makes the fact that Strauss rejected them particularly curious).

By unpacking some of the divergent, even contradictory ways in which the alienation between Strauss and Schoenberg during the years around 1909–14 can be interpreted in historiographical terms, my aim is not to opt for one reading over another. Instead, my concern is with the ways in which these different modes of historiographical interpretation sensitise us to the very challenges posed by any attempt to come to grips with the historical terminus of musical Romanticism. If we consider the view expounded by Benedict Taylor in the opening chapter of this volume that the concept of Romanticism may be best conceived as '*a mode of understanding* music rather than a style or historical era' (my emphasis), then the question concerning its 'end' can surely only be rendered approachable as a heuristic idea, in the way it prompts us constantly to question, challenge, and rethink the methodological foundations and historiographical categories, as well as the discursive strategies, based on which we – implicitly or explicitly, and be this in the arena of cultural and intellectual history, biographical hermeneutics or musical analysis – theorise the periodisation of late nineteenth- and early twentieth-century music history. In other words, discussion of the 'end' of musical Romanticism is contingent not merely on the empirical facts chosen to include as the subject for historical reflection, but already, in a much narrower sense, on the way we *choose* to approach them.

The Historiographical Challenges of Aesthetic Autonomy

This is no news. Ever since the publications of Leo Treitler's *Music and the Historical Imagination*, Leonard B. Meyer's *Style and Music*, and Carl Dahlhaus's *Nineteenth-Century Music*, all in 1989, this meta-discursive perspective has been well established in music history classes. This, however, has not rendered the question concerning the 'end' of musical Romanticism obsolete. Rather, modern-day scholarship has seen the rise of a number of powerful categories conceived to address the end of the long nineteenth century (to use the well-worn phrase), including 'late Romanticism', 'early modernism', 'maximalism', and '*Weltanschauungsmusik*'. In the hands of such writers as Peter Franklin, James Hepokoski, Richard Taruskin, and Hermann Danuser, to name but a few of the most influential voices from recent years, these categories have crystallised into fully fledged historiographical theories, each underpinned by its own set of methodological predilections. On the most fundamental level, these theories can be understood as different responses to the profound historiographical challenges emerging from the destabilised ontological foundation of the work-concept: the notion that the 'musical work' is an 'open' and 'regulative' category which hinges on a complex nexus between score, performance, and reception, cultivating and mediating ever-fluid productions of meaning, agency, cultural value, and social function.[20] These historiographical categories thus are not descriptive labels for easy stylistic categorisation, but rather represent distinct discursive operations.

It is in particular the writings of Carl Dahlhaus that continue to inspire controversial debate and serve as a critical reference amongst both his advocates and his critics. This is to no insignificant extent because of a provocative streak in his thought. There can be little doubt that Dahlhaus contributed to the theory of nineteenth- and early twentieth-century music historiography in a manner like no one else. His *Foundations of Music History* – a study inspired by his attempt to think through what he described as the 'practical difficulties'[21] he saw himself confronted with when working on *Nineteenth-Century Music* – remains, to this day, an unsurpassed juggernaut of (self-reflexive) methodological criticism. Broadly speaking, it sets out to tackle head-on the momentous aporetic question of how modern-day music scholarship in the face of the work-concept's destabilised ontological foundation can write of a 'history of music' – which is, for Dahlhaus, a 'history of musical *composition*' – at all. Resisting easy solutions, his response calls for a recalibration of our dialectical and epistemological sensibilities towards what he terms the 'relativity' of aesthetic autonomy. Thus, while in the opening of his study he maintains that it would be 'inconceivable in scope' to discard the aesthetic autonomy of the 'work' altogether,[22] the chapters that follow make a powerful argument for a nuanced engagement with post-Kantian questions of the artwork and the notion of disinterested aesthetic contemplation. In advocating a hermeneutic-contemplative and critical-rational approach to our understanding of musical works and their place in music history, the fierce dialectical efforts that lead Dahlhaus to assert the relativity of aesthetic autonomy actually push the concept precariously to its very limit – for Lawrence Kramer even beyond it: 'the relative autonomy of music', he writes succinctly, 'just *is* its lack of autonomy' (emphasis in the original).[23]

And yet, despite the tour de force in *Foundations of Music History*, the conclusion that Dahlhaus arrives at in *Nineteenth-Century Music* is puzzlingly orthodox. Instead of dissolving the question concerning the 'end' of nineteenth-century music into some kind of critical pluralism – into a set of loose 'ends'[24] – he chose to maintain, in fact to reinforce, the notion of an absolute 'end', in the singular. In his final chapter, suggestively entitled 'End of an Era', he contended with a nod to Adorno's *Philosophy of New Music* (albeit palpably dimming its polemical tone) that it is perfectly apt to 'end our history of "nineteenth-century" music in 1907, the watershed year of Schoenberg's transition to atonality', because, so he implied (and again, not uncontroversially), Schoenberg's accomplishments had a much more decisive impact on what 'constitut[es] the "genuine" modern music of our own [twentieth] century' than those of, say, Strauss or Stravinsky.[25] It is this unresolved tension in Dahlhaus's work – his manoeuvre undertaken in *Nineteenth-Century Music* to putty the craquelures inherent in the concept of aesthetic autonomy that *Foundations of Music History* so insightfully threw into focus – that makes his work provocatively resonant to this day.

One of the first scholars to have taken on the productive tensions pervading Dahlhaus's conception of the 'end' of musical Romanticism was James Hepokoski. In his now-classic essay on 'The Dahlhaus Project',[26] published in 1991, only two years after Dahlhaus had passed away, Hepokoski historicises Dahlhaus's theory of music historiography and illuminates the axiomatic configuration that gave rise to some of its most troubling, solipsistic tendencies – including Dahlhaus's linear conception of music history, his chauvinistic focus on the Austro-German canon, and his refusal to engage thoroughly with so-called 'lowbrow' genres – with such acuity that it is, without much of a stretch, possible to read his essay as an early attempt to outline the contours of what could today be called the 'Hepokoski Project'.

The ferments for such a project are fully articulated for the first time two years later, in Hepokoski's study of Jean Sibelius's Fifth Symphony. On the one hand, Hepokoski adopts Dahlhaus's term 'early modernism' to describe the period 1889–1914, and accepts the principal methodological premises built into it. Yet at the same time, he refurnishes the term, giving it a fresh historiographical spin, in at least three fundamental ways. *Geographically*, for one, he usefully instals a new dialectical axis oriented around issues of 'centre' and 'periphery', thus broadening the Austro-German local-topographical scope of Dahlhaus's discussion of 'early modernism' to include a more encompassing conception of modernism as a European event. Moreover, *historically*, Hepokoski liberates the concept of 'early modernism' from the suffocating Hegelian grip, espoused by Dahlhaus, of history as progress, breathing into it the life of a much more flexible and transgressive category. Whereas Dahlhaus, basing himself upon the influential Viennese cultural critic Hermann Bahr, amongst others, invites his readers to understand the 'breakaway mood' following 1889 – the year of Mahler's First Symphony and Strauss's *Don Juan* – as the 'dawning of "musical modernism"' (*Aufbruch zur musikalischen Moderne*) in the emphatic sense of the term, paving the way for 'the musical revolution captured in Schoenberg's dictum "emancipation of dissonance"',[27] Hepokoski blurs these clear-cut historiographical delineations. Commissioned by the Finnish government on the occasion of Sibelius's fiftieth birthday in 1915, the Fifth Symphony, strictly speaking, falls outside the historical confines of Dahlhaus's definition of 'early modernism'. And perhaps more crucially, the newly introduced formal categories of 'sonata deformation' and 'rotational form' by means of which Hepokoski seeks to elicit some of the symphony's compositional strategies are also, he implies, characteristic of the Romantic repertoire in general. These categories of sonata deformation theory thus cannot be thought of in terms of fetishised stylistic yardsticks for progress in the same way that, for example, 'developing variation', 'endless melody', or '"wandering" tonality' are for Dahlhaus.[28] Instead, for Hepokoski sonata form is primarily conceived of as a kind of centralising vehicle, a communicative matrix that is capable of engendering highly expressive contents and meanings.[29]

In this way, Hepokoski's use of the term 'early modernism' in effect not only diffuses into 'Romanticism', but also calls, thirdly, for a new *hermeneutic* practice, one that brings the aesthetic tropes at the heart of *Weltanschauungsmusik* – such as pantheism, symbolist naturalism, the uncanny, voluptuous eroticism, decadence, monumentality, historicism, exoticism, nationalism, imperialism, childhood nostalgia, bourgeois humanism, and pessimistic notions of metaphysical redemption[30] – into dialogue with solid, music theory-based analytical insights. By reorienting our attention to the interstice between 'absolute' and 'programmatic' strata and the ways in which they can help to illuminate each other and, as a consequence, open up hidden hermeneutic depths, Hepokoski's post-Dahlhausian concerns thus powerfully reveal the individual work as mediating on (not merely embodying a reflection of) the ideas that were widely proliferating at the turn of the century. In so doing, Hepokoski's study suggests new productive avenues for a critical reappraisal of Sibelius's Fifth Symphony and its place in music history (more than half a century after Adorno's trenchant polemical characterisation of the work as strangely out of touch with the historical situation[31]) as well as, indeed, of an entire generation of composers that '[came] of age in a post-Lisztian/ post-Wagnerian world'[32] yet resist easy categorisation along the stylistic and aesthetic occupations commonly associated with the Schoenberg circle, including such composers as Edward Elgar, Carl Nielsen, and indeed Richard Strauss. Hepokoski's concept of 'early modernism' has since served as a beacon in the sea of scholarship concerned with those composers whom Dahlhaus was quick to relegate, quite literally, to footnotes.[33]

If Hepokoski's theory can thus be understood as a critical continuation of Dahlhaus's historiography of 'early modernism', then Franklin's 'late romanticism' – a term dismissed categorically by Dahlhaus – is set out as a fundamental departure from it. Taking the cue from Taruskin's rejection of Dahlhaus's concept of (relative) aesthetic autonomy and its implied focus on the music's 'gnostic' dimension, Franklin's category of 'late romanticism' aims to provide an understanding of the ways in which music of that time is 'marked by implicitly communicated meaning, mediated as private subjective experience prompted in public among the "unmusical"'.[34] With his heightened concern for the 'unmusical', he draws renewed attention to those socially coded 'lowbrow' genres and forgotten works that fared badly in Dahlhaus's *Nineteenth-Century*

Music, yet enjoyed much popularity at the beginning of the twentieth century. In so doing, he makes a persuasive case for the rehabilitation of the 'unmusical' masses and their appreciation of the 'drastic',[35] not in order to launch a defence of their inexorable views but rather to (re)claim those views as worthy of serious critical and hermeneutic inquiry, indeed in a manner not dissimilar from the way Dahlhaus advocated for the 'autonomous' works of high art.

To illustrate the critical potential inherent in Franklin's agenda to 'reclaim' late Romanticism, we may wish to return, for one last time, to the anecdote presented at the beginning of this chapter. Once attuned to Franklin's sensitivities, Strauss's characterisation of the Berlin audience as being 'extremely conservative' can be cast in a new light. There is certainly no mistaking that this characterisation was intended to flatter Schoenberg. By implicitly elevating him to the status of a 'radical artist', Strauss played up Schoenberg's own self-cultivated image. Yet his instincts may have been profoundly ambivalent. As Franklin pointed out, '[b]y rejecting the bourgeois audience that had created the social possibility of nineteenth-century music, he [the radical artist, implying here Schoenberg] condemned himself to the role of the uncomprehended outsider, with only ironic counterfeits, mystic invocations and penitential silences with which to beg his keep from those same consumers of art that he had previously rejected'.[36] Strauss's reference to the 'extremely conservative' Berlin public is, in this sense, not simply diametrically opposed to the 'dawning of musical modernism' but must be understood as *integral* to it, as yet another response to the highly complex processes of aesthetic, cultural, and socio-political diversification at the turn of the century.[37]

In Lieu of a Conclusion: A Meditation

It seems, then, that with these post-Dahlhausian sensibilities, the historiographical challenges posed by the (relative) autonomy of music can be reframed as heuristic opportunities. Rather than asking whether *fin-de-siècle* music historiography would be better off with or without the concept of aesthetic autonomy, it appears apt to make full use of the varied arsenal of methodological and interpretative approaches available to us today in order to rethink how the end(s) of musical Romanticism can be conceived. For the purpose of promoting fresh historiographical perspectives, such an eclectic perspective is of crucial significance: it can, after all, serve to foster a healthy scepticism towards the historical baggage of this era and our own biases and blind spots as well as the ways in which the canonisation(s) of 'Romantic music', for the better or worse, has 'disciplined'[38] scholarly and cultural practices. Indeed, as the dust over so many hard-fought polemical debates about the end(s) of musical Romanticism has begun to settle, it seems more important than ever that we – as critical and imaginative thinkers, performers, and listeners – enter into an intellectually playful yet conscientious engagement with music's historical (un)situatedness, and feel encouraged to reinscribe our own subjectivity, modern-day sensitivities, and historical experiences, in the sense of a radical hermeneutic practice, into the tropes that make up the rich and variegated aesthetic imagination of turn-of-the-century music and its cultural life. Fed into such a hermeneutic metabolism, the idea of the 'end' of musical Romanticism can only be understood within and against contemporaneous cultural ideas and social values – that is, to speak after Julian Johnson, in the way that the discursive 'voices' that sing *through* the individual work resonate with our own.[39] So, for example, the pictorial depictions of forests, gardens, steppes, rural landscapes, mountainscapes, and seascapes as evoked in such works as Leoš Janáček's *The Cunning Little Vixen*, Frederick Delius's *In a Summer Garden*, Rued Langgaard's Fifth Symphony, Gustav Mahler's Third Symphony, Richard Strauss's *An Alpine Symphony*, or Claude Debussy's *La Mer*, not only touch upon crucial issues entrenched in nineteenth- and early twentieth-century thought but can moreover be read as vital contributions to recent discourses on historical ecology and human geography, in the ways that they engage us – at this challenging time of anthropogenic climate change, environmental catastrophes, and biopolitical 'governmentality' – in more fundamental questions of how humans construe their relationship with the natural world. Similarly, the way Salome, during her dance of the seven veils in Strauss's opera, is empowered yet also objectified by the male gaze poignantly addresses central issues relating to gender equality and power differentials. And indeed, with the cultural memory set smarting like a reopened wound (to adapt a famous phrase from George Eliot's *Middlemarch*), the imperialist imagination espoused in Elgar's *The Crown of India* raises far-reaching ethical and political questions in a world tinged with what Paul Gilroy has termed 'postcolonial melancholia'.

Once we acknowledge our very own cultural entanglement, musical Romanticism indeed 'persists' in the specific sense described by Richard Eldridge for the Romantic arts in general: as a concept that 'remains with us as a form of scrutiny of our human possibilities . . . because of its own persistence in the open itinerary of thinking about value, embodied in its own resistances to authoritative closure'.[40] But once we take the view that the question concerning the terminus of Romanticism thus pushes on us the very presuppositions of our own 'post-historical' era,[41] it turns out that the era of Romantic music is not one 'of the past' that has, in one way or another, come to an 'end', but is rather, to speak in Schlegelesque fashion, fragmentary and inconclusive – essentially open-ended.

Notes

* For Martyn Harry.
1. A transcription of the cited passage from Schoenberg's letter to Strauss from 14 July 1909 is provided in Nuria Nono-Schoenberg (ed.), *Arnold Schönberg 1874–1951: Lebensgeschichte in Begegnungen* (Klagenfurt: Ritter Verlag, 1998), 66. Unless otherwise stated, all translations my own.
2. H. H. Stuckenschmidt, *Schoenberg: His Life, World and Work*, trans. Humphrey Searle (London: John Calder, 1977), 61–76 (see here esp. 70–3), provides a reconstruction of the correspondence. The complex relationship between Schoenberg and Strauss during these years has been discussed by a number of commentators; these accounts usually owe a great deal to Stuckenschmidt's monograph.
3. Mahler's letter to Strauss from 6 February 1907 is reproduced in Herta Blaukopf (ed.), *Gustav Mahler – Richard Strauss: Correspondence 1888–1911*, trans. Edmund Jephcott (London: Faber and Faber, 1984), 96.
4. Strauss's letter to Schoenberg from 2 September 1909 is reproduced in Günter Brosche, 'Richard Strauss und Arnold Schoenberg: Mit unveröffentlichten Briefen', *Richard Strauss-Blätter* 2 (1979), 21–7, at 25.
5. Cited in translation after Stuckenschmidt, *Schoenberg*, 73; this statement is also referenced in Alma Mahler-Werfel, *Mein Leben* (Frankfurt: S. Fischer, 1960), 224.
6. A translation of the relevant passage from Schoenberg's letter to Richard Specht from 22 April 1914 is provided in Erwin Stein (ed.), *Arnold Schoenberg: Letters*, trans. Eithne Wilkins and Ernst Kaiser (Berkeley and Los Angeles: University of California Press, 1964), 50. The indiscretion can be partly reconstructed from the correspondence between Schoenberg and Mahler from February 1914, published in Haide Tenner (ed.), *Alma Mahler – Arnold Schönberg, 'Ich möchte so lange leben, als ich Ihnen dankbar sein kann': Der Briefwechsel* (Salzburg: Residenz Verlag, 2012), 67–71.
7. Berg's notebook is archived at the Österreichische Nationalbibliothek, Vienna, Musiksammlung, Fond Alban Berg; and a scan of Webern's letter to Schoenberg from 29 March 1914, held at the Library of Congress,

Washington, is provided by the Arnold Schoenberg Center, Vienna (ASC ID 22061). I am grateful to Regina Busch for drawing my attention to Berg's notebook as well as providing me with a transcription of Webern's letter.

8. This aspect of Adorno's music philosophy has been developed by Max Paddison in *Adorno's Aesthetics of Music* (Cambridge: Cambridge University Press, 1993), ch. 6.

9. I borrow this term from Arnold Whittall; see for instance his essay '1909 and After: High Modernism and "New Music"', *The Musical Times*, 150: 1906 (2009), 5–18.

10. Carl Dahlhaus, *Nineteenth-Century Music*, trans. J. Bradford Robinson (Berkeley and Los Angeles: University of California Press, 1989), 391.

11. I am referring here to Arnold Whittall, *Music Since the First World War* (London: J. M. Dent & Sons, 1977), Part I; and Robert P. Morgan, *Twentieth-Century Music: A History of Musical Style in Modern Europe and America* (New York: W. W. Norton & Company, 1991), ch. 3.

12. Anton Webern, *The Path to the New Music*, ed. Willi Reich, trans. Leo Black (Bryn Mawr: Theodor Presser Company, 1963), 48.

13. Carl E. Schorske, *Fin-de-Siècle Vienna: Politics and Culture* (New York: Vintage Books, 1981), 363.

14. Holly Watkins, *Metaphors of Depth in German Musical Thought: From E. T. A. Hoffmann to Arnold Schoenberg* (Cambridge: Cambridge University Press, 2011), 201.

15. Richard Taruskin, 'Revising Revision', in *The Danger of Music and Other Anti-Utopian Essays* (Berkeley and Los Angeles: University of California Press, 2009), 354–81, here at 373. Taruskin develops his criticism of Adorno's and Dahlhaus's music historiographies in various places, perhaps most prominently in his introduction, entitled 'The History of What?', to *The Oxford History of Western Music* (New York: Oxford University Press, 2005). For a discussion of Taruskin's strategy to 'erase' musical modernism, see J. P. E. Harper-Scott, *The Quilting Points of Musical Modernism: Revolution, Reaction, and William Walton* (Cambridge: Cambridge University Press, 2012), ch. 1.

16. Joseph N. Straus, *Remaking the Past: Musical Modernism and the Influence of the Tonal Tradition* (Cambridge, MA: Harvard University Press, 1990).

17. Richard Taruskin, *Music in the Early Twentieth Century*, volume 4 of *The Oxford History of Western Music* (New York: Oxford University Press, 2005), chs. 1 and 6.

18. Erik Wallrup, *Being Musically Attuned: The Act of Listening to Music* (Farnham: Ashgate, 2015), esp. 51–64.

19. Daniel M. Grimley, '"In the Mood": *Peer Gynt* and the Affective Landscapes of Grieg's *Stemninger*, op. 73', *19th-Century Music*, 40/2 (2016), 106–30, at 117.

20. The linchpin of this discourse is still Lydia Goehr, *The Imaginary Museum of Musical Works: An Essay in the Philosophy of Music* (rev. ed.; Oxford: Oxford University Press, 2007).

21. Carl Dahlhaus, *Foundations of Music History*, trans. J. Bradford Robinson (Cambridge: Cambridge University Press, 1983), 2.

22. Ibid., 6.

23. Lawrence Kramer, *Interpreting Music* (Berkeley and Los Angeles: University of California Press, 2011), 68.

24. Particularly important contributions in this context include Jim Samson (ed.), *The Late Romantic Era: From the Mid-19th Century to World War I* (London: Macmillan, 1991); Anthony Pople, 'Style and Languages Around the Turn of the Century', in Jim Samson (ed.), *The Cambridge History of Nineteenth-Century Music* (Cambridge: Cambridge University Press, 2001), 601–20; and Michael P. Steinberg, *Listening to Reason: Culture, Subjectivity, and Nineteenth-Century Music* (Princeton: Princeton University Press, 2004), ch. 6.

25. Dahlhaus, *Nineteenth-Century Music*, 391.

26. James Hepokoski, 'The Dahlhaus Project and Its Extra-Musicological Sources', *19th-Century Music*, 14/3 (1991), 221–46. For further detailed analyses of the specific ways in which the historical and political contexts of separated Germany shaped Dahlhaus's music historiography, see Anne Shreffler, 'Berlin Walls: Dahlhaus, Knepler, and Ideologies of Music History', *Journal of Musicology*, 20/4 (2003), 498–525; and the contributions gathered in Friedrich Geiger and Tobias Janz (eds.), *Carl Dahlhaus' Grundlagen der Musikgeschichte: Eine Re-Lektüre* (Munich: Wilhelm Fink, 2016). Another perspicacious, considerably more sceptical re-evaluation of Dahlhaus's work has been put forward by Matthew Riley, 'Musikalische Moderne: Dahlhaus and After', paper read at the conference *Elgar and Modernism*, held at Gresham College, London, on 14 December 2007.

27. Dahlhaus, *Nineteenth-Century Music*, ch. 6 (quotations from 330, 334, and 384).

28. I am thinking here of Carl Dahlhaus's essay entitled 'Issues in Composition', trans. Mary Whittall in collaboration with Arnold Whittall, in *Between Romanticism and Modernism: Four Studies in the Music of the Later Nineteenth Century* (Berkeley and Los Angeles: University of California Press, 1980), 40–78.

29. Cf. James Hepokoski and Warren Darcy, *Elements of Sonata Theory: Norms, Types, and Deformations in the Late-Eighteenth-Century Sonata* (New York: Oxford University Press, 2006), 8–13.

30. The term *Weltanschauungsmusik* has a long history in German-language music scholarship; for a revision of this category as part of a post-Dahlhausian project, see Hermann Danuser, *Weltanschauungsmusik* (Schliengen: Edition Argus, 2009).

31. Theodor W. Adorno, 'Gloss on Sibelius', trans. Susan H. Gillespie, in Daniel M. Grimley (ed.), *Jean Sibelius and His World* (Princeton and Oxford: Princeton University Press, 2011), 333–7.

32. James Hepokoski, *Sibelius: Symphony No. 5* (Cambridge: Cambridge University Press, 1993), 2.

33. While it is impossible here to give a full account of the literature which emerged in the context of this field of scholarship, notable major contributions include Stephen Downes, *Music and Decadence in European Modernism: The Case of Central and Eastern Europe* (Cambridge: Cambridge University Press, 2010); Daniel M. Grimley, *Carl Nielsen and the Idea of Modernism* (Woodbridge: Boydell Press, 2010); J. P. E. Harper-Scott, *Edward Elgar, Modernist* (Cambridge: Cambridge University Press, 2006); Matthew Riley, *Edward Elgar and the Nostalgic Imagination* (Cambridge: Cambridge University Press, 2007); and Matthew Riley (ed.), *British Music and Modernism, 1895–1960* (Farnham: Ashgate, 2010).

34. Peter Franklin, *Reclaiming Late-Romantic Music: Singing Devils and Distant Sounds* (Berkeley and Los Angeles: University of California Press, 2014), xiv.

35. Carolyn Abbate, 'Music – Drastic or Gnostic?', *Critical Inquiry*, 30/3 (2004), 505–38.

36. Peter Franklin, *The Idea of Music: Schoenberg and Others* (Houndmills and London: Macmillan Press, 1985), 164.

37. For the formation of this type of 'conservative modernism' and its proliferation during the Weimar Republic, see Nicholas Attfield, *Challenging the Modern: Conservative Revolution in German Music 1918–33* (New York: Oxford University Press, 2017).

38. Cf. Katherine Bergeron and Philip V. Bohlman (eds.), *Disciplining Music: Musicology and Its Canons* (Chicago: University of Chicago Press, 1992).

39. Julian Johnson, *Mahler's Voices: Expression and Irony in the Songs and Symphonies* (New York: Oxford University Press, 2009).

40. Richard Eldridge, *The Persistence of Romanticism: Essays in Philosophy and Literature* (Cambridge: Cambridge University Press, 2001), 11.

41. I borrow this concept loosely from Arthur C. Danto, *After the End of Art: Contemporary Art and the Pale of History* (Princeton: Princeton University Press, 1997).

Further Reading

Cook, Nicholas and Pople, Anthony (eds.). *The Cambridge History of Twentieth-Century Music* (Cambridge: Cambridge University Press, 2004).

Dahlhaus, Carl. *Between Romanticism and Modernism: Four Studies in the Music of the Later Nineteenth Century*, trans. Mary Whittall (Berkeley and Los Angeles: University of California Press, 1980).

Foundations of Music History, trans. J. Bradford Robinson (Cambridge: Cambridge University Press, 1983).

Nineteenth-Century Music, trans. J. Bradford Robinson (Berkeley and Los Angeles: University of California Press, 1989).

Danuser, Hermann. *Weltanschauungsmusik* (Schliengen: Edition Argus, 2009).

Franklin, Peter. *Reclaiming Late-Romantic Music: Singing Devils and Distant Sounds* (Berkeley and Los Angeles: University of California Press, 2014).

Harper-Scott, J. P. E. 'How We Got Out of Music History, and How We Can Get Back Into It', in Michael J. Kelly and Arthur Rose (eds.), *Theories of History: History Read Across the Humanities* (London, New York, Oxford, New Delhi, Sydney: Bloomsbury Academic, 2018), 37–59.

Hepokoski, James. 'The Dahlhaus Project and Its Extra-Musicological Sources', *19th-Century Music*, 14/3 (1991), 221–46.

Sibelius: Symphony No. 5 (Cambridge: Cambridge University Press, 1993).

Kramer, Lawrence. *Musical Meaning: Toward a Critical History* (Berkeley, Los Angeles: University of California Press, 2002).

Mauser, Siegfried and Schmidt, Matthias (eds.). *Geschichte der Musik im 20. Jahrhundert: 1900–1925* (Laaber: Laaber-Verlag, 2005).

Meyer, Leonard B. *Style and Music: Theory, History, and Ideology* (Chicago: University of Chicago Press, 1989).

Samson, Jim (ed.). *The Late Romantic Era: From the Mid-19th Century to World War I* (London, Basingstoke: Macmillan Press, 1991).

Taruskin, Richard. *Music in the Early Twentieth Century, volume 4 of The Oxford History of Western Music* (New York: Oxford University Press, 2005).

Treitler, Leo. *Music and the Historical Imagination* (Cambridge, MA: Harvard University Press, 1989).

Select Bibliography

Romanticism

Abrams, M. H. *The Correspondent Breeze: Essays on English Romanticism* (New York: Norton, 1984).

  The Mirror and the Lamp: Romantic Theory and the Critical Tradition (Oxford: Oxford University Press, 1953).

  Natural Supernaturalism: Tradition and Revolution in Romantic Literature (New York: Norton, 1971).

Beiser, Frederick C. *The Romantic Imperative: The Concept of Early German Romanticism* (Cambridge, MA: Harvard University Press, 2003).

Berlin, Isaiah. *The Roots of Romanticism*, ed. Henry Hardy (London: Chatto & Windus, 1999).

Bowie, Andrew. *Aesthetics and Subjectivity: From Kant to Nietzsche* (Manchester: Manchester University Press, 2003).

Charlton, D. G. (ed.). *The French Romantics*, 2 vols. (Cambridge: Cambridge University Press, 1984).

Eldridge, Richard. *The Persistence of Romanticism: Essays in Philosophy and Literature* (Cambridge: Cambridge University Press, 2001).

Ferber, Michael (ed.). *A Companion to European Romanticism* (Oxford: Blackwell, 2005).

Ferber, Michael. *Romanticism: A Very Short Introduction* (Oxford: Oxford University Press, 2010).

Ferguson, Frances. 'On the Numbers of Romanticisms', *ELH*, 58/2 (1991), 471–98.

Frank, Manfred. *The Philosophical Foundations of Early German Romanticism* (Albany: SUNY Press, 2003).

Frye, Northrop (ed.). *Romanticism Reconsidered* (New York: Columbia University Press, 1963).

Furst, Lilian R. (ed.). *European Romanticism: Self-Definition. An Anthology* (London: Methuen, 1980).

Hamilton, Paul (ed.). *The Oxford Handbook of European Romanticism* (Oxford: Oxford University Press, 2015).

Izenberg, Gerald. *Impossible Individuality: Romanticism, Revolution, and the Origins of Modern Selfhood, 1787–1802* (Princeton: Princeton University Press, 1992).

Lacoue-Labarthe, Philippe, and Nancy, Jean-Luc. *The Literary Absolute: The Theory of Literature in German Romanticism*, trans. Philip Barnard and Cheryl Lester (Albany: SUNY Press, 1988).

Lovejoy, Arthur. 'On the Discrimination of Romanticisms', *Proceedings of the Modern Language Association*, 39 (1924), 229–53.

Löwy, Michael, and Sayre, Robert. *Romanticism Against the Tide of Modernity*, trans. Catherine Porter (Durham, NC and London: Duke University Press, 2001).

McGann, Jerome J. *The Romantic Ideology* (Chicago: University of Chicago Press, 1983).

Peckham, Morse. 'Toward a Theory of Romanticism', *Proceedings of the Modern Language Association*, 66 (1951), 5–23.

Pratz, Mario. *The Romantic Agony* (London: Oxford University Press, 1933).

Remak, Henry H. H. 'West European Romanticism: Definition and Scope', in Newton P. Stallknecht and Horst Frenz (eds.), *Comparative Literature: Method and Perspective* (Carbondale, IL: Southern Illinois University Press, 1961), 223–59.

Safranski, Rüdiger. *Romanticism: A German Affair*, trans. Robert E. Goodwin (Evanston: Northwestern University Press, 2014).

Saul, Nicholas (ed.). *The Cambridge Companion to German Romanticism* (Cambridge: Cambridge University Press, 2009).

Wellek, René. 'The Concept of "Romanticism" in Literary History II: The Unity of European Romanticism', *Comparative Literature*, 1/2 (1949), 147–72.

Ziolkowski, Theodore. *German Romanticism and Its Institutions* (Princeton: Princeton University Press, 1990).

Romanticism and Nineteenth-Century Music

Cooper, John Michael (ed.). *Historical Dictionary of Romantic Music* (Lanham, MD: Scarecrow Press, 2013).

Dahlhaus, Carl. *Between Romanticism and Modernism: Four Studies in the Music of the Later Nineteenth Century*, trans. Mary Whittall (Berkeley and Los Angeles: University of California Press, 1980).

Nineteenth-Century Music, trans. J. Bradford Robinson (Berkeley and Los Angeles: University of California Press, 1989).

Frisch, Walter. *Music in the Nineteenth Century* (New York: W. W. Norton, 2013).

Rummenhöller, Peter. *Romantik in der Musik: Analysen, Portraits, Reflexionen* (Munich: Deutsche Taschenbuch Verlag, 1989).

Samson, Jim (ed.). *The Cambridge History of Nineteenth-Century Music* (Cambridge: Cambridge University Press, 2001).

Samson, Jim. 'Romanticism', in *The New Grove Dictionary of Music and Musicians*, ed. Stanley Sadie, 29 vols. (London: Macmillan, 2001), vol. 21, 596–603.

Primary Sources

Berlioz, Hector. *Memoirs of Hector Berlioz*, trans. David Cairns (London: Everyman's Library, 2002).

Hanslick, Eduard. *Eduard Hanslick's 'On the Musically Beautiful': A New Translation*, ed. and trans. Lee Rothfarb and Christoph Landerer (New York: Oxford University Press, 2018).

Hoffmann, E. T. A. *E. T. A. Hoffmann's Musical Writings: Kreisleriana, The Poet and the Composer, Music Criticism*, ed., annot., intro. David Charlton, trans. Martyn Clarke (Cambridge: Cambridge University Press, 1989).

Le Huray, Peter, and Day, James (eds.). *Music and Aesthetics in the Eighteenth and Early Nineteenth Centuries* (Cambridge: Cambridge University Press, 1981).

Lippman, Edward A. (ed.). *Musical Aesthetics: A Historical Reader, vol. II: The Nineteenth Century* (Stuyvesant, NY: Pendragon Press, 1988).

Schlegel, Friedrich. *Philosophical Fragments*, trans. Peter Firchow (Minneapolis: University of Minnesota Press, 1991).

Schopenhauer, Arthur. *The World as Will and Representation*, trans. E. F. J. Payne, 2 vols. (New York: Dover, 1958).

Schumann, Robert. *Schumann on Music: A Selection from the Writings*, trans. Henry Pleasants (New York: Dover, 1965).

Wackenroder, Wilhelm Heinrich. *Wilhelm Heinrich Wackenroder's Confessions and Fantasies*, trans. Mary Hurst Schubert (University Park, PA: Pennsylvanian State University Press, 1971).

Wagner, Richard. *Richard Wagner's 'Beethoven' (1870): A New Translation*, trans. and ed. Roger Allen (Woodbridge: Boydell Press, 2014).

Weber, Carl Maria von. *Writings on Music*, ed. John Warrack, trans. Martin Cooper (Cambridge: Cambridge University Press, 1981).

Specific Studies

Agawu, Kofi. *Music as Discourse: Semiotic Adventures in Romantic Music* (Oxford: Oxford University Press, 2009).

Bent, Ian (ed.). *Music Theory in the Age of Romanticism* (Cambridge: Cambridge University Press, 1996).

Bonds, Mark Evan. *The Beethoven Syndrome: Hearing Music as Autobiography* (New York: Oxford University Press, 2020).

  Music as Thought: Listening to the Symphony in the Age of Beethoven (Princeton: Princeton University Press, 2006).

Brittan, Francesca. *Music and Fantasy in the Age of Berlioz* (Cambridge: Cambridge University Press, 2017).

Chua, Daniel K. L. *Absolute Music and the Construction of Meaning* (Cambridge: Cambridge University Press, 1999).

Dahlhaus, Carl. *The Idea of Absolute Music*, trans. Roger Lustig (Chicago: University of Chicago Press, 1989).
Klassische und romantische Musikästhetik (Laaber: Laaber Verlag, 1988).

Danuser, Hermann. *Weltanschauungsmusik* (Schliengen: Edition Argus, 2009).

Daverio, John. *Nineteenth-Century Music and the German Romantic Ideology* (New York: Schirmer, 1993).

Donovan, Siobhán and Elliott, Robin (eds.). *Music and Literature in German Romanticism* (Rochester, NY and Woodbridge: Camden House, 2004).

Ferris, David. *Schumann's Eichendorff Liederkreis and the Genre of the Romantic Cycle* (New York: Oxford University Press, 2000).

Feurzeig, Lisa. *Schubert's Lieder and the Philosophy of Early German Romanticism* (Farnham: Ashgate, 2014).

Franklin, Peter. *Reclaiming Late-Romantic Music: Singing Devils and Distant Sounds* (Berkeley and Los Angeles: University of California Press, 2014).

Garratt, James. *Palestrina and the German Romantic Imagination: Interpreting Historicism in Nineteenth-Century Music* (Cambridge: Cambridge University Press, 2002).

Gelbart, Matthew. *The Invention of 'Folk Music' and 'Art Music': Emerging Categories from Ossian to Wagner* (Cambridge: Cambridge University Press, 2007).

Gooley, Dana. *Fantasies of Improvisation: Free Playing in Nineteenth-Century Music* (New York: Oxford University Press, 2017).

Loughridge, Deirdre. *Haydn's Sunrise, Beethoven's Shadow: Audiovisual Culture and the Emergence of Musical Romanticism* (Chicago: University of Chicago Press, 2016).

Lubkoll, Christina. *Mythos Musik: Poetische Entwürfe des Musikalischen in der Literatur um 1800* (Freiburg: Rombach, 1995).

Morton, Marsha L., and Schmunk, Peter L. (eds.). *The Arts Entwined: Music and Painting in the Nineteenth Century* (New York: Garland, 2000).

Perrey, Beate. *Schumann's Dichterliebe and Early Romantic Poetics: Fragmentation of Desire* (Cambridge: Cambridge University Press, 2002).

Reibel, Emmanuel. *Comment la musique est devenue 'romantique': De Rousseau à Berlioz* (Paris: Fayard, 2013).

Rosen, Charles. *The Romantic Generation* (Cambridge, MA: Harvard University Press, 1995).

Rumph, Stephen. *Beethoven After Napoleon: Political Romanticism in the Late Works* (Berkeley and Los Angeles: University of California Press, 2004).

Tadday, Ulrich. *Das schöne Unendliche: Ästhetik, Kritik, Geschichte der romantischen Musikanschauung* (Stuttgart, Metzler, 1999).

Taylor, Benedict. *Mendelssohn, Time and Memory: The Romantic Conception of Cyclic Form* (Cambridge: Cambridge University Press, 2011).

Vande Moortele, Steven. *The Romantic Overture and Musical Form from Rossini to Wagner* (Cambridge: Cambridge University Press, 2017).

Walton, Benjamin, and Mathew, Nicholas. *The Invention of Beethoven and Rossini* (Cambridge: Cambridge University Press, 2013).

Watkins, Holly. *Metaphors of Depth in German Musical Thought: From E. T. A. Hoffmann to Arnold Schoenberg* (Cambridge: Cambridge University Press, 2011).

White, Harry, and Murphy, Michael (eds.). *Musical Constructions of Nationalism: Essays on the History and Ideology of European Musical Culture 1800–1945* (Cork: Cork University Press, 2001).

Wood, Gillen D'Arcy. *Romanticism and Music Culture in Britain, 1770–1840: Virtue and Virtuosity* (Cambridge: Cambridge University Press, 2010).

Other English-Language Textbooks on Romanticism and Nineteenth-Century Music

Abraham, Gerald (ed.). *Romanticism (1830–1890), volume 9 of The New Oxford History of Music* (Oxford: Oxford University Press, 1990).

Einstein, Alfred. *Music in the Romantic Era: A History of Musical Thought in the 19th Century* (New York: W. W. Norton & Co., 1947).

Finson, Jon W. *Nineteenth-Century Music: The Western Classical Tradition* (Upper Saddle River, NJ: Prentice Hall, 2002).

Longyear, Rey M. *Nineteenth-Century Romanticism in Music* (Englewood Cliffs, N. J.: Prentice Hall, 1969).

Mellers, Wilfrid. *Romanticism and the Twentieth Century, volume 4 of Man and His Music: The Story of Musical Experience in the West* (London: Barrie and Rockliffe, 1962).

Plantinga, Leon. *Romantic Music: A History of Musical Style in Nineteenth-Century Europe* (New York: W. W. Norton, 1984).

Ratner, Leonard G. *Romantic Music. Sound and Syntax* (New York: Schirmer, 1992).

Ringer, Alexander (ed.). *The Early Romantic Era. Between Revolutions: 1789 and 1848* (London: Macmillan, 1990).

Samson, Jim (ed.). *The Late Romantic Era: From the Mid-19th Century to World War I* (London: Macmillan, 1991).

Taruskin, Richard. *Music in the Nineteenth Century, volume 3 of The Oxford History of Western Music, 6 vols.* (New York: Oxford University Press, 2005).

Whittall, Arnold. *Romantic Music: A Concise History from Schubert to Sibelius* (London: Thames and Hudson, 1987).

Index

For EU product safety concerns, contact us at Calle de José Abascal, 56–1°,
28003 Madrid, Spain or eugpsr@cambridge.org.

www.ingramcontent.com/pod-product-compliance
Ingram Content Group UK Ltd.
Pitfield, Milton Keynes, MK11 3LW, UK
UKHW030858150625
459647UK00021B/2750